1 MONTH OF
FREE
READING

at

www.ForgottenBooks.com

By purchasing this book you are eligible for one month membership to ForgottenBooks.com, giving you unlimited access to our entire collection of over 1,000,000 titles via our web site and mobile apps.

To claim your free month visit: www.forgottenbooks.com/free914924

ISBN 978-0-265-95386-0
PIBN 10914924

For support please visit www.forgottenbooks.com

SECOND ANNUAL

REPORT OF THE TRANSACTIONS

OF

THE PENNSYLVANIA STATE

A·GRICULTURAL SOCIETY.

VIRTUE LIBERTY & INDEPENDENCE

VOLUME II.

HARRISBURG:
A. BOYD HAMILTON, STATE PRINTER.
1855.

FEBRUARY 26, 1855.

Two thousand Extra copies ordered to be printed by the House of Representatives.

NOTICE.

The second volume of the Transactions of the Pennsylvania State Agricultural Society will not, probably, equal in size the one which preceded it, and which contained not only the proceedings of one year, but the history of the society from its organization to the year 1854.

Whatever is contained in this volume will be found properly to pertain to the transactions of this society and its auxiliaries for one year, in their mutual organizations for the improvement of agriculture, horticulture, the mechanic, domestic and household arts.

As the object to be attained in the publication of the transactions, is a reliable record of the progress of agricultural husbandry in Pennsylvania, too much attention cannot be given to a correct compilation of the proceedings of the county agricultural societies throughout the State. This could not be done the present year, for many of the societies have not reported their proceedings as required by law, and others have only given the fact of their organization, with merely the names of their officers. Although the county associations have rapidly increased within the year, still that wide spread information which should come up, duly endorsed, from every portion of the Commonwealth, cannot be complete until every county shall have its agricultural society, and their yearly proceedings brought side by side in the succeeding volumes of the transactions of this society.

The proceedings of some of the county agricultural societies, which will be found in this volume, can be referred to with pride, while there are others that show they are duly organized and ready, by another year, to add their experience in the good work. Should each county society hereafter make an annual report of their proceedings, embracing such agricultural information as can be gathered from the farmers of their respective districts, including the mode of culture of each competitor for premiums on field crops, &c., &c., and with the continuation of that enlightened liberality which has authorized the publication of the Transactions of the Pennsylvania State Agricultural Society, we may indulge the hope, that very soon we may be able to make this work what it should be, a faithful representative of the workings of the farmers of the whole State.

ROB'T C. WALKER, *Secretary.*

OFFICERS FOR 1855.

PRESIDENT.

James Gowen, Mount Airy, Philadelphia county.

VICE PRESIDENTS.

Isaac B. Baxter, Philadelphia.
Anthony T. Newbold, Philadelphia.
Wm. C. Rudman, Philadelphia.
Algernon S. Roberts, Philadelphia.
Thomas P. Knox, Norristown.
A. R. M'Ilvaine, Brandywine Manor, Chester county.
William Stavely, Lahaska, Bucks county.
Henry P. Robeson, Reading Furnace, Berks county.
John Strohm, New Providence, Lancaster county.
John P. Rutherford, Harrisburg.
Amos E. Kapp, Northumberland.
George W. Woodward, Wilkesbarre.
Chas. Augustus Lukenbaugh, Bethlehem, Northampton county.
William Jessup, Montrose, Susquehanna county.
H. N. M'Allister, Bellefonte, Centre county.
Jacob S. Haldeman, New Market, York county.
William Heyser, Chambersburg.
John S. Isett, Spruce Creek, Huntingdon county.
John M'Farland, Greensburg.
John H. Ewing, Washington.
John Murdoch, Jr. Pittsburg.
William Martin, Sr., Allegheny city.
William Waugh, West Greenville, Mercer county.
William Bigler, Clearfield.
James Miles, Girard, Erie county

ADDITIONAL MEMBERS OF THE EXECUTIVE COMMITTEE.

Frederick Watts, Carlisle.
John S. Evans, York.
A. O. Hiester, Harrisburg.
Isaac G. M'Kinley, Harrisburg.
Simon Cameron, Harrisburg.

CORRESPONDING SECRETARY.

Alfred L. Elwyn, Philadelphia.

RECORDING SECRETARY.

Robert C. Walker, Elizabeth, Allegheny county.

TREASURER.

George H. Bucher, Hogestown, Cumberland county.

CHEMIST AND GEOLOGIST.

S. S. Haldeman, Columbia.

LIBRARIAN.

David Mumma, Jr., Harrisburg.

LIFE MEMBERS, 1854.

James Gowen, Mount Airy, Philadelphia county.
Peleg B. Savery, Philadelphia.
C. B. Rogers, Philadelphia.
S. C. Stambaugh, Lancaster.
Algernon S. Roberts, Philadelphia.
Charles Augustus Lukenbaugh, Northampton county.
H. N. M'Allister, Bellefonte, Centre county.
Jacob S. Haldeman, New Market, York county.
Simon Cameron, Harrisburg.
A. O. Hiester, Harrisburg.
George H. Bucher, Hogestown, Cumberland county.
George Walker, Montrose, Susquehanna county.
P. R. Freas, Germantown.
William Sergeant, Philadelphia.
Craig Biddle, Philadelphia.
Frederick Watts, Carlisle.
George Boal, Boalsburg, Centre county.

William Marshall, Bellefonte, Centre county.
John Thompson, Half Moon, Centre county.
Jacob Struble, Zion, Centre county.
Robert Bryson, Carlisle.
J. Pemberton Hutchinson, Philadelphia.
J. Lacy Darlington, West Chester.
Robert C. Walker, Elizabeth, Allegheny county.
W. O. Hickok, Harrisburg.
James M. Meredith, West Chester.
Isaac G. M'Kinley, Harrisburg.
James Miles, Girard, Erie county.
John P. Rutherford, Harrisburg.
M. W. Baldwin, Philadelphia.
A. R. M'Ilvaine, Brandywine Manor, Chester county.
Amos E. Kapp, Northumberland county.
William F. Packer, Williamsport, Lycoming county.
Jacob Frantz, Mount Hope, Lancaster county.
William Hacker, Philadelphia.
John Rice, Philadelphia.
William Rice, Philadelphia.
Isaac Roberts, Norristown.
Anthony T. Newbold, Philadelphia.
William Penn Brock, Philadelphia.
Harry Ingersoll, Philadelphia.
John M'Gowan, Philadelphia.
Robert Wood, Philadelphia.
Chalkley Harvey, Chadd's Ford, Delaware county.
Philip Kramer, Philadelphia.
Edward K. Snow, Philadelphia.
George M. Keim, Reading.
Joseph Waterman, Philadelphia.
Richard E. Eli, Philadelphia.
Atlee G. Davis, Philadelphia.
Borrodaile Prichett, Frazer, Chester county.
Richard Wistar, Philadelphia.
Joseph W. Sharp, Philadelphia.
John Curwen, Harrisburg.
Andrew R. Chambers, Philadelphia.
W. S. Perot, Philadelphia.
H. T. Grout, Philadelphia.
- John Jordon, Jr., Philadelphia.
John Longstreth, Bristol, Bucks county.
John Hazeltine, Philadelphia.
Evans Rogers, Philadelphia.
Ward B. Hazeltine, Philadelphia.

William H. Hart, Philadelphia.
Stephen G. Fotterall, Philadelphia.
Thomas P. Hoopes, Philadelphia.
John M. Gries, Philadelphia.
Alexander Biddle, Philadelphia.
.George H. Brown, Philadelphia.
William C. Rudman, Philadelphia.
Henry F. Dettry, Philadelphia.
William H. Knight, Philadelphia.
A. Boyd Hamilton, Harrisburg.
George Boldin, Philadelphia.
Edwin Milford Bard, Philadelphia.
Isaac B. Baxter, Philadelphia.
George M. Lauman, Harrisburg.
William Stavely, Lahaska, Bucks county.
Samuel Pennock, Kennet Square, Chester county.
George Thomas, Belvidere, Chester county.
Richard Thatcher, Marsh, Chester county.
Isaac W. Van Leer, Wallace, Chester county.
E. V. Dickey, M. D., Oxford, Chester county.
H. P. Robeson, Furnace, Berks county.

AN ACT

To incorporate the Pennsylvania State Agricultural Society.

SECTION 1. *Be it enacted by the Senate and House of Representatives of the Commonwealth of Pennsylvania in General Assembly met, and it is hereby enacted by the authority of the same,* That George W. Woodward, James Irvin, E. A. Thompson, Frederick Watts, T. J. Bigham, and others, who have sub-scribed the constitution lately adopted by a convention assembled at Harrisburg, to improve the condition of agriculture, horticulture and the household arts, be and they are hereby created a body politic and corporate in law, by the name of " The Pennsylvania State Agricultural Society," and by that name shall have perpetual succession, and have capacity to sue and be sued, and may have a common seal, which at their pleasure may alter or renew; they may take by gift, grant, devise, bequest or otherwise, lands and tenements, goods and chattels, necessary for all the purposes for which the society was instituted: *Provided,* The annual income therefrom shall not exceed ten thousand dollars, independent of annual contributions by members, and the same to convey, lay out, apply and dispose of, for the benefit of the said society, as they under their charter and by-laws may direct.

SECTION 2. That the members of the said corporation shall have power to make and enforce such constitution and by-laws as may be necessary for the good government of the society, and the same from time to time to revoke, alter and amend, as they may think proper: *Provided*, That the same shall not be inconsistent with the Constitution and laws of this State.

SECTION 3. That the sum of two thousand dollars, out of any money in the treasury not otherwise appropriated, be, and the same is hereby appropriated to said society; and annually hereafter a sum of equal amount to that paid by the members thereof into its treasury, affidavit of which fact, and the amount so raised by the Treasurer of the society, being first filed with the State Treasurer: *Provided*, Such sum shall not exceed two thousand dollars in any one year.

SECTION 4. That when any number of individuals shall organize themselves into an agricultural or horticultural society, or any agricultural or horticultural society now organized within any of the counties of this Commonwealth, shall have adopted a constitution and by-laws for their government, elected their officers, and raised annually, by the voluntary contribution of its members, any sum of money, which shall have been actually paid into their Treasury, for the purpose of being disbursed for the promotion of agricultural knowledge and improvement, and that fact be attested by the affidavit of their President and Treasurer, filed with the commissioners of the county, the said county society shall be entitled to receive annually a like sum from the Treasurer of their said county: *Provided*, That said annual payment out of the county funds shall not exceed one hundred dollars: *Provided further*, That but one such society in any county shall be entitled to receive such appropriation in any one year, under this act.

SECTION 5. That the President of the Pennsylvania State Agricultural Society, who shall receive or expend any of the moneys hereby appropriated, shall, annually, on the first Monday of January, transmit to the Governor of the Commonwealth a detailed account of the expenditure of all the moneys which shall come into his hands under this act, and stating to whom and for what purpose paid; and a copy of the said report shall be transmitted to the Legislature at as early a day as practicable, and the original shall be filed in the office of the Secretary of the Commonwealth. And the presidents of the several county agricultural societies shall annually transmit, in the month of December, to the Executive Committee of the Pennsylvania State Agricultural Society, all such reports or returns as they are required to demand and receive from applicants for premiums, together with an abstract of their proceedings during the year. This act shall at all times be within the power of the Legislature to modify, alter or repeal the same.

JOHN CESSNA,
Speaker of the House of Representatives.

BENJAMIN MATTHIAS,
Speaker of the Senate.

APPROVED—The the twenty-ninth day of March, A. D. one thousand eight hundred and fifty-one.

WM. F. JOHNSTON.

CONSTITUTION OF THE PENNSYLVANIA STATE AGRICULTURAL SOCIETY.

The name of the society shall be the Pennsylvania State Agricultural Society. The objects of this society are to foster and improve agriculture, horticulture and the domestic and household arts.

SECTION 1. The society shall consist of all such persons as shall pay to the Treasurer not less than one dollar, and annually thereafter not less than one dollar, and also of honorary and corresponding members; the names of the members to be recorded by the Secretary.

The officers of county agricultural societies in this State, or delegations therefrom, shall be members *ex-officio* of this society.

The payment of ten dollars shall constitute life membership, and exempt the members so contributing from all annual payments.

SECTION 2. The officers of the society shall be a President, a Vice President from each Congressional district, three-fourths of whom shall be practical agriculturalists or horticulturists, a Treasurer, a Corresponding Secretary, a Recording Secretary, a Librarian, an Agricultural Chemist and Geologist, and such assistants as the society may find essential to the transaction of its business; an Executive Committee, consisting of the above named officers and five additional members.

DUTIES OF THE OFFICERS.

SECTION 3. The President shall have a general superintendence of all the affairs of the society. In case of the death, illness or inability of the President to perform the duties of his office, the Executive Committee shall select a Vice President to act in his stead, who shall have the same power and perform the same duties as the President, until the next annual meeting.

VICE PRESIDENTS.

It shall be their duty to take charge of the affairs of the association in their several districts; to advance all its objects; to call upon farmers to report as to the condition of agriculture in their neighborhood; to ask for information as to the modes of cultivation adopted by different farmers; and as far as in their power to make known the resources of their districts, the nature of its soil, its geological character, and all such matter as may interest farmers in every part of the State.

TREASURER.

The Treasurer shall keep an account of all moneys paid into his hands, and shall pay bills when audited and approved by the Executive Committee; each order for payment must be signed by the President or chairman of the Executive Committee.

CORRESPONDING SECRETARY.

The duty of this officer shall be to invite a correspondence with all persons interested in agriculture, whether in the State of Pennsylvania or elsewhere, but especially with our consuls in foreign countries, that new seeds, vegetables or live stock may be introduced, and. their fitness for cultivation and propagation in our climate be tested. At each stated meeting of the society he shall read his correspondence, which shall, either the whole or such parts as may be selected by the society, form a portion of the transactions.

He shall also correspond with the president or other officers of each State society in the United States, at least twice in the year, for purposes of combined and mutual action, and to be informed of the result and progress of each other's efforts; also, to invite mechanics to forward models or implements for examination and trial.

RECORDING SECRETARY.

The Recording Secretary shall keep the minutes of the society and of the Executive Committee; at the close of each year he shall prepare for publication such parts of the minutes and transactions of the society as may be designated.

LIBRARIAN.

The Librarian shall take charge of all books, pamphlets, &c., belonging to the society, and shall act as curator to preserve seeds, implements, or whatever property the society may possess.

EXECUTIVE COMMITTEE.

The Executive Committee shall transact the business of the society generally, and shall appoint annually, at their first quarterly meeting, a Recording Secretary and Treasurer, fix their salaries, and require security from the Treasurer, if they deem it necessary; shall superintend and direct the publication of such of the reports and transactions as they may deem proper, and shall designate the time and places for annual exhibitions, regulate the expenditures, examine all accounts, and keep such general charge of the affairs of the society as may best promote its interests.

They shall select their own chairman, and meet quarterly, and at any other time when convened by the President; five members shall form a quorum.

They shall call special meetings of the society when necessary.

SECTION 4. The society shall meet annually, on the third Tuesday of January, at Harrisburg, when all the officers of the society, not otherwise appointed, shall be elected by ballot for the ensuing year, and until another election. They shall also hold a general meeting at the time of the annual exhibition, and special meetings whenever convoked by the Executive Committee.

Fifteen members shall form a quorum for the transaction of business, but no member in arrears shall be entitled to the privileges of the society.

SECTION 5. This constitution may be altered or amended, at the annual meetings in January, by a vote of two-thirds of the members in attendance.

ACT OF INCORPORATION OF THE FARMERS' HIGH SCHOOL OF PENNSYLVANIA.

SECTION 1. *Be it enacted by the Senate and House of Representatives of the Commonwealth of Pennsylvania in General Assembly met, and it is hereby enacted by the authority of the same*, That there be and is hereby erected and established at the place which shall be designated by the authority, and as hereinafter provided, an institution for the education of youth in the various branches of science, learning and practical agriculture, as they are connected with each other, by the name, style and title of the Farmers' High School of Pennsylvania.

SECTION 2. That the said institution shall be under the management and government of a board of trustees, of whom there shall be thirteen, and seven of whom shall be a quorum, competent to perform the duties hereafter authorized and required.

SECTION 3. That the Governor, Secretary of the Commonwealth, the President of the Pennsylvania State Agricultural Society, and the Principal of the Institution, shall each be ex-officio a member of the board of trustees, and they with Doctor Alfred L. Elwyn and Algeron S. Roberts of the city of Philadelphia, H. N. M'Allister of the county of Centre, R. C. Walker of the county of Allegheny, James Miles of the county of Erie, John Strohm of the county of Lancaster, A. O. Hiester of the county of Dauphin, William Jessup of the county of Susquehanna, and Frederick Watts of the county of Cumberland, shall constitute the first board of trustees, which said trustees and their successors in office, are hereby erected and declared to be a body politic and corporate in law with perpetual succession, by the name, style and title of the Farmers' High School of Pennsylvania, by which name and title, the said trustees and their successors shall be able and capable in law, to take by gift, grant, sale or conveyance, by bequest, devise or otherwise, any estate in any lands, tenements and hereditaments, goods, chattels or effects, and at pleasure to alien or otherwise dispose of the same, to and for the uses and purposes of the said institution : *Provided however*, That the annual income of the said estates so held shall at no time exceed twenty-five thousand dollars ; and the said corporation shall, by the same name, have power to sue and be sued, and generally to do and transact all and every business touching or concerning the premises, or which shall be necessarily incidental thereto, and to hold, enjoy, and exercise all such powers, authorities and jurisdictions as are customary in the colleges within this Commonwealth.

SECTION 4. That the same trustees shall cause to be made a seal, with such devices as they may think proper, and by and with which all the deeds, diplomas, certificates and acts of the institution shall be authenticated, and they may at their pleasure alter the same.

SECTION 5. That at the first meeting of the board of trustees the nine named who are not ex-officio members, shall by themselves and by lot, be divided into three classes of three each, numbered one, two and three; the appointment hereby made of class number one, shall terminate on the first Monday of October, one thousand eight hundred and fifty-six, number two on the first Monday of October, one thousand eight hundred and fifty-seven, and number three on the first Monday of October, one thousand eight hundred and fifty-eight; and upon the termination of the office of such directors, to wit: on the first Monday of October in every year, an election shall be held at the institution to supply their place, and such election shall be determined by the votes of the members of the Executive Committee of the Pennsylvania State Agricultural Society, and the votes of three representatives duly chosen by each county agricultural society in this Commonwealth, which shall have been organized at least three months preceding the time of election; and it shall be the duty of the said board of trustees, to appoint two of their number as judges, to hold the said election, to receive and count the votes, and return the same to the board of trustees, with their certificate of the number of votes cast, and for whom; whereupon the said board shall determine who have received the highest number of votes and who are thereby elected.

SECTION 6. That on the second Thursday of June, after the passage of this act, the board of trustees who are hereby appointed, shall meet at Harrisburg, and proceed to the organization of the institution and selection of the most eligible site within the Commonwealth of Pennsylvania, for its location, where they shall purchase or obtain by will, grant or otherwise, a tract of land containing at least two hundred and not exceeding two thousand acres, upon which they shall procure such improvements and alterations to be made, as will make it an institution properly adapted to the instruction of youth in the art of farming, according to the meaning and design of this act; they shall select and choose a principal for the said institution, who, with such scientific attainments and capacity to teach as the board shall deem necessary, shall be a good practical farmer; he, with such other persons as shall from time to time be employed as teachers, shall compose the faculty, under whose control the immediate management of the institution and the instruction of all the youth committed to its care shall be; subject, however, to the revision and all orders of the board of trustees; there shall be a quarterly meeting of the board of trustees at the institution, and as much oftener as shall be necessary, and they shall determine; the board shall have power to pass all such by-laws, ordinances and rules, as the good government of the institution shall require, and therein to prescribe what shall be taught to, and what labor performed by the pupils, and generally to do and perform all such administrative acts as are usually performed by and within the appropiate duty of a board of trustees, and shall, by a secretary of their appointment, keep a minute of the proceedings and action of the board.

SECTION 7. That it shall be the duty of the board of trustees, as soon and as often as the exigencies of the institution shall require, in addition to the principal, to employ such other professors, teachers or tutors, as shall be qualified to impart to pupils under their charge, a knowledge of the English language, grammar, geography, history, mathematics, chemistry, and such other branches of the natural and exact sciences as will conduce to the proper education of a farmer; the pupils shall themselves, at such proper times and seasons as shall be prescribed by the board of trustees, perform all the labor necessary in the cultivation of the farm, and shall thus be instructed and taught all things necessary to be known by a farmer, it being the design and intention of this law to establish an institution in which youth may be so educated as to fit them for the occupation of a farmer.

SECTION 8. That the board of trustees shall annually elect a treasurer, who shall receive and disburse the funds of the institution and perform such other duties as shall be required of him, and from whom they shall take such security for the faithful performance of his duty as necessity shall require; and it shall be the duty of the said board of trustees annually, on or before the first of December, to make out a full and detailed account of the operations of the institution for the preceding year, and an account of all its receipts and disbursements, and report the same to the Pennsylvania State Agricultural Society, who shall embody said report in the annual report, which, by existing laws, the said society is bound to make and transmit to the Legislature, on or before the first Monday of January of each and every year.

SECTION 9. That it shall be lawful for the Pennsylvania State Agricultural Society to appropriate out of its funds to the object of this act, any sum not exceeding ten thousand dollars, whenever the same shall be required, and to make such further appropriation annually out of their funds as will aid in the prosecution of this object, and it shall be the duty and privilege of the said society, at such times as they shall deem expedient, by their committees, officers or otherwise, to visit the said institution and examine into the details of its management.

SECTION 10. That the act to incorporate the Farmers' High School of Pennsylvania, approved the thirteenth day of April, Anno Domini, one thousand eight hundred and fifty-four, be and the same is hereby repealed.

Approved March, 1855.

JAS. POLLOCK.

FOURTH ANNUAL MEETING OF THE PENNSYLVANIA STATE AGRICULTURAL SOCIETY.

The fourth annual meeting of the Pennsylvania State Agricultural Society was held on Tuesday, the 16th of January, 1855, as required by its constitution, in the Hall of the House of Representatives, at Harrisburg. In the absence of the President, Judge Watts, the Hon. John H. Ewing, one of the Vice Presidents, was called to the chair. The Recording Secretary read the report of the Executive Committee, which was unanimously adopted. It is as follows:

To the members of the Pennsylvania State Agricultural Society:

The ending of the fourth year in the transactions of the Pennsylvania State Agricultural Society, finds it in a position both creditable to the State and worthy of the cause intended to be benefitted. A great end has been accomplished in a short time, and a period has arrived when your society can step forth untrammelled from the pecuniary embarrasament which has retarded other State societies, and render material aid in fostering institutions for the benefit of the farmer and promotion of agriculture.

Since the memorable convention of farmers which established this society, in 1851, the spirit then infused has continued with unabated ferveney, and each succeeding year has outstripped its predecessor in adding to the accumulated benefit, until the year 1855 presents the pleasing spectacle of a society, although in its infancy, capable of assuming and maintaining a rank with those of longer standing and earlier birth.

The Executive Committee, who transact all the business of the society, have regularly met during the past year, as required by the constitution, and have disposed of all matters that were brought before them for their action.

At their meeting of the 14th of March, 1854, the following preamble and resolutions were offered by James Gowen, Esq., and unanimously adopted:.

" The death of Elliott Cresson, Esq., which occurred at Philadelphia on the 20th of February, 1854, in the 58th year of his age, has left a void in the ranks of philanthropy, benevolence and private worth, difficult to be supplied or filled, causing a deep sensation of sorrow and regret that his labors in the broad field of human rights and human progress had not been vouchsafed a longer day, with a slower setting sun, for the further development of his noble efforts, and to mitigate the grief of his bereaved relatives and friends. But they and the whole community have the consolation to reflect that, however short his probation, he did not live in vain; and ' though dead he yet speaketh' in the memorials he has left for their example and contemplation. In these regrets and in these memorials, this society is deeply a sympathiser and most gratefully a debtor.

" *Resolved*, That this society, at its first meeting since the decease of the lamented Elliott Cresson, offers its tribute of regret for the sudden and unexpected loss it and the community have sustained in the death of an enlightened philanthropist, an upright, benevolent citizen, and a public spirited benefactor.

" *Resolved*, That the generous bequest of five thousand dollars to this society, by the will of the late Elliott Cresson, towards the erection and support of an agricultural college, demands our grateful and unfeigned thanks, and commands the sympathy and respect of every farmer throughout the land.

" *Resolved*, That the Pennsylvania State Agricultural Society will and do hereby accept the bequest made to it by the will of the late Elliott Cresson, Esq., and hereby pledge the society to the faithful application of the same to the object designated by the will of the deceased.

" *Resolved*, That these proceedings be published in the daily and weekly papers of Philadelphia and Harrisburg, and that a copy of the same be presented to his venerable lady mother, as a token of the Pennsylvania State Agricultural Society's respect and gratitude to the memory of her noble son, and of deep sympathy in her bereavement."

In accordance with a resolution instructing the Secretary to procure a medal die, one has been furnished upon which the medals for the late exhibition have been struck. Through the courtesy of James Ross Snowden, Esq., of the United States Mint, at Philadelphia, the medals were there struck off, and the die there placed in safe keeping for the future use of the society. The artistic execution of the die is pronounced good, and was done by A. C. Morin, No. 86 Walnut street, Philadelphia.

According to a similar resolution of instruction, three hundred copies of the first volume of the transactions of this society, as authorized to be published by the Legislature, have been procured from A. Boyd Hamilton, State Printer, a part of which still remain in the library.

The life members of the society now number eighty-three, while the annual members exceed eight thousand. The amount thus received from life members is comparatively small, but can by another year, with a proper effort, be increased probably ten-fold.

The county agricultural societies have increased since our last annual meeting, until there is one in almost every county in the State, the reports of which, had they all been communicated to the State society, would no doubt have furnished desirable statistics from every part of the Commonwealth, which would add greatly to the information already obtained from some of these beneficial auxiliaries.

THE ANNUAL FAIR.

The fourth annual exhibition was held in the Twenty-fourth ward of the city of Philadelphia, on the 26th, 27th, 28th and 29th days of September last. The grounds used for the occasion were those known as the Powelton and Bingham estates, the use of which was gratuitously tendered the society by the board of directors of the Pennsylvania railroad company, and were in every way peculiarly adapted to the uses of such an exhibition. The fair was one of unusual attraction, and in amount of numbers in attendance, it exceeded any other exhibition probably ever held in the United States. The entry of articles and animals for exhibition on the books of the society, outnumbers by far the entry of any preceding year, and the whole fair, in every department, like the society itself, attained a greatness far beyond the anticipations of its most sanguine friends.

The premium list, as published for the exhibition, and including plate offered, and the premium list of the Pennsylvania Horticultural Society, which was adopted in addition, amounted to over eight thousand dollars, and the premiums themselves in every class were considerably larger than those of the preceding year. Fifty-four silver medals and one hundred and twenty diplomas were awarded and delivered.

It was expected that the Hon. Wm. M. Meredith, who had been invited for the occasion, would have delivered the customary annual address, but from indisposition he was unable to add to the exhibition this attractive feature.

Dr. Bryan, a gentleman of considerable experience in veterinary science, delivered a lecture on the fair ground upon this subject, the manuscript of which has been obtained for the society.

" The Philadelphia Society for the Promotion of Agriculture," by a resolution of its body, for the purpose of assisting the State society, and to throw the strength of their organization for the benefit of the State fair, determined to intermit their annual county exhibition, and appointed a committee of arrangement of their number to assist in making the necessary preparations.

The Pennsylvania Horticultural Society, at Philadelphia, also suspended their annual exhibition, and appointed a committee to superintend the horticultural department of the State Fair. The committees appointed by these two societies did efficient service in the discharge of the laborious duties, which were incumbent upon them in their respective capacities.

Philadelphia and her citizens did much to promote the interest of the society during the continuance of the fair, and great credit is due the people who attended the exhibition for their strict observance of temperance and good order. The mayor and police of Philadelphia extended the ægis of their municipal authority over all the ramifications of the fair, and protected alike persons and property until the society had wound up its exhibition, and the last article was removed from the ground:

2

The closing of the fourth year of the Pennsylvania State Agricultural ⸗ ⸗ ciety affords the members thereof great cause of congratulation, and promises for the future continued usefulness in the promotion of agriculture and encouragement of the domestic and mechanic arts.

The Treasurer, George H. Bucher, Esq., made his report of the financial concerns of the society for the past year, which was unanimously adopted.

TREASURER'S REPORT.

George H. Bucher, Treasurer, in account with the Pennsylvania State Agricultural Society,

DR.

1854.	To balance in treasury, as per settlement, 17th inst...	$6,058 64
Jan. 17.	Life membership fees paid by Messrs. A. R. M'Ilvaine, James Miles, J. M. Meredith, I. G. M'Kinley, A. E. Kapp, J. P. Rutherford and William F. Packer—each ten dollars	70 00
	Yearly membership fees paid by Messrs. Strohm, Carlisle, Herr, Smith, Horton, Jones and Gorgas—each one dollar	7 00
June 23.	Contribution of Messrs. Bakewell, Pears & Co., of Pittsburg	5 00
July 3.	Interest due 1st inst., on investments	239 62
Aug. 17.	Membership fee per Cyrus S. Haldeman	1 00
Sept. 13.	Do. do. A. Bolmar	1 00
	Amount received during the days of the annual exhibition—fees from members and single admission tickets—26th, 27th, 28th and 29th Sept.	24,842 31
	Life members' fees from Isaac B. Baxter, William H. Knight, William S. Perot, H. T. Grout, John Jordan, Jr., and John Longstreth—each ten dollars	60 00
October.	Maloy & Ford, premiums returned	9 00
	Wm. Penn Brock, premium exchanged for medal,	10 00
	John Sterrett & Co., do. do. for diplomas,	10 00
	Shibble & Lawson, do. do. do.	6 00
	Rent of ice cream and eating restaurants	700 00
	Balance paid by Harrisburg and Lancaster railroad company, exchanging sterling bond	10 00
	Amount of lumber sold at public and private sales	4,593 53
Dec. 13.	Amount of State appropriation	2,000 00
1855.		
Jan. 6.	Amount of life memberships paid R. C. Walker within the past year	290 00

Jan. 6. To amount paid into hands of Dr. Elwyn, treasurer
of funds collected in Philadelphia, towards expenses of the fair............................ $2,362 00
Interest due on investments to January 1, 1855.. 507 50

41,782 60

Note.—The investments of the society are, viz:

Harrisburg and Lancaster railroad company bonds............ $6,000 00
Hazelton coal company bonds............................... 2,000 00
Carlisle borough bonds.................................... 4,000 00
Deposit by committee...................................... 2,000 00
Philadelphia city bonds................................... 5,000 00

19,000 00

CR.

By payments as per vouchers, viz :
1854.

Feb.   Amount of premiums awarded on field crops......... $70 00
          Investment in Carlisle borough bonds, made by com-
          mittee.. 4,000 00

Vouchers.

No. 1. By Am't paid by R. C. Walker, as per statement $59 97
          From which deduct credits allowed—mem-
          bers' fees, &c............................ 20 50
                                                            39 47
     2.   Bill of North American and United States
          Gazette, printing...................... 4 06
     3.   Bill of M'Kinley & Lescure, printing...... 4 50
                                                            8 56
     4.   Bill of J. H. Brant, postages............. 8 23
     5.   Bill of A. J. Jones,   do............... 3 35
                                                            11 58
          Premiums paid A. & D. Chambers, and Bakewell,
          Pears & Co., omitted to be entered—being Com-
          mittee No. 31................................. 10 00
     6.   Bill of postages, stationery and stamps, paid by F.
          Watts, Esq., President......................... 20 00
     7.   Rent paid Mrs. C. Lescure, 9 months, to 31st July.. 75 00
     8.   Bill of A. B. Hamilton, for 300 copies of transactions
          of society, &c................................. 230 00
     9.   Bill of Henry Richardson, for engraving on premiums   53 45

No. 10. By am't paid William Schuchman, for design of diploma, $50 00
     11.   Paid L. N. Rosenthall, for 1,000 copies of diploma..   400 00
             Paid Robert C. Walker, Secretary, one year's salary
                to January, 1855............................. 1,000 00
             Paid George H. Bucher, Treasurer, one year's sala-
                ry, to January, 1855.........................   350 00

Expenses connected with the Fair.

     12.   Paid United States mint for medals furnished $252 50
     13.   Paid Conrad Bard & Son, for cups, engrav-
                ings, &c............................ 233 13
     14.   Paid Alex. C. Morin, for medal die, $150 00
             Paid by R. C. Walker..........   50 00
                                              ——— 100 00
                                                            585 63
             Paid for advertising and printing as per vouchers from
                15 to 30, inclusive............................ 1,142 93
     31.   Paid Jos. Blackburn, for rent of fair ground $100 00
     32.   Paid for use of ploughing ground to Owen
                Hughes............................ 200 00
                                                            ———
                                                            300 00
             Paid for hay, straw, &c., as per vouchers from 33 to
                36, inclusive..................................   801 82
             Paid for horticultural expenses, as per vouchers from
                37 to 40½, inclusive...........................   383 00
     41.   Paid J. & H. M'Ilvaine, lumber........ $1,982 75
     42.   Paid Dubois & Graves,   do.......... 1,977 31
     43.   Paid R. A. & J. J. Williams & Co., lumber 4,758 44
     44.   Paid J. Sidney Kean & Co.   do..   112 20
     45.   Paid J. & H. M'Ilwain, fence..........   336 38
     46.   Paid William H. Knight, hardware.....   324 43
                                                    ——— 9,491 51
             Paid expenses of business offices, night watch, gate-
                keepers, police and restaurant, as per vouchers
                from 47 to 67, inclusive 3,125 40
     68.   Paid Forsyth & Brother, hydrant water fix-
                tures................................ $229 60
     69.   Paid John Bayley, Amphion band........   240 00
     70.   Paid A. L. Archambault, steam engine.... 100 00
     71.   Paid J. A. Pringle, for Williams'
                tents.................... $450 00
             Paid by Dr. Elwyn.........   36 12
                                         ——— 413 88

No. 72.	Paid Kramer & Snow, carpenters	$307 00		
	Paid by Dr. Elwyn..........	150 00		
			$157 00	
73.	Paid Joseph Ritter, hauling.....	84 00		
	Paid by Dr. Elwyn..........	48 00		
			36 00	
74.	Paid C. Diffenback, work done..	63 00		
	Paid by Dr. Elwyn..........	27 00		
			36 00	
				$1,212 48

Labor, Hauling, &c.

75.	Paid Moore, Webster and others, as per vouchers to 92, inclusive.................................	359 69	
	Paid various persons by Dr. Elwyn, treasurer on the part of collections made in Philadelphia, as per vouchers.........$2,299 94		
	Balance in hands of Dr. Elwyn, as per statement........,.................. 62 06		
		2,362 00	
	Amount of cash premiums awarded at the late exhibition at Philadelphia in September last..........	4,823 00	
	Amount invested by order of Executive Committee,	7,065 00	
	Amount of postages and stamps paid by treasurer............................... $7 00		
93.	Amount paid E. Beatty, for printing 23 00		
		30 00	
	Amount paid Gilmore, Montgomery and others, as per vouchers from 94 to 103, inclusive..........	141 59	
		38,142 12	
	Balance in hands of Treasurer,..................	3,640 48	
		41,782 60	

We, the undersigned, having been appointed a committee to audit the above account of the Treasurer of the Pennsylvania State Agricultural Society, having examined the accompanying vouchers and compared them with the report, find it correct.

ISAAC G. M'KINLEY,
WILLIAM STAVELY,
S. S. HALDEMAN.

HARRISBURG, *January* 15, 1855.

FIELD CROPS.

The Committee on Field Crops for the year 1854, made the following report, which was also unanimously adopted, as was also a resolution thanking the author for the clear and comprehensive manner in which it was drawn :

To the Executive Committee of the Pennsylvania State Agricultural Society :

The Committee on Field Crops, organized by the appointment of John P. Rutherford, of Dauphin county, and John H. Ewing, of Washington county, to fill the vacancies occasioned by the absence of Thos. B. Bryson, of Cumberland county, and Jonathan Payson, of Chester county, respectfully report :

That owing to the very severe drought of the last summer, which affected injuriously every product of the farm, there has been no competition for the premiums on any of the field crops, except corn. George Drayton, farmer to Christopher Fallon, of Delaware county, and William Dripps, of Chester county, being the only applicants for the premiums on corn, John Ruthrauff, of Franklin county, the only applicant for the premiums on barley, and there being no applicants for any of the numerous other productions for which premiums were offered.

From the certificates and statement furnished by Mr. Drayton, farmer to Mr. Fallon, which are herewith presented and made part of this report, it appears that he produced from five acres of ground in one contiguous piece, accurately measured by a surveyor with chain and compass, five hundred and eight and one-fourth bushels of shelled corn, being one hundred and one bushels and twenty-seven quarts per acre, as ascertained by actual measurement of the whole in a sealed half bushel, between the 18th and 28th days of December last—all of which is certified to by the surveyor and two disinterested witnesses. The committee take pleasure, therefore, in awarding George Drayton, farmer to Christopher Fallon, the premium of fifty dollars for the best five acres of corn, as taking into view the great drought they consider that product highly commendable to the producer. Mr. Drayton, farmer to Mr. Fallon, also furnished more than half a bushel of shelled corn, besides a quantity in the ear, as a sample of his crop, together with a full statement of the mode of cultivation, thus complying literally with every requisition of the society.

They also award to William Dripps, of Chester county, the premium of twenty dollars for the second best five acres of corn—Mr. Dripps having produced on five acres and twenty-one perches of land, four hundred and nineteen and one-fourth bushels of shelled corn, being eighty-one bushels and twenty-one quarts per acre, as appears by the accompanying statement and certificates, which are also herewith presented and made part of this report.

By the statement and certificates furnished by Mr. Ruthrauff, which are also herewith presented and made part of this report, he appears to have produced on five and one-fourth acres of ground two hundred and sixty-four and one-fourth bushels of barley, being fifty and one-third bushels per acre, and on two acres and sixty-four perches one hundred and thirty-nine and one-half bushels, being fifty-eight and one-eighth bushels per acre. The product of the larger as well as the smaller lot, is highly creditable to Mr. Ruthrauff, and we therefore award him a premium of twenty-five dollars for the best five acres of barley. Mr. Ruthrauff presented a few quarts, but not the required quantity of the barley as a sample, which prevented the committee from testing its weight.

Your committee have noticed with pleasure the enlargement of the premiums offered for field crops, as well as the requisition from applicants of stricter evidence than in former exhibitions, of the measurement both of the ground and product. The award of premiums for an amount of produce per acre, which the great majority of the farming community believe (erroneously, if you please,) could not have been grown, keeps back competition, and tends to bring discredit upon the society. It is due, therefore, to the interests of the society, if not more to this incredulity itself, that the evidence upon which premiums for extraordinary productions are awarded, should be such as to satisfy, at least, the honest, intelligent, practical agriculturist. Would it be too much, therefore, to require the several certificates of the surveyor, the applicant and his assistants, not only to be full and explicit, but to be verified by affidavit? We are not aware of any objection to the substitution of affidavits for the certificates, that would not apply with equal force to the requisition of the affidavit in any case whatever, nor can we believe that the honest applicant for a premium would make any objection to the substitution of the one for the other. Certain it is, that if the solemnity of the affidavit induces caution, prevents evasion and gives additional credulity to the statements, it will answer a most beneficial purpose.

To insure accuracy and relieve the applicant from unnecessary embarrassment, your committee would most respectfully suggest the propriety of more specific requisitions and instructions in reference to the statement of the nature, depth and quality of the soil, the crop which for years was produced, the kind, quality and quantity of the manure used, the mode of cultivation, the kind of seed, and the manner of sowing it, together with the publication of the forms of certificates or affidavits for the surveyor, applicant and assistants. All of which is most respectfully submitted.

H. N. M'ALLISTER,
J. P. RUTHERFORD,
J. H. EWING.

———

STATEMENT OF GEORGE DRAYTON, FARMER TO CHRISTOPHER FALLON, UPPER DARBY, DELAWARE CO., PA.

To the Committee on Winter Premiums, Pennsylvania State Agricultural Society:

GENTLEMEN:—In compliance with the requisitions of the society, I herewith present a statement of the mode of cultivation and the kind of seed used by me in producing the corn, a sample of which has been entered for competition.

The soil upon which my corn was grown is a clay loam. Twenty-five loads of stable manure per acre were applied broadcast and plowed in to a depth of from eight to nine inches, then rolled before being thoroughly harrowed. It was then marked out and planted in hills three by four feet. Part of it was manured in the hill with a compost of soil, stable and poultry manure, and part with the improved super-phosphate of lime, manufactured by Prof. Mapes, of New York. It was planted on the 15th of May. It was suckered, leaving three stalks to the hill, and during the proper season thoroughly worked with the cultivator.

The seed was a mixture of the long White, Oregon, and Gourd seed; the White giving it length of ear, and the Oregon and Gourd seed depth of grain, having in the three combined qualities possessed by no single variety.

All of which is respectfully submitted.

GEO. DRAYTON,
Farmer to C. Fallon, Esq.

I do certify that on the twenty-fifth day of September, 1854, I surveyed and staked out for C. Fallon, Esq., five acres of corn in one contiguous piece, as described in the above draft, (draft omitted,) with chain and compass, according to the directions issued by the Pennsylvania State Agricultural Society.

Witness my hand and seal, this fifth day of December, Anno Domini, 1854.

N. F. WALTER, *Surveyor.*

UPPER DARBY, *January* 13, 1855.

This is to certify that we, the undersigned, did husk and crib, and between the 18th and 28th day of December, did shell and measure in a sealed half bushel, the corn which growed upon five acres of ground surveyed by N. F. Walter, surveyor, for C. Fallon, Esq. And we do furthermore certify, that there did grow upon the same, five hundred and eight bushels and one peck of shelled corn.

JOHN HARVEY, [L. S.]
WILLIAM PATTERSON, [L. S.]

STATEMENT OF WILLIAM DRIPPS, OF CHESTER COUNTY.

I hereby certify that on the 15th day of November last, I measured for William Dripps, on his farm in Valley township, Chester county, five acres and twenty-one perches of land, which had been planted with corn and was then standing in shock; said shocks in my opinion containing no more corn than had grown on the ground measured.

I also at the same time measured one acre in the same field, which also appeared to embrace only the corn grown upon it; that said measurement was made with compass and chain, and to the best of my knowledge and belief done correctly.

' JAMES B. MODE.

East Fallowfield, *Jan.* 3, 1855.

———

We do hereby certify that we husked, shelled, and measured the corn grown on the above ground, and that the five acres and twenty-one perches yielded four hundred and nineteen bushels and one peck of shelled corn, and the one acre yielded ninety bushels of shelled corn—all being measured in a sealed half bushel.

JOHN SMITH,
RICHARD STRODE,
For Thomas Burns.

Valley, *Jan.* 3, 1855.

———

The field that the five acres and twenty-one perches of corn was grown in, contained about eight acres; it had lain in grass five years; the soil was of a middling good quality; the subsoil was a yellow loam, laying on limestone. The situation of the field is from twenty-five to thirty-five feet above a small stream that runs through my place, with a fifteen acre field between it and the run. The land is rolling, without any spring or water in the field. Through the winter I bought stable manure, at such times as I could get it, and hauled on it at the rate of fifteen cart loads to the acre, (horse cart;) part of the five acres had no manure put on; about one-third of it. We commenced plowing about the first of May last; was plowed one foot deep, well harrowed and rolled, and half of the field was drilled in on the 23d of May. There was a very heavy rain the next day; we finished drilling the balance on the 6th of June; the rows were three feet nine inches, and the stalks fourteen inches apart. When the plants were about two or three inches above the ground we sprinkled some super-phosphate of lime (of my own manufacture,) on the rows, and when the plants were about four inches high, we run a hoe-harrow with the cultivator teeth out, and spike teeth in their place, through it once. When from eight to twelve inches high, we run the common hoe-harrow through it once. About the first of July we weed out by hand. I think we did not get the best part of the field in the five acres. We had no opportunity to select. When I left home to attend the State fair at West Philadelphia, I gave my man directions about husking, but he misunderstood me and husked the part I intended to have measured; we had to take what was left, and to get the proper quantity of ground in one piece, had to take in the part that was not manured, and also a tree and gully that the heavy rain had made in the spring, (24th of May.) I feel confident that the whole eight acres would have averaged eighty-five bushels to the acre. As evidence of that, the surveyor and myself could not discover any difference in the manured part, and I told him to measure off the one acre wherever it suited him best. That acre made ninety bushels shelled corn.

WILLIAM DRIPPS.

The plow used in the above cultivation, was the double Michigan.

STATEMENT OF JOHN RUTHRAUFF, OF FRANKLIN COUNTY.

SIRS :—The ground on which my barley grew last season, was a wheat stubble, plowed shortly after grain harvest. After laying some weeks it was well harrowed ; on the 20th of August I sowed in barley, three bushels to the acre, and plowed it in with the double shovel plow. When done seeding I rolled the ground with a heavy roller. The two acres and sixty-four perches had a light top dressing of manure previous to sowing.

I am, sirs,

Respectfully yours, &c.,
JNO. RUTHRAUFF.

PROSPECT HILL, *Fanklin co., Pa., Jan.* 8, 1855.

GREENCASTLE, *Franklin co., Pa., Dec.* 5, 1854.

To the Honorable Committee on Field Crops of the State Agricultural Society:

SIRS :—I surveyed accurately the pieces of ground Jno. Ruthrauff had in barley last season, and do certify that one lot contained five and one-fourth acres, and the other contained two acres and sixty-four perches—(5¼ acres ; 2 acres and 64 perches.)

JACOB HEICHERT, *Surveyor.*

GREENCASTLE, *Franklin co., Pa., Dec.* 15, 1854.

GENTLEMEN :—I measured accurately the barley raised by Jno. Ruthrauff, on the five and one-fourth acres of ground, and do certify that it made two hundred and sixty-four and a quarter bushels, being a fraction over fifty and a quarter bushels per acre—(5¼ acres, 264¼ bushels.)

I also measured the barley raised by Jno. Ruthrauff on the two acres and sixty-four perches, surveyed by Capt. Heichert, and do certify that it made one hundred and thirty-nine and one-half bushels of clean merchantable barley, making a fraction over fifty-eight bushels per acre—(2 acres and 64 perches, 139½ bushels.)

JAMES LONG.

The election of officers for the next year being in order, the chair stated that Judge Watts, the able and accomplished president of the society from its organization, in a letter addressed to the Secretary, peremptorily declined a re-election, and desired him to make this determination known at the annual meeting. The following is the letter:

CARLISLE, JAN. 15, 1855.

Robert C. Walker, Esq., Secretary:

DEAR SIR:—I have always said to you that it was my purpose to decline a re-election to the office of President of the State Agricultural Society. I desire that you will make this determination formally known at the annual meeting. I must not be understood to mean that I intend to abate, in any degree, the interest I take in the useful purpose which our society is destined to mark out; on the contrary, I will always be ready, in any subordinate position, to contribute all my ability to an enterprise which I estimate, in point of public economy, above all others.

It has always been a subject of regret to me that our annual meetings should necessarily be held at a period when professional duty commands my attention elsewhere. It would afford me great satisfaction to meet farmers from all parts of the State, and aid them to devise plans and means to promote their interest; I should especially be pleased to have an opportunity to urge upon them the assertion of their right to the establishment of a school, where their sons may be taught the science, as well as the practical operations of agriculture, at a cost commensurate with the profits of their business. But this opportunity is denied me, and I can only add the expression of a well matured opinion, that without that appropriate education which is sought and deemed essential to professional success, the progress and profits of agriculture must be slow, very slow.

I have the honor to be,
Very respectfully,
Your obedient,
FREDERICK WATTS.

Dr. A. L. Kennedy, A. M. Spangler and David Landreth were appointed a committee to prepare a resolution expressive of the sense of the society, on the declination of the Hon. Frederick Watts being a candidate for re-election to the Presidency of the society, who after a few minutes reported the following resolution:

Resolved, That the thanks of the society be and they are hereby tendered to the Hon. Frederick Watts, of Cumberland county, for the able, courteous and efficient manner in which from the organization of the society to the present, he has performed the duties of President.

The meeting proceeded to an election, which resulted in the choice of the following gentlemen:

PRESIDENT—James Gowen.

VICE PRESIDENTS—Isaac B. Baxter, A. T. Newbold, Wm. C. Rudman, Algernon S. Roberts, Thos. P. Knox, Abraham R. M'Ilvaine, Wm. Stavely, Henry P. Robeson, John Strohm, John P. Rutherford, Amos E. Kapp, George W. Woodward, Augustus Lukenbaugh, William Jessup, H. N. M'Allister, Jacob S. Haldeman, William Heyser, John S. Isett, John M'Farland, John H. Ewing, John Murdock, William Martin, Sr., William Waugh, William Bigler, James Miles.

ADDITIONAL MEMBERS OF THE EXECUTIVE COMMITTEE—Frederick Watts, John S. Evans, A. O. Hiester, Isaac G. M'Kinley, Simon Cameron.

CORRESPONDING SECRETARY—A. L. Elwyn.

CHEMIST AND GEOLOGIST—S. S. Haldeman.

LIBRARIAN—David Mumma, Jr.

The chair presented to the meeting the following letter, received by the Executive Committee from the Hon. James Miles, which was ordered to be published, and also referred to the corporators of the Farmers' High School.

HARRISBURG, JAN. 16, 1855.

To the Executive Committee of the Pennsylvania State Agricultural Society :

GENTLEMEN :—Believing the Agricultural interests of our State may be eminently promoted by the early establishment of the Farmers' High School, where a thorough practical and scientific education may be acquired by the youth of our State, who desire to make the tillage of the soil the business of their lives, I beg to make known to you, and through you to the gentlemen who are, or may be appointed trustees of the Farmers' High School of Pennsylvania, that I will give to the Institution, two hundred acres of land, situated in Girard township, Erie county, provided said school be located on said land.

Yours truly,

JAMES MILES.

David Mumma offered the following preamble and resolution, which were adopted.

WHEREAS, It is generally believed that a large portion of the several kinds of guano, now sold in our market, are, many of them, of a very inferior quality, and some of them almost worthless, and the frequent impositions practiced upon our farmers, in consequence of the great difficulty in discriminating between a good and an inferior article, has much lessened, if not entirely destroyed the confidence in this highly valuable manure; therefore,

Resolved, That we recommend, and respectfully urge upon the present Legislature the propriety of passing a law providing for the appointment of an Inspector of Guano for this State.

On motion of A. M. Spangler, it was

Resolved, That there be appointed by the chair, a committee consisting of five members to attend the annual meeting of the United States Agricultural Society for 1855.

On motion of Isaac G. M'Kinley, it was

Resolved, That the Pennsylvania State Agricultural Society takes a deep interest in the establishment of an institution for the instruction of the sons of the farmers of Pennsylvania in the most approved, practical and scientific mode of cultivating the soil; and inasmuch as the "act to incorporate the Farmers' High School of Pennsylvania," passed at the last session of the Legislature was, unfortunately, so defective as to prevent an organization under it, the present Legislature is earnestly invoked to modify said act in such manner as to secure the establishment of this most invaluable institution at the earliest practicable period.

On motion of Mr. Stavely, it was

Resolved, That when the meeting adjourns it adjourns to meet at half-past seven o'clock this evening.

Previous to the adjournment, Mr. Ewing, observing the President in the Hall, signified a wish to vacate the Chair, and after a few forcible and eloquent remarks gave place to Mr. Gowen, who upon taking the chair spoke as follows:

GENTLEMEN:—I return you my sincere thanks for the honor you have done me in electing me President of this society for the current year. With the profound sense of the obligation conferred, I must also acknowledge the apprehensions I feel that the time I can devote, as well as the ability I possess, will be inadequate to the proper discharge of the duties of the office to which you have elected me. But one thing I can promise, in all confidence, and that is, that whatever I can do to promote the interests of the society shall be done zealously and faithfully. It becomes me likewise to say that I consider it an honor to have been chosen to fill the place vacated by my predecessor, the Hon. Frederick Watts, who so ably presided over the society since its organization.

A resolution of thanks was tendered to the Hon. John H. Ewing, for the able manner in which he had presided at the meeting.

Adjourned till half-past seven o'clock.

EVENING SESSION.

A. L. Kennedy offered the following amendment to the fourth section of the constitution, which was not agreed to. Strike out last clause and insert:

"At the time and place of the annual exhibition, there shall be held, under the auspices of this society, a Convention of Delegates appointed for the purpose by the County Agricultural Societies, which convention shall elect its own officers, and be, in all respects, auxiliary to this society."

On motion of William Stavely, the first section of the constitution was amended so as to read:

" The society shall consist of all such persons as shall pay to the Treasurer not less than one dollar, and annually thereafter not less than one dollar ; the names of the members to be recorded by the Secretary."

On motion, it was

Resolved, That the thanks of this society be tendered to the members of the House of Representatives for the use of their Hall.

On motion the society adjourned.

ROBERT C. WALKER, *Recording Secretary*.

FARMERS' HIGH SCHOOL OF PENNSYLVANIA.

MEETING OF THE TRUSTEES.

In pursuance of the act of incorporation, a few of the persons designated by the act as trustees, met at Harrisburg on the 13th of June, 1854, for the purpose of considering its provisions. The members present did not constitute a quorum of the board. The Hon. GEO. W. WOODWARD presented the following resolution, which was agreed to:

Resolved, That FREDERICK WATTS, JAMES GOWEN and JOHN STROHM be a committee, whose duty it shall be to report to the next meeting of the board of trustees a plan of organization for the Farm School of Pennsylvania, with such modifications of the charter and such legislative appropriations as may be deemed advisable to apply for next winter.

The board then adjourned to meet at Harrisburg, in the room of the State society, on Thursday, the 13th of July, at two o'clock P. M., of which meeting it was directed that each member of the board should have personal notice.

ADJOURNED MEETING.

Thursday, the 13th of July, 1854. There were present, Messrs. Watts, of Cumberland, Mumma and Rutherford, of Dauphin, M'Ilvaine, of Chester, Boal, of Centre, and Baxter, of Philadelphia; there being no other member of the committee appointed at the last meeting, present, but the chairman, he submitted the following

REPORT.

The committee to whom was referred the subject of the organization of the " Farmers' High School of Pennsylvania," are of opinion that no good would result from any effort to organize under the existing law. It is radically defective in two particulars: First, in providing for a board of trustees composed of fifty or sixty members, many of whom are subject to constant removal by events having no reference to the interests of the institution, and living at so great a distance from any point, that there could be no hope of getting them together, to act at any time. Inasmuch as any service to be rendered by a trustee must be wholly gratuitous, it cannot be expected that individuals will make sacrifices so great as the provisions of this bill demand. The board should not consist of more than thirteen members, of whom the Governor, Secretary of the Commonwealth, Attorney General and President of the State Agricultural Society, should be members *ex-officio*. Nine should be named in the bill. The term of service of three of these should expire at the end of each year, whose place may be supplied by the election of three others, by the Executive Committee of the State society. This Executive Committee is composed of the officers of the society, who, by its charter, are elected by the members and taken from each congressional district, thus covering the whole ground and all local interests of the State. We know not where the responsibility of such election may be more safely reposed.

But the bill is defective because it makes no appropriation in aid of the project. There are many public spirited men in the State who believe that the establishment of a school where boys may be educated for farmers, is of more importance than any design which could occupy public attention. It is a fact universally known, that the literary institutions of the country, as at present constituted, educate young men to a state of total unfitness not only for the pursuits of a farmer but as a companion for his parents, brothers and sisters, with whom he is expected to spend his life. He is therefore driven from them—from his father's estate—and into a profession for which he has perhaps little capacity, and where he is subjected to all the temptations of an idle life; whereas, the Farm School proposes to impart an education which is appropriate to a farmer, which educates his body to the art as well as his mind to the science of farming, and which will have the feature of making the institution so nearly self-sustaining as to bring education, in point of expense, within the reach of every man who desires to make his son an educated farmer.

It is within the scope of our duty to make plain, through the medium of figures, a plan for the attainment of this object:

A farm of three hundred acres, at $60, would cost.............. $18,000
Additional buildings 10,000
Stock and implements.. 5,000
Furniture, books and instruments............................ 6,000
Contingencies... 1,000
                                                            ———————
                                                            40,000
                                                            ═══════

Let the State appropriate, in annual instalments of four
    thousand dollars.................................... $20,000
Appropriation of State society....................... 10,000
Mortgage loan....................................... 10,000
                                                     ——————— $40,000

To support the school will cost :

Salary of Principal...................................... $2,500
Two other Professors...................................... 3,000
One other Professor...................................... 1,200
To sustain the institution annually....................... 10,000
                                                          ─────────
                              •   16,700

Annual appropriation of State society.................... $5,000
Two hundred pupils, at $75 each.......................... 15,000
Produce of farm.. 4,000
                                                          ─────── 24,000
                                                          ─────────
Surplus.. 7,300

It cannot be doubted that if an opportunity be offered to the farmers of the State, by which their sons may be well instructed in all the elements which compose a good English education, embracing mathematics, chemistry, botany, mineralogy, and all those kindred natural sciences, the study of which can alone make a perfect farmer, they would be glad to avail themselves of it, when the entire expense shall not exceed seventy-five dollars a year. While the youth is being instructed in all those branches of science which at all pertain to agriculture, and his mind is being enlarged to greater capacity for thought, he will be engaged in the actual business of the farm ; so that when he returns to his family and home, it is but to continue his daily occupation, and with a zest which knowledge always imparts to labor. His attention will not be turned to those professional pursuits in which so few attain that degree of eminence which gives them even respectability of standing, and in which so many sink into utter worthlessness and even degradation.

To call a young graduate from the unmingled literary pursuits of a college and its concomitant associations, to the every day occupations of a farmer, of which he knows nothing, and to a society which he cannot appreciate, is a draft upon his endurance well calculated to excite disgust. But give him knowledge of the reasons which Nature's God has assigned for all those things in which he is engaged ; let him understand the mechanism of the implement he uses ; permit him to exercise the dictates of his own educated mind amongst his associates and others to whom it will be his pleasure and pride to impart his information, and this, too, with hands accustomed to labor, and you will ever after find him pursuing the happy occupation of a farmer, with profit to himself, great advantage to his neighbors, and a consequent benefit to the interests of the State.

If the Legislature, at its next session, will sanction this enterprise, by amending the bill and making such an appropriation as is here suggested, we have the most entire confidence in the ultimate success of the work, and that there will be more applicants for admission to such an institution than should be brought together at one point, and that this will be followed by others to be located at different points in the State.

All of which is respectfully submitted.

FREDERICK WATTS, *Chairman.*

This report having been read, and there not being a quorum present, legally competent to transact business, Mr. M'Ilvaine, of Chester, offered the following resolution, which was agreed to :   ·

Resolved, That the report just read be referred to Frederick Watts, Geo. W. Woodward and A. L. Elwyn, whose duty it shall be to address the people of the State on the subject, and ask the next Legislature to amend the bill, as indicated in the report, and that said committee make all necessary inquiries where the Farmers' High School of Pennsylvania may be most advantageously located, and that they invite propositions from all parts of the State, for its location.

ADDRESS.

TO THE PEOPLE OF PENNSYLVANIA.

We refer you to the foregoing proceedings for the subject upon which we address you, and we can offer little else to explain the object in view. There is no business in life which can derive more aid from the light of knowledge, than the pursuit of agriculture; there is no business which can conduce so much to human happiness as this; there is no business in which there are so many persons employed; all others, in the aggregate, do not make so many, and yet it is a fact that there is no school in our State adapted to educate a farmer. It may be truly said that the farmers of Pennsylvania have never derived any advantage from the large appropriations which have been made by the Legislature to the several colleges of the State. The price of an education at those institutions has always been beyond their means; and the quality of it, when obtained, has added comparatively little to benefit them. What we now propose, is to establish a school where practical farming and all the knowledge which pertains to a right understanding of that subject shall be taught, and that the product of the labor of the pupil shall be appropriated to his education and maintenance, to such an extent as to bring the price of learning within the reach of those whose business and habits require the study of economy. How many are there, who, knowing the value of an education, feel desirous that their sons should have its benefit, and yet look around in vain for an institution whose teachings are so practical as to prepare youth for the pursuit of agriculture? How many, too, fear the dissipations of a town—the temptations of a period devoted alone to study—the conviction that the son will be educated in mind and habituated in body, to a state of entire unfitness for practical and active life? If this want is to be supplied, it behooves those who are interested in agricultural pursuits every

3

where, to interest themselves in the establishment of a "Farmers' High School." Individuals who have no feelings to gratify and no interests to subserve, beyond the mere desire to do good, are willing to devote their time and their money to the organization of such an institution. They, too, propose to appropriate a much larger sum than that asked of the State, and the question is submitted to the reflection of the people, whether they will not take an interest in a project which so much concerns them, and urge upon their representatives the importance of the measure.

With a determined purpose that this design, which promises such important results, shall not fail for want of an effort, and anticipating the favorable action of the Legislature at its next session, we have been instructed to examine into the subject of where the "Farmers' High School" shall be located. It is very certain that its location will confer great advantages on the community around it. The example which it will afford—the knowledge it will impart—the expenditure it will annually make—are matters worthy of consideration, and will probably induce individual exertion to have it located at different points in the State. We are instructed to solicit and receive propositions on this point, to be submitted to the board of trustees as soon as the institution shall have been organized. Any communications on this subject, addressed to either member of the committee, will receive a right direction.

FREDERICK WATTS,
GEO. W. WOODWARD,
A. L. ELWYN,

July 21, 1854.   *Committee.*

PREMIUMS AWARDED AT THE ANNUAL FAIR AT PHILADELPHIA, 1854.

CATTLE.

No. 1—Short Horns.

To the President of the Pennsylvania State Agricultural Society:

Of the Committee of Judges appointed on Short Horns, Messrs. Keyser and Bolmar did not attend. Their places were filled in the way pointed out in the instructions given, by substituting Wm. Stavely and Jonathan Knight, of Bucks county; and after carefully examining the stock entered for exhibition, the committee award the following premiums:—Among so many good animals it was often difficult to discriminate, and owing to this difficulty, the committee has made some compromises by recommending special premiums. That the conclusions of the committee are entirely free from errors, or will in all respects meet the views and expectations of all persons, can hardly be hoped; having, however, acted according to the best of their judgment in good faith, the results are herewith respectfully reported.

Bulls three years old and upwards.

To Anthony Bolmar, of Chester county, Pa., for his bull "Harry,"
the first premium of.. $20 00

To Wm. Fernistone, of Easton, Pa., for his bull "Cato," the second
premium of... 15 00

To George Brinton, of Chester county, for his bull "Mars," the third
premium of... 8 00

Bulls between two and three years old.

To Dennis Kelly, of Philadelphia, for his bull "Lord Barrington,"
the first premium of....................................... 15 00

To Thomas Richeson, of Philadelphia, for his bull "Henry Clay,"
the second premium of...................................... 8 00

To Davis Hoopes, of Chester county, for his bull ——, the third premium of.. 4 00

Bulls between one and two years old.

To George A. Kreeble, of Montgomery county, for his bull "General
Taylor," the first premium of.............................. 10 00

To James Gowen, of Mount Airy, for his bull "Duke of York," the
second premium of... 5 00

To George Martin, of Philadelphia, for his bull "Strawberry," the
third premium of.. 3 00

Bull Calves under ten months old.

To Anthony Bolmar, of Chester county, for his "Charley," five
months old, the first premium of. 5 00

To John R. Barton, of Philadelphia, for calf "Woodbine," four
months old, the second premium of. 3 00

To Richard Cartwright, of Philadelphia, for his bull calf [not named,]
four months old, the pemium of............................ 1 00

Cows three years old and upwards.

To James Gowen, of Mount Airy, for his cow "Isabella," the first
premium of 20 00

To Anthony Bolmar, of Chester county, for his cow "Flora," the
second premium of... 10 00

To Owen Sheridan, of Philadelphia, for his cow "Sally," the third
premium of.. 6 00

Heifers between two and three years old.

To James Gowen, of Mount Airy, for his heifer "Young Lady," the
first premium of... 15 00

To Dr. John R. Barton, of Philadelphia, for his heifer "May Flower,"
the second premium of..................................... 10 00

To Thomas P. Remington, of Philadelphia, for his heifer "Beauty
Spot," the third premium of............................... 5 00

Heifers between one and two years old.

To David Meconkey, of Chester county, for his heifer "Rose," the first premium of $10 00

To John Clark, of Philadelphia, for his heifer "Kate," the second premium of 5 00

To James Gowen, of Mount Airy, for his heifer "Blossom," the third premium of 2 00

Heifer Calves under ten months old.

To Thomas P. Remington, of Philadelphia, for his "Donna Maria 4th," the first premium of 5 00

To Anthony Bolmar, of Chester county, for his heifer, five months old, the second premium of 3 00

To Thomas P. Remington, of Philadelphia, for his "Miss Barrington," the third pemium of 1 00

The display of Durham cattle was large and very good. Among the largest contributors were Messrs. James Gowen, of Mount Airy, Anthony Bolmar, of West Chester, and Aaron Clement, Dennis Kelly and Thomas P. Remington, of Philadelphia; the herds of the first named two gentlemen were exceedingly fine. There were also may other excellent specimens on the ground, and in view of the number and quality, the committee feel as if full justice could not be done to the enterprise and liberality of gentlemen who have given their attention and means to the improvement of this breed of stock, without the bestowal of some special premiums. No such power being vested in this committee, it respectfully makes the suggestion to the Executive Committee of the society, and recommends the following special pemiums:

To John A. Sheets, of Berks county, for his bull "Juno," over three years old $8 00

To Adrian Cornell, of Bucks county, for his bull "Pontiac," over three years old 8 00

To Thomas P. Remington, of Philadelphia, for his bull "Lord Barrington," between two and three years old 4 00

To William Devine, of Philadelphia, for his bull "General Scott," between two and three years old 4 00

To Lewis P. Hoopes, of Chester county, for his bull between one and two years old 3 00

To Thomas P. Remington, of Philadelphia, for his bull calf, ten months old 2 00

To Joseph Palmer, of Philadelphia, for his heifer "Lucy," between two and three years old 5 00

To Aaron Clement, of Philadelphia, for his heifer "Ellen," between two and three years old 5 00

To the same for his two heifers, "Flora" and "Beauty," each $2... $4 00
To same for heifer "Duchess.".. 2 00

Mr. Remington's heifers, "Fanny," four and a half months old, and "Flora," five months old, are worthy of especial commendation.

JOHN EVANS,
WM. STAVELY,
JONATHAN KNIGHT,
Committee.

No. 2—Devons.

To the President of the Pennsylvania State Agricultural Society:

The Committee appointed on Devon Cattle, No. 2, respectfully present the following awards:

Bulls of three years and upwards.

To Morris Longstreth, of White Marsh, Montgomery county, for his bull "Buck," three years and six months old, the first premium of $20 00
To C. P. Holcomb, of New Castle, Del., for his bull ——, four years old, the second premium of..................................... 15 00
To George A. Krieble, of Montgomery county, for his bull "Echo," seven years old, the third premium of............................. 8 00

Bulls between two and three years old.

To Thomas Hancock, of Burlington, N. J., for his bull "Winchester," two years and six months old, the first premium of............. 15 00
To Aaron Clement, of Philadelphia, for his bull, two years old, the second premium of.. 8 00
To Christopher Fallon, of Upper Darby, Delaware county, for his bull "Wm. Bigler," between two and three years old, the third premium of... 4 00

Bulls between one and two years old.

To Aaron Clement, of Philadelphia, for his bull, one year and four months old, the first premium of................................. 10 00
To Richard Pim, of Thorndale, Chester county, for his bull, one year and one month old, the second premium of....................... 5 00
To C. P. Holcomb, of New Castle, Del., for his bull "Granby," one year old, the third premium of................................... 3 00

Bull Calves under ten months.

To Charles H. Muierhead, of Philadelphia, for his bull, four months and two weeks old, the first premium of........................... 5 00

To C. P. Holcomb, of New Castle, Del., for his bull, six months old,
the second premium of.. $3 00

To same, for his bull, five months and two weeks old, the third premium of.. 2 00

Cows of three years and upwards.

To C, P. Holcomb, of New Castle, Del., for his cow "Betty," six
years old, the first premium of.................................. 20 00

To same, for his cow "Cherry," six years old, the second premium of 10 00

To William H. Stewart, of ——, for his cow, five years old, the third
premium of.............................. .... 6 00

Heifers between two and three years old.

For first premium—No merit.

For second do.   do.

To Morris Longstreth, of White Marsh, Montgomery county, for his
heifer, two years and six months old, the third premium of...... 5 00

Heifers between one and two years old.

To John Lippencott, of Bucks county, for his heifer, one year and
eight months old, the first premium of.......................... 10 00

To Richard Pim, of Chester county, for his heifer, one year and five
months old, the second premium of.............................. 5 00

To Morris Longstreth, of White Marsh, Montgomery county, for his
heifer, one year and six months old, the third premium of....... 2 00

Heifer Calves under ten months.

To C. P. Holcomb, of New Castle, Del., for his heifer, five months
and two weeks old, the first premium of.......................... 5 00

To same, for his heifer, eight months old, the second premium of.... 3 00

To Thomas Hancock, of Burlington, N. J., for his heifer calf "Violet,"
eight months and two weeks old, the third premium of......... 1 00

We beg to express our great satisfaction with the greater part of the animals
that came before our observation, and particularly commend Mr. Morris Longstreth's bull "Berry."

Although this is only the fourth exhibition of the society, we cannot let the
opportunity pass without assuring the President, and all who take interest in
the society, that we consider exhibitors have made unexampled improvement
in the cattle sent for competition.

We further beg leave to offer the following propositions for the consideration of the present and any future President and Committee of the Pennsylvania State Agricultural Society, viz:

1. That each separate and distinct breed of animals shall, in future, be so
placed in the stalls as to follow each other.

2. That each animal, intended for breeding from, shall have a name, and the exact age stated in years, months, weeks, and, in all very young ones, even days.

3. That each exhibitor shall give his exact address.

Should these suggestions hereafter become rules, we wish and hope that those who intend to send cattle for competition to future Fairs, will be particular in adhering strictly to them; for, by so doing, they will greatly facilitate the committees in their decisions, and benefit themselves.

ROBERT T. POTTS,
SAMUEL GILLELAND,
PASCHALL WORTH,
JOHN WM. GIBBONS,
*   Committee.*

No. 3.—HEREFORDS.

Nos. 4, 5 and 6.—AYRSHIRE, HOLSTEIN AND ALDERNEY.

To the President of the Pennsylvania State Agricultural Society:

The Committee on Ayrshire, Holstein and Alderney Cattle make the following report:

Ayrshire.

To A. R. M'Ilvaine, for the best bull between three and four years old, $20 00
To A. L. Pennock, for the best bull between one and two years old . . 10 00
To Aaron Clement, of Philadelphia, for the best cow three years old . . 20 00
To C. W. Harrison, for the best heifer between two and three years, 15 00

Holstein.

To John Worth, for the best cow three years old 20 00
To same, for the best heifer between one and two years old 10 00
To the same, for the best heifer calf ten months old 5 00

Alderney.

To Jonathan Knight, of Bucks county, for the best bull three years old, the first premium of 20 00
To Marshall Strode, of Chester county, for the second best bull, the second premium of 15 00
To Thomas P. Remington, of Philadelphia, for the third best bull, the third premium of 8 00
To Wm. Supplee, of Philadelphia, for the best bull between one and two years old 10 00
To Aaron Clement, for the second best bull between one and two years old 5 00

To Craig Biddle, of Philadelphia, for the third best bull between one
and two years old.. $4 00
To Thomas P. Remington, best bull calf ten months old............... 5 00

Alderney Cows.

To Peter Rose, of Philadelphia, for the best Alderney cow between
three and four years old.. 20 00
To Thomas P. Remington, for the second best.................... 15 00
To Wm. Supplee, for the third best............................. 6 00
To Thomas P. Remington, for the best cow between two and three
years old.. 15 00
To Lewis R. Hillard, of Montgomery county, for the second best,
between two and three years old................................ 5 00
To Wm. Supplee, for the best Alderney heifer between one and two
years old.. 10 00
To L. H. Twaddell, of West Philadelphia, for the second best between one and two years old.................................... 5 00

The committee consider the foregoing cattle in fine condition, and highly
creditable to the exhibition.

WM. KENNEDY,
JOHN J. ROWLAND,
Committee.

No. 7.—NATIVES AND GRADES.

To the President of the Pennsylvania State Agricultural Society:

Your Committee (No 7) on Natives and Grades respectfully report, that
they award the following premiums:

To James Gowen, of Mount Airy, for the best bull between one and
two years old... $6 00
To Isaac Newton, for the second best.......................... 4 00
To Reuben C. Lewis, for the best bull under ten months........ 3 00
A special premium is recommended to Aaron Clement for his grade
bull, eleven months old....................................... 5 00
To Robert Purvis, for best cow over three years old........... 12 00
To John J. Rowlin, for second best over three years old....... 10 00
To Jesse M. Williams, for third best over three years old..... 8 00
To Christopher Fallon, for best heifer between two and three years
old... 10 00
To C. W. Harrison, for the second best between two and three years
old... 8 00
To Isaac Newton, for the third best between two and three years old, 4 00

To Richard Cartwright, for the best heifer between one and two
years old.. $6 00

To Christopher Fallon, for the second best between one and two
years old.. 4 00

To Abraham L. Pennock, for third best between one and two years
old.. 2 00

To Isaac Newton, for best heifer calf under ten months old......... 3 00

To Richard Cartwright, for second best under ten months old 1 00

We also recommend special premiums to be given as follows:

To Peter Rose, for native heifer.................................. 5 00
To Christopher Fallon, for two grade cows........................ 10 00
To A. C. Jones, for a native cow................................. 5 00
To James Mars, for five grade cows............................... 20 00
To Richard Cartwright, for a native cow.......................... 10 00
To Bernard Devlin, for two heifers............................... 5 00
To John Turner, for one grade cow................................ 6 00
To W. P. Passmore, for one grade cow............................. 6 00
To same, one pair twin calves.................................... 4 00
To Francis Little, for two grade cows............................ 10 00
To Thomas D. Taylor, for two native cows......................... 10 00
To George Martin, for two grade cows............................. 10 00
To P. Lambert, for one grade cow................................. 6 00
To Nathan Ellmaker, for two grade cows........................... 10 00

SAMUEL ROBERTS,
DANIEL C. GETTY,
JOSHUA PAXSON,
Committee.

No. 8—WORKING OXEN.

To the President of the Pennsylvania State Agricultural Society:

The Committee on Working Oxen respectfully present the following report
as their awards:

For the premium offered by the society for the twenty yoke of working
oxen contended for by the Society of Chester, they award the premium of
fifty dollars, to be given to the agricultural society of that county, and also
recommend a silver medal to be offered to the same society.

For the best three yoke they assign the premium of twenty dollars to the
three yoke owned by Paschall Worth, Thomas S. Woodward and Lewis P.
Hoopes, of the county of Chester.

For the second best three yoke they award the second premium of fifteen
dollars to Geo. Blight, C. H. Muirhead and Thomas Dunlop.

The committee desire to express their admiration of a pair of Devon oxen, owned by Mr. Geo. Blight, that in every respect showed the best breaking and the greatest docility.

For the best single yoke they award the first premium of twelve dollars to Richard Pim, of Chester county.

A second premium of ten dollars to Joseph Powell, of the county of Delaware.

A third premium of eight dollars to Thomas B. Taylor, of Chester.

There were two or three other pairs of oxen entered for exhibition, but they were not brought before the committee, nor tested as to their working qualities. The committee cannot refrain from expressing their warmest admiration of the animals exhibited, possessing, as they did, all properties essential for the uses of the farmer.

The committee suggest to the Executive Committee the propriety of awarding a discretionary premium of eight dollars to George Newton, for a well bred and well broken pair of yearlings. Also, a similar mark of encouragement to Chauncey P. Holcomb, of the State of Delaware, for a beautiful pair of two year old Devon oxen.

The committee, in common with every farmer on the ground, cannot but speak warmly of the high interest displayed by the farmers of Chester county, in this exhibition, and to augur from the feelings displayed on this occasion, the happiest results to the agriculture of our State and country.

WM. A. NEWBOLD,
NATH'L ELLMAKER, Jr.,
RICHARD PETERS,
CHALKLEY HARVEY,
A. L. ELWYN,
Committee.

No. 9.—Fat Cattle.

To the President of the Pennsylvania State Agricultural Society :

The Committee on Fat Steers respectfully report that they award the first premium of fifteen dollars to Joseph Palmer, of Kingsessing, for his fine four year old short horn steer. Although there was no competition, the style, form, weight and quality of this animal was such as to entitle him to the above premium.

AARON CLEMENT, *Ch'n.*
CHAS. KELLY,
WM. J. LEIPER,
WM. EYRE, Jr.,
Committee.

No. 10.—Milch Cows.

To the President of the Pennsylvania State Agricultural Society:

The Committee, No. 10, on Milch Cows, beg leave to report that they have performed the duty assigned them, and find that Peter Rose, of the 24th ward, of the city of Philadelphia, is entitled to a premium of twenty dollars, for the best grade cow, "Milk Maid," seven years old; said cow having yielded or produced two hundred and twenty-eight quarts of milk in ten days, viz: from the 13th to the 22d of Sept., 1854, inclusive; that the weight thereof was five hundred and forty-seven lbs., and that it took eighteen quarts of said milk to make one pound of butter. Said cow calved on the 22d of August last. These facts are attested by depositions of Peter Rose and Hannah Rose, his wife.

GEO. WALKER,
STEWART TURTILL,
JACOB PAINTER,
Committee.

No. 11.—Foreign Imported Cattle.

To the President of the Pennsylvania State Agricultural Society:

The Committee of Judges on Foreign Imported Cattle, No. 11, two years old and upwards, report that they award for the best short horn bull, imported within twelve months, the premium of twenty-five dollars, and diploma, to Chas. Kelly, for his bull "Liberator." There was no other short horn bull of recent importation, of two years old, to compete with this animal. The committee, however, deemed him worthy of the premium.

To Christopher Fallon is awarded the premium of twenty dollars and diploma, for his very fine cow "Rose," she being considered the best short horn cow on the ground, imported within twelve months. Mr. Fallon exhibited another fine short horn cow, of recent importation, called "Nelly." Also, a fine young roan bull, under age, of much promise.

The committee cannot but commend Mr. Fallon, for his public spirit and judicious selection of the above imported cattle.

Thomas P. Remington exhibited "Rowena," a short horn cow, imported within twelve months; also, a young short horn white bull, under age and in very low condition. It is hoped that under good care these animals will reward their enterprising owner for importing them, and prove serviceable in the improvement of the breed of cattle in Pennsylvania. There were no Herefords, Ayrshires or Devons of recent importation exhibited, with the exception of a very fine young Devon bull of eleven months old, called "Devonshire," the property of Chauncey P. Holcomb, of Delaware.

JAMES GOWEN,
R. W. MUSGRAVE,
JOHN B. ADAMS,
Committee.

HORSES AND MULES.

No. 12.—Stallions and Mares for all Work.

To the President of the Pennsylvania State Agricultural Society:

The Committee, No. 12, appointed on Stallions and Mares, respectfully report, that they proceeded to examine the different animals exhibited in this class and division, in the order of their arrangement in the printed regulations of the society, and have awarded prizes as follows, viz:

Stallions of four years and upwards for all work.

To George Bellows, of Lancaster, N. H., for his stallion "Morgan
Black Hawk," ten years old, the first premium of.............. $30 00
To William H. Doble, of Penn'a, for his four year old stallion "Bashaw," the second premium of................................ 15 00
To Allen Fennimore, of New Jersey, for his stallion "Trafalgar," the third premium of.. 5 00

A complimentary diploma is recommended for Mr. George Bellows, of New Hampshire, for a very fine pair of young Black Hawk stallions, exhibited together.

Blood Mares of four years old and upwards, with foals at their feet, for all work.

To A. L. Pennock, Jr., of Holmesburg, Pa., for his seven year old
mare "Jane Eyre," first premium of....................... $30 00
To same, for his six year old mare "Dolly Sager," second premium of 15 00
To Francis King, of Philadelphia, for his eight year old bay mare, the third premium of................................... 5 00

Stallions of four years old and upwards, for heavy draught.

To Samuel Holman, of Chester county, Pa., for his six year old
"Duke of Normandy," first premium of...................... 30 00
To A. J. Stewart, of Huntingdon county, for his six year old "Juniata Fire King," second premium of........................... 15 00
To Thomas S. Davis, of Philadelphia, for his nine year old "Lebanon Farmer," third premium of................................. 5 00

A number of very fine animals of this class were exhibited, and the committee regretted they had not more premiums to award.

Brood Mares of four years old and upwards, with foals at their feet, for heavy draught.

To Joseph Lewis, of Delaware county, Pa., for this seven year old "Juliet," first premium of............................... $30 00

To John Scott, of Hestonville, Pa., for his twenty-five year old "Sally," second premium of.................................... 15 00

But two mares of this class were exhibited.

Stallions of four years old and upwards, for quick draught.

To J. M. Hamill, of Philadelphia, for his four year old stallion "Morgan Jackson," first premium of............................ 30 00

To Hosea Ball, of Philadelphia, for his seven year old stallion "Lone Star," second premium of.................................. 15 00

To John Clark, of Philadelphia, for his eight year old stallion "Tom Morgan,"... 5 00

Mares of four years old and upwards, for quick-draught.

To Hosea Ball, of Philadelphia, for his four year old mare "Fanny," first premium of... 30 00

Only one of this class exhibited.

Stallions of four years old and upwards, for draught.

To M. A. Kellogg, of Philadelphia, for his seven year old "Abdallah," first premium of... 30 00

To Gen. William Irick, of Burlington, N. J., for his nine year old "Toronto," second premium of............................... 15 00

To J. B. Schenck, of Bucks county, for his seven year old "Mackinaw," third premium of................................... 5 00

Mares of four years old and upwards, for draught.

None exhibited.

Stallions three years old and under four years.

To John Kline & Co., of Montgomery county, for their three year old "Perfection," first premium of.......................... 30 00

To Samuel R. Sager, of Holmesburg, Pa., for his three year old "Grey Sherman," second premium of....................... 15 00

To same, for his three year old "Black Sherman," the third premium of 5 00

Mares three years old and under four years.

To Hosea Ball, of Philadelphia, for his three year old "Fanny," first premium of... 30 00

To Thomas Leiper, of Delaware county, for his three year old "Fanny," second premium of.............................: $15 00

To George G. Leiper, Jr., of Delaware county, for his three year old "Di Vernon," third premium of.............................. 5 00

Stallions two years old and under three years.

To A. Reybold, of Delaware City, Del., for his two year old "Morgan Black Hawk," first premium of............................ 30 00

To A. L. Pennock, Jr., of Holmesburg, for his two year old "Bay Sherman," second premium of............................ 15 00

To Hosea Ball, of Philadelphia, for his two year old "Nebraska," third premium of.. 5 00

The horses exhibited of this class were so numerous, and many of them of so fine a quality, that the judges earnestly recommend for extra premiums, or complimentary diplomas, the following, viz :

To R. Plumpstead, of Upper Darby, Pa., for his two year old "Jackson Junior," ....Diploma

To Abraham Brower, for his two year old "Gen. Wayne,".........Diploma.

To William D. Clark, of Delaware City, Del., for his two year old "Rob Roy,"......................................Diploma

To Abraham Brower, for his two year old "Eclipse,"............Diploma

Mares of two years old and under three years.

To Joseph Lewis, of Delaware county, for his two year old "Fanny," first premium of... $30 00

To E. Hindle & Sons, of West Philadelphia, for their two year old "Betty," second premium of.............................. 15 00

Stallion colts of one year old.

To Hosea Ball, of Philadelphia, for his one year old "Lone Star," the first premium of...................................... 15 00

To William J. Quein, of Chester county, for his one year old "Mingo 4th," second premium of.............................. 10 00

To Francis King, of Philadelphia, for his one year old "General Duroc," third premium of................................. 5 00

Mare colts one year old.

To Hosea Ball, of Philadelphia, for his one year old colt "Fancy," first premium of.. 15 00 .

To Samuel Holman, of Chester county, for his one year old "Brown Filly," second premium of............................. 10 00

To same, for his "Iron Grey Filly," the third premium of.......... 5 00

At the request of the President, the committee examined two stallions described as thorough bred, of domestic origin, and award,

To Dr. Miller, of Philadelphia, for his eleven year old stallion
"Mingo," first premium of............................ $30 00
To Thomas Leiper, of Delaware county, for his five year old stallion
"Callender Irvine," second premium of..................... 20 00

G. H. CROSSMAN,
JAMES ANDREWS,
JOHN G. PALMER,
. *Committee.*

No. 12½.—MATCHED HORSES, GELDINGS, SINGLE MARES, JACKS AND MULES.

To the President of the Pennsylvania State Agricultural Society :

The undersigned, appointed to examine matched horses, geldings, single mares, jacks and mules, respectfully report that they have had great pleasure in discharging their several duties.

The exhibition of horses, in the class designated for your committee's report, has been large and attractive. Never, perhaps, has there been such a splendid collection of horses in Pennsylvania. Your committee expected the appearance of many specimens of the finest blood and action, but they have been agreeably disappointed by the variety and general excellence of the stock exhibited.

Before awarding the premiums, your committee ask permission to make a single remark: It is a fact that public attention has been directed for years to the improvement of the breed of cattle, hogs, sheep, and even chickens, while the horse, the noblest animal in the service of man, has been comparatively neglected. True, there are many superior horses in the State, and many have been presented for exhibition, but they are exceptions to the general rule. There is ample room for improvement in the introduction of thorough-bred horses—the moderate use of them, the selection of the finest mares for breeding, instead of those broken down by age and labor. Such a course might be more expensive, but the foals of such animals would command a full remuneration, and every one be benefitted by the style, action, power and endurance of thorough-bred horses.

Your committee award the first premium of thirty dollars, for best matched carriage horses, to Watson Newbold, of New Jersey; the second, of fifteen dollars, to John Emmett, of Philadelphia; the third, of five dollars, to Hosea Ball, of Philadelphia; and the first premium of twenty dollars, for matched mares, to Wm. R. Brown, of Bucks county.

The matched horses of Mr. Newbold, are well mated, and remarkable for superior style and gentleness; those of Mr. Emmett, for action and endurance; and those of Mr. Ball, as good roadsters and elegantly trained. The mares of Mr. Brown, are distinguished for symmetry and bottom, also for being admirably broken and fitted for service. A discretionary premium of five dollars is recommended for the Highland ponies exhibited by Zephania Campbell, of Philadelphia. For matched farm horses the first premium, of thirty dollars, is awarded to Geo. W. Hocker, of Montgomery county; the second, of fifteen dollars, to Hosea Ball, of Philadelphia; the third, of five dollars, to John Gilfillan, of Philadelphia; and a discretionary premium of ten dollars to Henry S. Kupp, of Berks county, for the best single draught gelding. The horses of Mr. Hocker exhibit fine size and great muscular development; those of Mr. Ball, for strength and kindness, and those of Mr. Gilfillan, are noted for general excellence as good farm horses. The bay horse of Henry S. Kupp indicates great strength, combined with light footedness; he is a superior specimen of his kind.

The first premium, of fifteen dollars, for farm mares, is awarded to Eli Logan, of Chester county.

The first premium, of ten dollars, for best gelding for saddle, is awarded to F. A. Shower, of Philadelphia; the second, of seven dollars, to Thomas Craig & Son, of Philadelphia.

The committee awarded to Charles T. Mathews, of the city of Philadelphia, a diploma for the best "*trained*" saddle horse of the "menage," of superior action, lightness, spirit and good disposition, trained according to the French system.

The first named is well gaited, gay, sure-footed, easy and graceful in motion; the second and third are fine horses, spirited, well broken and beautiful in action.

The first premium, of ten dollars, for the best gelding for harness, is awarded to Michael Trainor, of Philadelphia; the second, of seven dollars, to James G. Smith, of Philadelphia; the third, of five dollars, to Howard Tilden, of Philadelphia.

The first two named are remarkable for speed, blood and splendid action; the third is gay, docile and a beautiful traveler.

A discretionary premium, of ten dollars each, is recommended to be given to the following gentlemen:—Michael Trainor, O. G. Howard, Samuel K. Bye, Wm. P. Brock, Wm. F. Murray, Jacob Peters and Cyrus Haldeman, for their several horses. There was a number of splendid horses exhibited besides those already mentioned, but they were not entered for competition.

In advising the discretionary premiums, we do not wish to detract from the horses named as entitled to the regular premiums—these are selected from the entire display.

The first premium, of ten dollars, for the best mare for harness, is awarded to M. A. Kellogg, of Philadelphia; the second, of seven dollars, to Morris Spackman, of West Philadelphia, and the third, of five dollars, to J. W. Nicholson, of New Jersey. These are superior animals, of fine blood, style and action.

The first premium, of twenty dollars, for the best jack, is awarded to Wm. C. Henderson, of Lancaster county; the second, of ten dollars, to Aaron Clement, of Philadelphia; and the first premium, of twenty dollars, for the best jennet, to Wm. Cox, of Philadelphia.

The first premium, of twenty dollars, for best pair of mules, is awarded to George W. Hocker, of Montgomery county; the second, of ten dollars, to same, and the third, of five dollars, to Olom Lewis, Jr., of Delaware county.

The first premium, of twenty-five dollars, for the best team of mules, is awarded to F. A. Shower, of Philadelphia; the second, of fifteen dollars, to Eli Logan, of Chester county, and a discretionary premium, of ten dollars, to Morris Spackman, of West Philadelphia, for a very superior single mule.

Your committee, in conclusion, record their testimony to the very creditable stock exhibited.

JOHN H. BERRYHILL,
WILLIAM COLDER, Jr.,
A. E. KAPP,
Committee.

No. 13.—Foreign Imported Horses.

To the President of the Pennsylvania State Agricultural Society:

The Committee on Imported Horses award to Richard B. Jones, of Philadelphia, a diploma and premium of twenty dollars, for his imported stallion "Caliph." As Mr. Jones did not exhibit an authenticated pedigree of "Caliph," according to the regulations, he could not expect the premium of a "thorough bred"—but the committee have no doubt, from the appearance of the horse and the statements made, that he is of the Arab stock.

Two Spanish stallions, imported from Cuba, were exhibited by John Amey, of Philadelphia, to which we award a diploma and premium of five dollars.

WM. A. IRVINE,
W. M. BIDDLE,
Committee.

No. 14.—Sheep and Wool.

To the President of the Pennsylvania State Agricultural Society:

The Committee, No. 14, on Sheep and Wool, beg leave to report, that they have attended to the various duties assigned them, and have awarded as follows:

To John Worth, of Chester county, for the best Southdown buck, a premium of.. $10 00

To same gentleman, for second best, premium of................. 6 00

4

To Joseph Cope, of Chester county, for his Southdown ewes, first premium of... $10 00

To same gentleman, for second best Southdown ewes, second premium of.. 6 00

To same gentleman, for best Southdown lambs, a premium of....... 10 00

To same gentleman, for second best Southdown lambs, a premium of 6 00

To Lewis P. Hoopes, of Chester county, for four Southdown sheep, a complimentary premium of................................ 8 00

To Aaron Clement, of Philadelphia, for eight Southdown ewes, a complimentary premium of................................. 8 00

To George Drayton, of Delaware county, farmer to Christopher Fallon, for the best imported Leicester buck, a premium of........ 10 00

To same gentleman, for the best imported Leicester ewes, a premium of.. 10 00

To Bryan Jackson, of the State of Delaware, for the best Cotswold ewes, a premium of..................................... 10 00

To Aaron Clement, of Philadelphia, for the second best Cotswold ewes, a premium of..................................... 6 00

To Bryan Jackson, of the State of Delaware, for the best Cotswold lambs, a premium of..................................... 10 00

To same gentleman, for best Cotswold buck, a premium of......... 10 00

To Nathan Garrett, of Chester county, for second best Cotswold buck, a premium of...................................... 6 00

To Morthy & Flinn, of the State of Delaware, for the best mixed blood ewes, a premium of................................. 10 00

To George Drayton, of Delaware county, farmer to Christopher Fallon, for second best mixed blood ewes, a premium of.......... 6 00

To same gentleman, for a lot of mixed breed, a premium of........ 10 00

To Geo. D. Parris, of Burlington county, New Jersey, for a Leicester buck, a special premium of................................. 6 00

To Isaac Newton, of Delaware county, for his broad tailed or Tunis buck, and mixed blood lambs, a special premium of............ 10 00

To Aaron Clement, of Philadelphia, for Spanish Merino buck, a premium of... 10 00

To same gentleman, for the second best Spanish Merino buck, a premium of... 6 00

To same gentleman, for the best Spanish Merino ewes, a premium of 10 00

To same gentleman, for the second best Spanish Merino Ewes...... 6 00

To Morthy & Flinn, of the State of Delaware, for the lots of the best fat sheep, ten in number, a premium of 10 00

To John Worth, of Chester county, for second best lot of fat sheep, a premium of... 8 00

To A. T. Newbold, of Burlington county, New Jersey, for four sheep, eight months old, imported from Tartary in China, a special premium of.. 20 00

N. B.—These sheep breed twice a year, and have from four to six lambs at a birth ; the mutton remarkably excellent.   They were imported directly from Shanghai by Pratt & Sons, of Philadelphia.

To Dr. J. Bolton Davis, of Columbia, South Carolina, for one Cashmere buck goat, a yearling, and for two kids of the same, (one mixed with Nankin goat,) three months old................Silver medal

N. B.—These animals attracted general attention, and your committee believe they can be raised in Pennsylvania.

To Morthy & Flinn, of the State of Delaware, for the best fat sheep under two years old, a premium of.......................... $6 00

To George Drayton, farmer to Christopher Fallon, of Delaware county, for the second best fat sheep, a premium of................... 5 00

To Morthy & Flinn, of the State of Delaware, for the third best fat sheep.. 3 00

To Jonathan Knight, of Bucks county, for a fine mixed buck, a premium of.. 10 00

To Peter A. Browne, Esq., of Philadelphia, for his extensive and magnificent collection of "Pile," (hair and wool) from all parts of the habitable world...............................Silver medal

N. B.—This collection was an object of universal observation and admiration.

In conclusion, your committee report that they have had a very arduous duty to perform, and are sensible that meritorious animals have been necessarily ruled out in consequence of the wording of the list of premiums.   In some instances your committee have endeavored to surmount the difficulty by awarding special premiums.

Your committee respectfully recommend that the terms " long wooled," " middle wooled," and " short wooled," be no longer used.

ISAAC NEWTON,
BENJ. HICKMAN,
BRYAN JACKSON,
Committee.

No. 15.—SWINE.

To the President of the Pennsylvania State Agricultural Society :

Committee, No. 15, on Swine, report as follows :

Large Breed.

To Thomas Yedman, for the best boar over two years old, first premium of...$10 00

To Wm. Dripps, of Chester county, for the best boar over one year old, first premium of.. 10 00

To I. G. Updegrove, of Dauphin county, for the next best boar, second
    premium of.. $5 00
To Marshall Strode, of Chester county, for the best boar over six
    months old, first premium of.................................. 10 00
To Andrew Godfrey, of Philadelphia, for the best sow over two years
    old, first premium of.. 10 00
To same, for the next best over one year old, second premium of. ... 5 00
To Lewis P. Hoopes, of Chester county, for the best sow over six
    months old, first premium of. 10 00
To Francis Strode, of Chester county, for five pigs under six months
    old, first premium of.. 10 00
To Chalkley Harvey, of Delaware county, for five pigs under six
    months old; second premium of............................... 5 00

Berkshire Stock.

To James Gowen, of Mount Airy, for the best boar (white) over two
    years old, first premium of.................................. 10 00
To same gentleman, for the best boar (white) over one year old, first
    premium of.. 10 00
To same gentleman, for the best boar (white and black) over six
    months old, first premium of................................. 10 00
To same gentleman, for the next best boar (white) over six months
    old, second premium of...................................... 5 00
To Robert Purvis, of Philadelphia, for the best sow (black) over two
    years old, first premium of.................................. 10 00
To James Gowen, of Mount Airy, for the next best sow (black) over
    two years old, second premium of............................ 5 00
To same gentleman, for best sow (white) over one year old, first pre-
    mium of.. 10 00
To same gentleman, for next best sow (white) over one year old,
    second premium of 5 00
To same gentleman, for best sow (white and black) over six months
    old, first premium of.. 10 00
To Adrian Cornell, of Bucks county, for five pigs under six months
    old (black) first premium of................................. 10 00
To Robert Purvis, of Philadelphia, for six pigs under six months old,
    (black) second premium of................................... 5 00

Small Breed Suffolk Stock.

To Adrian Cornell, of Bucks county, for the best boar over two years
    old, first pemium of.. 10 00
To same gentleman, for best boar over six months, first premium of 10 00
To same gentleman, for best sow over two years, first premium of... 10 00

To same gentleman, for best sow over one year old, first premium of, $10 00
To same gentleman, for five pigs under six months old, first premium
of.. 10 00

Grade Stock.

To H. L. Strackbine, of West Philadelphia, for best sow, four years
old, of the Duchess county breed, the first premium of.......... 10 00
To John H. Miller, of Delaware county, for the best sow, six months
old, first premium of..................................... 10 00
To Cyrus Miller, of Lancaster county, for next best sow, six months
old, second premium of.. 5 00
To same gentleman, for the best boar, six months old, first premium
of... 10 00
To John H. Miller, of Delaware county, for next best boar, over six
months old, second premium of.............................. 5 00

Fat Stock.

To Thomas Yeaman, of Philadelphia, for best fat hog, one year old,
first premium of... 5 00
To James Gowen, of Mount Airy, for next best fat hog, one year old,
second premium of... 3 00

The committee would make honorable mention of a very fine boar, of the
Chester county stock, exhibited by Benjamin Hickman, of Chester county,
4½ months old ; also, a fine lot of shoats, of different ages, thirty-one in number, by the same gentleman. We think him entitled to a premium of $10,
for his very excellent display of stock.

MARSHALL PAINTER,
MARSHALL B. HICKMAN,
RICHARD PARKER,
Committee.

No. 16.—POULTRY.

To the President of the Pennsylvania State Agricultural Society:

The Committee, No. 17, on Poultry, beg leave to make the following report :

After a careful examination of the handsome display presented on the
ground, of the various kinds, the premiums are awarded as follows:

Shanghais.

Three, (one cock and two hens) to John Smith, of Harrisburg, the premium of... $3 00
Three, (one cock and two hens) to Robert Purvis, of Philadelphia.. 3 00

Dorkings.

To James Killen, of Germantown, for best lot of Dorkings, not less
than three.. .... $3 00
To George F. Curwen, of Delaware county, for second best........   2 00

Black Spanish.

To James Killen, of Germantown, for best pair of Black Spanish....   3 00
To Wm. Leonard, of Philadelphia, for second best................   2 00

Bucks County Fowls.   •

To George Vanartsdalen, of Bucks county, for best cage of Bucks
county fowls..   3 00

Brahma Pootras.

To Dr. James Crabb, of Philadelphia, for three Brahma Pootras,
(one cock and two hens)....................................   3 00
To Jonathan Dorwart, of Lancaster, for three Brahma Pootras, (one
cock and two hens)..   3 00

Cochin China. •

To Dr. James Crabb, of Philadelphia, for three Cochin Chinas,
(one cock and two hens)....................................   3 00
To Jonathan Dorwart, of Lancaster, for three Cochin Chinas, (one
cock and two hens)..   3 00
To Aaron Clement, of Philadelphia, for three Cochin Chinas, (one
cock and two hens)..   3 00

Chittagongs.   •

To George H. Yard, of Trenton, N. J., for one cock and two hens...   3 00

Bantums.

To Wm. M. Clark, of Philadelphia, one cock and two hens........   3,00
To same, one cock and two hens, black,...... ....   2 00 •

Game Fowls.

To Jonathan Dorwart of Lancaster, for best three, (one cock and two
hens) first premium....................... ....•...........   3 00
To Wm. Leonard, of Philadelphia, second best...................   2 00

Native or Dunghill Fowls.

To George Vanartsdalen, of Bucks county, for one cock and two hens   3 00
To Jonathan Dorwart, of Lancaster do.........do..........do....   2 00

Poland Fowls.

To Jonathan Dorwart, of Lancaster, one cock and two hens........ $3 00
To Wm. Leonard, of Philadelphia, for one cock and two hens...... 2 00

For the two best lots of Poultry exhibited.

To John Smith, of Harrisburg.............................. 10 00
To Robert Purvis, of Philadelphia........................... 10 00

Largest collection of Fowls exhibited.

To S. C. Radford, of West Philadelphia, five hundred fowls........ 10 00
To Jonathan Dorwart, of Lancaster, for second largest............ 8 00

Turkeys.

To Jonathan Dorwart, of Lancaster, for best pair of turkeys........ 8 00
To S. C. Radford, of West Philadelphia, for second best.......... 2 00

Geese.

To H. W. Ditman, of Philadelphia, for best pair of Bremen geese.. 8 00

Muscovy Ducks.

To Wm. Leonard, of Philadelphia, one pair Muscovy ducks........ 3 00

Common Ducks.

To Jesse M. Williams, of Philadelphia, best pair common ducks... 3 00

Pea Fowls.

To Wm. Leonard, of Philadelphia, best pair pea fowls............ 5 00

Guinea Fowls.

To Jonathan Dorwart, of Lancaster, best pair.................... 3 00

Pigeons.

To Wm. M. Clark, of Philadelphia, for best exhibition of pigeons... 5 00
To E. Heston, for second best exhibition of pigeons.............. 3 00

Imported Fowls.

To George H. Yard, of Trenton, N. J., for best pair of imported
fowls.. 5 00
To John M'Gowan, for second best pair of imported fowls........ 3 00

N. B.—The committee, in awarding the premiums, desire to say, that in consequence of the close competition in the best Shanghai and Cochin China fowls, and "best display," to do justice to the parties, agreed to award premiums of equal merit.

The committee, with great pleasure, state that they confidently believe the display of poultry, in every department, far exceeded any thing of the kind previously presented at any of our agricultural fairs; and the committee feel that those who add so much to the beauty and attraction of the grand display, deserve to be most favorably noticed. Many of the fowls were very superior, and, consequently, the competition very close. The committee, in some instances, transcended their powers, but believed it just to act as they did.

In addition to the premiums awarded above, the committee ask respectfully to recommend the following

DISCRETIONARY PREMIUMS.

To William A. Clark, of Philadelphia, for Silver Hamburg........ $3 00
To same gentleman for Golden Hamburgs...................... 2 00
To James Gillespie, of Philadelphia, for fine collection of Cochin
   China fowls...................................... 5 00
To same gentleman for handsome display of fowls............... 5 00
To Jonathan Dorwart, of Lancaster, Pa., for Harvey fowls........ 3 00
To same gentleman, for geese................................. 2 00
To same gentleman, for display of ducks....................... 3 00
To M. H. Cornell, of Bucks county, for Merino fowls............. 3 00
To James Killen, of Germantown, for Silky fowls................ 4 00
To same gentleman, for display of poultry...................... 8 00
To Hammond Holden, for Golden pheasants...................... 3 00
To same gentleman, for Silver pheasants....................... 2 00
To same gentleman, for Bolton Grays.. .... 2 00
To Peter Rose, of Philadelphia, for Bremen geese,............. 3 00
To G. & C. K. Engle, of Philadelphia, for Shanghai fowls......... 3 00
To same gentleman, for Cochin China fowls, bred from imported stock, 8 00
To A. Smith, of ———, for English Bantum.................... 3 00
To Aaron Clement, of Philadelphia, for fine collection............. 8 00
To William Leonard, of Philadelphia, for display of Bantums....... 3 00
To same gentleman, for display of Frizzled..................... 3 00
To same gentleman, for display of Golden pheasants............. 2 00
To same gentleman, for fine display........................... 5 00
To G. H. Yard, of Trenton, N. J., for eight fowls, weighing ten
   pounds each.. 5 00
To same gentleman, for very fine display of Chittagongs.......... 5 00
To J. C. Longstreth, of ———, for one coop of Bremen geese...... 3 00
To John Sloan, of ———, for two coops of handsome young Shanghais, 5 00
To George Vanartsdalen, of Bucks county, for very handsome dis-
   play and variety.. 5 00
To Joseph Breding, of ———, for display of Cochin and White
   Shanghais.. 5 00
To J. J. Hoopes, of ———, for handsome display................. 8 00
To Jesse M. Williams, of Philadelphia, for display of ducks, Java
   fowls, geese, &c.. 8 00

To R. L. Rutten, of ——, for one cage of Indian mountain game.. $3 00
To Pierce Byren, of ——, for three cages of Indian game, and one
    cage of fine Shanghais................................... 5 00
To same gentleman, for one imported English pheasant........... 3 00
To Dr. James Crabb, of Philadelphia, for fine collection of Bantums, 3 00
To same gentleman, for fine collection of imported hens.......... 2 00
To same gentleman, for fine collection of Indian mountain game.... 2 00
To same gentleman, for general display......................... 5 00
To S. C. Radford, of Philadelphia, for ducks, Poland fowls, Bantums
    and doves... 5 00
To same gentleman, for two cages of pigeons and Black Hamburg
    fowls.. 3 00
To same gentleman, for two cages of blue turkeys............... 3 00
To same gentleman, for one pair of Hongkong geese.............. 2 00
To John M'Gowan, of ——, for general display of Shanghais..... 8 00
To D. H. Brown, for one cage of California quails............... 3 00
To. W. W. Clark, of Philadelphia, for handsome cage of birds..... 3 00
To Michael Crock, of ——, for a display of forty-eight Ferrets... 5 00
To Geo. Curwen, of ——, for display of white and buff Shanghais.. 5 00
To Z. Campbell, of Frankford, for one basket Cochin China hen eggs,
    weighing three oz. each................................. 2 00
To same gentleman, for five cages of buff Shanghais............ 3 00
To same gentleman, for one cage of Bantums................... 3 00
To Z. Campbell, for general display,........................... 3 00
To H. W. Ditman, of Oxford, for fine Shanghai fowls,........... 3 00
To J. A. Gochering, for handsome Shanghais and Brahmas,........ 3 00
To John Lippincott, of ——, for display of wild ducks,.......... 3 00

             Respectfully submitted,

                     A. J. JONES,
                     CHAS. K. ENGLE,
                     ADRIAN CORNELL.
                             Committee.

No. 17.—Ploughing Match.

To the President of the Pennsylvania State Agricultural Society:

    The Committee, No. 17, on Ploughing Match, respectfully report, that they award a special premium of a silver medal to Newell French, for his Michigan double plough. The committee are of opinion that this plough is the greatest improvement of the age for deep ploughing. The committee also award a premium of fifteen dollars to Newell French, for ploughing with his Michigan double plough.

The committee award the first premium of $10 to George Buchanan, of ——, for his "Wiggins" plough, and the second premium of $8 to Jesse Paulding for his plough entered as "No. 10," and the third premium of five dollars to Prouty & Mears, for their plough.

To Jacob Sibbit, the first premium as ploughman,.................. $15 00

To George Blake, the second premium as ploughman,............. 10 00

To Robert Blake, the third premium as ploughman,.............. 8 00

To H. Rudolph Trego, for best ploughboy under eighteen years of age, premium of.. 10 00

To George Sackell, a boy over eighteen years of age, and under twenty-one, a premium of................................... 8 00

Respectfully submitted,
G. BLIGHT BROWNE,
JOHN JOHNSON,
GEORGE W. SHAEFFER,
WILLIAM BELL,
WILLIAM STAVELY,
ADRIAN CORNELL,
Committee.

No. 18.—FARM IMPLEMENTS, No. 1.

To the President of the Pennsylvania State Agricultural Society:

The undersigned committee, No. 18, beg leave to make the following report and award of premiums:

To Thomas Castor, for best farm wagon........................ $10 00

To Paschall Morris & Co., best square expanding harrows.......... 3 00

To C. B. Rogers, second best.............do.................... 3 00

To James Morris, for best corn cultivator, "Buckman's," a diploma, and... 5 00

To D. Landreth, for second best....do........................ 3 00

To S. & M. Pennock & Co., for best grain drill, exhibited by Paschall Morris & Co., diploma and................................. 15 00

To Stacy, for second best grain drill, diploma and................ 10 00

For third best grain drill, Lee & Thompson, "Moore's," exhibited by Paschall Morris & Co., diploma and........................ 5 00

For best seed planter, "Pennock's," exhibited by Paschall Morris & Co. 10 00

For second best seed planter, "L. Patee," exhibited by Paschall Morris & Co... 5 00

To Paschall Morris & Co., for best cultivator for general purposes, "Peckham's" patent, diploma and............................ 10 00

To C. B. Rogers, second best cultivator........................ $5 00
To D. Landreth, for best small seed sower....................... 10 00
To D. & H. Wolf, for second best do., exhibited by Paschall Morris & Co.. 5 00
To Paschall Morris & Co., for best roller...................... 5 00
To C. B. Rogers, for second best....do....................... 3 00
To Paschall Morris Co., for best fanning mill, "Roberts' United States," diploma and.. 10 00
To Paschall Morris & Co., for second best fanning mill, "Keech & Stillwell's "....................................... 5 00
To Paschall Morris & Co., for best corn stalk cutter, "O. U. Seely's" 5 00
To Paschall Morris & Co., for second best corn stalk cutter, "Daniel's" 3 00
To Paschall Morris & Co., for best vegetable cutter, " Ruggels & Co." 5 00
To Paschall Morris & Co., for second best vegetable cutter, " Whittemore's".. 3 00
To Paschall Morris & Co., for best corn and cob crusher, "Nichols'" 10 00
To D. Landreth, for second best corn and cob crusher, "Sinclair's" 5 00
To Paschall Morris & Co., for best clover huller, "Hunsicker & Co." 10 00
To Hibbs & Co., of Bristol, for second best clover huller.......... 5 00
To Paschall Morris & Co., for best horse cart, made by N. Coleman & Son, Philadelphia..................................... 5 00
To D. Landreth, for best ox cart............................. 5 00
To D. Landreth, for best horse rake, by Hibbs & Co., of Bristol...... 5 00
To D. Landreth, for second best horse rake, "Independent ".... ... 3 00
To Paschall Morris & Co., for best ox yoke..................... 5 00
To Paschall Morris & Co., for second best ox yoke, "Pennock's "... 3 00
To Paschall Morris & Co., for best corn sheller, hand and horse power, L. H. Davis' patent...................................... 10 00
To D. Landreth, for second best corn sheller, horse power, Reading's patent 5 00
To D. Landreth, best road scraper............................. 3 00
To C. B. Rogers, second best road scraper..................... 2 00
To Joseph Y. Collins, for best wheelbarrow....................Diploma.

Your committee beg leave to say, that there were many other articles on exhibition, which were well worthy of attention; but owing to the great amount of labor attending the duties of the committee, and a want of proper arrangement of the articles, we could not give them that examination which many of them merited.

We would respectfully suggest, that the duties of this committee, at another exhibition, be divided into not less than three committees.

We beg leave to report that we have examined the "Self-Shutting Farm Gate," deposited by Townsend Sharpless, exhibited by Paschall Morris & Co., and pronounce it admirable in every particular, and therefore award him diploma.

DAVID COCKLEY,
WM. H. HOLSTEIN,
ISAAC W. VAN LEER,
Committee.

No. 19.—FARM IMPLEMENTS, No. 2.

To the President of the Pennsylvania State Agricultural Society:

Your committee, No. 19, respectfully report that the Farm Implements submitted for their examination, as per catalogue, were of a superior quality, and they award the following premiums and diplomas:

To Paschall Morris & Co., for best churn, Spain's Atmospheric barrel churn.. $3 00
To D. Landreth, for second best churn........................... 2 00
To Melloy & Ford, Philadelphia, best twelve milk pans........... 3 00
To   do.   for second best...........do............... 2 00
To   do.   for best milk strainer........................ 2 00
To   do.   for second best do............................ 1 00

All the articles exhibited by Messrs. Melloy & Ford were of a superior quality.

To Paschall Morris & Co., for best potato masher.................. $3 00
To Charles Heite, of Philadelphia, for best grain cradle............ 2 00
To Paschall Morris & Co., best scythe and snathe..............Diploma.
To D. Landreth, for second best scythe and snathe................ $1 00
To Paschall Morris & Co., for best six hay forks, Sheble & Lawson.. 3 00
To D. Landreth, for second best six hay forks.................... 2 00
To Paschall Morris & Co., for best six grass scythes.............Diploma.
To Paschall Morris & Co., for second best six grass scythes......... $2 00
To Paschall Morris & Co., for best six axes, Beatty's.............Diploma.
To Paschall Morris & Co., for best manure forks, Sheble & Lawson's $3 00

Your committee would here observe that forks of all descriptions displayed by the firm of Sheble & Lawson were of the finest quality.

For best six Devonshire shovels and best six canal shovels—the display of these articles exhibited by D. Landreth, and by Paschall Morris & Co., were so good and similar that the committee award to each a...Diploma.
To D. Landreth, for best six spades................................Diploma.
To Paschall Morris & Co., for best six corn hoes................. $3 00
To D. Landreth, for second best six corn hoes.................... 2 00
To Paschall Morris & Co., for best lot of grain measures........... 3 00
To John H. Allen & Co., for best dozen of wire brooms............ 2 00

To John H. Allen & Co., for best dozen of Shaker or corn brooms... $2 00

To John H. Allen & Co., for best half dozen corn baskets.......... 5 00

To Paschall Morris & Co., for second best half dozen corn baskets... 3 00

A butter worker, simple in construction, and admirably calculated
for the making of butter, was invented and presented by Miss
Letitia A. Smith, of Chester county. It was exhibited by Paschall
Morris & Co. Your committee would award it a premium of... 3 00

To E. J. Dickey, exhibited by Paschall Morris & Co., for second best
butter worker, a premium of............:................ 2 00

To Henry A. Dreer, for a beautiful case of horticultural implements. 3 00

To Jonathan E. Rhoads, for a superior lot of scythe stones........Diploma.

To D. Landreth, for best hoisting hay forks..................... $3 00

An almost endless variety of implements were presented under this class,
No. 2, principally by Paschall Morris & Co., and D. Landreth, which were
not entitled to premiums by the printed catalogue.

Your committee would do violence to their feelings, and injustice to Messrs.
Paschall Morris & Co. and D. Landreth, did they not take further notice of
the very large and fine display of implements made by those gentlemen, of
every variety and of the finest quality for agricultural and horticultural purposes in the most extended applications of the term, giving an earnest to the
agricultural community that they are capable of supplying any demand made
on them for implements in all their variety. The committee feel much pleasure in awarding to each a............................ ....Silver medal.

In conclusion your committee would respectfully suggest the propriety of
having all articles that may be presented for exhibition hereafter, placed together under their respective classes or numbers. Such an arrangement would
save the judges trouble in their arduous duties, as well as much dissatisfac-
tion among contributors.

THOMAS P. KNOX,
JESSE GEORGE,
GUSTAVUS ENGLE,
Committee.

No. 20.—FARM IMPLEMENTS, No. 3.

To the President of the Pennsylvania State Agricultural Society:

The Committee, No. 20, on Farm Implements and Machinery have examined
with as much care as time would permit, the articles submitted to their inspection, and have been greatly gratified with the appearance of the exhibition, and feel that, although they have endeavored to do justic to the exhibitors, yet in much they possibly have failed. The great variety of implements
exhibited to us, and the necessity of examining each separately, prevent the
committee from particularizing.

The committee would most respectfully suggest that hereafter a separate committee be appointed on steam power and hydraulics, as a knowledge of farm implements and machinery does not necessarily imply a knowledge of either ôf the former.

Your committee have awarded premiums as follows, viz:

To John Stull, of Philadelphia, for the best portable saw mill...Silver medal.

To C. B. Rogers and David Landreth, for the next best, the sum of
$5 each... $10 00

To A. L. Archambault, for the best steam engine for farming purposes, easily portable, diploma and............................ 20 00

To Alduck & Sargent, for the best portable grist mill, C. W. Brown's patent... 20 00

To Straub & Balliet, for the next best ....Diploma.

The committee also award ten dollars to Henry Loyer for Levitt's improved corn and cob mill.

To Paschall Morris & Co., for Atkins' Automaton self reaper and raker..Silver medal.

To Lee & Thompson, for the Pennsylvania reaper and raker, exhibited by Paschall Morris & Co............................... $10 00

To S. G. Allen, of Salem, N. J., for improved combined reaper and mower, exhibited by Paschall Morris & Co., is awarded....Silver medal.

To David Landreth, for Hussy's reaper and mower................ $10 00

To Paschall Morris & Co., for Manny's reaper and mower, manufactured by Wm. Johnson & Co.................................. 10 00

To Paschall Morris & Co., for Manny's combined reaper and mower, with an improved separator.................................Diploma.

To Boyer & Bro., Harrisburg, for J. W. Hugit's self sharpening reaper and mower combined..................................... $10 00

To R. T. Elkinton, of Philadelphia, for M'Cormick's reaper and mower combined...Diploma.

To Jesse Urmy, of Wilmington, Del., for reaper and mower combined.. $20 00

To C. B. Rogers, for Allen's mower.........................Silver medal.

To Paschall Morris & Co., for Wood's mower, Manny's patent..... $10 00

To Wm. Manning, for North American mowing machine, with revolving knives, working with one or two horses................... 10 00

To Abner Garrett, of Chester county, for Hallenback's mowing machine, exhibited by Paschall Morris & Co.................... 10 00

To R. T. Elkinton, of Philadelphia, for the best sweep horse power, Pelt's horse power.. 10 00

To C. B. Rogers, for second best do. do......................... 5 00

To Alfred Blaker, of Bucks county, for the best railway horse power   10 00

To David Landreth, for the second best do...................... 5 00

To Paschall Morris & Co., for Gilbert & Rittenhouse's railway horse Power...Diploma.

To Alfred Blaker, of Bucks county, for the best threshing machine, a diploma and.. $10 00

To David Landreth, for second best do.. 5 00

To C. B. Rogers, for Wheeler, Melick & Co's., threshing, separating and cleansing machine combined.. 20 00

To R. T. Elkinton, of Philadelphia, for threshing, separating and cleansing machine combined...Diploma.

To W. W. Dingee, of York, for portable hay press, exhibited by Paschall Morris & Co.. $10 00

To Paschall Morris & Company, for E. Spain's patent Atmospheric churn..Silver medal.

To Thomas Palmer, for second best churn...........................Diploma.

To Alfred Blaker, of Bucks county, for best separator............... $10 00

To David Landreth, for second best.. 5 00

To Paschall Morris & Co., for Gilbert & Rittenhouse's threshing machine and separator... 10 00

To Paschall Morris & Co., for Deering & Dickson's Portable horse power hay press.. 10 00

To Paschall Morris & Co., for best dog power for churning machine.. 5 00

To Thomas Palmer, for best washing machine.................... 5 00

To John Pierce, for washing machine ....Diploma.

To Paschall Morris & Co., for Harris' Ohio Buckeye clothes washer...do.

To David S. Siner, for the best double acting lift and force pumps ....Silver medal.

To Maull & Brothers, for Barker's patent pump................. $10 00

Among the many and various pumps on exhibition, your committee were particularly interested in the great variety exhibited by Corning & Co., of Seneca Falls, N. Y.; among which are the iron, brass and side cistern pumps, especially used and adapted to the farmer; the out-door cistern and well pumps, with the iron and side force pumps, deserve particular attention; the tight-top well pump and brass force pump for house, are particularly commended; the deep well, railroad, double acting and iron house pumps, have a value, in the estimation of the committee, which should commend them to all persons requiring articles of the kind; the garden and fire engine pumps are more perfect than any other the committee have examined. For this collection the committee award a.............................Silver medal.

The committee have examined the various hydraulic rams for raising water, and they are pleased to observe, that there is great competition here, as in other matters connected with the duties of this committee, but disposed to do justice to all in the limited capacity in which they are acting, they award to Allan Ganthrop, for best Hydraulic Rams....................... $10 00

Morris Heston, for second best. ..do............................. 5 00

For the best hay and cattle weighing scales, they award to

George W. Colly, for Fairbank's scales, a diploma and............ $10 00

To Paschall Morris & Co., for Abbot's scales....................Diploma.

To A. B. Davis & Co., for scales.............................. $10 00

To George W. Colly, for the best weighing machine for general farm
purposes, Fairbank's patent ....Diploma.

To George W. Colly, for best lot of large and small scales........ $5 00

To Paschall Morris & Co., for best portable cider press, Krauser's
patent... ....Silver medal.

To David Landreth, for second best, Hickok's patent.............. 5 00

To E. Spain, for best variety of cooper work, exhibited by Paschall
Morris & Co......................................Silver medal.

To Paschall Morris & Co., for second best...................... $5 00

To Paschall Morris & Co., for best Lime spreader, entered by Lewis
Cooper.. 10 00

To Joseph W. Fawkes, for second best......................... 5 00

To Paschall Morris & Co., for best Guano spreader...........Silver medal.

To Paschall Morris & Co., for best collection of farmers' tools, arranged in a deposit...................................... $5 00

To Paschall Morris & Co., for the best invention for securing the run
of water in drains, manufactured by James Wardrop & Co., Pittsburg.. 5 00

To D. Landreth, for second best.............................. 3 00

To Paschall Morris & Co., for the best and most numerous collection
of agricultural implements, a diploma and.................. 25 00

To D. Landreth, for the second best.......................... 20 00

The committee, with pleasure, mention C B. Rogers and Charles Keite, of
Philadelphia, George Churnside, of Wilmington, Delaware, and James Robb,
of Huntingdon, Pa., as exhibitors of agricultural implements, and award them
each ten dollars.. $40 00

So many articles within their class have been exhibited, deserving of more
careful attention than the committee have been able to give, that they can
only suggest that hereafter the division of committees may be more extended,
so that more perfect justice may be done to exhibitors.

The committee also, without intending to "travel from the record of their
duty," may be permitted to suggest that permanency of place of the State
Fair would, in their opinion, render each succeeding exhibition more perfect
in its arrangements, and more generally useful and interesting.

E. W. STURDEVANT,

J. B. LEEDOM,

LEONARD SHALLCROSS,

Committee.

No. 21.—LEATHER AND ITS MANUFACTURES.

To the President of the Pennsylvania State Agricultural Society:

The Committee, No. 21, on Leather and its Manufactures, beg leave to make the following report, after a careful examination:

The goods deposited by Messrs. Lacey & Phillips, of Philadelphia, consisting of three sets of double harness, two ladies' and two gentlemen's saddles, bridles, horse covers, &c.; also, a very superior double carriage harness (previously exhibited at the Crystal Palace, and there received a silver medal.) We consider Messrs. Lacey & Phillips entitled to a special premium, or the highest award that can be given. We recommend for them a silver medal for harness, unsurpassed in style, richness and elegance of execution. The balance of their goods are superior in workmanship and style to any others exhibited.

The goods deposited by Moyer & Brother, make a good display. We award them a diploma.

Trunks, exhibited by A. L. Hickey & Co., we consider superior to others on exhibition, and consider them entitled to the highest award—a silver medal—for their superior workmanship.

Goods deposited by F. H. Smith, very pretty, and entitled to a diploma.

Leather deposited by B. A. Crawford—fair sides, slaughter sole leather— we consider the best, and award him a diploma.

To H. M. Crawford, for one dozen best calf skins, we award a.....Diploma.
To Thomas Coleman, half-dozen Calcutta kips..........................do.
To Samuel Armstrong, for harness leather.............................do.
   Do.............3 bundles leather, best ....do.
   Do...........1 bundle saddle skirting.................do.
   Do.............1 bundle splits.......................do.

To Daniel Stake, for three sides Spanish sole, manufactured at Franklin, Cumberland county, by Wm. M'Lain.....................do.

To Henry Deamer, for best cart harness............................ $5 00

To Charles P. Caldwell, for creditable exhibition of whips and canes, entitled to first premium..............................Diploma.

George H. Metz & Sons, bellows, foundry, &c.—We have only to say that they are good blowers, and consider them worthy the highest premium....................................Silver medal.

A. E. KAPP,
JAMES BOUSTEAD,
CHAS. T. MATTHEWS,
L. F. MYER,
Committee.

5

No. 22.—Dairy Sugar and Honey.

To the President of the Pennsylvania State Agricultural Society :

The undersigned, Judges on Products of Dairy, &c., (committee No. 22,) respectfully report; and regret that a very small number of articles of this class came under notice. The following are the awards of premiums for such articles as were presented for competition :

To Mrs. Job Hayes, first premium of twenty dollars for best butter, made from five cows, which were in profit since February last, producing one hundred and fifty-six pounds.

To Mrs. Job Hayes, for twenty pounds of butter made in June, first premium of.. $10 00

To George Walker, for best firkin of butter, made in September, a premium of.. 10 00

To Miss Jemima Miller, for best five pounds of butter, first premium.. Set silver tea spoons.

To Miss —— Howe, for second best five pounds of butter, second premium.. Silver cup.

To Mrs. Job Hayes, for fifty pounds of cheese over one year old, first premium... $10 00

To same lady, for fifty pounds cheese made this year, first premium, 10 00

To H. M. Hays, for fifty pounds cheese less than one year old, second premium 5 00

To Francis Parkeson, for best ten pounds of honey, first premium of 5 00

Also, to the same gentleman, a discretionary premium of three dollars is recommended for his very fine display of honey, it having been made in hives of his own construction.

To Wilson Baldwin, for second best ten pounds of honey, second premium of three dollars. This honey was made in Phelps's patent hive.

To John Smith, for third best ten pounds of honey, third premium of $2 00

The committee would state, that they examined three different kinds of bee hives.

Longstreth's hive, deposited by P. J. Mahon.

Phelps's hive, deposited by the patentee.

Parkinson's hive, deposited by the same.

Each is worthy of especial notice for different valuable qualities.

The committee would award a diploma for a lot of butter made from the Alderney cows, which did not strictly come under the rule for our decision. The butter was made by Mrs. Caroline Knight, and deposited by Craig Biddle.

LEWIS SHARPLESS,
ADAM C. ECKFELT,
JAMES A. MOORE,
Committee.

No. 23.—Flour and Corn Meal.

To the President of the Pennsylvania State Agricultural Society:

Your Committee, No. 23, on Flour and Corn Meal, respectfully report, that they have examined all the flour and other articles submitted to their judgment, and beg leave to award as follows, viz:

The first premium of ten dollars each on flour, is awarded to two barrels—one from Ashland mills, deposited by Smedley & Rudolph, and the other from Lewistown mills, John Sterrett & Co., deposited by L. G. Mytinger.—Both barrels made from white wheat, and very superior for family or bakers' bread.

The second and third premiums are awarded to Wm. B. Thomas, for his superior family flour; the second of five dollars, for his white wheat flour, and the third of three dollars, for his red wheat flour.

There was a small sample of rye flour exhibited by Charles L. Wampole, but the quantity being too small to enable the committee to form an opinion of the work produced, no premium is awarded to the depositor.

To Patrick Queen, the committee beg leave to recommend a premium of two dollars for his five bags Sea Island hominy. This article seems to be well prepared, and neatly put up for family use.

Of smut machines and grain separators, there were several varieties on exhibition. The committee regret that they had no means of testing the relative merits of these machines. All of them seem to be well constructed, and in their general principles, calculated to produce the desired result. But without other personal knowledge, the committee decline awarding any premium. The same remarks will apply to the bran dusters exhibited.

Of mill stones, some very fine looking specimens were on the ground, and showed superior skill in their construction; but as to their good quality in the grinding of wheat and other grains, the committee cannot pass judgment; practical experience alone being the true test of the quality of mill stones.

WM. M. HENDERSON,
H. W. SNYDER,
CALEB STRODE,
Committee.

No. 24.—Grain, Seeds and Vegetables.

To the President of the Pennsylvania State Agricultural Society:

The Committee, No. 24, on Grain, Seeds and Vegetables, report as follows:

To Richard Pim, best bushel white wheat	$3 00
To Joseph Hennings, second best, do.	1 00
To G. & C. K. Engle, best bushel of red wheat	3 00

To Jesse M. Williams, second best bushel of red wheat............ $1 00
To Charles L. Wampole, best bushel of rye...................... 3 00
To George Blight, second best.....do.......................... 1 00
To David Landreth, for the best bushel of white Flint corn......... 3 00
To G. & C. K. Engle, for best bushel of oats.................... 3 00
To David Landreth, for second best, do........................ 1 00
To James Sloan, best bushel of potatoes....................... 3 00
To A. L. Felton, second best, do.............................. 1 00
To Ira Gibson, for a very fine sample of "Foxite potatoes"........ 3 00
To Joseph Harrison, for best bushel of sweet potatoes, Pennsylvania
    growth.. 3 00
To Wm. Blair, best bushel field turnips....................... 3 00
To A. L. Felton, second best..do............................. 1 00
To A. L. Felton, best bushel of carrots....................... 3 00
To Wm. Blair, best bushel of parsnips......................... 3 00
To David Landreth, best bushel of flaxseed................:.. 3 00
To Job Hayes, best bushel of timothy seed.................... 3 00

The committee also notice a very fine collection of garden and field seeds, grown by David Landreth, Esq., at Bloomsdale, numbering over two hundred different kinds. Also, some white flour corn and "Adams's" early six weeks' corn.

Paschall Morris & Co. also exhibited a large and highly creditable collection of field and garden products, including over one hundred varieties of seed.

The contributions were large, and the quality of the different articles exhibited, uniformly good, notwithstanding the unfavorable season for many of them, evincing an increased interest on the part of our farmers, rendering it difficult for the judges, in many instances, to decide.

Among the contributions, we notice fine samples of corn from G. Blight, E. Hindle, E. T. Hoopes, Thomas Yeamans, W. Blair, J. Kinnear, Rev. J. Goddard, E. J. Dickey, and others.

Samples of wheat from A. Garrett, M. Clegg, T. Yeamans, J. Lidster, J. Cope, P. and G. P. Whitaker, G. Vanartsdalen and others.

The competition in potatoes was large. Among the contributors we notice G. Blight, T. Yeamans, J. Simpers, F. Scattergood, J. Kinnear, J. C. Kane, T. R. Bunting, H. W. Ditman and others, all of whom exhibited fine samples.

Messrs Craig & Bellas, A. Garrett, G. S. Fox, E. T. Hoopes, M. H. Cornell and C. M. Wampole, exhibited some good samples of oats.

JAMES S. HUBER,
On behalf of the committee.

No. 25.—Domestic Manufactures.

To the President of the Pennsylvania State Agricultural Society:

The undersigned Judges upon Domestic Manufactures, No. 25, respectfully report, that the exhibition under this head, was extremely meagre, when compared with other departments. The introduction of manufacturing establishments into our country has nearly banished that kind of household industry, which formerly produced articles of this class in such great abundance. Even among the articles exhibited, a number bore evidence of having been manufactured many years since. The committee have made the following award of premiums:

To David M. Everly, of Lancaster county, for best lot of cocoons.... $8 00
To Miss Harriet Sumney, of Lancaster city, for second best lot cocoons.. 5 00
To David M. Everly, best reeled silk............................. 5 00
To Miss Harriet Sumney, best sewing silk........................ 5 00
To same lady, best silk stockings............................... 5 00
To Anna F. Gordon, best linen diaper............................ 5 00
To Mrs. Job Hayes, second best linen diaper..................... 3 00
To Eli Logan, third best linen diaper........................... 2 00
To Miss H. M. Hayes, best double coverlet....................... 5 00
To Eli Logan, second best double coverlet 3 00
To F. Feggenbush, third best double coverlet.................... 2 00
To Mrs. Job Hayes, best home made shirt......................... 5 00
To Dr. John Curwen, second best home made shirt, made by the inmates of the Pennsylvania Lunatic Asylum................... 3 00
To same, second best home made woollen socks, made by same..... 2 00
To Mrs. George H. Bucher, best pair blankets..............Silver cup.
To Mrs. Job Hayes, second best pair blankets................... $5 00
To Eli Logan, third best pair blankets......................... 3 00
To Mrs. Job Hayes, best plain linen.......................Silver cup.
To Anna F. Gordon, second best plain linen..................... $3 00
To Mrs. Job Hayes, best woollen stockings...................... 3 00
To Eli Logan, second best woollen stockings.................... 2 00
To Miss M. B. Thomas, third best woollen stockings............. 1 00
To George Buckman, fifteen yards best rag carpet............... 5 00
Second best rag carpet, made in the Lancaster county prison.... 3 00
To Eli Logan, best home made flannel........................... 5 00
To Miss M. B. Thomas, best hearth rug.......................... 5 00

GEORGE SMITH,
NATHAN GARRETT,
EMANUEL HEY,
Committee.

No. 26.—Household Manufactures.

To the President of the Pennsylvania State Agricultural Society:

Your Committee, No. 26, on Household Manufactures, award the following premiums upon articles comprised within their schedule:

To Dr. John Curwen, for best ornamental needle work, made by inmates of Lunatic Asylum at Harrisburg.....................	$5 00
To Mary Brown, of West Philadelphia, for second best ornamental needle work..	3 00
To John C. Heald, of Philadelphia, for best Ottoman cover.........	3 00
To Martha C. Loughton, for second best Ottoman cover...........	2 00
To Anna E. Stroup, of New Bloomfield, Perry county, for best table cover..	3 00
To Mrs. S. T. Johnson, of Wilmington, Del., for second best table cover..	2 00
To Frederick Hapold, of Philadelphia, for best artificial flowers.....	3 00
To M. B. Thomas, of West Chester, for second best artificial flowers,	2 00
To Anna M. Mott, of Philadelphia, for best variety of worsted work	5 00
To Emily Welsh, of West Philadelphia, for the best worked cushion,	3 00
To Mary P. Wood, for the best quilt, a silk star quilt..............	3 00
To Mary M. Spangler, of Philadelphia, for second best quilt........	2 00
To Mrs. E. T. Miller, of Philadelphia, for the best lamp stand mat..	3 00
To M. B. Thomas, of West Chester, for second best lamp stand mat..	2 00
To Margaret G. Bradley, of Philadelphia, for best ornamental shell work..	3 00
To Mary A. Royer, for second best ornamental shell work.........	2 00
To Mrs. Job Hayes, of Chester county, for best home made bread...	5 00
To Sarah Jane Logan, of Chester county, for second best home made bread..	3 00
To Sarah Jane Logan, of Chester county, for the best pound cake...	3 00
To Mrs. Job Hayes, for second best pound cake..................	2 00
To Mrs. Job Hayes, for best sponge cake.......................	3 00
To Sarah J. Logan, for second best sponge cake..................	2 00
To Eliza G. Walker, of Allegheny county, for the best preserves..Silver cup.	
To Sarah Jane Logan, for second best preserves.................	$3 00
To Sarah J. Logon, for best tomato preserves...................Silver cup.	
To A. G. Walker, of Allegheny county, for second best tomato preserves...	$3 00
To Sarah J. Logan, for best tomato figs........................	5 00
To Miss Harriet Sumney, of Lancaster county, for second best tomato figs..	3 00
To Sarah J. Logan, best specimen of pickles....................	3 00

To Sarah J. Logan, for best quince butter....................... $3 00
To Mrs. Job Hayes, for second best quince butter.............. 2 00
To Mrs. Job Hayes, for best peach butter...................... 3 00
To Sarah J. Logan, for second best peach butter............... 2 00
To Mrs. Geo. H. Bucher, of Cumberland county, Pa., for the best
    home made soap... 3 00
To Mrs. Job Hayes, for the second best home made soap......... 2 00
To Mrs. Job Hayes, for the best fruit jelly................... 3 00
To Mrs. Eliza G. Walker, second best fruit jelly.............. 2 00

Special premiums.

To Matilda B. Thomas, of West Chester, for excellent crochet work, 2 00
To Mrs. Gillespie, for superior worked piano cover........... 2 00
To Miss Margaret Pogley, for ornamental leather box; &c....... 2 00
To Edward Remick, for fine worsted work, in frame............. 2 00
To Rebecca Githens, for demonstrative scale for cutting ladies' dresses, 2 00
To Miss Emily Welsh, of West Philadelphia, for needle-worked table
    mats... 2 00
To Mrs. E. T. Miller, of Philadelphia, for embroidered table cover.. 2 00
To Dr. John Curwen, for quilt made by inmates of the Lunatic Asy-
    lum, at Harrisburg....................................... 2 00

Respectfully submitted.
P. R. FREAS,
JOSEPH KONIGMACHER,
R. W. COLEMAN,
Committee.

No. 27.—MANUFACTURES OTHER THAN DOMESTIC.

To the President of the Pennsylvania State Agricultural Society:

Your Committee, No. 27, on Manufactures other than Domestic, report,
that they examined all the articles that came under their notice, and award
the following premiums, viz:

To Michael Lawn, for omnibus.................................Diploma.
To Lane & Co., for Germantown wagon.........................Diploma.
To Lane & Garner....do........do.............................Diploma.
To Lane & Garner, for Jenny Lind wagon, two seated, first premium, $10 00
To John Wagner............do.....do....do......2d....do.... 5 00
To Charles W. Conover, for top buggy, first premium.......... 10 00
To Lane & Garner...........do......2d....do................. 5 00
To Cyrus S. Haldeman, trotting wagon........................Diploma.
To J. J. Collins.............do.................................do.
To John Kneip, trotting wagon body............................do.

To Moses Hey, woollen knitting yarn, first premium................ $3 00
To James C. Ogden. .do.....do.............. .... Diploma.
To James C. Ogden, bed ticking...................................do.
To Lancaster county prison, cotton bags.........................do.
To same, woollen carpet..do.
To George Buckman, rag carpet..................................do.
To Rockhill & Wilson, fine display of clothing...................do.
To J. E. Colgrove, school desks................................do.
To Hortsman, military goods....................................do.
To B. Sherman, display of carpenters' tools, first premium........ $5 00
To John Colton. .do..............do......2d......do.......... 3 00
To William Goldsmith, display of carpenters' tools.............Diploma.
To George J. Henkels, display of furniture.................Silver medal.
To Courtney & Willitts, display of cottage furniture, enamelled......do.
To Dickel & Margan, birch wardrobe.........................Diploma.
To George W. Hocker, marble wagon.............................do.
To Amos Laman, child's vattent.................................do.
To same, Pennsylvania marble wagon............................do.
To Charles S. Swope, child's gigs and carriages..................do.
To John Pfaff, flute, (ivory)..................................do.
To J. Bancroft, fancy soaps...................................do.

All which is respectfully submitted.

E. P. THOMPSON,
WM. BELL,
HENRY C. EYER,

Committee.

No. 28.—WINTER PREMIUMS.

Winter premiums will be awarded at the annual meeting of the society, at Harrisburg.—See pages 22, 23, 24, 25, 26.

No. 29.—FRUIT.

To the President of the Pennsylvania State Agricultural Society:

Your Committee, No. 29, on Fruits, respectfully report, that they have awarded the following premiums, viz:

To D. Miller, Jr., of Carlisle, for best collection of apples and pears, $10 00
To E. A. Vickroy, of Johnstown, second best collection of apples
and pears.. 5 00
To J. Perkins, best bushel of apples........................... 2 00

To J. P. Lee, apples, best six native varieties.......................... $2 00
To J. C. Baldwin, 2d...do........do............................. 1 00
To Isaac Collins, for best quinces............................... 2 00
To L. Chamberlain, second best quinces........................ 1 00

And they recommend a special premium of $5 to L. Chamberlain, for Chinese quinces.

To W. Mackaw, best native collection of pears................... 10 00
To W. Mackaw, one peck of Seckel pears, best.................. 3 00
To C. B. Ott, second best Seckel pears......................... 2 00
To Mrs. Geo. Liggett, another variety, six specimens of Begnier... 2 00
To Mr. Mackaw, second do. do. Washington.................. 2 00
To Mr. Mackaw, foreign, best collection of pears................. 10 00
To. I. B. Baxter, do. 2d....do............do 5 00
To I. B. Baxter, variety Duchess D'Angouleme................... 3 00
To Mr. Mackaw, variety 2d Doyenne Blanc..................... 2 00
To Mrs. C. Whitaker, for Beurre Diel pears..................... 2 00
To I. B. Baxter, for Doyenne Blanc, 2d do...................... 2 00
To Charles Morris, best mountain sweet watermelons, 3 specimens.. 3 00
To Joseph Hatch, 2d..do................do................... 2 00

Special premiums for pears, viz:
To charles Cornell and Peter Parker, for Fondante de Malvines and Petre, $2 each.. 4 00

Wine.

To N. Longworth, of Cincinnati, for best home made Sparkling Catawba.. 3 00
To Mr. Haines, for best home made wine........................ 3 00
To   do.   for second   do............................... 2 00
To   do.   for best home made bounce..................... 3 00

Grapes.

To I. B. Baxter, best collection native...................Silver medal.
To Peter Raabe, second best do. do................................ $3 00
To A. L. Felton, best six bunches Isabella...................... 2 00
To Wm. John, second best . do.   do........................ 1 00
To Wm. Martin, Sr., best six bunches Catawba................. 3 00
To Henry Smith, second best   do.   do..................... 2 00
To T. Hilyard, best six bunches Elsinborough.................. 2 00
To Peter Raabe, second best do.   do......................... 1 00
To Wm. Savery, for another variety............................. 2 00
To Robert Buist, for best collection of foreign grapes, thirty varieties...Silver medal.
To David S. Brown, for collection of best foreign grapes, only fifteen varieties...Silver medal.

To Wm. Johns, for second best foreign grapes..................... $3 00
To D. S. Brown, for best black Hamburg, three bunches........... 3 00
To D. Murphy, second best   do.   do.................... 2 00
To H. Cowperthwaite, best Chasselas,........................ 3 00
To D. S. Brown, best white Muscat.......................... 3 00
To same, best Frontignac.................................. 3 00
To D. Murphy, second best do.............................. 2 00
To H. Cowperthwaite, another variety best.................... 3 00
To D. S. Brown, best Chasselas rouge........................ 2 00
To Andrew Craig, gardener to the Magdalen asylum, for best bushel
     of peaches.. 4 00
To I. B. Baxter, best peck of peaches........................ 2 00
To George Deakyne, second best do. do....................... 1 00
To Benj. Galice, best dozen peaches......................... 2 00
To Wm. W. Fraley, second best do. do....................... 1 00
To J. C. Zane, best mellons, Citron......................... 2 00
To A. L. Felton, second best do. do......................... 1 00
For the best and greatest number of choice varieties of peaches, three
     of each variety, to J. W. Thorne........................ 10 00
For second best do. do. to J. W. Summey..................... 5 00
To J. C. Zane, best specimen musk melon..................... 3 00
To G. W. Earle, second best   do.   do....................... 2 00
To Wm. Martin, Sr., of Allegheny county, for the best training of
     grape vines.....................................Silver medal.

Your committee, before closing their report, cannot but express regret that the unpropitious nature of the season, which has been almost unexampled for drought, has limited, in a great degree, the quantity and quality, especially of those rich varieties of fruits which, under more favorable circumstances, would have, in all probability, furnished the most splendid display ever presented for exhibition.

     All which is respectfully submitted.

     E. W. KEYSER,
     THOMAS HANCOCK,
     JAMES D. FULTON,
     W. E. BRINCKLE,
                              Committee.

No. 30.—FLOWERS, PLANTS AND DESIGNS.

To the President of the Pennsylvania State Agricultural Society:

Your Committee, No. 30, on Flowers, Plants and Designs have awarded the following premiums, viz:

For Private Collection of Green House Plants—20 varieties.

First premium to James Kent, gardener to J. Francis Knorr........ $20 00
Second premium to Thomas Robertson, gardener to B. A. Fahnestock 15 00
Third premium to gardener of Wm. W. Keen................... 10 00
Fourth premium to gardener of John Lambert................... 8 00
Fifth premium to Alex. Burnett, gardener to H. Pratt M'Kean...... 6 00

Collection of Green House Plants—20 Varieties—open to all.

First premium to John Pollock, gardener to James Dundas......... 20 00
Second premium to Robert Buist.............................. 15 00
Third premium to Isaac Collins............................... 10 00

Collection of Green House Plants—12 Varieties—open to all.

First premium to Isaac Collins, gardener to Gen. Robert Patterson.. 10 00
Second premium to John Pollock, gardener to James Dundas....... 8 00
Third premium to James Kent, gardener to J. Francis Knorr........ 6 00
Fourth premium to David Ferguson............................ 5 00

Collection of Specimen Plants—4 Varieties.

First premium to Peter Raabe................................ 5 00
Second premium to James Kent, gardener to J. Francis Knorr...... 6 00
Third premium to John Pollock, gardener to James Dundas........ 5 00

Collection of Conifers—6 Varieties.

First premium to Paschall Morris............................. 5 00
Second premium to John Gray................................. 3 00

Collection of Achemines.

First premium to Thomas Robertson, gardener to B. A. Fahnestock.. 4 00

Collection of Orchids.

First premium to Robert Buist................................ 5 00

Collection of Ferns.

First premium to John Pollock, gardener to James Dundas........ 2 00

Designs of Cut Flowers.

Premium to Peter Raabe..................................... 20 00
Premium to Henry Lynch, gardener to J. Rutter, West Chester..... 10 00

Designs of Cut Flowers, not exceeding five feet in height.

Premium to Henry A. Dreer.................................. 4 00
Premium to Robert Kilvingston............................... 3 00

Designs formed of Grasses.

First premium to Mary M'Ilvaine, West Philadelphia $5 00
Second premium to Wm. Berry, gardener to Alfred Cope.......... 3 00

Designs formed of Indigenous Plants.

First premium to John M'Intosh 5 00

Baskets formed of Cut Flowers.

First premium to Mrs. M. Newkirk............................ 3 00
Second premium to John Kindler, gardener to Thomas Dunlap 2 00
Third premium to Robert Kilwingston......................... 1 00

Boquets for the hand.

First premium to Charles Souchet 3 00
Second premium to Henry Lynch, gardener to J. Rutter, West Chester 2 00

Dahlias—24 Varieties.

First premium to Robert Buist........................Silver medal.

Roses—20 Varieties.

First premium to Robert Buist................................ 5 00
Second premium to Henry A. Dreer.......................... 3 00

Roses—Greatest Variety.

First premium to Paschall Morris............................ 3 00
Second premium to Robert Buist............................ 2 00

Verbenas—Greatest Variety.

First premium to Robert Buist............................... 3 00

German Asters—Best Collection.

First premium to Charles Souchet 3 00

The committee with great pleasure notice a handsomely prepared collection of "Marine Algae," or "Sea Weeds," by J. M. Somerville, of Philadelphia, and a beautiful collection of variegated plants by Robert Buist, together
with a handsome collection of plants from the garden of Dr. James Rush,
not entered for competition. They also notice an immense leaf of the "Vic-
toria Regia," and a fine specimen of "Nelumbrum Speciosum," from the collection of Caleb Cope, and a splendid specimen of "Lycopodium Coessium,"
from Mr. Joshua Robinson, Pittsburg, Pa. Mr. Peter M'Kenzie, of Philadel-

phia, has contributed 250 varieties of green house plants, but not for competition.

Respectfully submitted.

PETER M'KENZIE,
HENRY L. TRIPLER,
JACOB B. GARBER,
WALTER WHITE,
J. E. MITCHELL,
Committee.

No. 30½.—GARDEN VEGETABLES.

To the President of the Pennsylvania State Agricultural Society:

Your Committee, No 30½, on Garden-Vegetables, respectfully report, that they have awarded the following premiums, viz:

To James Jones, gardener at Girard College, for best 12 stocks of celery..	$3 00
To same person, for second best, another variety	2 00
To A. L. Felton, for 12 best white table turnips	3 00
To J. & C. K. Engle, for second best. .do	2 00
To James Jones, gardener at Girard College, for best dozen long red beets	3 00
To William Barry, gardener to A. Cope, best dozen parsnips	3 00
To George Blight, of Germantown, for second best dozen parsnips..	3 00
To William Barry, gardener to A. Cope, best dozen yellow onions..	3 00
To same, second best do do	2 00
To John Riley, gardener Insane Hospital, best three dozen yellow onions	3 00
To James Jones, gardener at Girard College, best three dozen white onions	2 00
To A. L. Felton, best six heads broccoli	3 00
To William Barry, A. Cope's gardener, best dozen tomatoes	3 00
To same, best peck do	3 00
To James Jones, gardener at Girard College, second best peck tomatoes	2 00
To George Blight, best egg plants, (second plants,)	3 00
To Henry Smith, Frankford, second best egg plants, (second plants,)	2 00
To James Jones, Girard College, best six egg plants	2 00
To Robert Buist, second best do. . do	1 00
To Jesse Rambo, Gloucester county, N. J., best dozen sweet potatoes,	3 00
To Amos Darlington, West Chester, second best do do	2 00
To William Barry, A. Cope's gardener, best half peck Lima beans..	3 00

To John Gray, best three garden squashes.............................. $3 00
To L. P. Hoopes, West Chester, best dozen ears yellow seed corn... 3 00
To John Kinnier, T. Dunlap's gardener, second best...do....do.... 2 00
To John Gray, best dozen ears white seed corn...................... 3 00
To M. B. Thomas, of West Chester, best dozen table potatoes...... 3 00
To John Kinnier, second best............do......do............. 2 00
To George Blight, best dozen carrots.............................. 3 00
To William Barry, second best dozen carrots..................... 2 00
To John Riley, best one dozen salsify............................... 2 00
To William Barry, A. Cope's gardener, best six dozen heads cabbage, 3 00
To John Riley, second best drum head cabbage................... 2 00
To James Jones, Girard College gardener, best red Dutch cabbage... 3 00
To James Jones, Girard College gardener, best of another kind, Sa-
voy... 2 00
To A. L. Felton, best six heads lettuce........................... 3 00
To William Barry, second best..do..'.............................. 2 00
To George Blight, best three dozen sweet corn.................... 3 00
To A. L. Felton, second best.....do....do...................... 2 00
To George Blight, best three specimens marrow squashes..,........ 3 00
To John'Riley, best two specimens pumpkins..................... 3 00
To H. W. Ditman, Oxford, second best..do 2 00

Display of Vegetables.

Best by market gardener, A. L. Felton, premium of............... $15 00
Best by amateur gardener, John Riley 10 00
Second best do., James Jones, Girard College gardener........... 5 00
Third best do., George Blight.................................. 4 00

Respectfully submitted.

CHARLES P. HAYES,
THOS. MEEHAN,
BENJ. GULLISS,

Committee.

No. 31.—STOVES.

To the President of the Pennsylvania State Agricultural Society:

Your Committee, No. 31, beg leave to submit the following report and award of premiums:

To Robert Wood, of Philadelphia, for

1. One large fountain, a silver medal.
2. Lamp stands, first premium.
3. Arbor seats and chairs, first premium.
4. Four vases, honorable mention.

5. Eight tree boxes, silver medal.

6. Four tables, creditable to maker.

7. "Lions and Dogs," images, silver medal.

8. Two sets stairs, manufactured from anthracite iron from Swede iron company, silver medal.

9. Lot of iron railing, silver medal.

10. Lot of ornamental castings, made for the Farmers' and Mechanics' Bank, manufactured from iron from the Swede iron company, silver medal.

11. Wrought iron carriage gate, well got up, and a beautiful specimen of wrought iron work.

12 Three bronze statues, well got up, creditable to maker and worthy of honorable mention.

Your committee consider that Mr. Robert Wood is deserving of more than ordinary credit, for the fine display made by him.

Andrew Moyer, one lot stoves for heating and cooking, worthy of notice.

Hammill & Rennage, two spiral heaters, beautiful castings, and worthy of notice.

Warnick & Liebrandt, one lot stoves, beautiful workmanship, creditable to makers.

Neman & Warwick, one lot stoves and portable forge, beautiful castings, and worthy of especial notice.

A. J. Gallagher, lot of stoves and fixtures, honorable mention.

T. H. Lachenmies, lot of railing and iron bedsteads, honorable mention.

Abbott & Lawrence, lot of stoves of various kinds, beautiful specimens of workmanship, and worthy of honorable mention.

F. Foering & Son, lot of stoves, beautiful articles, and worthy of honorable mention.

F. M'Ilvaine, hot air cooking range, made for heating an upper room, first premium, silver medal.

Keen & Co., one cooking range and warm air furnace, worthy of attention.

Reeder & Groff, lot of iron railing, deserving of honorable mention.

Josiah Kisterbock & Son, one wrought iron warm air furnace and worthy of honorable mention.

Rand & Hays, beautiful assortment of goods. We call particular attention to their ventilator and range.

Cox, Hager & Co., lot stove castings. We award them first premium, silver medal.

Peter & Johnson, for rotary roaster, a silver medal.

Cresson, Peterson & Stewart, fine assortment of stoves, worthy of notice.

Cresson, Peterson & Stewart, enamelled hollow ware, awarded a silver medal.

Thomas F. Williams, one Gorenier's cooking stove, awarded a silver medal.

S. A. Harrison, Chilson's warming and ventilating furnace, awarded a silver medal; and for grates, mantels, &c., honorable mention.

Respectfully submitted.

THOS. E. POTTS,
L. LEVIS,
THOS. C. WOOD,
Committee.

No. 32.—SILVER WARE, GLASS AND GLASS WARE, CUTLERY AND BRITANNIA.

To the President of the Pennsylvania State Agricultural Society:

Your Committee, No. 32, on Silver Ware, &c., award the following premiums, viz:

To Franklin Smith, of Philadelphia, for best stained glass for windows...Silver medal.

To Conrad Bard & Son, Philadelphia, best specimen of silver ware, a fine collection....................................Silver medal.

To Wm. J. Kerr, Philadelphia, for samples of cut glass ware....Silver medal.

To Calverty & Holmes, Philadelphia, for variety of Britannia ware...Silver medal·

To S. H. Wilder, for display of clocks...........................Diploma.

To John O. Mead & Co., Philadelphia, for display of plated silver ware...Silver medal.

To Philadelphia Glass Company, for sky lights, vault lights and window glass...Diploma.

Respectfully submitted.

C. W. HARRISON,
HEZEKIAH KING,
SAMUEL WALKER,
Committee.

No. 34.— INVENTIONS.

To the President of the Pennsylvania State Agricultural Society:

The judges of articles enumerated in invoice, No. 34, entitled Inventions, report that they have bestowed as much time as the brief continuance of the Exhibition permitted to the examination of the specimens allotted to them, some of which do not appear to come fairly under the designation of inventions. This remark applies especially to the display of "hats, caps and furs," which appears to your committee to be highly creditable; but as they have no practical knowledge of such matters, they must decline making any award other than a diploma to each of the following exhibitors, viz:

To Charles Oakford, for a most extensive and beautiful assortment of hats, caps and furs.

To John S. Young, for a case of hats and caps of beautiful finish, and to Messrs. T. A. Boyce and John C. Pfeil for a similar display.

Among the inventions that appear to be really such, the committee notice the following, viz:

A hydraulic ram of large size for supplying railroad depots and towns, deposited by Mr. Joseph Strode, of West Chester. It is deemed worthy of a discretionary premium of ten dollars, as being the most complete yet produced.

They would also notice the vibratory engine of Gardener's improvement, as deserving of a diploma.

The premium of three dollars for the best specimen of pressed brick is awarded to J. W. Andrews, of Norristown, for his specimen of brick burned with coal.

Diplomas are also awarded to the following, viz:

Galvanized iron, manufactured by M'Cullough & Co., of Wilmington, Del., deposited by J. C. Adams.

To Bayliss, Darby & Lynn, collection of wire work.

To Robert C. Justis, for double span rotating gate, open without alighting.

To E. Woolman, self-closing gates and hinges.

To N. B. Harris, automaton weighing and packing machine.

To same gentleman, for hominy and samp mill, to manufacture from dry corn for sea purposes.

To G. R. Blakiston, lot of hydraulic cement.

To A. C. Gallahue, of Pittsburg, machine for pegging boots and shoes.

To W. F. Scheible, four seal presses.

To Stewart & Thomas, composition roofing.

To Prof. James, for safety locomotive bars.

To Stephen Ustick, for brick machine.

To Wagner & Lindlay, for bricks.

To J. W. Andrews, for bricks.

To Paxon & Phipps, for bricks.

To Stratton & Bro., for gas apparatus.

To Jacob Zook, for self-acting carrier for lathes.

To C. B. Daniel, for roofing slate, iron girders and shutters.

To Isaac T. Ford, for expansion bits.

JOHN C. CRESSON,
C. M. CRESSON,
E. T. HYATT,
Committee.

No. 35.—MISCELLANEOUS ARTICLES

To the President of the Pennsylvania State Agricultural Society:

The Committee, No. 35, on Miscellaneous Articles, respectfully offer the following report, and award the following premiums:

To Richards & Betts, for Chrystallographs ....Silver medal.
To M'Leese & Germon, for Chrystallotypes.......... ....do.
To D. B. Richards and M'Leese & Germon, for Daguerreotypes, each
    a..Diploma.
To A. W. Williams, for mezzographs........................... do.
To. L. N. Rosenthal, for tinted lithographs..................Silver medal.

From the excellence of the Daguerreotypes of M. A. Root, your committee regret that his contribution was received too late for competition, and leave the award to the Executive Committee.

To M'Curdy, Jones, White & Co., for excellence of manufacture of
    artificial teeth..................................:........Silver medal.
To Dr. Charles Neil, for block and plate work...................do.
To William C. Eastlack, for block and plate work...............do.
To Robert Bates, for his case of instruments for the cure of stammer-
    ing, the committee would recommend the special premium of a. .Diploma.
To Wm. Calvert, dentist, for improvement in enamelling and mould-
    ing block teeth, a...Silver medal.

           Respectfully submitted.

                    A. L. ELWYN,
                    PAUL B. GODDARD,
                    ALFRED S. KENNEDY,
                             Committee.

No. 36.

To the President of the Pennsylvania State Agricultural Society:

The special committee respectfully report, that owing to the great variety and number of articles submitted to their inspection, the merits of many of which could only be decided by actual trial, precluded by the circumstances under which a State Fair is held, they have not felt at liberty to award premiums to a large number of probably deserving exhibitors. When a number of exhibitors in the same line presented their claims, they have *not* pretended to decide upon their relative merits, inasmuch as their opportunity for examination was inadequate to the proper discharge of their duty. The following premiums are recommended:

For a very interesting collection of Pathological specimens, illustrating
    the diseases of the horse and other domestic animals, deposited by
    the American Veterinary Society, a.....................Silver medal.
For the display of chandeliers, gas fixtures, &c., made by Cornelius
    Baker & Co., a...Silver medal.

To Allen & Needles, C. Cummings, C. B. Rogers, G. A. Leinau, for fertilizers, each a...Diploma.

To Peyton & Thomas, for display of hemp and cotton in bails, exhibited by Paschall Morris & Co...........................Diploma.

To W. F. Murphy, of Philadelphia, for display of blank books, bank ledgers, &c...Diploma.

To A. Mann, of Philadelphia, display of blank books and stationery, Diploma.

To James R. Reed, & Co., of Pittsburg, for one set of engineering instruments.......................................Silver medal.

To F. Reed, of Canton, Mass., case of cordwainer and garden tools, exhibited by Paschall Morris & Co..........................Diploma.

To Daniel Halliday, of Ellington, Conn., for patent wind mill or engine, exhibited by P. Morris & Co........................Silver medal.

To P. Morris & Co., for patent angular hames. ....Diploma.

To Paschall Morris & Co., for Stauffer's bolting apparatus.........Diploma.

To P. Morris & Co., for Canby's grain winnower................Diploma.

To Durand & Tourtelot, for syrups, &c........................Diploma.

To Thomas Butler, Philadelphia, for a beautiful display of superior copper and tin ware......................................Diploma.

To Hartman & Saxe, for display of surveying instruments.........Diploma.

To R. C. Walborn, Philadelphia, display of shirts, collars, stocks and wrappers..Diploma.

To Wm. Rose & Brothers, plasterers' and bricklayers' trowels.....Diploma.

To E. D. Hatch, domestic hardware...........................Diploma.

To Charles Bradfield, Philadelphia, for turning lathe and improved belting....... ....Diploma.

To J. E. Mitchell, Philadelphia, grind stones and mill stones......, Diploma.

To James Wood & Sons, Philadelphia, for patent imitation Russian sheet iron..Diploma.

To J. F. Hammitt, Philadelphia, for improved railroad car seat.....　do.

To E. G. Chommer, for case of dies ....　do.

To —— Krup, for essence of coffee.............................　do.

To Bohler & Co., for essence of coffee..........................　do.

To H. S. Hitner, specimens of iron ore.........................　do.

To Hitner, Cresson & Co., for pig metal........................　do.

To A. Winter, for machine for sawing fire wood.................　do.

To Thomas Fisher, for "Mathematics simplified" ....　do.

To F. Ford, Philadelphia, for display of window blinds...........　do.

To James H. Bryson, No. 2 North Sixth street, for his printing press in operation on Fair ground, and for his card printing, a....Silver medal.

Respectfully submitted.

JAMES A. M'CREA,
G. BLIGHT BROWNE,
Committee.

To the President of the Pennsylvania State Agricultural Society:

The undersigned, having been requested to serve as a committee, and to examine the piano fortes exhibited at the fair of the Pennsylvania State Agricultural Society, respectfully report: ,

That only six piano fortes have been sent to the Fair, for exhibition. Of these, four, manufactured by Messrs. Hallet, Davis & Co., of Boston, are exhibited by Mr. J. E. Gould, of Philadelphia. Two were made and are exhibited by Mr. Geo. Voigt, of Philadelphia.

The large open building in which this portion of the exhibition is held, is not as favorable to sound as an enclosed room, and perhaps the instruments do not appear in their most favorable light. However, a square piano forte, of 6½ octaves, made by Messrs. Hallet, Davis & Co., is found to be a superior instrument; and, in consideration of the reasonableness of the price, it is deemed worthy of especial commendation.

It is seldom that an instrument of good quality can be obtained at moderate cost; and when a maker combines, in his pianos excellence and cheapness, he has certainly achieved a great merit.

The cost of the piano above designated, is three hundred dollars; and it is the united opinion of the committee that it is the best instrument exhibited, and entitled to receive the first premium which the society offers for the "best piano," a...Silver medal.

PIERCE BUTLER,
Chairman of Com. on Piano Fortes.

PHILADELPHIA, *September* 29, 1854.

REPORTS

OF THE

TRANSACTIONS OF COUNTY SOCIETIES,

AS FAR AS RECEIVED.

ADAMS COUNTY.

GETTYSBURG, *March* 1, 1855.

To the President of the Pennsylvania State Agricultural Society:

SIR :—The Adams County Agricultural Society has been in existence only a little over a year, and not having yet held an exhibition, (the intense drought in this region last season having prevented,) its proceedings, although interesting to its members, would afford but little of value to those beyond its own sphere. Something has been, and is being, done, however. Our society believing that the establishment of the office of State Agricultural Chemist, and the appointment thereto of an eminently qualified gentleman, would result in largely promoting the agricultural interests of the Commonwealth, (and surely no other branch of industry is more deserving of justice at the hands of our legislators,) addressed a circular to the different county societies, requesting their co-operation in securing, by legislative enactment, the desired object. Whether our efforts will result in accomplishing anything, cannot now be said, but if not, " let the fire be kept up" as long as the necessity exists.

Our society is now discussing the various subjects connected with agriculture, and considerable interest is being felt in those discussions. The application of lime to land engaged the attention of the society for several successive meetings, and many facts of an interesting, and no doubt valuable, character were elicited from those who have limed more or less largely, and have noted results. I regret that I did not take a sketch of the debates, as I believe that their publication would be of service. I am fully persuaded that if no greater good should result from the establishment of our society than is brought about by these discussions, that all the time and means required have been repaid over and over again. They are, indeed, a most valuable feature of our organization.

The present officers of the society are:

PRESIDENT.—Hon. John M'Ginly.

VICE PRESIDENTS.—Maxwell Shields, F. Diehl, Wm. B. Brandon, Amos Lefever, Philip Donohue, Wm. B. Wilson, Joseph Fink, Peter Diehl, Joseph Kepner, Jacob Shank, John Lehman and Solomon Powers.

MANAGERS.—Thomas A. Marshall, John Gilbert, Abraham Krise, of P., Samuel Durboraw, David M. Myers, Joseph Wierman, James J. Wills.

RECORDING SECRETARY.—H. J. Stahle.

CORRESPONDING SECRETARY.—D. M'Conaughy.

TREASURER.—George Arnold.

We hope to be able to have a county fair next fall.

Yours truly,

H. J. STAHLE, *Secretary.*

ALLEGHENY COUNTY.

PITTSBURG, *March* 28, 1855.

To the President of the Pennsylvania State Agricultural Society:

DEAR SIR :—I have the honor to transmit to you, in obedience to the fifth section of the act of Assembly of March, 29, 1851, the following report of the finances of the Allegheny County Agricultural Society, for the year ending January 1, 1855:

The society's annual fair was held in the Ninth ward of the city of Pittsburg, during four days, in the latter part of October, 1854, on the grounds occupied last year by the State fair.

The cost of fences, buildings and fixtures was.......	$3,971 14	
Incidental expenses	1,125 26	
Cost of medals.................................	743 36	
Cash premiums paid.............................	1,049 00	
		$6,888 76
The gross receipts of the fair amounted to..........	5,829 18	
State appropriation for the year 1854..............	100 00	
Cash on hand on January 1, 1854.................	1,252 25	
		7,181 43
Leaving a balance of.....................................		292 67
Together with all our buildings and fixtures worth............		3,500 00

upon the grounds, of which we have a lease for four years from the date of last fair.

PAUL A. WAY, *President.*

O. P. SHIRAS, *Secretary.*

BEAVER COUNTY.

To the President of the Pennsylvania State Agricultural Society:

SIR :—The second annual meeting of the Beaver County Agricultural Society, was held in the court house, on Monday evening of March court, 1854. The following officers were elected to serve for the year, viz :

PRESIDENT.—R. L. Baker, Economy.

VICE PRESIDENT.—D. Minis, Falston borough.

RECORDING SECRETARY.—William Henry, Beaver borough.

CORRESPONDING SECRETARY.—A. R. Moore, Brighton township.

TREASURER.—James Allison, Beaver borough.

BOARD OF MANAGERS.—Thomas Thornily, Falston ; Daniel Dawson, Ohio ; Thos. M'Kinley, Chippewa ; Robert Potter, Raccoon ; James Darragh, borough; Robert Nelson, New Sewickley; Dr. J. H. Dickson, Rochester; Dr. S. Cunningham, Beaver; H. Irwin, Rochester township; W. Shrodes, Moon.

The board of managers at their first meeting, March 31, 1854, resolved to enlarge the fair ground occupied by the society for the last year's exhibition, by enclosing two acres more, making over four acres, including last year's enclosure. The additional ground was enclosed with a substantial board fence, eight feet high, to correspond with the fence built last year. The stalls for horses and cattle were doubled in number; the pens for sheep and swine remain the same in number as last year.

Additions were made to the floral hall and mechanics' hall doubling their capacity for holding articles for exhibition. An additional office was built for the use of the treasurer and his assistants; also an eating room large enough to accommodate from fifty to one hundred persons at once at table. A ring, containing about one-sixth of a mile in circuit, was also enclosed with substantial posts and boards, within, and at one end of the fair ground, for the more thorough display of horses, carriages, &c. The fair ground (which lies east of the borough of Beaver, and immediately adjoining it,) will, with a few additional improvements, which can be made the coming season at small cost out of the surplus money in the treasury, be complete in all its parts for its intended use, and will compare favorably with any county fair ground, perhaps, in the United States.

At the meeting of the board referred to above, a letter from R. L. Baker, Esq., president elect of our society, was received, declining to fill the office, on account of the multifarious duties pressing upon him, as principal of the Harmony society of Economy. Every member of the board regretted his declination of the office. Possessing, as all knew he did, the talents and experience in an eminent degree, to fill the post with honor to himself and advantage to our society, and the regret was not lessened when reference was made to the constitution, that it contained no provision for filling the vacancy; and that, by a law of our State establishing the Farmers' High School of Pennsylvania, we could not be represented—not having the proper officer required by law, to meet with others to organize a board for that institution. At an adjourned meeting of the society held on the 11th September last, this omission in the constitution was remedied, and vacancies can now be filled.

Thomas Thornily, Esq., was chosen president of the board of managers, and James Darragh, Esq., secretary. Committees were also appointed at the first meeting of the board, to superintend the fair ground, with discretionary power to enlarge and alter the buildings erected last year; to arrange the premium list, and to procure tickets for the present year. It was also resolved that the board meet on the last Friday of every month until the fair. This was carried into full effect—not an appointed day passing without having a quorum, and generally a full board.

Herewith you will find appended a list of premiums awarded. The annual fair was held on Thursday and Friday, the 21st and 22d of September last.

The weather was as fine as could be desired—the fair ground and buildings in good order. The floral hall was beautifully decorated, by a pretty large committee of the ladies and gentlemen of the neighborhood, with evergreens and flowers; our friends of the Harmony society of Economy, furnishing more than their proportion of flowers for the occasion. A large proportion of the articles on the premium list was well represented, and some were not surpassed by the State fair held the previous year at Pittsburg.

The fat ox, for instance, exhibited by the Harmony society, was the same which took a premium on that occasion, 'and much improved. The French Merino buck, by Caughey & Glass, and also the blooded horse, by J. W. Welsh. Some of the classes on the premium list were better represented, and others not so well as last year. But taken as a whole, it was considered equal by the thoughtful and intelligent.

Those whose observation and philosophy never extend beyond brick walls and brick pavements thought it inferior to our last fair. The season in this section of the State, was one of the most unpropitious for a fair that has occurred since the first settlement of the country. The unprecedented drought, scorching sun, and blighting wind, checked, and in some localities nearly destroyed the hopes of the husbandman. Had our fair fallen greatly below last year's exhibition, it would not have been a matter of surprise to the cultivators of the soil. To such, the wonder was, that so much could be produced and of such a quality in so unfavorable a season.

The attendance on both days of the fair was good. On the last day not less than six or seven thousand were on the ground at one time, being nearly equal to one fourth the population of the county.

We have over four hundred members, and the receipts from all sources will be over nine hundred dollars. Our expenses will be something over seven hundred dollars, leaving a balance in the treasury from one to two hundred dollars, when all claims are paid.

The address was delivered at two o'clock of the second day, by our worthy and respected fellow citizen, R. P. Roberts, Esq., and was listened to with marked attention by a large concourse of citizens, their wives, their sons and their daughters.

Late on the afternoon of the second day the fair closed, having passed off without any accident or occurrence to mar the harmony and general hilarity of the occasion.

On the 19th of October the ploughing match came off, on the ground selected for the purpose, by the committee, about half a mile west of the borough of Beaver.

Herewith is appended the report as published in the Beaver Argus, of all that is thought necessary on that subject.

D. MINIS, *Vice President.*

PLOUGHING MATCH.

The second annual Ploughing Match of the Beaver County Agricultural Society, came off on last Thursday. Fifteen ploughmen, with the following ploughs, entered the field as competitors for the premiums, viz:

James Irvin, Hall & Speer's Iron Cutter, No. 5.
Samuel Walton, R. Hall's Half Patent Lever.
Samuel Purvis, Hall's Patent Lever, No. 5.
David Ferguson, Kinkead's, No. 9.
John Small, Hall's Centre.
Candless Wilson, J. S. Hall & Speer's Valley Forge Iron Centre, No. 16.
James Laird, Hall & Speer's Centre Draft.
John M'Farland, Hall's Centre Draft, No. 5.
Ritchey Eakin, Wood's Centre.
Ruel R. Wray, Hall & Speer's Iron Coulter, No. 8.
Solomon Spangler, M. & S. H. Darragh's Hill Side.
John Given, Hall & Speer's Iron Coulter, No. 8.
Joseph Wray, Jr., Darragh's.
John Garrard, Hall & Speer's Iron Coulter.

At twenty minutes of twelve o'clock the signal being given by one of the managers, the horses were started, their drivers vieing with each other in time as well as skillful and scientific ploughing. The ploughing on the whole, considering the ground, being a light sandy soil, we heard practical farmers pronounce as very clever.

The premiums were awarded as follows:

First premium, Candless Wilson.................................... $6 00
Second...do...John M'Farland..................................... 5 00
Third....do...John Garrard....................................... 4 00
Fourth....do...Ritchey Eakin..................................... 3 00

Russell Vanoisdell did not enter for competition, but commenced on an unappropriated land when the others were nearly done, using M. & S. H. Darragh's Centre Draft, D. D. plow, which did such good work that a discretionary premium was recommended and awarded.

While we were pleased to see the presence of many from the distant townships of the county, we regretted that a greater number had not brought their teams and ploughs to exhibit their skill in turning the furrow. We hope that by the next 'match,' those of our agriculturists that were only spectators on this occasion, may be participators, and thus add interest to the "Ploughing Match."

List of premiums paid by Treasurer of Beaver County Agricultural Society, awarded at the Second Annual Fair held in Beaver, on 21st and 22d of September, 1854.

Thomas Watton, best Bolton gray chickens	$1 00	
Mrs. Watton, best gloves	50	
		$1 50
Miss A. Ferguson, best print butter		5 00
Thomas Thornely, second best largest collection of apples	$ 50	
Do.......best half bushel of apples	1 00	
Do.......best peck of pears	50	
Do.......best living hedge	1 00	
		3 00
T. M. Long, best pen drawing, (discretionary)		3 00
John W. Welsh, best blooded stallion		5 00
Eli Reno, best half bushel of apples		1 00
Thomas H. Mason, best draught mare, (discretionary)		2 00
Lewis & Hart Darragh, best game chickens	$1 00	
Do ....best Neshanock potatoes	1 00	
		2 00
Ephraim Smith, best pony		1 00
Joseph Cunningham, best pair of turkeys	$1 00	
Do..........best Java ducks	1 00	
		2 00
Henry Reed, best three acres of barley		3 00
Charles J. Dickey, best Bramah Pootra chickens		1 00
M. L. Todd, best quilt		1 00
Samuel Patterson, second best heavy draught horse	$1 00	
Do.......best jack	2 00	
		3 00
Martin S. Lyon, best Devonshire cow		1 00
Mrs. Clarissa Shively, best bread		1 00
Miss E. M. Morehead, best fruit jelly	$ 50	
Do...........best card case	50	
		1 00
Miss Adaline Morehead, best card basket		50
Lemuel Woodruff, best buggy horse	$3 00	
Do.......best Malay chickens	1 00	
		4 00
Miss Mary Ann Coyle, best ornamental needlework		1 00
J. W. Moore, best Shanghai chickens		1 00
William Given, best butter three months old	$2 00	
Do.....best coverlet	1 00	
Do.....best pair of blankets	1 00	
Do,.....best diaper	50	
		4 50

William H. Stokes, best double set of car harness $3 00
    Do .... best single set of ear harness 1 00
    Do .... best bridle and martingale 50
                                —— $4 50

Joseph Morehead, best corn in ear, ten bushels 1 00
    Do ...... best bridle harness 1 00
    Do .... best upper leather 1 00
                                —— 3 00

George Engle, best and largest collection of apples 1 00
Miss C. Moore, O. T., second best patch work quilt .... $ 50
    Do .... best woollen stockings 50
                                —— 1 00

Miss M. Moore, O. T., best thread lace 50
William G. Wolf, best heavy draft horse $3 00
    Do .... best Durham calf 1 00
                                —— 4 00

James Todd, best seed wheat, two bushels 2 00
John S. M'Coy, best boar pig 2 00
Daniel Dawson, best Leicester ewes $3 00
    Do ..... best sweet pumpkins 50
    Do ..... best cultivated farm 5 00
                                —— 8 50

Mrs. P. Stewart, best collection of chickens 1 00
Mrs. C. M. Stewart, best preserves .... $ 50
    Do .... best patch work quilt 1 00
                                —— 1 50

Cole & Co., best patent tubs 1 00
William Bryan, best Catawba grapes .... $ 50
    Do ..... best hearth rug, (discretionary) 1 00
                                —— 1 50

John D. Stokes, best harness leather 1 00
    Do ...... best kip skins 1 00
                                —— 2 00

John Culbertson, best Timothy seed 1 00
H. N. Frazier, best two horse carriage 2 00
John Sutherland, best seed oats, two bushels $1 00
    Do ...... second best coverlet 50
                                —— 1 50

George Robinson, best sow and pigs 2 00
John Imbrie, best yoke of oxen $3 00
    Do ... best two horse wagon 2 00
                                —— 5 00

James Darragh, best saddle horse 3 00
    Do ..... second best winter apples 50
    Do ..... best heavy sole leather 1 00
                                —— 4 50

J. J. Anderson, best cooking stove.. .... $2 00
     Do..... best castings, generally 1 00
                                        ——$ 3 00

Ritchey Eakin, best three years old colt........................ 3 00
James Scott, best sweet potatoes........................ $1 00
     Do... best cabbage................................ 50
                                     —— 1 50

Mrs. Fisher, best coverlet.. 1 00
Philip Hill, best grain drill..................................... 2 00
John Weaver, best stone ware.................................. 1 00
Miss Nannie Power, second best leather work box.............. 50
Hon. Joseph Irwin, best Poland chickens...................... 1 00
Stacy D. Engle, best specimen of peaches..................... 1 00
Mattison Darragh, second best blooded stallion.................. 3 00
M. & S. H. Darragh, best two horse plough $2 00
     Do......... best one horse plough................. 1 00
     Do......... best shovel and corn plough........... 1 00
                                     —— 4 00

Abraham B. Wolf, best Durham bull two years old.......... 3 00
     Do....... best Durham heifer calf................. 1 00
                                     —— 4 00

James Sterling, best machine to gather clover.................... 1 00
Samuel M'Manemy, best seed, white wheat.....·............ 1 00
John R. M'Donald, best three acres of oats..................... 3 00
William Spencer, second best two years old colt 1 00
Candless Wilson, first premium for ploughing.................... 6 00
John M'Farland, second premium for ploughing.................. 5 00
John Garrard, third premium for ploughing...................... 4 00
Ritchey Eaken, fourth premium for ploughing 3 00
Russell Vanoisdell, discretionary premium for ploughing............ 1 00

                                     147 00

BEDFORD COUNTY.

The annual meetings of our society are held on the Monday evenings of our February courts, when the reports of the transactions of the preceding year are presented, and officers for the ensuing year elected.

The first meeting of the past year was held February 15, 1854, when, after the transaction of the usual business, the following officers were elected:

PRESIDENT.—Major Samuel Davis.

VICE PRESIDENTS.—Thomas M. Lynch, John Dickey, Michael Halderbaum, Benjamin R. Ashcom.

RECORDING SECRETARY.—John Mower.

CORRESPONDING SECRETARY.—Wm. Hartley.

TREASURER.—Samuel Brown.

The next meeting was the first of May, when the only business done was the appointment of a committee of five, to make arrangements for the fair in the fall.

The committee appointed at this meeting had another meeting called on the 7th of September, when it was proposed that in consequence of the very unfavorable season through which we had passed, the fair should be postponed. After a long discussion the proposition was overruled, and the committee instructed to proceed in their arrangements.

Our fair was held on the 18th, 19th and 20th days of October, occupying the court house and grounds around it, as in previous years. Compared with former ones, the exhibition was meagre. Field products and vegetables were scarce; so also were fruits, excepting apples, which were very fine; poultry and stock as numerous, and perhaps finer, than those of previous years; but many things were missed from the exhibition, which serve to fill up and impart interest. The season had been so unfavorable the people were discouraged, and seemed to regard the effort rather a failure. There was also a large falling off in the number of members, but to what cause that was attributable I do not know.

Only one meeting was held since the fair, which was the regular annual meeting.

The reports of the committee of arrangements and treasurer exhibit the present condition of the society.

Amount received by committee for admissions.................... $106 40

Amount expended by committee for sundries 106 94

Due committee... 54

Balance in treasury February 15, 1854........................ $262 24½

Received for memberships for 1854............................ 162 00

Received from county... 100 00

524 24½

By amount of premiums paid $242 62½

By amount paid for lumber........................ 32 81

By amount paid for labor, &c....................... 73 56

By amount of uncurrent funds..................... 24 00

373 00

Balance in treasury... 151 24½

Leaving us considerably worse off, pecuniarily, than at the beginning of the year.

At the same meeting the society adopted the following resolutions:

1. That it is not only expedient but absolutely necessary for the permanence and future usefulness of the society, that a suitable lot of ground be purchased for its exhibitions.

2. That a committee of three persons be appointed to select the ground and make the purchase.

3. That the President be authorized to issue life tickets to members on payment of ten dollars, and tickets for ten years on payment of the sum of five dollars.

The officers elected for the present year are—

David Patterson, President, Bedford township.

John M'Vicker, Vice President, Bedford P. O.

Capt. Geo. Smith....do........Bedford township.

A. R. Craine.........do.......'...Bedford township.

Samuel Vondersmith..do........Bedford borough.

Samuel Brown, Treasurer, Bedford borough.

Wm. Hartley, Corresponding Secretary, Bloody Run P. O.

John Mower, Recording Secretary, Bedford borough.

The interest in the society and its operations seems to have not only flagged but fallen off very materially during the past year; but there are some men who have its welfare at heart, and who, by their intelligence, perseverance and zeal, will be able to place it on a firm and lasting foundation, accomplishing for and by it all that is proposed to be effected by such institutions.

Respectfully, &c.,

JNO. MOWER.

BRADFORD COUNTY.

Officers of the Society for 1854.

PRESIDENT.—Col. Gordon F. Mason, Towanda.

VICE PRESIDENTS.—Gen. D. Bullock, Smithfield; Hon. Harry Acla, Tuscarora; Rogers Fowler, Monroe; Jesse Edsall, Columbia; John W. Griffin, Canton.

CORRESPONDING AND RECORDING SECRETARY.—William C. Bogart, Towanda.

TREASURER.—William Elwell, Towanda.

MANAGERS.—Emanuel Guyer, Burlington; M. H. Laning, Wysox; M. C. Mercur, Towanda; G. F. Redington, Troy; Zebulon Frisbie, Orwell; C. N. Shipman, Athens; Joseph Towner, Rome; J. F. Means, Towanda; B. Laporte, Durell.

EXECUTIVE COMMITTEE.—E. Guyer, Burlington; M. H. Laning, Wysox; M. C. Mercur, Towanda.

REPORT OF THE EXECUTIVE COMMITTEE.

The Executive Committee, in pursuance of their duty under the Constitution, make the following report:

In accordance with a resolution of the society, passed at its regular meeting in February, the committee made the necessary arrangements for holding its second annual fair at the borough of Towanda, on the 6th and 7th of October.

The unprecedented drought which visited with dire consequences almost the entire length and breadth of our country, caused many to fear, and almost to doubt the practicability of holding a fair. A universal failure of the crops was apprehended on all sides, and to a very considerable extent the fears of our farmers were alarmingly realized. Many who had commenced the opening of the season with high hopes and expectations of receiving a due share of the plaudits and admiration of the thousands that would attend the annual exhibition of the society, to witness the noble results of industry, science and skill, were called to view with deep regret and concern, their fair fields and gardens scorched and withered to unsightly wastes, and their fruits either utterly blasted, or stunted, and rendered tasteless and unwholesome by this desolating scourge.

Thus, amid these discouraging circumstances, was the success of the exhibition rendered exceedingly doubtful; but it was deemed entirely advisable by the committee to make full and ample preparations as the circumstances and the means of the society would admit; and it is a source of gratification that their efforts were most nobly seconded by almost every department of industry within its bounds.

The court house and public square, which were again kindly presented by the commissioners of the county for the use of the society, were suitably arranged for exhibiting the different articles and animals presented for competition and exhibition. Pens and stalls, ample in size and number, were erected on two sides of the enclosure to accommodate animals of all kinds, and hay and water provided for their subsistence. Two large and well arranged sheds were erected for the exhibition of mechanical and farming implements, fruit, vegetables, and other agricultural products. The centre and south portions of the grounds were arranged for the exhibition of horses and working cattle.

The court room, under the skillful and tasteful hands of the young ladies of Towanda, was most beautifully decorated with evergreens and flowers. In the centre of the room was a beautiful floral temple, raised upon a mound of moss. From the mouth of a rich horn of plenty poured luscious fruits and beautiful flowers, in every variety, down the green slope of the mound. Several cages of beautiful birds, furnished for the occasion by Mr. James Nevins, of Towanda, and interspersed and hidden among the winding evergreens, poured forth strains of sweet song, lending a most cheerful and pleasurable effect to the already delightful scene. The spacious room during the evening, was

7

brilliantly illuminated, presenting to the beholder a beautifully varied and
gorgeous picture. Immediately in front of the judge's desk, and near the
entrance to the room, were long tables, richly laden with the most costly productions of ingenuity, skill and labor. Here was seen the handiwork of the
fair women of our country, in every variety of form and grade of workmanship,—the most delicate and richly wrought needlework, requiring months of
assiduous application and labor, with the no less surprisingly beautiful products of the spinning-wheel and loom. Here, too, was seen in tempting pro-
fusion, breads of every variety, from wheat of alabaster whiteness, to the rich
and inviting brown loaf of the rye; cakes, preserved fruits, raspberry and
other vinegars, pickles, preserved meats, soaps and numerous other articles of
the household department—all demonstrating the superior skill of the fair
contestants. A large number of paintings and drawings, several of them by
young ladies of this county, were on exhibition, many of them evincing superior artistic skill, and all deserving praise. A beautiful sample of cocoons
and manufactured silk, were exhibited by Mrs. Adelaide Delpeuch, of Sheshequin, deserving the highest regard of the committee. The articles on
exhibition in the ladies' department, considerably exceeded in number and
variety those of last year, especially those of the more useful character. The
large number of articles in this department compels the committee to forego
their desire to give them a more detailed notice.

The committee, in reviewing another portion of this department of the
exhibition, desire to note with especial commendation, the rich and beautiful
specimens of fancy and other articles manufactured and exhibited by several
enterprising mechanics of this county. Among these, their notice was directed to a magnificent set of parlor furniture, and two beautiful sets of cham-
ber furniture, made by A. O. Hart, of Athens; two tastefully arranged cases
of gentlemen's boots and ladies' shoes, exhibited by Mr. W. H. Fritcher, of
Athens. These articles were of unsurpassed beauty of workmanship. A set
of single carriage harness, by Ual Porter, of Standing Stone, and a case of
single carriage harness, by Messrs. Culp & Kirby, of Towanda, both specimens
reflecting the highest credit and praise upon the manufacturers. Two fine
specimens of rifles and shot guns, by Mr. J. Harder, of Athens, and J. V.
Geiger, of Towanda, their beautiful and elaborate finish doing great credit to
their makers. A superior specimen of saddles, exhibited by C. S. Smith, of
Towanda, and a lady's side saddle, by J. F. Bosworth, of Waverly, exceeding
in beauty of design and finish anything of the kind that has come to the notice
of the committee.

The committee also examined with great pleasure, a number of specimen
Daguerreotype likenesses, by Mr. L. N. Howard, of Athens; also a case of
the same, beautifully executed, by Messrs. Hathaway & Wood, of Towanda,
denoting great proficiency in this branch of the arts.

The committee cannot speak in too high praise of a magnificent piano,
manufactured by Messrs. Light, Newton & Bradbury, of New York city, and
exhibited by Mr. E. Hosford, of Owego, N. Y. This instrument, in elegance

of finish and superiority of tone, surpassed any that has come under their notice, and evinces, in a highly honorable degree, great merit in the part of its makers. Mr. Hosford also exhibited a superior melodeon, made by Carhart & Needham, of N. Y. city, with various other instruments of fine quality, all deserving of commendation.

In passing to notice the more heavy branches of mechanical manufactures, the committee feel that it is due to many of the competitors and exhibitors, that their review should be somewhat in detail. While the limits of this report will not admit of a particular reference to each article in the list, yet several of those on exhibition were deservedly worthy, and seem to demand special notice. Among these, their attention was called to a steam engine from the manufactory of Messrs. Shipman & Welles, of Athens, and exhibited on the grounds in full operation by Mr. Clark, the accomplished constructing mechanic. This was a beautiful specimen of machinery, very simple in construction, and finished in a very superior manner, evincing a high order of mechanical skill and workmanship. It is due to say, that this is but another evidence of the enterprise characteristic of these gentlemen, which has placed their works among the first in the country, and made them an honor to our county. The committee also refer with great pleasure to the extensive assortment of agricultural and household implements exhibited by Mr. R. M. Welles, of Athens, embracing labor-saving machinery for almost every department of agricultural and household economy. These articles were generally of superior character, both in excellence of workmanship and utility. Mr. Welles is deserving of high commendation for the zeal and enterprise with which he has engaged in this department of business. In this connection, also, the committee refer with pride and satisfaction to several newly invented and improved ploughs, horse powers, threshing machines, churns, stoves, and other agricultural and household implements, made and exhibited by several of the enterprising manufacturers and mechanics of the county, among whom were Messrs. Hall & Russell, A. Mix & Co., Youngs & Fowler, Lamereaux & Co., J. Irvin, G. C. Hill, J. Jones, S. Shiner and others. These articles were all of superior character, doing great credit to their inventors and manufacturers. There were a large number of mechanical implements and constructions on exhibition, highly meritorious, which are fully and properly noticed in the report of the Awarding Committee.

Great credit is due to the exhibitors for the display of valuable horses presented in competition—every class in the list being fully represented, and claims to premiums nobly contested by the finest specimens of their kinds. A large number of young animals of great merit were on the grounds, many of them the progeny of stock of unquestionable reputation, at present on exhibition, affording undoubted evidence of a superior character of animals in preparation soon for market. Full descriptions will be found in the reports of the Judging Committees.

The exhibition of neat cattle largely exceeded in number and quality, the most sanguine expectations of the committee. To those anxious for the promotion of the agricultural prosperity of the county, this display of stock must have been of deeply absorbing interest. No observer, acquainted with the agricultural history of the county, could have failed to discover the vast improvement here so manifestly apparant, especially in breeding and dairy cattle. A new impulse seems to have been given to this department, by several enterprising farmers in different parts of the county, which must eventually place her in the very highest class of successful competition in the cattle market. It is with no ordinary pleasure and satisfaction that the committee bring to the notice of the society and the public, the names of several of the gentlemen alluded to, who have expended considerable sums of money in introducing several of the imported breeds of cattle into the county, for the purpose of improving the quality of our stock; several of whom, it will be seen by the reports of the Judging Committees, were exhibitors of very superior breeders, of late introduction. Among these are Messrs. Redington, Wilber and Horace Pomeroy, of Troy; P. S. Furman and Jesse Edsall, of Columbia; Hiram Spear, of Springfield; V. E. & J. E. Piolett, of Wysox; Col. J. F. Means, B. S. Russell and M. C. Mercur, of Towanda. It is but due to say, that a large amount of the best stock cattle exhibited, was the result of the enterprise and liberality of several of these gentlemen. There were other cattle exhibited, exciting the admiration of all who beheld them. Among those more particularly brought to the notice of the committee, were those of Messrs. Thomas Hyatt, J. Lloyd, Hiram Elliott, W. Wood, Wm. Scott, Wm. Braund, E. Guyer, I. A. Park, W. W. Easterbrooks, Harry Mix, Hon. D. Wilmot, F. Ackley, D. O. Chubbuck, John Foyle, George Gard, N. P. Brown, John Fox, George Walborn, H. S. Mercur, T. Smith, N. N. Bowen, Samuel Kellum, 2d, Thomas Hyde, Lyman Wright and several others, the names of the exhibitors were not ascertained.

While in this connection, the committee would urge upon the attention of our farmers, a single suggestion from the judges on working cattle. In this department, there was an evident lack of interest, hardly to have been expected in a county, which, it is believed, ought to be able to compete successfully with any other in the State, both in number and quality of her working cattle. It is to be hoped that this seeming want of interest in this one particular, will be more than made up at our next Fair.

The number of sheep on exhibition, the committee regret to say, was not so large as there was good reason to expect. The quality of several specimens presented was very fine.

The committee observed several fine breeding hogs, and several litters of pigs, which were extra. The number on exhibition was not large, yet a decided improvement over that of last year.

The display of poultry, as usual, was exceedingly fine, and of choice character. It is not too much to say, that in this department we are fully equal to any in the State, both in quality and variety.

It is a source of regret and annoyance to the committee that there should have been any cause to lay aside the several applications for premiums on field crops. It was thought that the rule of our first annual fair, regulating the measurement of the land, and of the crop, was liable to lead to error, and consequent injustice. It was accordingly abandoned, and another, more stringent and definite adopted in its place. This, with the other rules of the society, was published at an early day in the season, with the hope that it would be read and understood by every competitor, that its strict observance might lead to a ready disposition of each application. But it is somewhat remarkable, that in no single instance, so far as the committee have ascertained, has this rule been complied with in scarce any particular, thus leaving the committee no other alternative but to lay aside the application.

The specimens of garden vegetables were more numerous and much finer than there was any expectation of witnessing. The display, under the circumstances of the drought, was one that did great credit to the exhibitors.

The exhibition of fruit was large, and in many instances of great merit. Every year gives evidence of increased interest and improvement in this important branch of agriculture in our county. The committee refer with pleasure to the report of the Judging Committee upon this department.

Attention is called to the report of the Committee on Dairy, as showing an increased interest in this important branch of the exhibition. It is evident, however, that the benefits of a large display in this department, are not fully appreciated by our dairymen. This certainly cannot be the result of any lack of excellence in the article manufactured. Our county ought to rank at least with the best in the quality and amount of her dairy products.

The committee would call attention to the interesting reports of the judges on horse and ox shoeing, and ploughing, together with several other reports on classes of animals and articles, not named in this report.

The Executive Committee, in their review, have been thus particular in many of its details, because it was deemed justly due to those of whom they have spoken and brought to the favorable notice of the society.

The weather, during the exhibition, was highly favorable. The show rooms and grounds were thronged throughout by an immense concourse of people—all delighted and deeply interested. A temporary platform was erected on one side of the enclosure for the accommodation of the speakers and officers of the society; the court room, although very large, being entirely too small to contain the large numbers anxious to hear the address. At two o'clock, on the 6th, the President introduced the Rev. George Landon, who delivered a highly interesting and practical address, which was listened to with rapt attention, frequently eliciting bursts of the most hearty applause.

The committee would urge upon the attention of the society the propriety and necessity of securing, by lease or otherwise, sufficient and proper ground upon which to erect permanent and necessary buildings and fixtures for holding its annual exhibitions. The experience of other societies of long standing, has led them to adopt this as the only security to ultimate and certain success. The committee was subjected to much inconvenience and difficulty, and the society to considerable expense, for want of sufficient and necessary room for the proper arrangement of articles for exhibition.

Since the last annual meeting of the society, the Rev. J. Towner, a highly esteemed and most efficient member of the board of managers, has been called from this to a better and more glorious existence above. In the death of Mr. T., his family have lost a beloved head, and the society and community a valuable and worthy member.

In conclusion, the committee would congratulate the society upon its more than anticipated fair prospects. With a firm determination on the part of its friends to secure its permanent existence and prosperity, the certain benefits resulting from its establishment to the great industrial pursuits of our county, must place us in every respect at least equal to the first in the State.

Respectfully submitted.

E. GUYER,

M. H. LANING,

M. C. MERCUR,

Executive Committee.

JUDGES' REPORTS AND AWARDS.

REPORT ON STOCK HORSES.

To the Executive Committee:

Your committee respectfully report, that after an examination of the stock on exhibition, they award premiums as follows:

Best stallion for heavy draught, over four years old, "John of Jersey," to C. Cummings, Jr.

Second best do. "Revenge," to J. G. Towner.

Best stallion for light draught, over four years old, "Eclipse," to B. S. Smith.

Mr. Edmund Horton had on exhibition "Young John of Jersey," a four years old stallion, which your committee think peculiarly fitted for general use.

Best three years old stallion, to Salisbury Grace.

Second best do to C. Cummings.

Mr. Hiram Elliott presented a very fine three years old stallion, "The Native," which your committee think worthy of recommendation to stock breeders.

Best blood mare, to I. A. Park.

Second best do. to Horatio Gamage.

C. FURMAN,

ADDISON M'KEAN,

J. T. D. MYER.

REPORT ON CARRIAGE AND DRAUGHT HORSES.

To the Executive Committee:

The undersigned Judges on Carriage and Draught Horses, at the second annual exhibition of the society, having observed that certain omissions occur in the published list of premiums in the class assigned to them, therefore beg leave to submit the following list of premiums as actually awarded. A few words of explanation from the undersigned, are necessary, in the first place, to show the facts in the case, and the considerations which influenced their decisions.

The published proposals of the committee invited competition with *horses*, *mares* or *geldings*, including the three in one class. The judges on examination, found that there existed among their number considerable difference of opinion in regard to the respective value of horses or geldings and mares, a diversity depending upon the sex only, irrespective of other considerations. The difference of opinion, on this point, was so great, that the judges under their arrangement published by the committee, despaired of being able to do justice to all the competitors. They therefore concluded to subdivide the class submitted to them, into two classes, including horses and geldings in one, and mares in the other, so as to admit the awarding of premiums to each class, irrespective of the other. This they did after consultation with two members of the committee, and as they understood by their consent.

The judges also regret that the published proposals did not allow them to award premiums on single draught horses. A large number of such were on exhibition of superior quality, and the judges would have been pleased to compliment the owners with premiums, had the regulations of the committee allowed them to do so. They therefore respectfully recommend that this omission be supplied on occasion of any future exhibition.

First premuim for best pair matched carriage horses, to Job P. Kirby

Second best do., to Frank Overton.

First premium for best pair of draught horses, to Silas Shiner.

Second best do., to J. Stevens.

First premium for best single carriage horse, to H. N. Fish.

Second best do., to W. M. Watts.

First premium for best saddle horse, to H. Fox.

Second best do., to M. F. Ransom.

First premium for best pair of matched colts, three years old, to Stephen Strickland, Jr.

Second best do., to A. P. Bowman.

Frist premium for best pair matched carriage mares, to B. S. Russell.

Second best do., to George Hill.

First premium for single carriage mare, to D. C. Hall.
Second best do., to Finley M'Kean.

JOHN W. GRIFFIN,
D. C. SCOVILLE,
SAMUEL KELLUM, 2d,
S. C. NAGLEE,
L. S. KINGSBURY.

REPORT ON COLTS.

To the Executive Committee:

The undersigned judges on two years old, yearling and sucking colts, after examination award as follows:

First premium to Black Bertrand stallion, two years old, owned by H. M. Fish, Troy.

First premium to Messenger colt, owned by B. M. Calkins, Columbia.

Second premium to a two years old colt, sired by Sir Patrick, owned by John Elsbury, Ulster.

A premium to a one year old mare colt, sired by John of Jersey, owned by John Bowman, Monroe.

Second premium to a two years old roan colt, sired by Durock, owned by J. B. Smith.

First premium to two years old sorrel mare colt, sired by John of Jersey, owned by Morris Coolbaugh.

First premium to a sucking horse colt, sired by Shark, and owned by S. B. Holcomb, of Ulster.

A premium to a dark bay colt, owned by H. Gamage, Burlington.

W. S. DOBBINS,
HORACE POMEROY,
C. M. BROWN,
J. W. BARTLETT,
JAMES W. CARTY.

REPORT ON JACKS AND MULES.

To the Executive Committee:

The undersigned Judges on Jacks and Mules, report as follows:
Best jack, first premium to John W. Smith.
Best pair of mules, first premium to Chester Pierce.
Best mule colt, premium to D. Coolbaugh.

S. S. BRADLEY,
J. B. SMITH,
JOHN BLACKWELL.

REPORT ON STOCK CATTLE.

To the Executive Committee:

Your Committee on Stock Cattle, after a careful examination, report the following awards:

Durham—Full Bloods.

Best bull, three years old and upwards, first premium to M. C. Mercur.
Second best do. to H. Pomeroy.
Best bull, two years old, first premium to E. Guyer.
Second best do. to G. F. Reddington.
Best bull, one year old and upwards, first premium to J. F. Means.
Second best do. to B. S. Russell.
Best cow, three years old, first premium to H. Pomeroy.'
Second best do. to Jesse Edsall.
Best cow, two years old and upwards, first premium to G. F. Reddington.
Second best do. to P. S. Firman.
Best heifer, one year old, first premium to B. S. Russell.
Second best do. to H. Pomeroy.
Best bull calf, first premium to H. Pomeroy.
Second best do. to P. S. Firman.
Best heifer calf, first premium to H. Pomeroy.
Second best do. to P. S. Firman.

Grades—Durham.

Best bull, three years old and upwards, first premium to J. Loyd.
Second best do. to same.
Best bull, two years old, first premium to Hiram Elliott.
Second best do. to W. Wood.
Best bull calf, first premium to Wm. Scott.
Second best do. to H. Pomeroy.
Best four yearlings, first and second premium to Wm. Braund.
Best pair twins, two years old heifers, first premium to G. Walburn.
A premium for fine grade bull, two years old, to John Foyle.
Best one year old stags, first premium to E. Guyer.

Devons—Full Bloods.

Best bull, one year old, first premium to Thos. Hyatt.
Best heifer, two years old, first premium to same.
Second best do. to same.
Best heifer, one year old, first premium to same.

Natives.

Best bull, three years old, first premium to F. Ackley.
Second best do. to Jno. M. Fox.

Best bull, two years old, first premium to W. W. Eastabrooks.

Best do. one year old, to I. A. Park.

Second best do. to same.

Best heifer, two years old, to W. W. Eastabrooks.

Best do. one year old, to D. O. Chubbuck.

Best calf, to George Gard.

Your committee found it difficult, indeed, to select and name the stock most deserving of premiums, from the unusual number offered, and nearly all of choice quality, of their kinds. Though some, no doubt, will be disappointed, yet we could not give all premiums. We take pride and pleasure in saying, the stock exhibited here is fully equal to the best we have seen at any county fair, and many fully equal to the best stock exhibited at the annual State Fair, and does great credit to the farmers of Bradford county ; and those who have failed this year, try and do better next.

CHAS. F. WELLES, Jr.,
CHESTER WELLES,
C. FRISBIE,
M. F. RANSOM.

REPORT ON WORKING CATTLE.

To the Executive Committee:

The Judges on Working Cattle respectfully submit the following report :

Best pair of working cattle, over five years old, (exhibited, but not in time, under the rules) owned by Lyman Wright.

Second best, premium to N. N. Bowen.

These were the only two yokes exhibited in this class: the first, a cross of the Durham and Devon, very beautiful in build and color ; the second, a cross of the Devon with the Native.

First premium for the best yoke of three years old working cattle, to W. W. Eastabrooks, the only yoke offered in this class. These were very fine.

Your committee submit that the farmers of Bradford have been too remiss in presenting their working cattle for exhibition at our county fair. They believe that Bradford may safely challenge any county in the State to produce more or a better quality of cattle of this class.

JUDSON BLACKMAN,
ANDREW WEBB,
J. C. RIDGEWAY,
PETER STERIGERE,
DANIEL BAILEY.

REPORT ON MILCH COWS.

To the Executive Committee :

The Committee of Judges on Milch Cows, respectfully report the following premiums :

First premium for best Durham milch cow, to Horace Pomeroy, Troy.
Second best do., Jesse Edsell, Columbia.
First premium for best grade milch cow, to Harry Mix, Towanda.
Second best do., to W. W. Eastabrooks.
First premium for best native milch cow, to Wm. Scott, Wysox.

CHARLES WRIGHT,
JOHN PORTER,
JARED WOODRUFF,
MARTIN ELSBREE.

———

REPORT ON FAT CATTLE.

To the Executive Committee :

Your Committee of Judges on Fat Cattle, after examination, award premiums as follows :

Best pair of fat steers, three years old, first premium to G. F. Reddington, of Troy.
Second best do., two years old, to Samuel Kellum, 2d.
Best two years old fat heifer, first premium, to Thomas Hyde.
Second best do., to B. S. Russell.

The committee also examined a very fine fat yearling heifer exhibited by H. S. Mercur, Esq., and commend the same to the attention of the Executive Committee.

J. B. M'KEAN,
ROBERT COOPER,
JESSE EDSALL,
H. H. MACE,
C. STOCKWELL.

———

REPORT ON SHEEP AND WOOL.

To the Executive Committee :

Your Committee of Judges on Sheep and Wool, after a careful examination, report the following awards of premiums :

Best fine wool buck, first premium to Mercur & Smith.
Second best do., to William M'Cabe.
Best buck lamb, to W. W. Eastabrooks.

Mixed wool, or crossed.

Best buck, first premium to Richard Bennet.
Best six lambs, to Mercur & Smith.
Second best do., to Salsbury Cole.

Coarse wool.

Best buck, first premium, to Jesse Edsell.
Second best do., to Mercur & Smith.
Best six ewes, to William Braund.
Best six lambs, to John M. Guyer.

There were also six beautiful Southdown ewes brought in too late for competition, by Lyman Wright. The committee regret this very much, as they were highly meritorious. There was, also, a full blood Leicester buck, exhibited from Standing Stone, very fine, but also too late for competition under the rules.

> J. B. G. BABCOCK,
> JOSEPH INGHAM,
> WILLIAM BURTON,
> J. M. BEACH,
> WILLIAM BLACK.

REPORT ON SWINE.

To the Executive Committee:

The Judges on Swine report the following awards:

First premium for best six months old boar, to M. C. Mercur.
First premium for best breeding sow, to William Braund.
Second best do., to M. C. Mercur.
Premium to R. Brower for a fine litter (six) of six months old pigs.
First premium to William Braund, for best litter of pigs.
Second do. to George Gard.

> DAVIS VANDYKE,
> HARRY MIX,
> JOHN MORROW,
> BYRON KINGSBURY.

To the Executive Committee:

The Committee on Seeds report the following awards :

For the best bushel timothy seed, first premium to J. F. Chamberlain. Second best do., to Roswell Luther.

> G. HILL,
> W. PATTON,
> S. M'CORD,
> J. LAPORTE.

———

To the Executive Committee:

Your Committee on Poultry respectfully report, that they have examined the various specimens of poultry on exhibition, and have awarded premiums as follows :

Best pair of Brahma Pootra fowls, to Jared Woodruff.

Best pair of Brahma Pootra chickens, to W. W. Kinney.

Second best do., to Hugh Hicks.

One pair superior Polands, to Thomas Smith.

One pair superior Dorkins, to David Cash.

One pair superior English red game, to George Golden.

For superior game of the cat bird variety, to I. Myer.

Largest and best variety of Shanghais, to Addison M'Kean.

Second best do., to Daniel O. Chubbuck.

One pair superior black Chittagongs, to Jesse Woodruff.

One pair superior white Shanghais, to Danford Chaffee.

Four pair cross of Ostrich and Cochin China varieties, to Joshua Kilmer.

Superior Cochin Chinas, to Jared Woodruff.

For superior Muscovy ducks, to William J. Delpeuch.

One pair superior white turkeys, to James Santee.

One pair superior black turkeys, to Thomas Smith.

Largest variety of superior turkeys, to Benjamin Davidson.

The committee award a high degree of merit as follows :

For eleven cross Brahma and Cochin China, to Jared Woodruff.

One pair of game of the large red variety, to I. Myer.

Three pair Cochin China chickens, three months old, to Charles Mercur.

Two pair Brahma Pootra chickens, three months old, to H. Hicks.

Two pair Shanghais, to Charles Page.

Three Brahma Pootra chickens, to Daniel O. Chubbuck.

One superior silk fowl, to Jesse Woodruff.

The committee feel it due, as an act of justice to the competitors, to say that they have found it very difficult to decide in most of the cases, so nearly equal in merit were specimens to each other, and although there was not quite so great a variety of breeds exhibited this year as last, there has been a very decided improvement upon last year's exhibition, which proves the adaptation of our climate to the profitable rearing of this valuable variety of stock by our people.

WM. BROWNING,
WM. DELPEUCH,
GEO. F. HORTON,
W. PATTON,
E. H. MASON.

REPORT ON GARDEN VEGETABLES.

To the Executive Committee:

The Committee of Judges appointed to adjuge and award premiums on Garden Vegetables, make the following report:

Best variety of garden vegetables, first premium to W. Chase and C. F. Welles, Jr.

Second best variety of garden vegetables, to B. S. Russell.

Best half dozen heads cabbage, to R. Luther.

Best half peck early garden potatoes, to C. P. Upson.

Best six stalks of celery, to M. H. Laning.

Best dozen carrots, to Asa Stevens.

Best sample egg plants, to M. H. Laning.

Best sample of Lima beans, to Wm. Mix.

Best variety of radishes, to Samuel Kellum, 2d.

Best sample tomatoes, to J. C. Ridgeway.

Best sample onions, to Addison M'Kean.

Best sample sweet corn, to H. Spear.

Best sample sweet pumpkins, to B. S. Russell.

Best sample sweet potatoes, to same.

Best sample cabbage turnips, to same.

Best sample marrowfat beans, to H. Spear.

ISAAC MYER,
S. P. STALFORD,
HIRAM SPEAR,
F. W. BROWN,
WM. BAKER.

REPORT ON HONEY AND SUGAR.

To the Executive Committee:

Your Committee on Honey and Sugar, respectfully report, that there were but few specimens of honey and sugar on exhibition; those, however, were very fine. We award as follows:

First premium for best honey, to J. L. Johnson.

First premium for best sugar, to W. Black.

MRS. SAMUEL KELLUM, 2d,
MRS. C. F. WELLES, Jr.,
BURTON KINGSBURY.

REPORT ON DAIRY.

To the Executive Committee:

The Committee on Dairy respectfully submit the following report, and award premiums as follows:

First premium on firkin or tub butter, to Andrew Webb.

Second premium do. to Jared Woodruff.

First premium on roll butter, to Jared Woodruff.

Second premium do. to J. B. M'Kean.

Cheese.

First premium, to G. C. Gore.

Second do. to G. C. Hill.

They also beg leave to submit the annexed few practical rules on butter making; also the annexed instructions by Mrs. Gore on cheese making.

F. BLACKMAN,
A. BUDD,
J. HOLCOMB,
JAMES ELLIOTT,
P. FURMAN.

The newer and sweeter the cream, the higher flavored will be the butter. The air must be fresh and pure in the room or cellar where the milk is set. The cream should not remain on the milk over thirty-six hours. Keep the cream in tin pails or stone pots, into which put a spoonful of salt at the beginning; then stir the cream lightly each morning and evening. This will prevent the cream from moulding or souring. Churn as often as twice a week, and as much oftener as circumstances will permit. Upon churning add the cream upon all the milk in the dairy. Use nearly an ounce of salt to a pound of butter. Work the butter over twice, to free it from the buttermilk and brine, before lumping and packing. The air must be pure in the room where the butter is kept and worked, and the butter should be exposed to th air as little as possible. Be certain that it is entirely free from buttermilk or coagulated milk, and it will keep sweet forever.

To the Executive Committee:

Being a competitor on cheese, I will give you my mode of making, as requested by you, to wit:—To the milk from ten cows add about one tea cup full of rennet; after it is sufficiently curdled it is then carefully cut up and drained. Then put into a tub, and scalded with hot whey, drained again, and after it is cool it is chopped up and salted and ready for the press.

MRS. LUCY GORE, aged 81 years.

———

REPORT ON FLOUR AND MEAL.

To the Executive Committee:

Your Committee on Flour and Meal award the following premiums :
First premium for best flour, to Elias Thompson.
Second do. for second best, to R. Luther.
First premium for best sack of corn flour, to S. Decker.
Second do. for second best, to R. Luther.

W. BROWNSON,
F. D. BEARDSLEY,
MOSES CANFIELD,
H. WILLEY,
J. L. JOHNSON.

———

REPORT ON EARLY FRUIT.

To the Executive Committee:

The Committee on Early Fruit beg leave to report, that soon after their appointment in June last, they gave public notice in the papers that they would have a daily session, and invited samples of fruit to be left for their inspection. The past season has not been a favorable one for fruit, and yet the samples and varieties presented to us have been very large, and in some cases the committee have felt a good deal embarrassed in awarding the premiums. This has been the case especially with apples and peaches, and in the awards we have made, care has been taken to comply strictly with the rules laid down by the society, and to do justice to each depositor. The committee would direct special attention to the fact which they think the present season has established, and that is, that our climate and soil is remarkably well adapted to the cultivation and growth of all the early varieties of apples, pears, peaches and plums, and it only requires a little attention, at the proper season, to budding and grafting, for each farmer and gardener to surround himself with a succession of fruits for the entire season. It must be borne in mind that a tree to bear well must be fed—that is, properly manured, from year to year, with the refuse of the house and barn, such as ashes, decayed leaves, fermented barn-yard manure, and any and all of those little fertilizing materials which will aid the tree bearing fruit from year to year and renew its strength. The man who plants a tree loves his race and is a public benefactor. The committee award the following premiums:

Cherries, largest and best variety, to Stephen Powell.

Second best variety, to William E. Bull.

Best single specimen, to Rogers Fowler.

Apples, largest and best variety, to M. H. Laning.

Second best variety, to W. J. Delpeuch.

Best dozen, single specimen, to Asa Stevens.

The committee would notice some choice specimens of golden sweet apples, presented by J. M. M'Afee, of South Towanda; by C. R. Darling, of Orwell, of a number of beautiful bow apples, and by Wm. Coolbaugh, of Durell, of a handsome variety of early fall apples.

Plums, largest and best variety, to Wm. M'Cabe.

Second best do., to Stephen Powell.

Best dozen, to Wm. H. Van Dyke, for sample of large imperial Ottoman. Two choice varieties of green gage and prune plums were presented by Harry Mix, of Towanda, but not in sufficient numbers to compete.

For sample early sweet harvest pears, to Jared Woodruff.

For sample very fine seedling pears, to W. J. Delpeuch.

Peaches, largest and best variety, to M. H. Laning.

Second best do., to J Woodruff.

Best dozen, to Thomas Elliott, for sample of Honest Johns.

Second best do., to John Mix. Some choice specimens of early freestones were also presented by Mrs. Miles Carter, of Towanda, E. Guyer, of Burlington, and Byron Kingsbury, of North Towanda.

For best three watermelons, to Samuel Kellum.

For best three muskmellons, to same.

For best variety of cantelopes, to M. H. Laning.

Gooseberries, largest and best variety, to Harry Mix.

> BENJ. S. RUSSELL,
> J. D. MONTAYNE,
> D. F. BARSTOW,
> H. S. MERCUR,
> C. M. MANVILLE.

REPORT ON LATE FRUIT.

To the Executive Committee:

Your Committee on Late Fruit respectfully report the following awards of premiums:

For the largest and best variety of fall apples, first premium to M. H. Laning.

Second best do., to Salsbury Cole.

Best dozen fall apples, to Joshua Kilmer.

Largest and best variety of fall pears, to Jared Woodruff.

Largest and best variety of late peaches, to Charles Manville.

Second best do., to M. H. Laning.

Best dozen peaches, to Thomas A. Jennings.

Largest and best variety of grapes, to Harry Mix.

Best dozen clusters, to Wm. Elwell.

Second best do., to same.

Best dozen quinces, to D. F. Barstow.

Best late watermelon, to Samuel Kellum 2d.

E. REED MYER,
I. A. PARKS,
C. G. GORE,
M. J. COOLBAUGH,
G. H. VANDYKE,
ORRIN M. EMERY.

REPORT ON AGRICULTURAL IMPLEMENTS.

To the Executive Committee:

The committee appointed to adjudge and award premiums on agricultural implements, report the following awards:

For best plough, first premium to A. Mix & Co.

Second best plough, to Lamoreaux & Co.

Best fanning mill, first premium to R. M. Welles.

Best threshing machine, to Youngs & Fowler.

Best grain cradle, to S. Shiner.

Best ox yoke complete, to G. C. Hill.

Best hand churn, to J. Jones.

Best log chain, to W. W. Eastabrook.

We also commend to your attention, and the attention of the public, a corn sheller, a corn-stalk cutter, and a power churn, exhibited by R. M. Welles, of Athens, as being superior articles, and worthy the attention of those in want. All of which is respectfully submitted.

D. O. CHUBBUCK,
H. GIBBS.

REPORT ON MECHANICAL MANUFACTURES.

To the Executive Committee :

Your Committee of Judges on Mechanical Manufactures, after a careful examination of the several articles presented for exhibition and premiums, report the following awards :

Best specimens in finishing of iron and brass. The committee would notice with laudable commendation the steam engine of Shipman & Welles, of the "Junction Iron Works," of Athens, five horse power, horizontal, five inch cylinder, twelve inches in the crank. All parts of this beautiful engine were made at the works of the exhibitors, and chiefly of Pennsylvania iron, from Astonville works, Lycoming co., and will vie with the work of the best shops in the country. Other specimens of work in this line were exhibited by S. W. Welles, of Athens, a horse shoe and an augur bit. But the premium for this item was finally awarded to an ingenious, and, as the committee were informed, self-taught minor, C. T. Hull, of Athens, for a set of dies or stamps, for lettering.

Blacksmith's work.—Premium to Wm. S. Wiggins, of Athens. The committee hesitated long between the horse shoes exhibited by Mr. Wiggins, and C. M. Van Winkle, of Rome, to whom the second premium was finally awarded. Both of the shoes show a proper conception of the structure of the horse's feet, in making the bearing upon the outer edge of the hoof ; and that for which the premium was awarded is admirably adapted for cases of hoofbound horses.

For the best two horse carriage, G. H. Drake, of Towanda.

Best single carriage, D. Magner, of Wysox.

Best two horse carriage harness, Jerre Culp, Towanda.

Best single carriage harness, U. Porter, of Standing Stone. A well made and tasteful single harness was exhibited by J. Culp.

Best saddle, C. T. Smith, made by the late Elhanah Smith, of Towanda.

Best cooking stove, Lamoreaux & Co., Towanda.

Best parlor stove, Lamoreaux & Co., Towanda.

A single chair, with a very beautiful worsted work seat, by Mrs. Wm. Rockwell, of Towanda, and another with back and seat of mosaic piece work, by Mrs. E. A. Parsons, of Towanda, attracted the attention of the committee, but the rules of the society did not allow a premium.

Best lot of cabinet ware, A. O. Hart, of Athens ; very beautiful and well made.

Best pair of fine boots, sewed, W. H. Fritcher, of Athens.

Best pair of fine boots, pegged, C. C. Brooks, of Athens.

Best pair of ladies' shoes, W. H. Fritcher, of Athens.

Best side of upper leather, A. A. Bishop, of Wysox.

Best dressed calf skin, A. A. Bishop, of Wysox.

Best side of harness leather, Nichols & Co., LeRaysville.

Best flour barrel, Jacob Jones, of Athens.

Best butter firkin, Russell Pratt, of Towanda.

Best made rifle gun, Jacob Harder, of Athens.

Best shot gun, J. V. Geiger, of Towanda.

Best tin-ware, R. M. Welles, of Athens; exceedingly well made, with copper and brass wire and hinges.

Many articles were simply on exhibition, and not intended as competitors for a premium, that your committee feel compelled to notice as worthy of general interest. Among these was a specimen of "patent expanding window sash," made and sold by Mr. L. Post, of Towanda. Spiral springs are inserted in the sides of the sash frames, and appear to have all the advantages of weights and pulleys, besides being much less complicated and expensive. This sash is always tight by the expansion of the springs, and dust and air are entirely excluded. This improvement is the more useful, as it can be applied to old windows without extra expense.

A lady's side saddle, with raised side, and very fancifully ornamented, was exhibited by J F. Bosworth, of Waverly.

C. L. WARD, Chairman.

REPORT ON HORSE AND OX SHOEING.

To the Executive Committee:

The undersigned committee, in pursuance of their appointment, beg leave to notice the following report:

Anything tending to a laudable emulation in mechanism, the arts and sciences, and the promotion of individual interests and happiness, is a natural consequence, and it is apparent that agricultural societies are a powerful auxiliary to the natural aids in the work of human philanthropy. The undersigned, fully impressed with this view of the question, and desirous to add their mite in the general issue and result of the county society's undertaking, have faithfully discharged the duties assigned them. The committee have referred to the U. S census, for 1850, and find in that year in Bradford county there were seven thousand two hundred and thirty-three horses. When we consider the importance and great value of that noble animal, their convenience and the amount of capital invested in them by the people of this county, it is not strange that we find a lively interest, every where felt, in promoting their usefulness. How often do we painfully witness a well proportioned animal crimpling along with a half hitch, caused by bad and careless shoeing? This is an every day sight. But while your committee acknowledge the truth of this fact, they take pleasure in announcing the evidence of the great interest felt by the numerous competing blacksmiths for the premium for the best specimen of horse shoeing. This is an encouraging circumstance, and witnessed with pleasure. A very large number of fine horses were presented for our examination, and it is due to ourselves to say, that our decisions were made without knowing the names of the mechanics. The specimens presented exhibit skill and good workmanship; all deserve commendation. In some instances it was quite difficult to determine which was the best horse shoeing in all its parts. The first premium, however, the committee, with great unanimity, awarded to a span of young spotted horses, belonging to Frank Overton, and shod by Wm. B. Dodge, of the borough of Towanda. The award to the second best shoeing, was decided in favor of a breeding mare, owned by Charles Ellsworth, and shod by Cyrus Van Winkle, of Rome. A fine stud horse, owned by B. L. Smith, and shod by E. Smith, of Rome; and also, a black horse of M. F. Ransom, of Smithfield, were specimens of good workmanship and judicious shoeing.

No oxen were presented for our examination.

> D. M. BULL,
> G. W. GRIFFIN,
> E. S. MATHEWSON,
> WM. A. PIERCE.

REPORT ON PLOUGHING.

To the Executive Committee :

Your Committee on Ploughing and Ploughs, respectfully report, that they attended to the duty assigned them, and the following is the result:

Guy G. Irvine ploughed forty-five square rods in forty-one minutes, having ploughed best with John Irvine's plough, which we consider the best plough on trial.

Mr. L. Pratt ploughed forty square rods in thirty-five minutes—not as well ploughed as Mr. Irvine. We recommend him to a second premium.

> J. E. PIOLLET,
> JOHN CHAMBERLAIN,
> G. RUSSELL,
> C. PIERCE,
> LAWRENCE H. SCOTT,
> S. W. TOWNER,
> JULIUS RUSSEL,
> E. W. HALE.

REPORT ON UNENUMERATED ARTICLES.

To the Executive Committee :

The Committee on Unenumerated Articles have instructed me to make the following report, to wit:

A premium of ten dollars to Shipman & Welles, of the Junction iron works, at Athens, Pa., for best steam engine.

A premium of one dollar to Horace Pomeroy, of Troy, for a horse hay fork, being awarded for its utility and saving of labor.

A premium of one dollar to Mrs. E. Guyer, for a corn husk bed, being for its superior work in the preparation of the husks.

. A premium of one dollar to Hiram K. Stevens, for best specimen of wooden ware, awarded for superior workmanship.

A premium of two dollars to L. N. Howard, of Athens, for best specimens of Daguerreotypes, for good execution and likenesses.

A premium of three dollars to Mrs. Adelaide Delpeuch, of Sheshequin, for specimens of cocoons and silk manufactured therefrom, for the skill and enterprise manifested.

The committee further award the commendation of the society to R. M. Welles, of Athens, for a clover huller, and a morticing machine, both of which were well manufactured, and admirably adapted to the purposes designed, but were neither of them made in Bradford county. The object of the committee is, to have the favorable notice of the society given to these articles; also, the commendation of the society to J. H. Latham, agent for "Smith's improved wheel and water case," for the reasons last above stated. Also, the commendation of the society to Hathaway & Wood, for specimens of Daguerreotypes, being well executed. Also, the commendation of the society to J. Q. Ingham, for a small escrutoire, made by him before he was sixteen years old, as exhibiting ingenuity and good workmanship. Also, the diploma of the society to the fire company, "Franklin, No. 1," for their fire engine.

MILLER FOX, Chairman.

REPORT ON HOUSEHOLD MANUFACTURES.

Class No. 1.

To the Executive Committee:

Your Committee on class No. 1, of Household Articles, make the following report of awards:

For best white flannel, first premium to Mrs. John M'Afee.

Best plaid do., to Mrs. Elisha Keeler.

Best wool carpet, to Mrs. J. F. Satterlee, Jr.

Second best do., to Mrs. John Record.

Best rag carpet, to same.

Second best do., to Mrs. S. Spalding.

Best tow cloth, to Mrs. John M'Afee.

Best brown twilled linen, to Mrs. Jonathan Stevens.

Best table cloth, to Mrs. Allen M'Kean.

Second best do., to Mrs. W. W. Browning.

Best bleached linen, to Mrs. John M'Afee.

Best linen thread, to Mrs. Alanson Lovelace.

Second best do., to Miss Abel.

Best linen yarn, to Mrs. S. Decker.

Best stockings, to Mrs. H. Kinney.

Best socks, to Mrs. Thomas Ingham.

Second best do., to same.

Best fringed mittens, to Mrs. John Record.

Best fringed gloves, to same.

Best striped mittens, to Mrs. S. Kellum 2d.

Best made shirt, to Mrs. James Macfarlane.

Second best do., to Miss C. Miller.

Best patchwork, to Mrs. James B. Wilcox.

Second best do., to S. S. Hill.

Best pieced quilt, to Mrs. D. Bullock.

Second best do., to Mrs. C. Manville.

Best double counterpane, to Mrs. Joseph Allen.

Second best do., to Mrs. J. Woodruff.

Best single counterpane, to Mrs. S. Decker.

Second best do., to Mrs. Wm. Burton.

Best white counterpane, to Mrs. John Record.

Best spread, to Mrs. Horace Kinney.

Best woollen yarn, to Mrs. John Morrow.

Second best do., to Mrs. Charles Stevens.

Best door mat, to Mrs. E. C. Welles.

Best chip mat, to C. R. Darling.

Best specimen of darning, to Miss Mary Ann M'Cormick.

Many of the articles were so nearly alike in excellence that the committee had much difficulty in awarding the premiums, and many of those which did not receive premiums are worthy of high commendation. A table cloth, made by a lady in Scotland, attracted much attention for its great beauty; a white quilt, also, exhibited by Mr. Colt, was a remarkable specimen of industry and fine workmanship.

> MRS. M. H. LANNING,
> MRS. JAMES ELLIOTT,
> MRS. MILLER FOX,
> MRS. J. F. LONG.

Class No. 2.

To the Executive Committee :

The undersigned, Committee on Household Manufactures, respectfully submit the following report. After a careful examination we have awarded premiums as follows :

Best bread, premium to Mrs. M. H. Lanning.

Second do., to Mrs. Allen M'Kean.

Third do., to Mrs. Wm. Scott.

Best biscuit, premium to Mrs. Samuel Kellum 2d.

Second do., to Mrs. Allen M'Kean.

Best cup cake,* premium to Miss Elizabeth Myer.

Best peach butter, to Mrs. E. Guyer.

Best apple butter, to same.

Best raspberry vinegar, to Mrs. J. P. Kirby.

Best tomato catsup,* to Mrs. C. Warford.

Best spiced peaches,* to Mrs. J. Beidleman.

Best preserved peaches,* to Mrs. S. C. Naglee.

Best toilet soap,* to Mrs. E. Guyer.

Best soft soap, to same.

We beg leave to say, that other biscuit and bread, also rusks of superior quality, were on exhibition. We would recommend to your especial commendation a loaf of rye bread, made by Mrs. Kellum, and also one of superior quality, by Mrs. B. Kinesbury. There was an excellent potato pie, the only one exhibited of any kind. There was much competition in raspberry vinegars—all very fine. We consequently found some difficulty in deciding on a preference. We found 267 to be equal in flavor to any presented, and much superior in clearness and beauty of appearance. There was on exhibition some very superior maple molasses, and one glass of very fine apple jelly, the only specimens presented. No recipes were given. There was also a specimen of apple butter two years old in good condition. We earnestly recommend exhibitors of this class to attach a recipe to each article, for the benefit of the community.

MRS. W. S. BAKER,
MRS. H. S. MERCUR,
MRS. J. HOLCOMB,
MRS. JAS. CHUBBUCK.

NOTE.—The articles marked thus * were the only ones of the kind presented.

Class No. 3.

To the Executive Committee:

The committee on class No. 3, report as follows:

Best lamp mat, first premium to Miss S. Canfield.

Second best do. to Miss R. N. Horton.

Best paper flowers, to Miss Cooper.

Best fancy knitting, to Miss H. M. Pierce.

Best specimen of netting, to Mrs. M. H. Lanning.

Best crochet work, to Mrs. J. Culp.

Best variety of worsted work, to Miss R. N. Horton.

Much difficulty was experienced in awarding premiums to these last named articles, there being so many deserving. The premiums were finally given to those that had neatness of workmanship, combined with beauty of design.

MRS. J. MACFARLANE,
MISS. M A. MASON,
MISS ELIZA SMITH,
MISS F. E. ABLE, ·
MISS COLE.

Class No. 4.

To the Executive Committee:

The undersigned committee having examined the articles presented in this class, report the following awards:

First premium for faucy needlework to an elegant cushion, most elaborately and beautifully embroidered with silk, worsted and beads, by Mrs. C. L. Ward.

First premium for best specimen of mosaic work on a chair, to Mrs. E. A. Parsons.

First premium for best specimen of worsted work on cloth, to Mrs. Miller Fox. '

Second do. for beautiful specimen of worsted work on canvass, to Mrs. James H. Phinney.

Two specimens by Mrs. Henrietta Page, worthy of high commendation.

First premium for a lace cape, embroidered with braid, without a pattern, being beautifully done, by Mrs. Beidleman.

Second do. to a pair of lace sleeves, beautifully embroidered with linen floss, by Mrs. Henry Vandyke.

First premium for French needle work, to Miss Elizabeth Myer.

A beautiful cloak and bonnet, for a child, the cloak richly embroidered with white silk upon pure white cashmere, and the bonnet with the same upon white satin, by Mrs. J. W. Mercur, exhibited by Mrs. W. C. Bogart, but not for premium, was worthy of the highest commendation.

MISS MARY A. BUFFINGTON,
MISS SUSAN MYER,
MISS H. NOBLES,
MISS LAURA BAILY.

Class No. 5.

To the Executive Committee:

The undersigned respectfully report. This class embraces millinery, mantuamaking and fine needle work. Of the first of these articles, we regret to say that there was no specimen presented.

For dress-making, the premium was given to A. M. Morley—a child's dress neatly made and embroidered by a child but eight years old; a piece of work which would do credit to a person of more advanced age.

For fine needle work, the first premium was awarded to Miss Helen Carter, for skirt of a tasteful design, and well executed. The second premium was given to Mrs. M. C. Jones, for pair of sleeves, the work of which was equally good, but the second premium was given in consideration of its being a much smaller piece. There were, also, beautiful specimens of work exhibited, belonging to a lady who did not reside here, but which were worthy of high commendation. There was an infant's embroidered hood, also, by Mrs. Geo. Sanderson, which is ingeniously made, and deserves to be favorably noticed.

MRS. VANDYKE,
MISS MARY SWEENY,
MRS. C. L. WARD,
MISS BRINK,
MISS MILLER.

REPORT ON PAINTINGS, DRAWINGS, ETC.

To the Executive Committee:

The judges on the sixth class of articles, including paintings, drawings and fancy articles, submit the following report :

The number of articles under this class, is quite limited. Our citizens have been either too generally absorbed in the various departments of productive industry, to devote much attention to the fine arts, or else our native artists have been too modest to submit their performances to the public view. The judges have found among the paintings presented for competition, some pieces of considerable merit, and have awarded the following premiums:

Best oil painting, castle, with water scenery, premium to Miss M. A. Mason.
Best water color, flower piece, to Miss Able.
Best Monochromatic drawing, magic lake, to Miss E. Drake.
Best pencil drawing, four heads, to Mrs. James Macfarlane.
Best fancy article, card basket, by a child, Miss Helen Powell.
Second best do., fancy tidy, to Mrs. H. Kinney.

We also take the liberty to call attention to a beautiful landscape painting, on exhibition, by Mr. Montalant, the property of C. L. Ward, Esq. It is a distant view of Towanda borough and the surrounding hills, with the Susquehanna winding among them, as seen from a point near the mouth of the Towanda creek, at sunset. The subject is a beautiful one, and the artist has studied and labored it with great success. Not being the production of an artist residing within the limits of the county, the regulations of the society prevent us from testifying our appreciation of its merit by a premium. We would also notice two paintings exhibited by B. S. Russell—a cattle piece, of remarkable merit, by Kuyp, and "Canadian ponies," by Etter; both good paintings, but excluded from competition by the rules of the society. The view of Towanda borough from the hill on the opposite side of the river, deserves much commendation as a portraiture of the town, for the accuracy of the drawing, and the great faithfulness and distinctness with which the distant objects are represented, but is defective in coloring.

H. BOOTH,
THERESA PIOLLET,
WM. H. PERKINS,
MISS M. E. CHILD,
MRS. C. A. BURCH.

REPORT ON MUSICAL INSTRUMENTS.

To the Executive Committee:

The judges on musical instruments, respectfully report:

As there were no instruments presented for competition and premium, the committee have only to speak in terms of commendation of the following:

E. Hosford, Esq., of Owego, had on exhibition a superb 7 1-1 octave rosewood piano, from the manufactory of Lighte, Newton & Bradbury, New York city. The workmanship of the instrument, exhibits mechanical skill of the highest order, it being finished back, having papier mache plate, pearl keys, and scroll legs in the style of Louis 14th, and altogether presenting a beautiful and unique appearance. The bass is deep and heavy, and the upper notes are of exquisite tone. The committee would commend the following, from C. M. Cady, of the New York Musical Review, as fully expressing their sentiments with reference to this beautiful instrument :—"I take pleasure in calling attention to this instrument, as a triumph of mechanical art of which any American piano forte maker might well be proud, whether considered with reference to the beauty of its external finish, or the superior quality of its tone, so full, even and resonant, and yet so pure, silvery and brilliant."

The melodeon presented by the same gentleman, is also a neatly finished instrument, manufactured by Carhart & Needham, N. Y., having a pedal of improved action. The instrument in tone is a superior one. We desire, also, to mention favorably, a violin, an eight-keyed flute, a French guitar and an accordeon with a flutina arrangement—all of which are superior instruments.

MISS BLACK,
MISS BALLARD,
MISS A. NEWELL,
MISS ELLEN WARD,
MRS. WM. DELPEUCH,
MR. R. C. SIMPSON,
MR. WM. DIETRICH.

Report of the Treasurer upon the finances of the Bradford County Agricultural Society.

William Elwell, Treasurer, in account with said society.

DR.

To balance on settlement for 1853..........................	$293	70
To memberships and admission to fair of 1854................	705	04
To amount from Bradford county, per act of Assembly.	100	00
To amount for boards, &c., sold.	100	00
	1,189	74

CR.

By redeemed orders..............................	$372	74		
Paid premiums for 1853..........................	6	75		
Do. 1854..........................	287	50		
By uncurrent funds..............................	2	00		
			668	49
Balance in the treasury, February 1, 1855............			530	25

Amount of premiums—paid and unpaid.

Amount of premiums awarded at the fair of 1854..............	$399	50
Do. paid on do. do...................	287	50
Balance unpaid premiums of 1854........................	112	00
Do. do. 1853........................	13	00
Total unpaid premiums..............................	125	00

All of which is respectfully submitted.

WILLIAM ELWELL, *Treasurer.*

February 5, 1855.

CENTRE COUNTY.

To the President of the Pennsylvania State Agricultural Society:

The Centre County Agricultural Society, auxiliary to the Pennsylvania State Agricultural Society, presents the following abstract of the proceedings of the society for the past year:

That the society continues in a prosperous condition is shown in the increase of members, the general attendance usually given to the meetings, and the interest taken in its welfare and prosperity by the farmers and citizens generally of the county. The society has held four quarterly meetings during the past year. At these meetings discussions upon a stated point or question in agriculture, horticulture and fruit culture are held, in which members participate, and much useful instruction imparted by the debaters upon controverted points in agriculture and its branches. The society numbers about three hundred members, and held their third annual exhibition at Bellefonte, in the month of October last. This exhibition was highly creditable to the society, from the very large display made of horses, stock generally, the products of the field, dairy, and handsome display of household manufactures, together with agricultural implements, &c. The society paid out in premiums awarded about $400. The annual election takes place at Bellefonte, on the fourth Tuesday of January next, for officers for the ensuing year.

All of which is respectfully submitted.

GEORGE BUCHANAN, *Secretary.*

SPRING MILLS, *December* 27, 1854

CHESTER COUNTY.

WEST CHESTER, *March* 16, 1855.

To the President of the Pennsylvania State Agricultural Society:

The second annual exhibition of the Chester County Agricultural Society was held in this borough on the 8th and 9th of September last.

In the stock department, where we had reason to hope for the most eminent success, our expectations were more than realized. The display was truly a noble one—comparing favorably with the best exhibitions of the kind held under the auspices of the State Society.

In the various manufacturing departments, also in fruits, grains, vegetables, &c., &c., the display, though not large, was quite respectable.

In household productions, the ladies contributed with their accustomed good taste and liberality, and made a tempting display of the good things of this life.

The number of entries of all kinds for competition, reached over seven hundred, and the amount of money awarded in premiums (besides numerous diplomas) was five hundred dollars.

The society numbers at present between seven and eight hundred members.

The officers of the society for the current year are:

PRESIDENT—Isaac W. Van Leer.

VICE PRESIDENTS—Hon. A. R. M'Ilvaine, John Parker, Gen. George Hartman, Lewis Brinton.

RECORDING SECRETARIES—James H. Bull, William Torbert Ingram.

CORRESPONDING SECRETARY AND TREASURER—J. Lacey Darlington.

EXECUTIVE COMMITTEE—Paschall Worth, Nathan Walton, Dr. Geo. Thomas, Marshall B. Hickman, Thomas R. Trimble, Dr. E. V. Dickey, Dr. Isaac R. Walker, Abner Garrett, Lewis P. Hoopes, John H. Kinnard.

Very truly yours, &c.,

J. LACEY DARLINGTON, *Cor. Sec'y.*

CRAWFORD COUNTY.

To the President of the Pennsylvania State Agricultural Society:

I herewith send you a statement of the Crawford County Agricultural Society, for the year 1854, which is the second year of its existence. The first fair was got up on a very short notice, and was merely a preliminary effort, and very few premiums were paid.

Statement of Receipts and Expenditures.

Balance from 1853...	$94 25	
Receipts for year 1854.................................	471 84	
Due from county..	100 00	
		$666 09
Premiums paid and incidental expenses for the year 1854.........		380 86
Balance in treasury, January 1, 1855......................		285 23

Every effort will be made to make the Crawford County Agricultural Society, in a few years, compare favorably with any of our sister counties in the State.

Very truly yours, &c.,

J. E. PATTON,
President Crawford County Agricultural Society.

CONNEAUTVILLE, *February* 17, 1855.

DAUPHIN COUNTY.

To the President of the Pennsylvania State Agricultural Society:

On behalf of the Dauphin County Agricultural Society, I submit to you the following report for the year 1854:

The society held its first exhibition at Harrisburg, on the 13th, 14th and 15th days of September last. The exhibition far exceeded the expectation of the most sanguine friends of the society; and was highly creditable to the citizens of Dauphin county. Owing to the liberality, on part of the society, in admitting families without limit to number of persons, upon a ticket of membership, the receipts for admission to the fair grounds fell far short of what they should have been from the number of persons who visited the exhibition, and were less than the actual expenses of the exhibition, premiums included. The society was, however, promptly released from this otherwise embarrassed condition, by the liberality of the exhibitors who were entitled to premiums, most of whom remitted the premiums to which they were entitled.

On the last day of the exhibition John H. Berryhill and David Taggart, Esqs., delivered addresses to a large concourse of gentlemen and ladies on the fair grounds.

The gross receipts of the society during the year were......... $1,617 41
Expenses, premiums, &c., were............................. 1,515 89

Balance in treasury................................. 101 52

Amount of premiums awarded at fair....................... $617 00
Number of members of the society at this time.............. 632

With the printed list of premiums the following address by David Mumma, Jr., President of the society, was printed and circulated among the citizens of the county :

Address to the Citizens of Dauphin County.

The Dauphin County Agricultural Society, relying confidently upon the aid and co-operation of the farmers, citizens, and ladies of the county, have determined to hold an Agricultural Exhibition at Harrisburg on the 13th, 14th and 15th days of September next. To make this exhibition what it should be, it will be necessary that all persons should feel a lively interest in it. Not only the farmer, but the mechanic, the fowl fancier, and the ladies, too, must lend a helping hand. Some of the most interesting departments of the exhibition can be successful only with the assistance of the latter.

There are many reasons why Dauphin county should have a well organized agricultural society. And the success of the society depends upon the success of this their first exhibition.

It is now an admitted fact, that these exhibitions tend most effectually to arouse the sleeping energies of the producers, and direct the attention of the farming community to the subject of scientific reform, and give a healthy tone to public opinion. It is a fact universally admitted, that agriculture is the most ancient, as well as the most honorable, of all human pursuits; and upon examination we find, that in all ages of the world, it has been the legitimate and favorite pursuit of the wise and good, who have both patronized and exercised this vocation. Agriculture claims pre-eminence above manufactures and commerce on account of its superior utility. It may truly be said, that it is the breast from which society derives its nutriment and support. It is the mother of civilization and refinement. There is no nation now existing, however great and powerful it may be, but owes its origin to this source.

In ancient Egypt, the country from which art, civilization and government were first derived, agriculture was the chief employment of the people; and the agricultural class was the first in importance, and the power of the state was in their hands. In Rome it occupied that dignified position it will ever maintain in a healthy state of public opinion. In the palmy days of her splendor and power, it was considered the only honorable and dignified pursuit. Her consuls and dictators were taken from the plough, and the first honors of the republic were surrendered without regret, for the congenial avocations of rural felicity. So high was it held in public estimation, that all commercial employments were considered unworthy the dignity of freemen.

The moral effects resulting from the pursuits of agriculture make it the duty of all good members of the community, to do all in their power to encourage and promote its success. There is no pursuit that brings to mind so continually the presence of God, as agriculture. The farmer looks upward toward the throne of the Most High for the perfection of all his labors. He commits his seed to the earth and expects from above the moisture necessary for germination. Indeed there is nothing the farmer can do, in the legitimate line of his duty, but brings to his mind the visible presence of God. He sees the footprints of the great I AM in his smiling fields, and acknowledges His goodness in His bountiful gifts. He lives, and breathes, and walks, amid the manifestations of His goodness and power.

But agriculture also merits our support on the score of interest. Its intimate connection with the wants, the comforts and interests of every man; its controlling influence over the mighty commerce of the States, and the relation it sustains to the manufacturing and mechanical interests of the country, will ever rank it as the most important branch of national labor. It is the foundation of our commercial superstructure. It gives employment to our shipping, and impels onward the car o commerce, and is the nursery of every industrial pursuit. It is the first in order, the strongest in necessity, and the highest in usefulness, of all the multiplied interests of our country. The other branches depend upon it, are sustained by it, and without it could not exist. Such then is agriculture. Need we say more to induce every citizen to lend a helping hand in promoting its success. Because notwithstanding its great importance, it has, in this country, always been most neglected.

A systematic course of training has ever been considered necessary to prepare the novitiate to exercise successfully any of the commercial or mechanical pursuits, while the simplest practical experience has been thought sufficient to entitle its possessor to the highest wages in agricultural employment. While the manufacturer and mechanic are moving Heaven and earth to improve the quality of their fabrics, in order to obtain a speedy sale, the agriculturalist has been content to follow in the old beaten path, and depend upon the seasons and Providence for an abundant crop. But this reproach is rapidly being wiped away, by the labors of agricultural philanthropists, aided by the various agricultural societies that have been formed within the last few years. Through their efforts agricultural improvement has been revived as it were, and is now advancing with rapid strides. Instead of being considered a mere exertion of physical abilities, it is rising to the dignity of a science. In many of the states of this Union every county has its agricultural society. In Pennsylvania, too, over thirty counties have well organized societies. In nearly all of these exhibitions were held last year, all of which were attended with astonishing success. To establish the Dauphin county society upon a firm basis, the proposed exhibition must be successful. To make it so needs but the will of our citizens. We have the ability and the means; our farmers are as intelligent and industrious; raise as fine horses, cattle, swine, sheep, shanghais, fruit, vegetables, &c.; and their wives and daughters are as skillful in producing and preparing the necessaries and luxuries of life, as those of any county in any state of this Union. Our mechanics are as ingenious and industrious as those of any other community. To make the exhibition as attractive as it should be, the household and floral department should be well filled and well arranged. For the success of this we have a sufficient guaranty in the industry, taste and intelligence of the ladies of Harrisburg and the county generally.

Let us all then give this subject a proper hold upon our feelings and interest. Let this interest increase to such an extent, that the holding of agricultural exhibitions in this county will become as regular and as much a matter of course as the return of the seasons. Let these exhibitions be consecrated to the great work of agricultural improvement. Let all the people come to these annual and joyous festivals, and most happy will be the results to the social and pecuniary interests of our county.

Officers of the Society.

PRESIDENT—David Mumma. Jr.

SECRETARY—J. M. Beck.

TREASURER—W. L. Trewick.

LIBRARIAN—W. S. Boyer.

With one Vice President from each township in the county. All of which is respectfully submitted on behalf of the society, by

DAVID MUMMA, Jr.,

President of the Dauphin County Agricultural Society.

HORSES AND MULES.

The Committee on Horses and Mules very respectfully report, that they have carefully examined all the stock presented for their inspection, and are highly gratified in being able to state that a clever number and variety of horses came under their notice; fairly showing that in this department of stock our people are alive to improvement.

In our opinion the best stallion for quick draught was the " English Clifton," owned by Mr. J. Reed, Dauphin county, entitled to a premium of.. $8 00

Black stallion for saddle, "Red Bird," owned by Mr. J. Reed, Dauphin, entitled to a premium of 6 00

Bay stallion, "King William," draught and saddle, owned by Captain Henry Brightbill, Dauphin county, entitled to a premium of...... 6 00

Bay stallion, "Plow Boy," heavy draught, owned by Abner Steever, Dauphin county, entitled to a premium of 8 00

Dark brown stallion, "Independence," heavy draught, owned by L. M. French, Dauphin county, entitled to a premium of.............. 4 00

Roan stallion, "Canada Roan," quick draught, owned by L. M. French, Dauphin county, entitled to a premium of 2 00

Light bay stallion, "Young Lion," owned by John Brooks, Dauphin county, special premium of...................................... 2 00

Dark bay stallion, three years old, "Clifton Colt," owned by Samuel Huston, Cumberland county, is entitled to a premium of........ 5 00

Two black stallion colts, one year old, Clifton stock, owned by Samuel Huston, Cumberland county, entitled to a premium of........ 5 00

For the best pair of carriage horses the committee award to D. J. Unger, Harrisburg, a premium of............................. 5 00

For the second best pair of carriage horses the committee award to J. Elder, Harrisburg, a premium of............................. 3 00

For the best family horse, "Dick," owned by Hon. A. O. Hiester, Dauphin county, the committee award a premium of............ 5 00

[This horse was not left on the ground for exhibition, and is not entitled to a premium under our rules.]

For the second best family horse, "Jack," owned by T. & H. Willson, Harrisburg, the committee award a premium of............ 3 00

[Not entered for exhibition.]

For the best saddle horse, "Frank," owned by Miss Sarah Rutherford, Harrisburg, the committee award a premium of............ 5 00

[Not entered for exhibition.]

For the second best saddle horse, owned by Dr. E. L. Orth, Harrisburg, the committee award a premium of...................... $3 00

[Not entered for exhibition.]

For sorrel mare for saddle, owned by F. Swartz, Harrisburg, entered by Geo. A. C. Seiler, the committee award a premium of........ 3 00

For one pair brown horses, quick draught, owned by H. Clay, Harrisburg, the committee award a discretionary premium of.......... 3 00

For brown horse, "John," for speed in single driving, owned by Wm. Metzgar, Harrisburg, we award a preimum of................ 5 00

[Not entered for competition.]

For family driving horse, owned by John Riley, Dauphin county, we award a discretionary premium of.............................. 3 00

Two handsome bay mares, draught, owned by Major G. M. Lauman, Dauphin county, the committee award a premium of........... 8 00

Eay mare, quick draught, owned by Major G. M. Lauman, Dauphin county, the committee award a premium of.................... 5 00

Sorrel mare, "Dolly," quick draught, brood mare, owned by S. T. Jones, Jr., Harrisburg, the committee award a premium of............... 5 00

One black horse colt, three years old, Clifton stock, owned by Samuel Huston, Cumberland county, we award a premium of........... 3 00

One chesnut sorrel colt, between three and four years old, owned by John Wetzel, Dauphin county, we award a premium of.......... 3 00

One mare colt, black, two years old, Clifton stock, owned by Samuel Huston, Cumberland county, we award a premium of 3 00

One mare colt, roan, two years old, owned by Isaac Mumma, Dauphin county, we award a premium of 3 00

[Remitted by claimant.]

One brown mare colt, owned by Geo. Garberich, Dauphin county, we award a discretionary premium of........................... 2 00

[Refunded.]

One two years old horse colt, owned by James Wilson, Dauphin county, we award a premium of............................. 3 00

One black mare colt, one year old, owned by E. G. Gray, Dauphin county, we award a premium of.............................. 3 00

One pair of mules, ten years old, owned by Robert Bryson, Cumberland county, we award a premium of........................ 3 00

One pair of mules, two years old, owned by Abner Rutherford, we award a premium of..................................... 3 00

The display of pairs of carriage horses was not as large as we expected, from the marked proverbial character of the people of Harrisburg in regard to this valuable and beautiful stock, but have no doubt that our future exhibitions will have a decided improvement.

The committee take pleasure in noticing the fact that the Hon. William F. Murray, Harrisburg, exhibited a fine family horse with great speed, but under the regulations was registered too late for competition.

Mr. Whitby, proprietor of the "Railroad Circus," appeared in the ring with two beautiful mares, perfectly trained, and entertained the audience to admiration with their performance. The committee regret that they were registered too late for competition.

Mr. E. Byers presented on the ground and in the ring a formidable array of heavy draught horses, each drawing a cart containing one ton of coal. They moved with great strength and beauty.

Col. J. P. Espy appeared in the ring with a very gentle and pleasant riding horse.

Capt. John Nevin registered a "Rob Roy" horse, which is no doubt a reliable and good animal. He was not brought to the special attention of the committee in the ring.

All of which is respectfully submitted.

WM. COLDER, Jr.,
RICHARD FOX,
GEO. M. LAUMAN,
WM. R. GORGAS,
A. J. JONES,
Committee.

BLOOD CATTLE.

The Committee on Blood Cattle respectfully report, that being restrained, by their appointment, to the examination of blood cattle, their duties are confined to narrow limits, inasmuch as the duty of examining and reporting on grade cattle, will devolve on another committee. We regret that the absence of Mr. John Evans, of York, one of the committee, has deprived us of his invaluable experience on the subject of our examination and report.

The display of cattle, although not very large, is highly creditable for the first exhibition for the county, showing some of the very finest specimens of the pure blood, which will, doubtless, soon diffuse itself throughout the whole stock of the country.

From among those produced, we have awarded

To George M. Lauman, for the best short horn Durham bull "Rodrick," a premium of...................................... $8 00

For the second best to Dr. John Curwen, of the Lunatic Hospital, a premium of... 4 00

For the best short horn Durham bull calf to George M. Lauman, a premium of... 2 00

For the second best.. ———

For the best short horn Durham heifer to George M. Lauman, a premium of.. $4 00
For the second best to Jacob Stouffer, a premium of.............,... 2 00
For the best Alderney bull to George M. Lauman, a premium of..... 8 00
For the best Alderney cow to.......do........do.......do...... 5 00
For the second best to Dr. John Curwen, a premium of............ 3 00
For the best Devonshire bull, we have awarded to Christian Eberly,
. of Cumberland county, a premium of....................... 8 00
For the best Devonshire bull calf, a yearling, to Jacob Hite, a premium of.. 2 00
For the best Devon cow to George M. Lauman, first premium....... 5 00
For second best Devon cow and calf to Jacob Hite, a premium of... 3 00

The committee cannot close their report without making honorable mention of the fine display of stock by Mr. Haldeman, of York county, which, though not the recipients of premiums under the rules governing the committee, do credit to the taste and judgment of the purchaser.

They also make honorable mention of a part Alderney bull, exhibited by Dr. Curwen, and a part Alderney cow, by A. J. Jones.

DAVID R. PORTER,
ABNER RUTHERFORD,
ROBERT BRYSON,
A. O. HIESTER,
Committee.

———

NATIVES OR GRADES.

The Committee on Natives or Grades, respectfully report, that they have attended to the duty assigned them, and in coming to their decision, have given such time and attention, in their examination, as its importance demands.

Your committee were much gratified to find so large a number of fine cattle on the ground for exhibition.

The following comprises the list of premiums awarded:

J. G. Lauch, Swatara, the best bull............................. $5 00
George Garverich, Susquehanna, second best.................... 3 00
E. G. Gray, Susquehanna, the best bull under two years.......... 2 00
F. P. Haehnlen, Susquehanna, the best bull calf................. 1 00
Cyrus Gingrich, Derry, best cow and calf....................... 5 00
J. Young, Harrisburg, second best cow and calf................. 3 00
E. G. Gray, Susquehanna, best heifer.......................... 2 00

Abram Franer, Harrisburg, second best.......................... 1 00
Robert Bryson, Cumberland, best yoke of oxen.................. $8 00

All of which is respectfully submitted by

> ISAAC MUMMA,
> JOSEPH HERSHEY,
> JOSHUA ELDER,
> JOHN RIFE,
> NICHOLAS REEMSHART,
> *Committee.*

SWINE.

The undersigned Committee on Swine, having examined the same, do make the following report:

Large Breed.

For the best boar, we award the premium of three dollars to Isaac G. Updegrove, of Susquehanna township.

For the second best boar, we award the premium of two dollars to Robert Bryson, of Cumberland county.

For best breeding sow over two years old, we award the premium of three dollars to John Wetzel, of Swatara township.

For the best pair of pigs, we award the premium of three dollars to George M. Lauman.

Small Breeds.

For the best boar, Chester county breed, we award the premium of three dollars to Dr. Curwen, of the State Lunatic asylum.

For the second best boar, half Chester county and half China, we award the premium of two dollars to Dr. Curwen, of the State Lunatic asylum.

All of which we respectfully submit.

> J. B. RUTHERFORD
> SAMUEL HOSLER,
> ROBERT STEWART,
> HENRY GINGRICH,
> *Committee.*

SHEEP.

The Committee on Sheep make the following report:

Robert Bryson, of Cumberland county, exhibited four fine Southdown sheep, and there being no others on exhibition, your committee award him the first premium of three dollars.

Though the few sheep on exhibition were good and well worthy of a premium, your committee cannot but regret that this important branch of farm stock has not received more of the attention of the farmers of this county. Your committee believe that this is, to a great extent, owing to the fact that such a large number of vicious dogs are kept unrestrained in the county, that it is entirely unsafe for farmers to keep large flocks of sheep. This fact renders large tracts of land in the county, well adapted to sheep grazing, almost entirely unproductive. Some fair and proper legislation on this subject would, no doubt, result in great advantage to the farmers of the county.

JACOB S. HALDEMAN,
SAMUEL MUMMA,
ABNER CASSEL,
Committee.

POULTRY.

The Committee on Poultry report, that they have awarded the premium of one dollar on each of the following varieties, to the persons named herein, viz:

For the best pair of buff Shanghais, to John Smith, of Harrisburg.

For the best pair of white Shanghais, to same.

For the best pair of Brahma Pootras, to same.

The committee recommend a premium to be awarded to H. A. Mish, Esq., for a very fine lot of Shanghais, of one dollar.

For the best pair of Jersey blues, to W. R. Verbeke, of Harrisburg.

For the best pair of China geese, pure, to Henry Herr, of Harrisburg.

For best pair of large geese, to Michael Brubaker, of Swatara.

For the best pair of musk ducks, to G. W. Felix, of Harrisburg.

For the best pair of puddle ducks, to John Witmoyer, of Susquehanna.

For the best pair of fantail pigeons, to John Shanklin of Harrisburg.

For the best pair of ruffs, pigeons, to G. W. Felix, of Harrisburg.

For the best pair of croppers, pigeons, to same.

For the best pair of nems, tumblers, carriers and trubits, each to same.

The committee recommend the same premium to John Shanklin, for a very fine lot of ruff neck pigeons.

For a hybrid Guinea fowl and chicken, to Martin Goss, of Swatara.

The committee also recommend the same premium to Col. G. M. Lauman, for a very fine white turkey gobler.

For the largest collection of fowls, a premium of four dollars to G. W. Felix.

For the next largest collection of fowls, a premium of two dollars to John Smith.

Mr. G. W. Felix exhibited a large collection of buff and white Shanghais and Brahmas, of pure blood, but were not in first rate condition.

Very fine Shanghais were exhibited by Rev. John Winebrenner, Master Hummel Kerr, Dr. A. Patterson, Michael Newman, David Harris, Esq., Wm. Dock, Esq., Geo. A. Bender, Master Geo. A. Gross, Master Valentine Berghaus, James Gowan, David Witmoyer and James M. Jack.

Fine games were exhibited by G. W. M'Kee, John Shanklin and W. Till.

Fine bantums were exhibited by G. W. M'Kee and Mrs. Verbeke.

Major Brady exhibited a very good pair of musk ducks.

The display of poultry is large and good, and very creditable for the first effort of the Dauphin County Agricultural Society.

Respectfully submitted.

A. PATTERSON,
LEWIS HECK,
DAVID TAGGART,
D. W. GROSS,
Committee.

AGRICULTURAL IMPLEMENTS.

Class No. 1.

The Committee on Agricultural Implements, class No. 1, beg leave to make the following report:

After a careful examination of the implements exhibited, they have awarded premiums as follows:

For the best two horse plough, (Proutty & Mears,) Boyer & Brother exhibitors, a premium of..................................... $4 00

For the second best two horse plough, (Eagle,) Boyer & Brother exhibitors, a premium of..................................... 2 00

For the best one horse plough, (Savery's Eagle,) Boyer & Brother exhibitors, a premium of.................................... 2 00

For the best cultivator, to Boyer & Brother, a premium of.......... 2 00

For the best harrow, Boyer & Brother 2 00

For the second best harrow, E. G. Gray........................ 2 00

For the best roller, Boyer & Brother.......................... 2 00

For the best Subsoil plough, Boyer & Brother................... 2 00

All of which is respectfully submitted by

ROBERT M'CHURCH,
JOSEPH ELSER,
DANIEL A. KEPNER,
Committee.

Class No. 2.

The Committee appointed to examine Agricultural Implements, class No. 2, report the following premiums:

Best drilling machine, (Pennock's,) entered by Boyer & Brother.... $4 00

Second best, (Hunt's) entered by Boyer & Brother................ $2 00
Best drill for corn, (M'Farlane's,) Boyer & Brother.............. 2 00
Second best, (Keller's,) Boyer & Brother....................... 1 00
Best mowing or reaping machine, (William J. Huyett's,) patent self
    sharpening, Boyer & Brother............................. 5 00
Second best, (Maney's,) J. Winebrenner........................ 3 00
Best ox yoke, Boyer & Brother................................ 1 00
Best grain cradle, M. P. Dill, Shiremanstown, Cumberland county... 2 00
Best guano and lime spreader, Boyer & Brother................. 2 00

The display of agricultural implements is not very large, but good of the kind, and the committee think they have discharged their duty to the best of their ability.

JNO. B. COX,
A. STURGEON,
GEO. GARVERICH,
JOHN HORST,
Committee.

Class No. 3.

The Committee on Agricultural Implements, class No. 3, after carefully attending to the duties imposed upon them, submit the following report, viz:
Jeremiah P. Smith, Hummelstown, Dauphin county, hand power corn
    sheller, premium.. $2 00
To Boyer & Brother, exhibitors, as follows:
Pennock's double corn sheller, very highly recommendable.
Longett's single corn sheller ......do..........do.
Yankee straw cutter, No. 6, twenty knives, premium............. 2 00
    Do....do....No. 6, sixteen knives, highly recommendable.
    Do....do....No. 2, highly recommendable.
Nichols' corn and cob crusher and grinder...................... 2 00
Brown's horse power grist mill................................ 2 00
Eberly & Co., horse power corn cob breaker.................... 2 00
Pennock's clover huller....................................... 2 00
Wm. J. Huyett's corn stock cutter and grinder, horse power....... 2 00
Potts' corn stock cutter and grinder, horse power, highly recommen-
    dable.
Hamden's corn sheller, recommendable.
Reading's horse power corn sheller............................ 2 00

JACOB SHELL,
JOHN H. FOX,
WILLIAM REED,
H. W. HOFFMAN,
SAMUEL REEL,
Committee.

Class No. 4.

The Committee on Agricultural Implements, class No. 4, respectfully report, that they have carefully examined the several implements submitted for their inspection, and award the following premiums:

To Samuel Heffelfinger, of Cumberland county, for his revolving
horse rake, No. 28.. $1 00
To Boyer & Brother, for their vegetable cutter, No 3.............   1 00
 Do.........for their two prong fork, No. 20.................   1 00
 Do.........for their Spain churn, No. 4, entered No. 6....   1 00
 Do..........for their hoe, No. 18, a good article, the com-
    mittee recommend a premium of.........   50
 Do.........for manure fork, No. 19....................   1 00
 Do.........for their reversable steel teeth cultivator, No.
    13....................................Diploma.
 Do.........for hay knife, No. 29.....................Diploma.
 Do.........for seed drill for root crops, No. 2........... $1 00
 Do.........for their six prong manure drag, No. 12......   50
 Do.........for iron teeth rake, No. 24..................Diploma.
 Do.........for Keller's shaking fork, No. 22...........Diploma.
 Do.........for a set of doubletrees, No. 16.............. $1 00
 Do.........for bee hive, No. 15.....................Diploma.
 Do.........for patent scythe snathe, No. 17........... $ 50
To Michael Wise, of Shiremanstown, for a lot of handrakes, No. 1,   1 00
To Boyer & Brother, for oscillating churn, No. 5..............Diploma.
To Jacob Mish, for farm and market wagon, No. 31.............. $1 00
To Boyer & Brother, for a case of horticultural implements, No. 6..   1 00
 Do.........for a chest of....do..........do....No. 27,   1 00
 Do.........for scoop, No. 2, entered No 4...............Diploma.

The committee also award the premium of eight dollars to Boyer & Brother, for the best and most numerous collection of agricultural implements.

Your committee also feel, that the exertions and energy displayed by Boyer & Brother, to further the interests of the agriculturalist in his many arduous duties, are worthy of all praise.

      SAMUEL MUMMA,
      JACOD D. HOFFMAN,
      WILLIAM ALLEN,
        Committee.

AGRICULTURAL PRODUCTIONS.

The Committee on Agricultural Productions, Tobacco and Vegetables, have given their extensive department a careful and impartial examination, and award the following premiums:

Best bushel of white wheat, Geo. M. Lauman........................ $1 00
Best bushel white Mediterranean wheat, Boyer & Bro............. 1 00
Best bushel rye, J. E. Fisler 1 00
Best bushel barley, same.. 1 00
Best bushel gourd-seed corn, Jacob Hite......................... 1 00
Best sample Stowel evergreen corn, Jacob Mish 1 00
Best sample tall Oregon corn on stalks, Philip Hoak............. 1 00
Best bushel of Mercer potatoes, Henry Clay...................... 1 00
Best bushel orange potatoes, Benjamin Olwine................... 1 00
Best bushel seedling potatoss, Pennsylvania State Lunatic Hospital, 1 00
Best bushel sweet potatoes, H. W. Hoffman 1 00
Best dozen white beets, W. K. Verbeke.......................... 1 00
Best dozen red beets, John Wetzel 1 00
Best half dozen acorn pumpkins, H. W. Hoffman,................. 1 00
Best Jersey cashaw, Henry Fortney.............................. 1 00
Best egg plants, Pennsylvania State Lunatic Hospital............ 1 00
Best peck onions, John Wetzel 1 00
Best dozen carrots, same 1 00
Best dozen cabbage, Wm. Hummel............................... 1 00
Best Boston marrow squash, Jacob Mish......................... 1 00
Best sample of beans, same.................................... 1 00
Best basket tomatoes, Jacob Hite............................... 1 00
Best sample of ripe peppers, same.............................. 1 00
Best sample of tobacco, J. R. Eby.............................. 3 00
Best sample of Valparaiso squash, Daniel Sheesley.............. 1 00

The committee would respectfully recommend the following discretionary premiums :

Best half dozen cabbage, Frederick P. Haehnlen. $1 00
Best sample green peppers, H. W. Hoffman...................... 1 00
Best sample kale, John M. Shock............................... 1 00
Best sample broom corn, do.................................. 1 00
Best sample endive,   do.................................. 1 00

They would also make honorable mention of a prairie sweet pumpkin by Master S. M. Oyster.

WILLIAM J. ROBINSON,
JONAS MILLER,
CHRISTIAN EBERLY,
JOHN WETZEL,
AARON BOMBAUGH,
Committee.

———

FLOUR.

The Committee on Flour report, that they have awarded premiums as follows, viz:'

To C. Eberley, of Cumberland county, the first premium of........ $4 00

[This lot the committee think will bake the best of any exhibited.]

To Willson & M'Cullough, of Harrisburg, the second premium of..   2 00

[This is a good article, and is clearer of specks than the other, but is a little too clammy ; and your committee think will not bake quite as well.]

T. B. Bryson, of Cumberland county, also exhibited a barrel of good flour, but there being but two premiums, your committee could not award one for it.

All of which is respectfully submitted.

JACOB STAUFFER,
LEWIS KIBLER,
JOHN KUNKEL,
Committee.

FLOWERS.

To the President of the Dauphin County Agricultural Society:

Sir :—The Committee on Flowers beg leave respectfully to report, that they have attended to the duties assigned them. They regret that the display in this branch of the exhibition was not better, both in amount and variety. They believe, however, that it was not owing to a want of productions of this kind, but to a lack of a proper spirit of enterprise in the citizens in exhibiting what the committee know they possess of this beautiful and interesting branch of horticulture. They recommend the award of premiums as follows, viz:

To John Shannon, for the greatest and best variety of flowers, a premium of.. $3 00

To Dr. J. H. Fager, for the greatest variety of camellias, a premium of.. 2 00

To J. A. S. Trullinger, for a lemon and an orange tree, a premium of   2 00

To John H. Briggs, for the greatest variety of cut flowers, a premium of.. 1 00

To Miss Clara M'Kinley, for the second best variety of cut flowers, a certificate of honorable mention.

To Sarah A. Black, for a vase of artificial flowers, a certificate of honorable mention.

The committee would remark, that they observed several beautiful boquets and growing plants, but not having been entered for competition, they do not consider them as within their cognizance.

G. H. SMALL,
JOHN ROBERTS,
JOHN FAGER,
Committee.

DAIRY, HONEY AND FRUIT.

The butter exhibited were beautiful specimens of the dairy, and reflect much credit on each of the contributors. Mrs. James Mahon, of Susquehanna township, exhibited five pounds of butter of very fine flavor and color. This butter was made of the cream of one cow, gathered in a spring house, and churned in the ordinary way in a barrel churn. Mrs. Daniel Houck, of Susquehanna township, exhibited three pounds of excellent butter, remarkable for its sweetness of flavor and good color. Mr. Allen, of West Hanover, and Henry Lauman, of Upper Swatara, also exhibited specimens of excellent butter. The committee award the following premiums:

To Mrs. Jas. Mahon, for the best five pounds butter, first premium .. $2 00

To Mrs. Daniel Houck, for second best three pounds of butter, second
    premium......... ....   1 00

Peaches.

Those exhibited were of a very superior quality, but the variety not large, being principally of the large "Griffith" seedling variety. There were several competitors for this peach. Those exhibited by Mr. James B. Thompson, of Harrisburg, were the largest and best, many of the specimens weighing fourteen ounces, and measuring twelve and a half inches in circumference, and of very fine flavor.

G. M. Lauman, Esq., Dr. C. L. Berghaus, John Shanklin, of Harrisburg, and Jacob Reinard, of Susquehanna, exhibited very large and fine specimens of the same variety. Geo. W. Harris, Esq., of Harrisburg, exhibited a basket of rare Ripes of much merit; Mr. John Wetzel, of Susquehanna, a basket of very fine large clings of the "Monstrous Pompoon" variety.

The committee recommend the following premium:

To John B. Thompson, Harrisburg, for the largest and best peaches... $3 00

The committee recommend a diploma to each of the following:

Maj. G. M. Lauman, Dr. C. L. Berghaus, John Shanklin, for fine specimens of yellow Griffith seedling peaches.

To John Wetzel, for specimens of superior clings, of the "Monstrous Pompoon" variety.

Apples.

But few exhibited. Mr. Alfred Milleisen, of Upper Swatara, exhibited a basket of very large apples of six different varieties; Jacob Wert, a basket of Rambos of very superior quailty; Jacob Mish, a lot of "Cadwallader" Pippins and Rambos.

The committee recommend the following premium:

To Alfred Milleisen, for the greatest number and best varieties of
    apples, the premium of....................... .... $3 00

They also recommend a diploma to the following :

To Jacob Wert, of Susquehanna, for his fine display of Rambos.

To Jacob Mish, for his excellent "Cadwallader" Pippins.

Pears.

There were but two contributors of this fruit. Mr. Jno. A. S. Trullinger exhibited a basket of very large and luscious pears, the variety not named by the contributor, and unknown to the committee. G. W. Harris, Esq., exhibited a lot of very fine "Bartlet."

The committee recommend the following premiums :

To J. A. S. Trullinger, for the best lot of pears exhibited, a premium
of.. $3 00
To Geo. W. Harris, a diploma for his very fine "Bartlet" pears.

Quinces.

Mr. Jacob Mish and Mrs. E. Brenizer, each exhibited a basket of very fine quinces. The committee recommend the first premium,

To Mr. Jacob Mish, for the best quinces........................... $3 00
Also, to Mrs. E. Brenizer, a discretionary premium for very fine quinces, of.. 1 00

Grapes.

Dr. J. H. Fager exhibited a lot of very fine Catawba grapes ; Mrs. Jane M'Lellan, and Mr. Adam M'Afee, each a specimen of Isabella grapes, very fine ; Mr. Geo. Bergner, white Malaga, and Henry Fortney white German wine grape.

The committee recommend the following premiums:

To Dr. J. H. Fager, for his Catawba grapes........................ $3 00
To each of the above contributors of grapes, a diploma of merit.

Plums.

Hon. Wm. Dock exhibited a lot of very fine large yellow plums of the "Gen. Hand" and "Egg" varieties ; Miss Hynecka, a basket of very fine "Orleans" plums ; and Geo. Bergner a lot of blue plums, names unknown.

The committee recommend the following premiums:

To Hon. Wm. Dock, for his very fine plums of "Gen. Hand" and
"Egg" varieties, a premium of................................... $2 00
To Miss Hynecka, for her fine Orleans plums, a diploma of merit.

Honey.

Mr. John Young of Harrisburg, exhibited two boxes of one pound each of very fine white pure honey, taken from the bees without destroying them.

This honey is very pure and fine. There being none other exhibited, the committee award him the premium of three dollars for the best honey.

All of which is respectfully submitted.

E. G. GRAY,
ALFRED W. MILLEISEN,
JOEL HINCKLEY,
MICHAEL HOERNER,
SOLOMON LANDIS,
Committee.

MISCELLANEOUS AND DISCRETIONARY PREMIUMS.

The Committee on Miscellaneous and Discretionary Premiums have decided upon the following awards, viz:

For one ten-horse power engine, Gilliard Dock................... $10 00
For one iron standing press, Gilliard Dock....................Diploma.
For U. S. standard weights, Gilliard Dock...................... $1 00
For two church bells, Kelker & Bro............................ 6 00
For platform scales, Kelker & Bro...........................Diploma.
For one standing press, W. O. Hickok ....Diploma.
For one cider press, W. O. Hickok............................. $3 00
For two sides of harness leather, J. & J. K. Greenawalt........... 1 00
For half a doz. calf skins, J. & J. K. Greenawalt................. 1 00
For one improved Scotch horse collar, J. B. & G. W. Brownsberger, Diploma.
For one patent harness bridle, J. B. & G. W. Brownsberger........ $1 00
For railroad washing machine, Boyer & Bro.....................Diploma.
For one set of horse shoes, S. P. Jeffries......................Diploma.
For up and down wood saw, H. Hants...........................Diploma.
For lumber counting machine, W. O. Hickok.................... $1 00
For stave jointer, David Drawbaugh............................ 1 00
For boring machine, David Drawbaugh.......................... 1 00
For fancy marble work, John Smith............................ 3 00
For Parian marble lamb, H. A. Miller.........................Diploma.
For pictures, by Mrs. A. B. Carpenter......................... $1 00
For miniature ship, Wm. Till..................................Diploma.
For specimens of penmanship, T. K. White....................Diploma.
For plain and ornamental card writing, T. K. White.............. $1 00
For shell boxes, L. Weaver................................... 1 00
For specimens of Daguerreotypes, A. B. Tubbs.................. 3 00
For specimens of Daguerreotypes, A. C. Smith.................. 2 00
For specimens of Daguerreotypes, M'Clees & Germon...........Diploma.
For specimens of Chrystalotypes, M'Clees & Germon............. $3 00
For specimens of water color painting, Mrs. J. F. Mesick......... 1 00
For specimens of card writing, Mrs. L. M. Lawrence............Diploma.
For oil paintings, David Lingle....... .... $2 00

For specimens of Short Mountain coal..........................Diploma.
For case of insects, H. L. Harris..............................Diploma.
For hammer, Wm. Buehler, Jr..................................Diploma.
For plumb bob, J. Paxton.....................................Diploma.
For horn basket, Mrs. S. Snyder...............................Diploma.
For leather picture frame, Miss Rebecca Hynecka............... $1 00
For plumb bob, W. H. Collins..................................Diploma.
For prospective drawings and landscapes, Wm. S. Rawson..... Diploma.
For topographical and machine drawing, Wm. S. Rawson........ .. $1 00
For fancy baskets, Miss Anna J. Schleight.....................Diploma.
For moss wreath, Miss Hettie Bryson..........................Diploma.
For collection of insects, Edmund Shell.......................Diploma
For four bottles parsnip wine, David Espenshade................... $2 00
For two bottles currant wine, John Wetzel...................... 1 00
For wrought and cast iron railing, Wm. Bush.................... 3 00
For washing machine, Owen Seip...............................Diploma.
For Venitian blinds, Wm. F. Poorman.......................... $3 00
For lot of stone ware, T. H. Willson & Co...................... 3 00
For Chilson furnace, M. A. Swiler.............................Diploma.
For shoes, Mrs. E. Brenizer...................................Diploma.
For plate of wax fruit, Mrs. A. Cookman.......................Diploma.
For case of horse and cattle powders, D. W. Gross..............Diploma.
For best collection of hats and caps, Speel & Zollinger..........Diploma.

HENRY GILBERT,
J. B. M'ALLISTER,
JACOB R. EBY,
B. F. ETTER,
M. A. SWILER.
Committee.

————

HOUSEHOLD MANUFACTURES.

The Committee on Household Manufactures, after due examination of the specimens presented for their consideration, do award as follows, viz:
For best bed quilt, first premium to Pennsylvania Lunatic hospital... $2 00
For second best quilt, Mrs. M. Metzger.......................... 1 00
For cotton counterpane, Mrs. Mary Lutz........................ 2 00
For woollen counterpane, Mrs. M. C. Wiestling................... 1 00
For the best home made blanket, Mrs. Jane Mahon 1 00
For best home made Venitian carpet, Mrs. I. G. Updegrove........ 1 00
For best home made rag carpet, Mr. Hopkins, weaver.............. 1 00
For best woollen hose, Mrs. Mary Geiger........................ 1 00
For best cotton hose, Mrs. S. E. Wallace....................... 1 00
For ladies' fancy collar embroidery, Miss C. E. Hetzel........... 1 00
For worsted embroidery, rural scene, Miss A. C. Steele..........Diploma.

For needle work, seat chair, Mrs. William Colder.................... $1 00
For Applique mantilla, premium, Miss C. A. Freaner................. 1 00
For black silk mantilla, Applique, Mrs. Hutter....................Diploma.
For best bread, Curry Taylor...................................... $1 00
For bread, Mrs. John Young.....................................Diploma.
For best pastry, Mrs. D. Herr..................................... $1 00
For pickles, Mrs. E. Brenizer...................................... 1 00
For best preserved cherries and strawberries, Mrs. Newhard,........ 1 00
For best preserved peaches, Mrs. R. F. Kelker 1 00
For best preserved crab apples, Mrs. Geo. Bergner................. 1 00
For best preserved jelly, Mrs. C. Kemble.......................... 1 00
For fine display of millinery, Mrs. M. C. John....................Diploma
For beautiful card basket, Miss Mary Orth.........................Diploma.
For embroidered ladies' collar, Miss Isabella Jackson.............Diploma.
For a vase of paper flowers, Mrs. Cookman........................Diploma.
For embroidered bag, Mrs. Newhard...............................Diploma.
For two bags by a lady sixty-five years of age....................Diploma.
For worsted work, Mrs. A. B. Carpenter...........................Diploma.
For embroidery, Mrs. A. C. Keifer................................Diploma.
For raised worsted work on canvas, chair seat, Mrs. F. W. Boley..... $1 00
For best home made table linen, Mrs. Sarah E. Wallace...........Diploma.
For raised worsted work on hair cloth, chair seat, Mrs. G. C. Barnitz, $1 00
For raised worsted work ottoman cover, Mrs. Prudent Smith......... 1 00
For embroidery with cheneel suspenders, Miss H. Wenrich........Diploma.
For book marks, Charles Wilson...................................Diploma.
For flowers, drawn, Miss Alice Hickok............................Diploma.
For ottoman seat, Mrs. M. Berghaus .... Diploma
For tidy for chair, Miss Sarah Sloan.............................Diploma.
For artificial flowers, Jacob Wertz...............................Diploma.

The number and beauty of needle-worked articles on exhibition, and the neatness with which they are executed, render it most difficult for the committee to decide. The chair seats made by Mrs. P. K. Boyd, and fire screen, are very fine and worthy a diploma. In this department it is truly pleasing to see the embroidery executed by young misses from ten to fourteen years of age, whose industry and skill cannot fail to excite your admiration, and to whom we awarded diplomas, viz: Miss Lizzie Kerr, Miss Till, Miss Shannon, Miss Eliza Ross and Miss Clara M'Kinley.

MRS. JOSEPH WALLACE,
MRS. HERMAN ALRICKS,
MRS. GEORGE W. HUMMEL,
MRS. GEO. P. WEISTLING,
MRS. JOSHUA ELDER,
MRS. JOSIAH ESPY,
MRS. J. F. MESICK.
Committee.

FAYETTE COUNTY.

FAYETTE COUNTY, *February* 24, 1855.

To the President of the Pennsylvania State Agricultural Society:

The Fayette County Agricultural Society is now in a more flourishing condition than it has yet been. From the increased interest felt in its success, and in its annual fairs, there is just reason to believe it will continue prosperous. The progress we are making can be better illustrated by a brief report of our last county fair. Our recent annual fair was held on the farm of Eli Cope, one and a quarter miles east of Brownsville. The grounds are handsomely located on the National road and near the Monongahela river. The lot is enclosed with a good tight board fence, and also well provided with stalls for stock and other necessary fixtures for the use and accommodation of exhibitors and spectators. Notwithstanding we have went to considerable expense, we have managed to regularly increase the amount of premiums offered and paid each year, and yet have a surplus annually in the treasury. The attendance of visitors has always been very large, embracing every avocation and profession. The number of entries has always been very large. The general condition of agriculture is on the increase. The spirit of improvement is quite manifest in every department, there being an inquiry for better cattle, sheep, horses and hogs; better seeds and better farm imple-, ments. The stock of cattle are mostly native, but they are fast giving way to the large and fine Durham.

Horses.

We are now experimenting with the Morgan. They are considered fine for riding or driving, but some think too light for heavy hauling.

Sheep.

The French sheep, with their various crosses, are becoming quite numerous and very popular on account of their great size and large fleeces of fine wool; the Spanish, with their crosses, are quite numerous and much liked; the Saxons have had their day with us and their is a strong prejudice against them; the Cotswold, Southdown and other coarse woolled sheep have some advocates on account of their mutton qualities abroad; the Silician have but few friends and fewer advocates on account of their near resemblance to the Saxons.

Hogs.

We have few distinct breeds of hogs, except the Suffolk, which is very popular, and will soon be seen throughout our county.

Fruit.

A great improvement in the quality of fruit grown is manifested ; we now see fine, large and luscious fruit instead of the little knotty and sour things of a few years since.

Officers.

PRESIDENT—John S. Goe, Jefferson township.

VICE PRESIDENTS—William L. Lofferty, J. S. Krepps, J. G. Maple, all of Brownsville.

RECORDING SECRETARY—William C. Johnson, Redstone township.

CORRESPONDING SECRETARY—A. H. Shaw, Brownsville.

TREASURER—D. Dayermon, Jefferson township.

MANAGERS—U. Hickenbothen, Luzerne township, William Miller, Jr., Luzerne township, H. Gades, Menallen township, W. Y. Roberts, Luzerne township, Eli Cope, Redstone township, T. C. Ternen, Brownsville, S. Brown, Jefferson township, William G. Patterson, Jefferson township, William Waggoner, Redstone.

Very respectfully yours, &c.,

JOHN S. GOE, *President.*

———

HUNTINGDON COUNTY.

STOVER'S PLACE, HUNTINGDON COUNTY, *March* 7, 1855.

To the President of the Pennsylvania State Agricultural Society:

I can only express my regret, that our society is yet in a state of embryo, or nearly so, but we hope that in future we will be able to make annual reports which will be creditable to our county.

But at present I can only report, that our first meeting for the purpose of forming an agricultural society, was held in Huntingdon in November last. Our last and only subsequent meeting was held on the 9th day of last January, when the Huntingdon County Agricultural Society was organized by electing the undersigned, President ; J. S. Barr, of Huntingdon, and John S. Isett, of Spruce Creek, Recording Secretaries ; Dr. John Gemmell, of Alexandria, Corresponding Secretary ; Hon. James Gwin, of Huntingdon, Treasurer, and Thomas H. Cromer, Esq., Librarian.

Very respectfully yours,

JONATHAN M'WILLIAMS, *President.*

JUNIATA COUNTY.

To the President of the Pennsylvania State Agricultural Society:

The society, after making due allowance for those that have died or re-moved from the county, numbers about two hundred and thirty members.

Our annual fair for 1854 was held at Perrysville, in said county, on the 11th, 12th and 13th days of October, and was very well attended. Owing to the great drought of the season the exhibition of the agricultural products of the county was not so good as the previous year; still it was respectable, and evinced a degree of perseverance, on the part of the agriculturalists, that was commendable. The display of stock, poultry, &c., was very fine; so also of agricultural implements, &c. The amount of funds realized by the society from the fair and other sources, for the year, was five hundred and eighty-one dollars. The amount of premiums awarded by the several appro-priate committees, at the fair, was about two hundred and sixty dollars. These premiums have all been paid out of the funds of the society received for the year, and the balance of said fund has been fully exhausted in the payment of the necessary expenses of the society—so that you will perceive that it is with our society as it is with many individuals, just about able to make the two ends of the year meet.

At the annual meeting of the society, held at the court house in Mifflintown, on the 6th of last month, an election for officers of the society for the ensuing year was gone into, according to the requirements of our constitution, and resulted in the election of Joseph Pomroy, Esq., as President; James Ander-son, William Banks, J. H. M'Allister, Jacob Koons, William O'Kesan, John Woodside, Samuel M. Adams, Daniel Westfall and David Cassel, as Vice Presidents; Jacob A. Christy, as Treasurer and Secretary; E. L. Jameson, Corresponding Secretary; and Jerome N. Thompson, John Jacobs, Samuel Brown, E. P. Thompson, William Starrett, Joseph Rothrock and Gen. Wil-liam Bell.

Respectfully yours, &c.,

J. A. CHRISTY, *Secretary.*

MIFFLINTOWN, *March* 5, 1855.

LANCASTER COUNTY.

NEAR NEW PROVIDENCE, LANCASTER Co.,
February 24, 1855.

To the President of the Pennsylvania State Agricultural Society:

DEAR SIR:—In compliance with the act of incorporation of the Pennsyl-vania State Agricultural Society, I forward to you the enclosed abstract of the proceedings of the Lancaster County Agricultural Society during the preceding year. During the period referred to, the Lancaster County Agricultural Society held their first agricultural exhibition at Columbia. The time at first fixed upon for holding the exhibition was the 13th, 14th and 15th of September; but in consequence of the cholera breaking out with great violence at that place, a few days previous to the above dates, the exhibition was postponed until the 18th of the succeeding month, (October.) This postponement interfered, materially with the arrangements of many that had contemplated attending the exhibition. And, notwithstanding all traces of the disease had disappeared, and the town being as healthy as usual at the time of holding the exhibition, rumors and reports of a contrary character prevailed throughout the county, and hundreds were deterred from participating either as contributors or spectators, from their apprehension of danger in visiting a place that had recently been so severely afflicted. Owing to these circumstances the exhibition was not so well attended as the intelligence, enterprise and dense population of the county had induced the managers to expect.

The display of horses was very fine, and the competition spirited. The animals for which premiums were awarded, were worthy of the distinction accorded to them; whilst others, by the judges considered inferior, were so nearly equal to the best as to leave but a shade of difference between them, and that slight difference, by some, decided to be in favor of the latter.

In other stock the exhibition was rather limited, and though some of the animals exhibited were of superior quality, there was not so much competition as would have been desirable, nor so large a display as the county of Lancaster ought to have presented. In agricultural implements, machinery and inventions of various kinds, the exhibition was quite respectable and highly gratifying to those in attendance; and specimens of various mechanic arts, reflected credit on the workmen, and will, no doubt, redound to their advantage.

The vegetable and floral department was also well supplied, fully attesting the skill and industry of those whose attention was directed in that line. The display of poultry was ample and interesting, affording high gratification to those who indulge a fancy for the various kinds of poultry lately introduced in this county. But it was in articles of household and domestic manufacture that the exhibition appeared to the best advantage. The display of useful, ornamental and fancy needle-work, and of various kinds of preserves and jellies, was highly creditable to the ladies of Columbia and the immediate vicinity, they being the principal contributors; there being but few ladies from other parts of the county that manifested any interest in the subject.

The competition for field crops was very limited, owing probably, in addition to the reasons above suggested, to the fact that the premiums were not published until after harvest, and farmers not having their attention directed to the subject, had not taken the precaution to have their ground accurately measured, and the produce thereof kept and threshed separately, so as to ascertain the exact yield; and the latter part of the season being unusually dry, the corn crop fell far short of the usual average, so that the best corn was not much superior to an ordinary crop, and farmers seemed unwilling to enter the list of competition with a yield, that, in favorable seasons, would be obtained by numbers of their neighbors. Miss Catharine Yeates, of Lancaster city, received a premium of five dollars for a yield of thirty bushels to the acre, on two acres of wheat. This was a good crop, and being the only one offered, Miss Yeates was fairly entitled to the premium, though under favorable circumstances, on our good wheat lands, in this county, a larger crop is not unfrequently obtained under the ordinary mode of cultivation.

To Jacob B. Shuman, of Manor township, was awarded a premium of ten dollars for a crop of seventy-five bushels to the acre, on five acres of corn. There being no other corn crop offered, there was no hesitation in awarding the premium to Mr. Shuman, though the managers are fully satisfied that in favorable seasons, eighty bushels to the acre is frequently obtained on good land in this county, without any extraordinary effort. Mr. Shuman himself thinks, that if the season had been good, he would have had a yield of one hundred bushels to the acre.

Mr. Shuman submitted a statement of his mode of cultivation, which I regret that I have not in my possession to forward you a copy, but it did not vary much from that practiced by most of the good farmers in this county. The ground was ploughed in the fall to the depth of eight or nine inches, turning in a heavy crop of clover. In the spring, before planting, it was well pulverized by using a large cultivator. Whilst the crop was growing the ground was kept loose and clear of grass and weeds by the use of the small cultivator, and, I think, received one dressing with the plough. Enclosed I send you a list of the other premiums awarded at our exhibition.

Very respectfully yours,

JOHN STROHM, *President.*

AWARD OF PREMIUMS OF THE FIRST ANNUAL EXHIBITION OF THE LANCASTER COUNTY AGRICULTURAL SOCIETY.

Horses and Mules.

David Styre, best filly, heavy draught.	$6 00
David Styre, best brood mare.	12 00
J. M. Strickler, best colt, one and a half years old.	4 00
Thomas Moderwell, best heavy draught colt.	12 00
Jacob Rohrer, best stallion, two and a half years old, heavy draught	6 00
Robert Duncan, stallion, two years old, heavy draught.	4 00
Jacob Stauffer, best stallion, four years old, heavy draught	8 00
E. F. Hoover, brood mare.	8 00
John Stehman, best pair of mules.	8 00
D. Peart, best team of mules.	8 00

James Mullison, second best team of mules...................... $4 00
T. S. Richards, best ladies' saddle mare......................... 3 00
T. S. Richards, best match horses............................... 8 00
James Mullison, best mare, quick draught...................... 12 00
Thomas Himes, best pair mules, two and a half years old.......... 4 00
Thomas Himes, best light saddle horse........................... 3 00
Gen. D. Miller, Philadelphia, blood family horse.................. 5 00
Jacob Garber, best family mare ....,................... 5 00
A. K. Rohrer, second best carriage horse........................ 5 00

Cattle.

D. Peart, best Durham bull, two and a half years old.............. 4 00
Mrs. Brown, best Durham cow.................................. 8 00
Mrs. Brown, best Devonshire cow............................... 8 00
Asa Louden, second best, two Durham cows..................... 4 00
Asa Louden, one bull, (discretionary)........................... 2 00
C. B. Herr, two steers.. 5 00
Asa Louden, Durham cow and calf.............................. 5 00
Asa Louden, calf, six months old............................... 1 00

Sheep.

Jos. Schock, best Southdown buck..................... 5 00
Jos. Schock, best ewe ....Diploma.
Cyrus Miller, second best buck................................. $3 00
Cyrus Miller, ewe, cross....................................... 2 00
Miss C. Yates, best ram.....................................Diploma.

Swine.

John Stehman, best boar, over one year old...................... $5 00
Cyrus Miller, best boar, over six months and under one year old.... 5 00
Cyrus Miller, five best pigs, five weeks old...................... 4 00
Augustus Pelan, best fat hog................................... 5 00
Oliver Paxton, second best..................................... 3 00

Poultry.

Jonathan Dorwart, best Shanghai fowls.......................... 2 00
Jonathan Dorwart, best Poland fowls............................ 2 00
Albertus Welsh, best Black Spanish............................. 2 00
Albertus Welsh, best Chittagongs............................... 2 00
Mrs. Brown, best Bantums 2 00
J. Dorwart, best lot of poultry.................................. 4 00
A. Welsh, largest collection of fowls............................ 4 00
J. Dorwart, best pair of turkeys................................ 1 00
A. Welsh, best Muscovy ducks.................................. 1 00

A. Welsh, best common ducks.................................... $1 00
J. Dorwart, best spangled Shanghais............................ 2 00
A. Welsh, second best... 1 00
A. Welsh, best lot of game fowls.............................. 2 00

Farming Implements.

N. Bear, best horse power and threshing machine, Haines' patent. ... 8 00
Beecher & Bro.'s, second best do............................... 4 00
Paschall Morris & Co., best reaper, mower and raker, Atkins' patent,
  diploma and... 8 00
John Winebrenner, reaper and mower, with Wood's improvement,
  Farm Journal and.. 4 00
Paschall Morris & Co., best portable cider press............... 3 00
Paschall Morris & Co., best subsoil plough.................... 5 00
Paschall Morris & Co., best and most extensive collection of agricul-
  tural implements.. 4 00
Roberts & Biggs, second best collection....................... 2 00
Lewis & Cooper, best lime spreader............................ 2 00
A. K. Bowers & Co., best corn sheller, diploma and............ 2 00
A. & H. Stoner, best fanning mill, diploma and................ 4 00
Samuel Keelan, second best.................................... 2 00
Paschall Morris & Co., best hay and straw cutter, Daniel's patent, di-
  ploma and... 2 00
Dr. S. Keller, best seed planter, diploma and................. 4 00
Cottrell & Diller, best and most numerous collection of farming im-
  plements, diploma and..................................... 3 00
Bowers & Co., best cam gearing, diploma and................... 5 00
A. & H. Stoner, second best drill............................. 3 00

Ploughs.

Jos. Heidler, best plough..................................... 5 00
Cottrell & Diller, second best plough......................... 4 00

Carriages.

Mr. Dock, best carriage, buggy and hunting wagon.............. 3 00
Mr. Dock, for carriage plate hooks, by Decker, Atlee & Co........Diploma.

Dairy.

Mrs. D. Peart, best butter, diploma and....................... 1 00

Bread and Flour.

J. R. Appleby, fair article of flour.......................... 1 00
J. R. Appleby, bag extra flour................................ 2 00

Grain.

S. C. Slaymaker, best twelve ears white seed corn................ $1 00
Casper Hiller, best bushel Mediterranean wheat.................... 2 00
Mrs. Shuman, best yellow seed corn............................ 1 00
C. B. Herr, best bushel white blue stem wheat................... 2 00
C. B. Herr, best bushel corn................................... 2 00
S. Heller, M. D., cabbage seed, nine kinds, wheat, corn, &c.....Dis. Premium.

Vegetables.

S. C. Slaymaker, best bushel turnips............................ 1 00
S. C. Slaymaker, best sugar beets.............................. 1 00
S. C. Slaymaker, best twenty-five varieties of vegetables.......... 1 00
Henry Bitner, M. D., best tomatoes............................. 1 00
J. H. Hershey, two best purple egg plants....................... 1 00
Mrs. Shuman, best lot of table vegetables....................... 4 00
J. H. Mifflin, best bushel Mercer potatoes...................... 1 00
J. H. Hershey, best half bushel sweet potatoes.................. 1 00
Jonathan Dorwart, best half bushel white onions................. 1 00
E. F. Hoover, best bushel blue Mercer potatoes.................. 1 00
Casper Hiller, best carrots.................................... 1 00

Other than Domestic.

P. F. Fry, best pair of woollen blankets.....................Diploma.
P. F. Fry, best bleached sheeting...........................Diploma.
P. F. Fry, best unbleached sheeting.........................Diploma.
P. F. Fry, best bleached shirting...........................Diploma.
Davis & Forney, best steam engine........................... $4 00
Davis & Forney, best pump..................................Diploma.
Davis & Forney, best steam pump............................. $4 00

Field Crops.

Catharine Yeates, fifty bushels clay wheat, best, but no proof submitted.
J. B. Shumam, best five acres common wheat, no proof submitted.

Fruit.

Rudolph Willmans, best variety apples........................ $4 00
J. L. Detweiler, second best variety apples................... 2 00
Elizabeth Peart, best dozen fall apples....................... 2 00
John Frazer, second best dozen fall apples.................... 1 00
J. H. Hershey, best variety peaches.......................... 2 00
J. M. Summy, second best variety peaches..................... 1 00
J. M. Summy, best variety pears.............................. 2 00
Oliver Paxson, best variety cooking pears..................... 1 00

J. M. Summy, best variety quinces.............................. $2 00
Mrs. Dickey, best collection grapes............................. 2 00
J. M. Summy, second best....................................... 1 00
John Summy, best home-made wine............................... 2 00
Mrs. J. L. Wright, second best.................................. 1 00

Flowers.

Miss M. O. Garber, best collection dahlias....................... 2 00
Jos. Youdell, gardener for Mifflin & Houston, best collection of roses 2 00
Jos. Youdell, best collection of verbenas........................ 2 00
Jos. Youdell, best collection of green house plants............... 2 00
John Zimmerman, green house plants, discretionary.............. 2 00
Miss Isabella A. Slaymaker, best basket flowers.................. 1 00

Stoves.

Cottrell & Diller, best cook stove, for coal, the " Morning Star ".... 3 00
H. Pfahler, second best, " William Penn ".......................... 2 00
Cottrell & Diller, best wood cook stove, " Girard "................ 3 00
H. Pfahler, cook stove, wood, Philadelphia....................... 2 00
Cottrell & Diller, best cooking ranges........................... 3 00
H. Pfahler, best ornamental parlor stove, " Diadem ".............. 3 00
J. D. Schalf, best hall stove.................................... 2 00
H. Pfahler, best hollow ware.................................... 2 00

Fancy.

Miss Entriken, best embroidery.................................. 2 00
Miss Harriet Patton, second best................................ 1 00
Mrs. James Vaughen, best worsted work.......................... 2 00
Mrs. Edwin Haldeman, second best.............................. 1 00

Unenumerated Articles.

A. K. Bowers & Co., best turned bed-posts, diploma and.......... 1 00
Davis & Forney, lot of brass cocks 1 00
P. F. Fry, best lot of glassware................................. 2 00
Reeves, Buck & Co., Safe Harbor, best assortment of iron........Diploma.
B. F. Spangler, case of books and fancy articles, diploma and...... 1 00
Philip Shreiner, musical clock and watch tools.................. 2 00
A. K. Bowers & Co., hive and bees............................. 1 00
J. W. Fisher, two sewing machines............................Diploma.
G. W. Beitzel, steam wash boiler............................... $2 00
Dr. W. M. Long, case of dentistry.............................. 1 00
John Shenberger...Diploma.
John Shultz, sausage cutter..................................Diploma.

J. F. Spangler, one churn......................................Diploma.
A. M. Spangler, atmospheric barrel churn...................... $1 00
J. C. Pfahler, harness and fly nets, diploma and................... 1 00
Grover, Baker & Co., sewing machine..........................Diploma.
A. Underwood, harness, diploma and........................... $1 00
H. Pfahler, flat iron heater and coal stove ....Diploma.
Jacob D. Schall, parlor stove, diploma and..................... $3 00
John M. Stauffer, patent farm gate, diploma and.................. 1 00
Harriet Summy, cocoon silk.................................... 2 00
Harriet Summy, raw silk, diploma and.......................... 1 00
Mrs. Lowry, best quince preserves............................. 1 00
Mrs. Peart, best preserved water-melon, diploma and.............. 1 00
Mrs. John L. Wright, best preserved peaches.................... 1 00
Miss Evans, best apple jelly.................................. 1 00
Mrs. Peart, best spiced quinces................................ 1 00
James Cross, best fancy hair work.............................Diploma.
Mrs. Brown, best home made carpet............................ $3 00
Mrs. Myers, second best home made carpet..................... 1 00
Mrs. Fanny Shuman, best silk quilt............................ 2 00
David Lankford, second best silk quilt......................... 1 00
Mrs. John L. Wright, best home made blankets.................. 2 00
Mrs. J. P. Stehman, best counterpane.......................... 2 00
Mrs. J. P. Stehman, best bureau cover......................... 1 00
Mrs. Harnley, best patch quilt................................ 2 00
Catharine Moderwell, second best quilt........................ 1 00
Mrs. C. Green, home made table linen 2 00
Mrs. Anna R. Uhler, second best table linen.................... 1 00
Mrs. Susan W. Pownall, best starch............................ 1 00
Mary Green, best home made stockings......................... 1 00
Anna Peart, worsted work....................................Diploma.
Mrs. Shrœder, ladies' shoes, diploma and...................... $3 00
Dr. J. Keller, largest assortment surgical instruments, seeds, &c., di-
     ploma and.. 2 00
Wm. Brady, two boxes superior finished edge tools..............Diploma.
Henry Myers, duck gun, made by his father..................... $1 00
Lewis Tredenick, case superior hats, highly finished............Diploma.
Christian Focht, two dressed sheepskins....................... $1 00
G. W. Beitzel, bell hanging, &c...............................Diploma.
Miss Josephine Hamilton, worsted work, reception chairs.........Diploma.
Miss Letitia Caldwell, one boquet of flowers..................Diploma.
Miss Rebecca Pfahler, one boquet.............................Diploma.
Miss Rebecca Welshans, one boquet............................Diploma.
Agustine Mayberry, improved mangle...........................Diploma.
L. S. Garber..Diploma.

John Bliss, improved horse shoes....................................... $1 00
W. F. Shetter, best hames... 2 00
Cohn & Gross, best hydraulic ram, diploma and.................... 2 00
J. C. Pfahler, best lot saddles, diploma and......................... 5 00
J. C. Pfahler, group of sixty-two portraits on one plate, taken by J.
    R. Williams, of York..Diploma.

———

Lancaster, January 13, 1852.

Dear Sir :—By unanimous vote of the Lancaster County Agricultural Society, we have been instructed to request a copy for publication of your able,
practical and useful address, this day delivered. In obeying the instructions
of the society, we can, with perfect truth, assure you that the request which
we now make is not a mere compliment to you, but that your compliance will
be the means of spreading before our farming community a mass of information which, we believe, will be at once pleasing and profitable to them.

Very respectfully, your friends,
ABRAHAM KAUFFMAN,
JAMES EVANS,
THOS. H. BURROWES.

James Gowen, Esq.

———

January 14, 1852.

Gentlemen :—The motive that urges you to ask for the publication of the
address, was the same that induced me to deliver it, and I therefore most
cheerfully comply with your request. Permit me to add, that it will afford
me the liveliest gratification should your laudable intention be properly appreciated, and your anticipations of usefulness be fully realized, through its
reception by " our farming community."

With great respect,
I am, gentlemen,
Your obedient servant,
JAMES GOWEN.

Abraham Kauffman, James Evans, Thos. H. Burrowes, Esqrs.

———

ADDRESS.

Mr. President, and gentlemen of the Lancaster County Agricultural Society :—Had I been called upon to address an assemblage of citizens of Lancaster upon any subject other than one falling within the purview of your
society, I should, from conscious inability, have shrunk from the performance
of a task that could not fail, if attempted, to place me in a position of great

embarrassment—an embarrassment not to be overcome by any resolution I could summon to sustain me, under the pervading sense of my insufficiency to even measurably acquit myself before so enlightened an audience as Lancaster can, on all occasions, present to the apprehension of one acquainted, as I am, with the character of its citizens. Nay, even on the subject of agriculture, I cannot but distrust my competency to fulfil the expectations naturally suggested by the call you did me the honor to make upon me, inferring as I may, the estimate you put upon my services, from the standard of your own reputed excellence in the theory and practice of agriculture.

Yet notwithstanding these apprehensions, I shall, with due deference and to the best of my abilities, attempt to improve this occasion, the first anniversary of your society, by adverting to the expediency of agricultural societies, the characteristics proper for membership in view of usefulness, the apathetic condition of farmers, and the means best calculated to enlist their sympathies in behalf of improvement, subjoining some brief remarks upon the practice of farming.

The advantages of agricultural societies have, from experience and observation, been impressed upon my mind for a series of years. Wheresoever I sojourned in Pennsylvania, and with whomsoever I conversed, capable of properly appreciating the expediency of establishing them throughout the State, my influence was directed to that object. These societies I considered not only as necessary to the improvement of the husbandry of the localities where they might be formed, but to further the grand object of a State agricultural society, embracing and commanding the combined talent and experience of the county associations, and capable of diffusing a spirit of improvement in culture and husbandry, throughout the whole length and breadth of the Commonwealth. The effect of such an organization I believed would be, primarily, to increase the products of the soil and to elevate the character of the husbandman; and, secondly, to be a means of improving the financial concerns of the State, by enabling the tax payers, the farmers, to bear their burdens with greater ease and convenience, from increase of profits, growing out of a condition of improved practice in farming—which improvement, in my mind, could only be effected by a combined effort, through the medium of a State society. The impulse thus to be given, would tend to bring under profitable culture the waste or neglected lands, to the advantage of their owners as well as the public—enhance their value to a highfold state—capacitate them to proportionate taxation, and, by this means, diminish the rate to the payers on old improved lands, by reason of the addition of the newly-improved lands being subjected to taxation on an increased value. This increase, and increasing operation of the material to be taxed, while it lessens the rate, by dividing individual burden, seemed to me the safest and surest basis of revenue to be relied upon by the Commonwealth for the extinguishment of its debt, compatible with progressive prosperity to all the industrial classes.

In contemplating the benefits to accrue from a combined effort in favor of agriculture, and the means by which it could be effected, the wealth and influence of Lancaster county, so proverbial at all times, could not fail to lead me to regard its moving in the cause as essential to success. Hitherto, " The Philadelphia Agricultural Society for Promoting Agriculture" had labored singly and alone in the work; and having its shoulder at the agricultural wheel, could, with a good grace, call upon others for help to move it from the rut of apathy in which it had so long been imbedded. That call was graciously responded to by almost every county in the State, and by none more cordially than Lancaster. Her broad shoulders were put with a will to the machine, which was soon seen to move and roll onward to Harrisburg, the centre of the State, where last January it was dedicated to the work of agricultural progress. Your share, gentlemen, in this achievement, was in every respect worthy of your noble county; and your society, which I now have the honor to address, exhibits a striking evidence of the determination of Lancaster to persevere in the great undertaking, and furnishes a guarantee that so far as it depends upon her, the work of progress will be carried on with zeal and fidelity. I repeat, that I ever thought that no State agricultural society could be effected, until Lancaster moved in the matter; and it is equally clear to my convictions, that, so far as Eastern Pennsylvania is concerned, the State society must languish unless Lancaster, through its agricultural society, lends to it the commanding influence of its name and energies. This must be conceded, I think, by all who are conversant with her position and character as a farming district. The relation she bears to York, Cumberland, Dauphin and Berks, through associations of maternity and filial regard, cannot but render her action of the utmost importance. Her supineness hitherto, was held by many, in other sections, as excuse for holding back, while she stood still. This was cause of regret to several of her own cherished citizens, among them the venerated Redmond Conyngham, who corresponded with me, and who has been translated from an earthly* to a heavenly Paradise, to receive the reward of his many virtues. If he were living, how it would rejoice him to witness the scene in which we are now permitted to participate. He, with many of his venerable cotemporaries, has been gathered to the great Harvest Home where we all must be garnered; but Lancaster still, as ever, abounds with laborers capable of carrying on the good work. Any county of the State may be challenged to present a greater array of gifted minds than Lancaster can point to among her citizens—men capable of filling every station in which talent, patriotism, and sterling worth are deemed prerequisites. Surely, then, it will not be asking too much of them, to lend the influence of their names to the cause in which we are embarked. Most of them have been brought up on farms, or have in youth mingled in the scenes of rural life, and it cannot be but their youthful recollections, as well as a just appreciation of the labors of the husbandman, will incline them

---

*His residence was in Paradise, Lancaster county.

to join with you in redeeming the time, and in placing the agriculture of your county in fact, where it ever was supposed to be, in the first rank. And here permit me to say, that so far as regards the prosperity of your society, and the advancement of the interests it was instituted to promote, it should be your aim to invoke the aid and countenance of such men. I allude to gentlemen of the learned professions, and other intelligent and influential citizens, not specially engaged in farming.

The great body of farmers, those whose sphere of action is circumscribed within the limits of the fields they cultivate, however naturally strong in good sense and understanding, are, from their habits of quiet and seclusion, averse to placing themselves in stations, even in an agricultural society, which might demand the exhibition of capabilities commensurate with the duties of the places their associates would gladly see them fill. Hence, if the founding and conducting a society were to depend upon the farmers themselves, few agricultural societies would be formed or carried on with the zeal, tact and energy necessary to their progress and usefulness; and this must be apparent to every observer who has had the opportunity of acquainting himself with the retiring habits of the tillers of the soil. Therefore, it is not only expedient but indispensable to the advancement of the cause, that agricultural societies should rank among their members men respectable and distinguished of whatever profession. It needs no argument to demonstrate the advantages to be derived from the co-operation of such men.

To illustrate, however, the benefits that have been conferred upon agriculture by the labors of professional gentlemen, I need but refer to the Philadelphia society, and its successful career through a period of nearly seventy years. Its presiding officers, for the greater part of that time, were the distinguished and talented Judge Peters and Nicholas Biddle; and I may safely say, that it was owing to their labors and influences, with other respectable citizens not farmers, that gave to that agricultural society such a celebrity. To this day it exhibits on its list of members individuals of the medical and legal professions, and of the commercial community, who prove themselves zealous and useful members. It should, however, be remarked, that the great bulk of the society at all times, was made up of those owning and living upon farms.

The aid rendered by literary and professional men in carrying out the design of the society, was not the only benefit growing out of the associating of characters so apparently opposite in their habits and manners as the rustic and the polished gentleman, by no means. A community of feeling as well as of interest sprung up between them, through the medium of the intercourse established at the meetings of the society, held for a special purpose—"the promoting of agriculture." The reciprocal advantages to both classes were soon strikingly manifest. The hand that held the plough no longer despised the hand that held the pen, since it began to perceive that it was not so idle nor so useless a hand as had been supposed. The cultivator of the soil and chopper of wood began to think the cultivator of speech and chopper of logic not so contemptible as he had imagined, since he had so frequently heard him explain, with force and fidelity, principles which he himself understood and maintained, but could not commend or establish, from having thought the faculty of speech not worth cultivating. He was sorry to think, that while he kept every implement on the farm bright and in good condition, using them freely when occasion required, he had neglected one implement, the tongue, it having been considered of little service upon the farm, and therefore suffered to rust for want of use. On the other hand, the man of tact and talent discovered, that though his taciturn fellow member was not fluent in speech, yet he said much in a few words, and frequently with grace deferred to him, as when his unpracticed adversary maintained an opposite opinion, founded in experience and good judgment. Moreover, the man of polish and learning could not but perceive, perhaps, that if the burnishing bestowed on him had been given to his sturdy though unassuming opponent, he would have developed a brighter and deeper lustre than that which he himself reflected; and that though the farmer might be deficient in head, according to the "cute go ahead principle," yet that deficiency was atoned for in the largeness and goodness of the heart that God had implanted in his bosom, and which had never been permitted to rust, but was ever active in the works of true benevolence and genuine hospitality, and in the exercise of the best sympathies of our nature, intuitively kept in play by its own generous disposition.

The seemingly dissimilar points of character of these respective classes gradually became modified through contact and association, and inspired confidence in each other, while every joint effort to promote the cause for which they had associated, imbued all with a better understanding of the principles of rural economy—making of one, amateur agriculturists—of the other, enlightened practical farmers—each class contributing, in their repective spheres, to the advancement of the theory and practice of agriculture. This conventional feeling led to individual intimacy, highly beneficial to their improvement. The professional or mercantile gentleman would make visits to the dwellings of his fellow members, the farmers, where he was received with kindness and becoming hospitality. Here the love of rural pursuits, imbibed at the meetings of the society, was heightened by all he saw around him. The unpretending commodious farm house—the noble barn—the well kegt garden—the ample orchard—the shady trees—the beautiful meadow—the finely cultivated fields—the rich pastures, with the sheep and cattle, could not but call forth the oft-repeated expression, that "God made the country and man the city," and lead him to contrast the peaceful scene before him with the bustle, din, and dust of the thronged mart, from which he had escaped to breathe, but for a short space, a purer atmosphere; and to determine, whenever fitting opportunity occurred, to quit the city, with all its conventional rules and artificial modes, to spend the remainder of his days in the enjoyment of the quiet and simple habits of country life. And thus have many wealthy and influential citizens been merged in the great family of agriculturists, adding weight, character, and influence to the profession. The taste, enterprise, and public spirit of these gentlemen, led to making large outlays in improving land, experimenting in culture, erecting fine buildings, ornamenting grounds, importing choice breeds of cattle, sheep and swine, and patronizing agricultural journals. These investments inured more to the benefit of the country than to the individuals by whom they were made, and were mainly undertaken in the spirit of a lofty and generous patriotism. The man most entitled to praise, in this connection, in Pennsylvania, is John Hare Powell. Had his efforts been properly appreciated, and his example followed in the selection and breeding of cattle, it would have added to the value of the live stock, beef, and dairy products of the State, some millions of dollars annually.

The illustration, so feebly sketched as it has been, in reference to the benefits accruing to the cause, through an union of individuals of different callings and professions, will serve, however, I trust, to show the propriety of some effort on the part of those who think the promoting of agriculture commendable, and whose tastes, talents and patriotism fit them for the work.

In view of the great necessity for such combination, it is only necessary to glance at the condition of the working farmer, and the impediments that naturally prevent him from devising or pushing forward any plan promotive of increase of profit with less toil, or the elevation of his obscure and humble vocation ; for be it remembered, however poetry may gild or invest his calling with charms, it is, in plain and truthful prose, one of depressing drudgery— excluding the mere farmer, from habit, as well as from the prejudice of fashionable society, from taking rank with members of many other professions in the scale of gentility. This position I would fain ameliorate, if not invert— and to that end I would invoke the aid of every able and generous mind around me.

The isolated position of farmers generally deny to them the opportunities and advantages of social intercourse, and means of improving, enjoyed by almost every other industrial class. The mechanic, with entire ease and convenience, may and does associate daily in the same shop, or weekly or monthly in the society room, with his fellow artizans, in any village, town, or city. So of the manufacturer. The lawyer and physician, from the nature of their functions, are ever within or under each other's eye and that of the public, while struggling for distinction, which serves to stimulate to renewed effort, should they pause for a moment in their emulous career. The country trader is kept ever lively waiting upon his customers, while his skill is tasked in the selection of supplies suited to their wants, and to yield a fair profit.— The merchant is relieved from the tedium of the counting-house by appearing on change, among the enterprising class that daily crowd that animated scene of commerce and speculation. All have means and incentives peculiar to their pursuits, which instruct, inspire and gratify. Not so with the unpretending

11

habitant of the farm, whose constant and unremitting labors confine him wholly
to the barn, the stable and the field.   He has but few opportunities of associating even with those of his own calling, much less with others better
versed than himself in the ways of the busy world.   Each day so spent lessens
the desire to look abroad, or change in any respect his practice or routine,
and thus he settles down in a state of apathy, apparently insensible to the
necessity of improvement, till Time, with its witherings, numbers him with
the clods—with which, while living, he seemed little more than a fit associate.

In drawing this sketch, let me not be understood as designing to disparage
the calling of the farmer, or to impute to the simple and inoffensive swain
aught that would cast a shadow on his brow, or a blemish on the spotless integrity of his unsophisticated nature: far be it from me.   A worthier motive
moves me to call your attention to the condition of the thousands that uncom-
plainingly toil on, day after day, bowed in body and spirit by incessant, and
in general unremunerating labor—shifting, when no longer able to bear it, the
same undiminished burden on the shoulders of their sons, which had been
cast by their fathers upon themselves.   It is to lighten this load, that I thus
appeal to the generous sympathies of their more enlightened brethren, the enterprising and intelligent farmers of Pennsylvania, of whom I am certain she
holds within her rich and beautiful domain as many noble specimens as any
state in the Union can boast.   To them I would especially appeal to advance
the character of their profession, and promote the influence of the landed interest, and to place the husbandman in the position he should occupy in the
scale of intelligence, and in the consideration due to him morally, physically
and politically.

It may be asked, how can this be done?   I answer, by educating liberally
the rising generation; by encouraging and patronizing the Agricultural Press,
thereby sowing broadcast, as it were, the seed of information, so that every
farmer may be provided with a crop, if not for reaping at least for reading;
and by holding Agricultural Exhibitions, in which all should participate,
either as contributors or spectators.   But these plans cannot be carried out
without a combined effort through County Associations and a State Society.
The State Society is formed, but societies such as yours should be maintained
by every county.   When every county shall have its Agricultural Society represented in the State Society, it will then be easy to carry out the necessary
plans for the improvement of the whole.

The most feasible and practical plan to arrest the attention of the farmers
of the present day, and call them forth from their solitude to mingle in the
interesting and stirring scenes of competition and display, is the Agricultural
Exhibition and Cattle Show.   It was held by the venerable Judge Peters,
already alluded to, that one good agricultural exhibition was of more avail in
stirring up the dormant energies of the careless and indifferent farmer, than
all the essays ever written.   In this every intelligent man, having experience

in such matters, must concur. How can those be reached who will not read—who, from habit, would deem it a harder job to turn over a few pages than as many furrows? When, therefore, precept fails to be available, we must rely upon example. The Agricultural Fair and Cattle Show are as cabalistic words, operating magically upon the curiosity of the farmer—impelling him and his family to go, where every body is expected to go, to see such sights of horses, cattle, sheep and swine, agricultural products and implements.—What book or essay could be half so interesting and instructive to such a man, as the broad and varied page presented to him in the imposing tableau of a well arranged exhibition? Here are living pictures of animals that breathe and move—aye, speak in tones and language more eloquently and forcibly to his comprehension and appreciation, than any thing you or I could say or write. These noble horses, of various degrees of excellence in action, blood, bone and sinew, rivet his attention, and bring him to think and compare them with the dull, unsightly beasts upon his farm, that consume so large a portion of his corn, oats and hay, without an equivalent, and his conclusion will be, that the next colt he raises shall be a animal worth looking at, worth its feed, and worth money when he wants to part with him. Then there are the bulls, cows, heifers and calves, of various breeds, under his eye and within his reach—Durhams, Ayreshires, Devons and Aldernies—each challenging comparison in size, beauty, handling, feeding and milking. He examines, compares, and ventures an opinion upon respective ones, and anxiously awaits the award of the judges, to learn whether he is anything of a judge himself through their decision, should it or should it not tally with his opinion as affecting his favorites in the matter of premiums. He turns to the sheep, swine, poultry and implements, which serve to keep up the interest he felt on entering the show grounds. He is astonished, not bewildered, because he knows the use and meaning of every thing. He is only surprised that animals and things so common and familiar to him, should have been brought to such perfection—should have undergone such extraordinary change, and he should not have known it sooner.

What effect may it be supposed this lesson will exert upon his future practice? None other than a beneficial one. The emulation implanted in the breast of every right-minded man will inspire him to make an effort to produce things equivalent to what he has seen, so far as stock is concerned, and to hope that at some not distant period he will return to such a scene, not only as a mere spectator, but as a contributor and competitor. Once this resolve is made, a new era dawns upon the condition of his farm—for who would have fine cattle, sheep and swine, but would naturally desire to have fine pastures, well-tilled fields, good fences, comfortable stables, large manure heaps, and heavy crops, all of which being compatible and indispensable to the position he designs in future to hold among his spirited brother farmers; and hence he will become a useful man in his neighborhood, stirring up by his example the apathetic and careless, who witnessing the results consequent upon his skill and energy, cannot fail of being stimulated to adopt a similar practice. Here, then, is one of the many advantages resulting from Agricultural Exhibitions, one which my own experience and observation have fully confirmed. What has rendered the agriculture of New York of late years so prominently conspicuous among her sister states, but her well established agricultural societies—which, through a spirited effort made at first by a few notable and patriotic individuals, persevered in under many discouraging circumstances, proved so successful, that there is not a county I believe in the Empire State that is not impressed with the seal and attestation of the beneficial effects of agricultural associations—while the whole United States views the annual exhibition of the New York State Agricultural Society more in the light of a national affair, in which all feel a just pride, than a mere state institution. Ohio, our western neighbor, is following with rapid strides the example New York has set. So with Maryland, who has entered the field, determined to wreathe her brows with a leaf from the palm of distinction.

With these animating examples before her, it would have ill become Pennsylvania, with all her acknowledged capabilities to compete with the greatest and the best, to fold her giant limbs and look on unmoved, an unconcerned spectator of this race of progress, and not make one invigorating bound to keep them in condition, or by way of showing that neither one nor many states could make a patriotic demonstration, without Pennsylvania participating in it. State pride, and every ennobling impulse that nature in her finest mood puts in play, could not but urge her to contend, now, as ever, for precedence in whatever can exalt, dignify, or adorn! Impelled by these aspirations, she stood nobly forth at her capital the beginning of the last year, and entered the field of competition, under the title of "The Pennsylvania State Agricultural Society," and in the name of "Virtue, Liberty and Independence." Her Agricultural Exhibition last fall showed she was perfectly in earnest; and if it did not prove her in advance of her sister states, it demonstrated she was not far behind those who had gone the farthest. The cause which has been cherished for ages by the most enlightened nations is worthy of Pennsylvania; and it should be our ardent desire, that for the character of the State, the honor and prosperity of her citizens, our good old Commonwealth should gain for herself an imperishable name, in raising to the highest rank, through a generous and liberal policy, the peaceful and interesting pursuits of agriculture—that she may be the victor in the race now being run, and be crowned with a chaplet, more to be prized, than ever decked the brow of the most successful warrior of the tented field!

From the rank which it was my pride to aspire to, and to which I may in some degree claim to have attained among those who have labored to promote agriculture, it may be expected that I should speak of the principles of scientific culture in connection with chemistry; but were I competent to the task, it would be of doubtful expediency to investigate or refine upon principles of science on an occasion like the present. But a more pertinent reason may be given, a reason quite satisfactory to myself that I should not attempt it, and that is, I am so deficient in the science that I should only render myself ridiculous, did I undertake to elucidate the elements and agents which nature so mystically employs in the process of vegetation. They alone are competent to unfold its mysteries, who have devoted their time and talents in acquiring a knowledge of its principles and laws through scientific research and philosophical experiment—the graduates of the laboratory. For my poor part, I must be content to worship at a distance; not daring to enter the temple, into whose portals the initiated only should claim admission. But there are matters and things within our reach and comprehension, which, without being presumptuous, we may claim the right to touch, handle, and understand; I mean the simple practice of every-day husbandry.

Before entering upon that, permit me a word of warning, not irrelevant to our object. All experience has shown that no discovery in science or philosophy has been made, but was put in jeopardy so soon as it had claimed some degree of popularity, by pretenders and charlatans. I would then, for the sake of the cause for which you have associated, and in which I have spent time, money—I will not say talents, but such abilities as I could command from a too scanty stock, earnestly admonish you not to countenance the speculative quacks, who, for mere lucre and contemptible notoriety, will spring up, relying upon the easy credulity of others and their own brazen effrontery, and profess to teach and lecture upon scientific agriculture. We have seen of late sad specimens of professors, besides those who lately figured in Clairvoyance, Prevision, Retrovision, Mesmerism, Phreno-Magnetism, Psychology, and other mysterious ologies and isms, which, like live coals blown to cinders, have been puffed to death by these philosophic bellows blowers. And now, since Scientific Agriculture is getting into vogue, it would not surprise if some of the "wise men" would turn their mother-wit to profitable account by turning their hand to teaching Vegetable Physiology and Agricultural Chemistry. If they should, and meet with the least encouragement, it will retard the improvement you and other true and disinterested men have essayed to advance. Why? Because it cannot be disguised that among the generality of farmers, there is a distrust of the means resorted to through the press, appealing to their reason and good sense in well authenticated facts and results, bearing upon their practice, which, from the prejudice against "Book Farming," they are prone to not heed or credit. If these pretenders get loose among them, they will sicken and surfeit them to loathing, by technical jargon and arrant quackery. Beside, which is most to be feared, the truly well educated professor, whose services would be of the utmost benefit to the cause, will, through self-respect, refuse to officiate as "Professor of Rural Economy," when he perceives the title has been assumed by others through impudent pretension, and the station defiled by the sheerest humbuggery. This is not all: the legislature to whom we look for aid in furtherance of Agricultural Education, might, when appealed to, be diverted from the importance due to its consideration, should some clever member, not having the fear of God before his eyes but the manner in which these self-styled professors perform their functions, turn the whole subject of Agricultural Education into burlesque and ridicule. For these and many other cogent reasons, it behooves the friends of agriculture to protect it from every taint and speck of quackery. That agriculture is largely indebted to the science of chemistry, is but a feeble acknowledgment of the benefits already conferred upon it. And to say that much more is yet in reserve for it from the same beneficent abundant source, is less presumptive than authoritative; for, from what has been done, it is plain that more can and will be more ably done. Results suggest results, and ever will, till mind and matter shall be wholly resolved, and time be no more!

Since the developments made by Liebig, in the application of Organic Chemistry to agriculture and physiology, mighty efforts, no doubt, are being made by chemists in Europe and in this country upon these and kindred subjects, which must give to agriculture results at once practical and miraculous. I have read or heard it somewhere stated, that ere long it will not surprise to see as much manure compressed within the compass of a pocket handkerchief as would be sufficient to dress an acre of ordinary land for growing wheat. Notwithstanding the confidence I have in science, I must say, that when this shall happen, there will be a decline in the price of farm horses and working oxen; and without meaning to be irreverent, would pray to be helped in my unbelief. But our doubts are not a proof that the thing is impossible, for many of us are old enough to have witnessed achievements in science now so perfectly familiar to our apprehension as not to challenge our special wonder, which, before having been practically demonstrated, appeared as visionary, as that a handkerchief full of fertilizing ingredients would at no very distant day be found sufficient to manure an acre of ground.

When Fulton, who was born in your county, first designed to supplant wind, sails and cordage, by navigating with steam, what faith would it have required then to have believed that steam should in so brief a space, less than the length of our own fleeting day, drive wingless ships across the Atlantic in ten or eleven days ; or that in a shorter period, the grass would be growing on your great turnpike, where, but as lately innumerable Conestoga wagons lumbered along with the products of your industry to the Philadelphia market ; and heavy four-horse stages carried you over that road to the city in the prodigious short space of one day, allowing time for the best breakfasts and dinners at the best taverns, ever passengers were comforted with. When that is compared with the rapidity every thing is whisked over the same distance now on the railroad, by Fulton's agent, steam, not allowing time to beget an appetite for a morsel, nor for a glance at the beautiful farms through which we are steamed with giddy velocity, it is enough to bring the tears into eyes like mine, when reminiscences of the Lancaster turnpike crowd upon the memory, reminding us of the mutability of human affairs! I repeat, what degree of faith would it have required to have believed that those things would come to pass, when your neighbor Robert Fulton was meditating their accomplishment? Why, it would have needed the faith that could remove mountains to have assented to the bare possibility that such things should ever be. And what of the Magnetic Telegraph, and numerous other things that cause old folks to think that they no longer inhabit the same world in which they were born?

My object in adverting to those wonderful discoveries, is, to ask of you, brother farmers, to admit the possibility of great changes being made in the practice of culture and husbandry, and what is equally important, to admit that changes are really needed to bring us on a footing or along side of other callings, who, by some short cut have got the start of us, and can turn out better work and more of it than they did or could do forty years ago; while we remain pretty much in the same condition we were in then; working as hard and making as little as at any time within our recollections; wheat, corn, roots, grass, etc.,scarcely maintaining their former average per acre, while the cost of producing them, is certainly not diminished. Well, having as I hope you have admitted all this, I would take occasion to ask you to go a step further, and that is, for every one to resolve, by every means in his power, through observing, experimenting, reading, and comparing, to gain more knowledge and throw more light on the theory and practice of agriculture, for the purpose of improving his own practice, raising the character of the profession, and increasing the wealth of the State, by increase of products and bringing the lands into higher condition.

Inspired with the hope that you are prepared to listen to suggestions tending to improvement, from even the least pretending source, I now return to the remarks I had intended to make on the practice of every-day husbandry.

It is a good old maxim, that "whatever is worth doing at all, is worth doing well," and, that "we should begin at the beginning." Agreeably to this, I shall begin at the manure, which, if not the basis of good culture, is indispensible to the production of crops on such lands as we cultivate. The manure heap is aptly termed the farmer's golden mine, from which he extracts the veritable ore itself, through a process of assay and coinage, elaborated on his fields, by Nature's self, through every stage of vegetation, from the embryo germ to the perfect maturation of every plant. No skill, no shift, that I have witnessed, ever did succeed in producing even a tolerable crop of grain or roots without a liberal application of manure, proportioned to the condition of the land, and the nature of the crop to be raised, without exhausting it to a greater degree in value than the profit realized from the wretched product forced from the impoverished soil. How essential then is it that every degree of care, every expedient should be resorted to by the farmer, to increase and preserve in the best condition, every thing within his reach having, the character and quality of manure; and, how lamentable to witness the general inattention so prevalent among farmers to this first indispensable point in a good husbandman! You may visit any number of farms, on none of which, but it is almost certain to find the farmer at work—even hard work—and yet, a glance at the condition of his stables and barn-yard is sufficient to show that he is laboring in vain, while the stables and yard are neglected, and the manure permitted to waste so shockingly—one day's waste in this quarter, if prevented, would repay perhaps a week's work of such labor as engages his attention. Now it is not pretended that in looking to the manure, he should neglect the other work; both can, and should be attended to; the thing required is proper attention to both, conformably to economy and good management. If the stables and pens have not been emptied or cleaned for a week or a month; if the manure heap is not well constructed to prevent washing and waste—if the droppings of the cattle in and about the yard are not constantly taken up while fresh and thrown among the lighter substances upon the heap, but are left to be burnt to cinders by the sun, and tossed about with the winds, or washed by the rain, or frozen with the frost; of what avail is labor on land thus cheated of its nourishment while being worked to death? If such things be, it were less than full measure of justice to call them disgraceful; on the other hand, if duly attended to, the porpriety of doing these things is so self-evident, and the ease with which they may be performed under a proper system, so apparent, that but little commendation is due for the service. He, who would be deserving of praise in this respect, should be found adding to the manure heap, gatherings from ditches, decayed wood, leaves, weeds, bones, and the droppings of horses and cattle on the roads and lanes near to the farm, with many other things not necessary to mention here, all of which, from time to time, might be collected at little expense of time. It may be asked what can be done with the bones? The best way of converting them into manure, would be to grind them; an apparatus might be profitably employed for the purpose. They can easily be reduced by saturating them with a solution of one part sulphuric acid (oil of vitriol) and two parts water, when placed in a heap, underlaid and surrounded with mould, as sand is placed round lime to make mortar, throwing in the mould occasionally to unite and catch the falling substance from the bones. As all may not be reduced by the first sprinkling, another heap may be formed of so much of the old one as remains unreduced. proceeding as at first till all is reduced. If this method be considered too troublesome, the bones will be found to be worth all the trouble of gathering them, for placing in the manure heap, to be thrown aside when the manure is being hauled out, to be again deposited in the succeeding heap. Their decomposition will be slow, it is true, but their presence in the heap will more than repay the trouble of keeping them from year to year. They may be put away at once by burying them near the roots, at a suitable distance from the stems, of pear and other fruit trees, and grape vines; the fine fruit that will in after years be produced by the trees thus treated, will attest their value. I am thus particular in pointing to bones, not only on account of their fertilizing properties, but to awaken attention to the necessity of husbanding every thing available for manure.—

It seemed strange that we should witness the gathering of bones at our very doors, along our rivers and canals, to be shipped at Philadelphia to England for manure, and not avail ourselves of an article that the English farmers consider worth importing from so great a distance. It is asserted that over four millions of dollars' worth of bones are annually consumed in England for agricultural purposes. Then to think of the folly of purchasing guano, imported fron Peru, at forty dollars per ton, when it is in our power to make a full supply of manure at home. The farmer who cannot maintain his land in high condition by the manure made upon his farm, is not worthy the name of husbandman. How should this be done? I answer, by keeping a large stock of cattle, and letting nothing go to waste. "Waste not, want not," is a saying worthy of special regard. The quality as well as the quantity should be taken into account: one load of well-preserved manure, from the heap of a pains-taking farmer, is worth two loads of his who is careless—this is fifty per cent. in favor of the former. Guano cannot be objected to as a manure, for it abounds in fertilizing ingredients, but its cost is objectionable. In our climate, the same amount in money paid for guano, if invested in stable-yard manure, would be of more benefit to the land in the long run. No manure is more to be relied upon than that furnished by horses, cattle, sheep and swine. In the year ending the 30th June, 1850, there was imported into the United States no less than twenty-one thousand two hundred and forty-three tons of guano; this, at forty dollars per ton, amounts to eight hundred and forty-nine thousand seven hundred and twenty dollars. At the port of Philadelphia alone, in 1851, four thousand nine hundred and eighty tons were imported; if sold at the price quoted, it would amount to but little less than two hundred thousand dollars.

Of all the concentrated or extraneous manures, poudrette, when properly manufactured, is the best and cheapest, and for obvious reasons should be most encouraged. A large supply of this excellent article may soon be expected, from the works about being established by Professor Peyson, a clever French chemist and engineer, who has made arrangements with the Board of Health of the city of Philadelphia for disinfecting or deodorizing cess pools, and the converting sewerage and putrescent substances into poudrette. I witnessed an experiment by him on a cess pool at my residence last May, when he deodorized the contents of an old deep well in the space of fifteen minutes. The object of having it done under my inspection, was for the purpose of taking charge of the disinfected mass, at the instance of the Philadelphia Agricultural Society, to ascertain whether the process he conducted would not destroy the fertilizing property of the fecal matter. To this end I applied it to a part of a patch laid off for ruta baga turnip, to be compared with other very strong manure, principally from a slaughter house. I found the poudrette, through all the stages of growing the crop, equally as effective as the other manure, and giving as good a yield in turnips. This is instanced, to show what science can do for agriculture, and to point to resources not often taken into account by farmers. The turning this offensive matter, which among a dense population is a source of inconvenience and disease, into a state to be handled with less unpleasantness than good stable manure can be, is a triumph of science, and if properly encouraged will add to the agricultural products of the State thousands upon thousands of dollars annually.

To speak of lime, as I feel bound to do, in connection with manure, requires no small degree of courage, knowing the great value you place upon it. Broadly, then, I hold it not to be a manure, in the common acceptation of the term; and that its so frequent application upon a large portion of your land, the heavy loam and clay lands, is not only destructive of the real manure applied to those soils, but to the inherent organic fertility found in them. Quick lime, spread on or with manure, evolves or liberates the most active elements or fertilizing ingredients in the manure, facilitating their escape into the air. Not only so, but so long as its causticity continues, which, from the large portion of magnesia generally found in lime—the burning process, if I may be allowed the expression—is likely to be kept up for a long time, during which the vegetable ingredients in the soil are being too rapidly and unnecessarily wasted, to the great detriment of the soil, and to the injury of almost every subsequent crop raised upon it. In no case can such lime be safely applied in quantity, as is customary, except where the soil is overcharged with vegetable mould, or abounds in fibrous roots. If dressing after dressing of fifty or more bushels of caustic lime to the acre be applied every four or five years, nothing can save the soil from the accumulated injuries thus heaped upon it, but the application of a great deal more barn-yard manure than, under the condition of no lime, would be needed, to counteract or repair the mischief doing, or already done, by the lime. Here, then, is a needless expenditure of lime and manure, which, if time would permit to go into a calculation for a few years, would show an astounding amount in dollars. As well might you be found heaping wood on a fire to keep up a comfortable temperature in a house on a cold day, while you kept the street door open to let in the cold, when half the fuel would serve to keep the house warm if the door were shut, as to apply caustic lime to heavy limestone land, in quantity as it is usually applied, thereby rendering it so necessary to put on so much more manure to modify it.

By way of illustrating the opposite tendencies of lime and manure, suppose a heap of rich manure removed from where it had stood sometime in a field, the spot on which it stood being surcharged with the liquid it had absorbed from the heap. If seeded in this condition, the grain would not head or fill—at best it would be rusted or choked with weeds. In such a case, what would be the readiest method a farmer could adopt to restore this over-rich spot to usefulness? Why, nothing more nor less than to administer to the soil a strong dose of quick lime, by trenching and mixing it well in, throughout the spot affected. This would put its plethora to a purgation, and soon render it lean enough for active service. On the other hand, a scabby spot, left on a field by a heap of lime, can be restored by pouring a quantity of liquid manure upon it, or by trenching in well rotted barn-yard manure, in excess. By this it would seem that lime, in some degree, is as antagonistic to manure as the sun is to moisture. But it may be claimed that lime is made use of as an agent to prepare food for plants: be it so then, and allow that in some cases its services are useful; would that justify its indiscriminate application as a feeder, as well where there is nothing for him to do in his line, as where there was something he could do lawfully?

In the general, lime is so wasteful and ravenous a cook, that he sometimes consumes more than he furnishes to the family of plants it is intended he should provide for; nay, it may be suspected, that when his allotted means fail to appease his gnawing appetite, he will feed on the plants themselves, though they may have a little of his own blood in them. Do not, I pray you, take this as a wholesale condemnation of lime. As an agent, it is useful in meliorating certain conditions of soil, if judiciously applied. Light sandy, micacious or isinglass, red shale and slaty soils, may in general be benefited by dressings of lime; but on clayey limestone soil I should deem its application unnecessary, if not injurious. To mix in a good dressing of common sand, would be more rational by far than throwing lime into it. The sand would be harmless at least; the lime, in my judgment, could not be so. If the value of the lime, so inappropriately applied, were expended in wood ashes and pulverized charcoal, it would show results incomparably remunerative. In thus pronouncing so unequivocally upon the merits of lime, I am aware of the risk incurred; but if it should serve no other purpose than to lead to a closer observation of its effects by others, I shall feel fully compensated, and content me, in abiding an unprejudiced verdict, on the opinion so frankly avowed.

This leads me to say a word on another agent, Gypsum, or Plaster of Paris: and here I feel at perfect liberty to admit its surprising beneficial effects on soils and vegetation. That so small a modicum of this cheap and easily applied mineral should exhibit such wonderful influence in conservating the fertility and capability of land to sustain it so ably under the exhausting process of producing, must astonish every experienced and experimental farmer! The question, as to how it acts, is one that has challenged the observation of many inquiring minds, and seems at this day not to be fully settled. Some hold that it supplies, in itself, an element necessary to the development, growth and perfectability of plants, inasmuch as gypsum, and the sulphuric acid it supplies, are found in the ashes of the plants. Others maintain that its beneficial agency consists in its conservative capacity to husband, or prevent the escape of ammonia and other subtile elements of fertility in the manure and soil, fixing or retaining them in the soil, so as the plants may feed upon them through all the stages of vegetating. To this latter theory I am fully inclined. Those who adhere to the other opinion, rely upon, as already stated, the evidence of gypsum being found in the plants; and hence the necessity of an adventitious supply of gypsum, lest the land should be destitute of this indispensable ingredient. But taking this plausible deduction into view, how could so small a quantity as a bushel of plaster, sown on the surface of an acre of land, considering its insolubility, be taken up in so short a period as the season of growth by a plant, such as wheat for instance, whose roots penetrate so far below the surface of the ground? The shortness of the period of growth will more forcibly apply to clover and grass for mowing, which, from the time the plaster is applied till the harvesting of these crops, less than three months, would be too short a period to expect they could have taken up the plaster sown upon them. That they did not take it up, or any of it, is probable: that they did take it up, could only be proven by chemical tests, hardly possible, it is presumed, to conduct to any positive certainty.

The theory, then, that the gypsum exerts an influence merely, or only, in holding in solution, as chemists would say, the fertilizing gases for the use of the plants, seems unquestionable. I am strengthened in this by experience in sprinkling plaster daily in my stables, for years, on the removal of the litter and dung; its effect is, to abate at once the effluvia, showing the influence it exerts over the ammonia. Let any one try its effects on a foul stable, and he will soon be convinced of the nature of the service it performs, and its great utility in preserving the volatile portion of the manure, so essential to its strength and good quality. An excellent opportunity was afforded me last July for proving its effects in this regard. The manure used on the 'ruta baga patch already alluded to, in juxtaposition with the poudrette, was principally from a slaughter house; it was particularly odorous, and had it ploughed in as soon as possible. A few days afterwards there came on a heavy rain, succeeded by a sultry sun, and the patch became very noisome; had a bushel of plaster immediately sown upon it; was present when the sowing commenced, but left, and returned to the patch as the operation was finished, and was gratified to find that in so short a period, about an hour, the disagreeable odor had almost entirely subsided. From this, is it not manifest that it was owing to the action of the gypsum that the offensive smell was abated, and that the strong effluvia was nothing more or less than the ammonia escaping from the soil, which had so recently been impregnated to a high degree by the putrefaction from the slaughter house manure? Then, did the gypsum neutralize or destroy the fertilizing gas, which was poisoning the atmosphere? or did they both unite, from the principle of affinity or attraction? I believe they united. The plaster, in descending, may have carried so much of the gas with it as fell in its way, purifying or relieving the air of it so far; and, when lodged on the ground, became a receiver to take in, or a lid to cover the volatile elements of fertility that would escape—holding them until rains and dews should wash them from its embrace to enrich the soil, and furnish food to the rootlets of the plants that nestle beneath, waiting for the precious tricklings. If this simple explanation shows, with some degree of accuracy, the action and influence of gypsum, how insensible then must the farmer be to his own interests, who will not provide a suitable supply of this perfect God-send of a substance, wherewith to sprinkle his stables, his manure and his fields?

While treating of plaster, clover, from association, naturally presents itself; and as time will not permit to enter upon cropping and culture, I feel inclined to make a passing remark upon it here. There is a prevailing opinion that clover is favorable to the land, as a non-exhauster, if not an enricher of soil. If it derive this character from the idea that it draws more nourishment from the air than the soil, I beg leave to dissent. I am not much of a believer in the doctrine of atmospheric nutriment, and yet I am not prepared to reject it in toto. A close observation will establish, I think, that it is owing to the shade the clover imparts to the land, that it exhausts so little of the soil. Buckwheat furnishes another instance, with this difference, that the supply required to fill the head or mature the grain in the buckwheat, is greater than what is needed to form the flowers of the clover. Shade is a wonderful conservator of soil; and this suggests how careful we should be to expose our land as little as possible, in a bare or naked state, to the severity of our summer suns and winter frosts. But to shade may be reckoned a loss sustained in the clover, and consequent *gain* to the land, from so much of it being left on the field at hay making, especially when the clover is grown with timothy, a practice that cannot be too strongly condemned. The top dressing thus given involuntarily to the land, from the best and strongest parts of the clover, the fine leaves and flowers, strewn around, contributes in no small degree to the good condition claimed for the soil after crops of clover; add to this, the quantity of clover roots spewed out upon the land through freezing and thawing, left to rot upon it, and you have almost the sum total of the causes which lead to the hypothesis that clover is a non-exhauster, or improver of the soil. If this be the case, is it not proper we should look closer into cause and effect, and not blindly follow illusive practices, so subversive of our own prosperity? I must not be understood as condemning the practice of growing clover: I condemn it not, but insist that every crop grown should be well husbanded, and put to its proper use, and not wasted on the field where it is grown. And here it may not be out of place to explain why clover and timothy should not be grown together. One ruling objection is, they don't ripen at the same time. If the clover be cut when ready for mowing, the timothy cut with it is of little account, having not attained its growth; it shrivels astonishingly in the sun while drying; what's of it is acid, disagreeable in taste, and unwholesome, from not having matured or elaborated its sap. If on the other hand, the timothy is left to ripen, the clover then is almost a total loss, nothing of it reaches the barn fit for cattle, or even fit to supply the place of straw. Independently of this, if a fine sod is desirable, as it undoubtedly should be, it never can be found with timothy and clover. Why? Because, from the start at growing till the end of their respective terms, they are in habit, taste and condition uncongenial, and there

fore inappropriately put together. While growing together the first season,
the bushy head of the clover pushes aside or smothers the tiny blades of the
young timothy; next spring, much of the clover has been forced from the
ground by the frosts of winter, leaving the stems and roots of the timothy
sadly exposed to the freezing and thawing of March, with its occasional chill-
ing winds; and hence the impossibility to find a continuous, compact sod, on
any field thus cropped. And who takes the pains to calculate the loss on
spaces left bare where the clover stood, or reflects on the impropriety of wasting land and labor? When timothy is required, it should be sown alone, and
permitted to mature suitably for hay. Orchard grass and clover may be sown
together, because they ripen at the same time, and delight in the same soil; but
where a good, well-set sod is wanted, to last for several years, no red clover
should be sown with the timothy or orchard grass. The clover should be kept
by itself, and confined to fields or patches intended soon to be broken up.

There is another remark, however it may conflict with preconceived opinion
or established usage, a sense of duty compels me to make; and that is, of all
the time-wasting, land-cheating practices, none is more to be deprecated than
that of turning in green crops, as a succedaneum for manure. In whatever
place this is practised, however strong the land may be at the start, the system, if persevered in, must inevitably bring the land, its owners and the country into a state of poverty. No good husbandman would think of pursuing
such a course. Think of the time lost in preparing ground for a crop, seeding it, and instead of allowing it to mature, to be gathered to the barn, ploughing it under, to serve as manure to the land on which it was raised! Manure,
indeed! To call the acidulated water, which the decomposition of partly
grown clover, buckwheat, &c., produce, manure, would be a misnomer—the
calling of a thing by the wrong name. Where a winter crop in the spring
shows unmistakable signs of proving a failure, a clever farmer should, and
would plough it in, and substitute a summer crop in its stead, so as to provide
against loss of time in producing, and to get what he could for the manure he
had bestowed upon the winter crop the previous fall. It is intolerable the cant
of want of vegetable matter in the soil, as excuse for turning in green crops.
No soil that is well supplied with barn-yard manure, and laid down to grass
occasionally through a judicious rotation, can be destitute of vegetable matter.
If the turning in, year after year, scant crops of clover and the like, be persisted
in, the land so treated must, in a brief period, become not only destitute of
vegetable mould, but of every other organic ingredient necessary to fertility.

Two considerations should ever govern the practical farmer. The first is,
the absolute necessity of maintaining his land in high condition—"good
heart," as it is termed. The second is, the system best adapted to impair as
little as possible the first or main object, through a judicious adaptation of
of crops, in view of profitable yield, at the least possible loss to the soil. In
proportion as these considerations shall influence, in like proportion will be
the good or bad culture and husbandry on the farm.

To maintain land in good condition, there is no resort within my experience equal to soiling, on old well-cleared farms; if in no other respect, the increase of manure dropt in the stables and yard, at hand for preserving, instead of its being wasted on the lanes, fields and ditches, would be sufficient to recommend it to the provident husbandman. This increase of manure, giving increase of fertility to the soil, and by consequence increase of products, is so progressive, and mutually so self-sustaining to the cattle and land as to defy calculation. The enlightened farmer, who has experimented on it, can only compute or appreciate its multiplying results. It is easier, however, to illustrate the evils of depasturing exposed uplands, than to calculate the benefits accruing from the system of soiling cattle; but the one will, in some degree unfold the other. Suppose we begin with fifteen head of grown cattle, and inquire how many acres, under our fervid suns, would it require to pasture them from May till November, on fields of artificial grass, denuded before the previous winter had set in to impoverish them farther with its killing frosts—the cattle to be turned out on the first of May in condition as is usual in such cases? Why, not less than thirty acres. Now I aver, that five acres of well prepared land, near to the barn, under patches of rye, clover, and orchard grass, lucerne and corn, to be cut green, and fed judiciously in the stables or sheds—the cattle having a spring in some spot to be driven to for water and exercise—would sustain these fifteen head of cattle better than the thirty acres appointed for them to graze on. Here, then, is a saving of twenty-five acres of land by this operation. And how much better would be the condition of this land under grain, or grass for mowing, than it could be under the continual biting of the cattle, and the scorching heat of the sun? And in how much better condition would be the cattle, having plenty of juicy food, with time to rest and ruminate in the shade, to that of ranging all day under a burning sun, tired and fatigued in limbs and jaws, gathering a scanty, scorched herbage, that but mocks their restless cravings? Add to this the quantity of manure that may be saved in these two months, with the increase of dairy products, and you can form some idea of the beneficial workings of the system of soiling. It may be objected, that the additional expense in wages or labor incurred, in cutting and feeding, has not been brought forward. Well, let us examine this item. These cattle must be turned out, and brought in from the fields, daily to be milked; this under the circumstances, by no means rare, of the fields being distant and fences not very good, consumes time and breeds confusion, from the frequent interruption to other work having to be suspended while looking after the cattle, that have, perhaps, broken into some forbidden field or thrown the bars down. Then allow for so much time and labor as is thus spent in the common way, and you have to take into account only the additional unconsumed time of a man or well grown boy, who would be required to attend constantly on the cattle while being soiled. A boy who can milk, clean stables, mow a little grass, clover or corn, wheel it on a barrow to the stables, or hitch a horse to haul it, would be sufficient for the undertaking; but even should a full hand be required, the wages for two months would not exceed thirty dollars; but who would think of wages, when the work is chiefly getting manure for the mere wheeling it out, as would be the case if the stables be cleaned out as they should be, three times a day. In this way, forty to fifty head of cattle might be kept for milking and breeding, upon any commonly good farm of from seventy to one hundred acres; admitting at the same time of more efficient cropping, through a series of years, than if but some eight or ten head were kept in the ordinary way, and even these to be turned out on the roads and lanes while the crops are in, as is sometimes the case, until turned in upon the stubble and young grass with the swine, so soon as the grain is removed from the fields. The soiling should not be continued longer than two months. The cattle from July should have the range of the mowed grass fields the remainder of the season, with the stubble land in due time. In July the orchard grass and clover, the best artificial grass for hay and pasture, will be ready for second cutting; but no good husbandman, who values the condition of his land, would think of mowing second crop—the cattle only should eat it. Second crop makes poor fodder, and to turn in the cattle so soon as the scythe has ceased mowing either first or second crop, be it meadow or upland, to exterminate the roots of the grass during fall, completely denuding the fields when winter shall have set in, is not only bad policy but wasteful economy; an acre or more of turnip, and other roots, would serve a better purpose for winter food than second crop grass and clover.

It is a reproach to Pennsylvania that her cattle and dairy products should fall so far short of New York. The census of 1840, if it can be relied upon, with that of 1850, as far as have been given, show that we fall below New York in dairy products about eight millions of dollars annually. This is a large item in one product, and is just so many millions a year abstracted or lost to the income wealth of our Commonwealth. Another item is no less startling—it is, that New York produced, according to the former census, twenty millions of bushels potatoes more than Pennsylvania. The difference in dairy products cannot surprise, when the difference is perceived in the quality of our butter and that of New York—I allude to salted or preserved butter for winter use; ours scarcely average eight cents a pound—a considerable portion of it sells from five to six cents per pound for grease—whilst that of New York averages eighteen cents a pound. I have taken some pains to ascertain the quantity of New York butter that is sold annually in the Philadelphia market—some of it, no doubt, consumed in Lancaster and neighboring counties—and from the most reliable sources am led to believe that it falls little short of three hundred thousand dollars! Here, then, is the money of farming Pennsylvania going into the pocket as it were of New York, for butter alone, to the tune of three hundred thousand dollars every year, to say nothing of cheese and potatoes. Is not this startling, if not shameful; and should it not serve to rouse us to a better sense of our own interests. Now, a cow of same breed and quality will cost as much in New York as in Pennsylvania. The land and climate of the latter are as good, if not better, than those of the former. What, then, makes the difference? Nothing, but that the skill of the one in dairy products and the management of cattle, is greater and better than the other—a difference which we should endeavor, by all means, to equalize at least.

The time I had intended to occupy has elapsed, and therefore must bring my remarks to a close. The preparation of the soil and adaptation of crops, with their culture, are necessarily excluded. My principal object, as you may have perceived, was to promote the furtherance of societies such as yours, believing as I do that in no other way can the improvements needed in culture and husbandry, on public considerations as well as on individual account, be so effectually accomplished as by a combined effort of enlightened and patriotic minds, devoted to that object. One word as to the adaptation of crops to the soil. There is scarcely a farm of any considerable size, much less a district of country, but exhibits some variety in soil, and which does not require a special and judicious discrimination in adapting the crops to its peculiarities. To follow, then, a common rotation, as if the soil of the whole were common or equal, must end in disappointment to the hopes of the farmer, and peculiar loss to the public in general. Whether from this, the waste of manure or the neglect to husband it, or inaptness in resource, it is apparent the lands are not as productive as they should be. If they be ill used, wasted or robbed of their fertility, what is to become of Pennsylvania when they shall not yield their adequate and natural increase? Thousands of acres of fine land are being doomed annually to deterioration, through a vicious system, by their owners, who are little better than cumberers of the ground, and by the destruction wantonly perpetrated by tenants. This latter class are as wolves among flocks, ever prowling about, and victimizing wherever they come. There may be some honorable exceptions to this sweeping charge; but it may be asked, where is the farm under rent, for a few years, but has its character sunk and its fertility destroyed? In England, and some parts of Europe, this evil is well provided against by remedies, founded as well on public policy, conservative of the landed interest, as protective of private rights; and he who wantonly deteriorates the soil there, is held in little less detestation than a public robber.

If, in filling up the broad outline broached at the beginning, with such detail as in my judgment seemed best calculated to subserve the great cause of agriculture, I have drawn too largely, gentlemen, upon your time and patience, fidelity in purpose, and zeal in executing, must plead my excuse for any seeming diffusiveness. The attentive hearing, however, you have afforded to my remarks, leads me to hope no other apology is necessary. One thing at least is certain, that I have fallen far short of the service I could have wished to have rendered to the cause your kind partiality designated me to promote.

To the President of the Pennsylvania State Agricultural Society:

In accordance with the act of Assembly of March 29th, 1851, sections four and five, I submit to you the following report of the Agricultural and Horticultural Society of Lawrence county, for the past year. Names of officers for the ensuing year:

PRESIDENT—Thomas Pearson.

VICE PRESIDENTS—Thomas Cunningham and William Hamilton.

SECRETARY—J. W. Reynolds.

TREASURER—William M'Clymonds.

MANAGERS—William Brown, John Simpson, William Blanchard, J. P. Cowden, William Williams and Philip Crowell.

In our last year's report it was shown, that our society had assumed a character of permanence and prospective determination, by the leasing for a term of ten years a beautiful and highly eligible field on one of the prominences which overlook the active and flourishing borough of New Castle, and that the site had been enclosed by a permanent board fence, and commodious and spacious buildings erected thereon, for the protection and exhibition of all kinds of articles offered by competitors, together with such other fixtures and appurtenances as were deemed necessary for the accommodation of all the members and spectators who should attend our annual fairs.

Our annual exhibition took place on the 5th, 6th and 7th days of October, and was well attended and highly satisfactory to all who felt an interest in the advancement of our agricultural progress, though the excessive and unparalleled drought of the season had greatly enfeebled and indeed almost annihilated every species of vegetation. Yet still even in this department many excellent articles were on exhibition, and our animal and mechanical specimens showed a most laudible and encouraging improvement.

We give the reports of some of our agriculturists as to their crops, but at the same time ask due allowance to be made for the entire want of refreshing showers for the space of almost four months of the period of their growth.

Our citizens show an increasing interest in the society, and we think we may say with safety that our society has done much already in driving hence the native fear and contempt felt by our farmers for "Book farming," as it was termed, and has created a desire for a more scientific knowledge of their business. Hence the circulation of good agricultural and horticultural papers are greatly increased.

The society numbers about two hundred and seventy-five members.

A premium list was offered amounting to five hundred and fifty dollars, of which three hundred and fifty dollars was awarded and paid. Whole receipts amounted to one thousand dollars. Incidental expenses amounted to óne hundred and seventy dollars.

Statement of Hiram Watson in relation to corn:

"I husked five hundred and forty-eight bushels of shelled corn on ten acres of ground, it was the second successive corn crop on the same ground. About three acres was manured with horse manure. I ploughed the ground the first week in May, from eight to ten inches deep, and furrowed three and one half feet each way, rolled my seed in plaster and planted on the fifteenth of May; worked three times with cultivator and ploughed once—plastered once before working first time. The corn planted was the red cob gourd."

Statement of same gentleman in relation to oats:

"I threshed four hundred and thirty-two bushels of oats from nine acres of ground; the ground being corn stubble, on creek bottom. Ploughed the ground last week in March—sowed April 4th, two and one half bushels per acre—ploughed from six to eight inches deep."

Statement of P. Mershimer:

"I raised from one acre one hundred and four bushels of red potatoes and fifty bushels of Neshanock potatoes. Ploughed eight to ten inches deep on the 7th or 8th days of May—planted on 10th day of May, on black loamy soil; planted fifteen bushels red and five bushels Neshanock potatoes to the acre. Furrowed about three feet one way—harrowed and hoed once, and ploughed twice. This is the tenth successive crop of potatoes raised on the same ground."

Our crops were all light—not near enough for home consumption. Wheat is worth in our county two dollars per bushel; corn one dollar; oats fifty-six cents; rye one dollar and twelve and a half cents; potatoes one dollar and fifty cents, and hay eighteen dollars per ton.

THOMAS PEARSON, *President.*

J. W. REYNOLDS, *Secretary.*

LEHIGH COUNTY.

To the President of the Pennsylvania State Agricultural Society:

The formation and permanent existence of an agricultural society in this county, which but three years ago was a doubtful experiment, is now an "accomplished fact," and the managers of the association take great pleasure in announcing to the public, that of its future prosperity and usefulness there is now no doubt. The first meeting on this subject was held in the court house, at Allentown, on Tuesday, the 5th day of February, 1852. The meeting was not large, but was composed of men who were convinced of the importance of the measure, and who were determined to effect it, if possible. After an address on the subject, by ROBERT E. WRIGHT, Esq., the society was organized by electing as

PRESIDENT—Edward Kohler, Esq.

VICE PRESIDENTS—Paul Balliet, North Whitehall; Henry Diefenderfer, Upper Milford; Benjamin S. Levan, Washington; John Shiffert, Lower Macungie; John Lichtenwalner, Upper Macungie; John H. Helfrich, Weisenburg; Joel Klotz, Lowhill; Joseph Moser, Lynn; Charles Wittman, Upper Saucon; Martin Kemmerer, Salisbury; Solomon L. Keck, Hanover; Godfrey Peter, Heidelberg; Augustus L. Ruhe, Allentown; Peter Troxell, Jr., South Whitehall; George Beisel, Northampton.

RECORDING SECRETARY—J. M. Line.

CORRESPONDING SECRETARY—David O. Moser.

TREASURER—Owen Schrieber.

CHEMIST—Lewis Schmidt.

LIBRARIAN—E. D. Leisenring.

Preparations were made with considerable energy for the first exhibition, which was opened on Wednesday, the 7th day of October, continued for two days and was successful beyond the hopes of its warmest friends. The fair was held on the property of Messrs. Pretz & Weinsheimer, in Allentown, where some three or four acres of ground were surrounded by canvass purchased and presented to the society for this purpose, by the citizens of Allentown. The articles exhibited were so numerous, and the crowd of visitors so large, that the managers were induced to make the institution a permanent one.

They accordingly purchased the ground now owned by the society, in the township of South Whitehall, on the western border of Allentown; and immediately commenced preparing for the second annual exhibition on the most liberal scale.

The grounds, containing eight acres, were enclosed in a substantial fence; a large building with extensive sheds, for the reception of the articles intended for exhibition, were erected, which though not finished in time, afforded convenient, but by no means ample accommodation for those who attended on that occasion. The success which they then met with, encouraged a further expenditure, and the exhibition of 1854, which has just closed, the transactions of which are here recorded, was held in an enclosure and buildings, which we can safely say, for beauty and convenience, are not surpassed by any in this country.

The site is on the most elevated spot near Allentown, overlooking the whole town, and the magnificent panorama of hills and vales which surround it. The space includes eight full acres, perfectly even, with a light inclination towards the south; and is surrounded by a close fence eight feet high. The main entrance is on the south-west corner, opposite the northern terminus of Sixth street; at which point there is erected a most beautiful Swiss cottage, occupied by the person who has charge of the grounds, and used during the fair as a ticket office, and by the various committees appointed to award the premiums. Passing through the spacious gate-way, the eye is at once arrested by the main exhibition hall, a stately building one hundred feet long by fifty wide, and thirty feet high, surmounted by a splendid gallery or observatory; with a heavy ornamental cornice and brackets surrounding the eaves and projecting gables—the whole exterior being neatly and tastefully painted.

The appearance of this building, covered as it is during the exhibition, with flags and streamers, and of the observatory filled with spectators, is exceedingly beautiful. Passing along the western side of the enclosure, to the left of the main entrance, the first building met with is the poultry house, which is a neat ornamental building, one hundred and fifty feet long, by thirty feet wide. Beyond that on the same side, is the range of stabling for horses presented for exhibition, two hundred feet long, by twenty feet wide, and furnished with every requisite accommodation. This building extends northward to about the middle of the western line. Beyond this, and occupying the northern half of the enclosure is a trotting circle, one thousand nine hundred feet in circumference, and fifty feet wide, enclosed on both sides by a substantial fence, so constructed as to afford a full view of the course from all points, while it effectually prevents all accidents that might happen to the spectators from unmanagable horses. Indeed, by a regulation of the society no horses are admitted on that part of the grounds appropriated to the use of the visitors. In the centre of the plot of ground which is inside the trotting course, there is a building eighty feet long, by thirty feet wide, (with an observatory,) intended for the exhibition of pleasure carriages, &c.

On the eastern side of the enclosure there is a building two hundred feet long, by twenty feet wide, intended for the exhibition of neat cattle, and adjoining it on the same side, are a row of pens, occupying two hundred and fifty feet in length, for the use of sheep and hogs.

On the southern side, near the main entrance, are a row of well arranged restaurants, ten in number, which are readily disposed of, and produce a handsome return to the society for this investment.

The ground on the southern side of the enclosure, and around the centre building, has been laid out most beautifully in walks and circles, along which several hundred choice shade trees have been planted, which when fully grown, will make this a most delightful promenade. Directly in front of the main building there is a space left for a fountain, which in all probability will be finished by the next exhibition.

In short, the whole thing is one that the county may be proud of, and which cannot fail to be for many years a source of rational pleasure and profit to our best citizens. We invite the aid of all good men in its behalf.

EDWARD KOHLER, *President.*

A. L. RUHE, *Secretary.*

At an annual meeting of the Lehigh County Agricultural Society, held at the house of Charles Ihrie, in the borough of Allentown, on Tuesday, the 7th day of February, A. D. 1854, the following officers were elected for the ensuing year :

PRESIDENT—Edward Kohler.

VICE PRESIDENTS.—A. G. Reninger, J. M. Line, J. G. Schimpf, Allentown; Charles Fiot, Salisbury; Charles Witman, U. Saucon; Aaron Dubs, L. Milford; Charles Foster, U. Milford; Benjamin Jarret, L. Macungie; Hiram J. Schantz, U. Macungie; Jacob Grim, Weisenberg; Peter Weida, Lowhill; Samuel J. Kistler, Heidelberg; Charles Peter, Washington; Paul Balliet, N. Whitehill; Peter Troxel, S. Whitehill; Solomon L. Keck, Hanover; Samuel Thomas, Catasauqua; Joseph Moser, Lynn.

RECORDING SECRETARY—A. L. Ruhe.

CORRESPONDING SECRETARY—Dr. D. O. Moser.

TREASURER—Owen L. Schreiber.

CHEMIST—Lewis Klumpf.

LIBRARIAN—E. D. Leisenring.

The success which the society met with during the two years of its existence, encouraged a further expenditure. Preparations were made to finish the main exhibition hall, which last year was left unfinished; pleasure walks and circles were laid out and planted with shade trees; the trotting course was enlarged; a ticket office and a number of restaurants were built, and other improvements were made. According to previous notice, the third annual exhibition was opened on Wednesday, the 4th day of October, and continued for three days. The weather was exceedingly fine and pleasant throughout; a shower on the day previous to the opening of the exhibition, settled the dust, which rendered the roads as agreeable as if prepared to order.

On Thursday afternoon, Robert E. Wright, Esq., delivered the third annual address, (which is hereto annexed,) and on Friday afternoon the Rev. Josiah Yeager delivered the closing address in the German language, in which the calling and dignity of a farmer was ably discussed.

AWARD OF PREMIUMS.

The following is a list of the premiums awarded by the association at their annual exhibition of 1854, in accordance with the reports of the several committees appointed for that purpose :

No. 1.—FIELD CROPS.

There was no competition for the premiums offered by the society this year for field crops.

No. 2.—Horses and Mules.

The committee inform the society that the competition this year far exceeded that of last, and also that, in distributing the premiums, they found it exceedingly difficult, in some instances, to give their decision. A beautiful black mare, four years old, owned by Dr. Franklin B. Martin, a pair of carriage horses owned by Jacob Stein, and a brood mare owned by Paul Balliet, are reported as deserving the notice of the public.

For the best stallion for heavy draught, to Levi Shelly, of Bucks county, name of horse, " Rockingham," seven years old...........	$6 00
Second best, to William Walbert, name of horse, " English," seven years old...	3 00
Best brood mare, heavy draught, to Isaac Hartman, name of mare, " English,"..	4 00
Second best, to Paul Balliet, name of mare, " Morgan,"...........	2 00
Best stallion, quick draught, to George Beisel....................	6 00
Second best, to Jonas Wieant.....................................	2 00
Best horse colt, between two and four years old, to Reuben Kline...	4 00
Second best, to Isaac Hartman....................................	2 00
Best mare colt, between two and four years old, to Robert Oberly...	4 00
Second best, to Aaron Landis.....................................	2 00
Best pair of farm horses, to Hiram J. Shantz.....................	4 00
Second best, to John Bortz	2 00
Best pair of mules, to Andrew Keck..............................	4 00
Best pair of carriage horses, to Charles Seagreaves..............	4 00
Second best, to Thomas Hoffman.................................	2 00
Best gelding, between two and four years old, to Charles Seider....	3 00
Second best, to Tilghman Kleppinger.............................	1 00
Best suckling horse colt, to Paul Balliet, name " General Taylor,"..	2 00
Best road horse, to John L. Hoffman.............................	3 00
Second best, to Charles Kline....................................	1 00
Best speed horse, to Charles Witman.............................	3 00
Second best, to Robert Kramer..................................	1 00

No. 3.—Neat Cattle.

The Committee on Cattle reported that in this branch of the farmer's wealth they already see a decided improvement since the formation of this society, the result, undoubtedly, of the information the members and visitors have obtained at these exhibitions. The display of cattle was exceedingly fine. They especially notice those contributed by Charles Seagreaves, John Bortz, Paul Balliet, George Beisel, Joseph Amey, Aaron Landes, Charles W. Cooper, Owen L. Schreiber, William H. Gruber; John Gross, Hiram J. Schantz, David Mertz, Edward Schreiber, William H. Blumer, Enos Erdman, P. Newhard and Christian Nicholas.

Owing to the very large number of some of the grades exhibited, the committee found it very difficult, in some cases, to decide which was entitled to the greatest praise; but after mature deliberation, awarded as follows:

Best Devon bull, over three years, Charles Seagreaves $6 00
Second best, Joseph Amey...................................... . 3 00
Best Devon bull, under three years, C. W. Cooper............... 4 00
Second best, John Bortz....................................... 2 00
Best native bull, O. L. Schreiber............................. 4 00
Second best, Paul Balliet 2 00
Best Devon bull calf, under six months, John Bortz............ 2 00
Second best, John Gross....................................... 1 00
Best Durham cow, over three years, H. J. Schantz.............. 6 00
Second best, Paul Balliet..................................... 4 00
Best Devon cow, C. W. Cooper.................................. 6 00
Second best, Charles Seagreaves............................... 4 00
Best native cow, H. J. Schantz................................ 6 00
Second best, O. L. Schreiber.................................. 4 00
Third best, David Mertz....................................... 4 00
Best Devon heifer, under three years, John Bortz.............. 3 00
Second best, George Beisel.................................... 2 00

No. 4.—SHEEP.

Though the sheep presented were all of a good quality and blood, the number was this year very limited. Premiums were awarded as follows:

Cotswald buck, Xenophon Kohler............................... $4 00
Spanish mixed buck, Thomas Knecht............................ 4 00
Southdown and Lesterville, crossed, Paul Balliet............. 4 00
Best pen of three ewes, Bakewell, full blood, John Bortz..... 4 00
Second best, three ewes, Bakewell and Southdown, crossed..... 4 00
On the following the committee recommended premiums as follows:
For a Spanish mixed lamb, Thomas Knecht...................... $1 00
Two Cotswald lambs, Xenophon Kohler......................... 1 00
One Southdown ewe, Christian Nicholas....................... 1 00
One Southdown and Scottsville mixed ewe, Paul Balliet....... 1 00

No. 5.—SWINE.

There was but a small number of swine exhibited, but those which were here were of a superior breed.

For the best boar, Lestershire, six months, twenty-four days old,
  Hiram J. Shantz.. $2 00
The best boar pig, Lestershire, thirteen weeks old, George Beisel... 2 00
The best sow, Lestershire, six months, twenty-four days old, Hiram
  J. Shantz.. 2 00

The best sow, Lestershire, between two and six months old, George
Beisel $2 00
The second best sow, Lestershire, between two and six months old,
George Beisel... 1 00
The best lot of pigs, between and over four weeks old, John Bortz... 2 00
The best pork hog, eighteen months old, Henry Roth.............. 2 00
The best pair pork hogs, twelve months old, William Baer......... 2 00

No. 6.—AGRICULTURAL PRODUCTS.

The number of grain exhibitors was very small, and no oats came under the
notice of the committee. Samuel A. Bridges, Esq., exhibited a small quantity
of white wheat, which he received from the Patent Office, at Washington, and
which, in the opinion of the committee, is of a very superior quality. Specimens can be had of A. L. Rhue, Secretary of the Society, by applying at his
shoe store. The variety and quality of the potatoes was unusually fine, and
the committee found it some instances, difficult to decide who was entitled to
premium:

For the best white wheat, Hiram J. Shantz....................... $1 00
Troxell's wheat, Peter Troxell, Jr............................Diploma.
Best Med. wheat, Dr. John Romig............................... $1 00
Second best, John Bortz.....................................Diploma.
Best red wheat, Nathan Bauer.................................. $1 00
Best rye, Owen Faust 1 00
Best white rye, James Troxell, Jr............................. 1 00
Second best rye, Paul Balliet ....Diploma.
Next best, Hiram J. Shantz...................................Diploma.
Best yellow corn, William Grim................................ $1 00
Second best, Paul Balliet...................................Diploma.
White rye, Peter Troxell, Jr................................Diploma.
Red corn, Paul Balliet ....Diploma.
Best buckwheat, Peter Troxell, Jr.............................. $1 00
Second best, William Weidner ....Diploma.
Best timothy seed, Joseph Wint $1 00
Best clover seed, Joseph Wint................................. 1 00
Best Mercer potatoes, William Weidner........................ 1 00
Best Pink-eyed potatoes, William Weidner..................... 1 00
Red potatoes, extra, William Weidner ....Diploma.
Best Irish potatoes, Peter Romig.............................. $1 00
Best Christie potatoes, Benj. Jarret.......................... 1 00
White Halifax potatoes, C. Pretz.............................. 1 00
Pink-eyed potatoes, Joseph Wint.............................Diploma.
Red Halifax potatoes, Jacob Hagenbuch.......................Diploma.
Red Halifax potatoes, William Grim..........................Diploma.
Red potatoes, J. W. Engleman.................................. $1 00

Best sweet potatoes, John Metzger.................................. $1 00
Second best, J. W. Engleman..................................Diploma.
Half dozen pumpkins, cushion, Joseph Wint..................... $1 00
Large pumpkin, Stephen Lentz................................. 1 00
Do.   do.   Amandas Trexler............................Diploma.

No. 7.—AGRICULTURAL IMPLEMENTS.

The committee regret that the display of agricultural implements, though
large, was still not what is needed in this grain growing county, and would
respectfully urge our mechanics to exhibit next year a greater display, believing it to be to their own interest as well as those of the farming community. Premiums were awarded as follows :

Charles Witman, of Upper Saucon, for a six mule team, full rigged. . $5 00
Reuben Lawall, of Montour county, for a corn plough and cultivator
   combined, No. 80... 1 00
Jonas Weber, of Upper Macungie, and Charles Beitler, of Allentown,
   each exhibited highly finished and well made corn ploughs, they
   being so alike in principle that the committee were unable to decide upon the merits, as no opportunity was presented of testing
   them, they however recommend a premium to Jonas Weber for No.
   530 and 529... 1 00
Charles Beitler, for No. 829.................................... 1 00
Edward Knauss, of Allentown, who exhibited two well made and
   highly finished ploughs....................................... 2 00
Samuel Tinsman, of New Jersey, who exhibited two horse power
   corn shellers, one with a fan, and the other without it.......... 1 00
David Lintz, of Hamburg, for a hand corn sheller, No. 176, Xander's
   patent... 1 00.
Lee & Thompson, of Chester county, for Allen's mower........... 3 00
Ben. Yeakel, of Berks county, for Hussey's mower and reaper....... 3 00
Edward Beck, of Allentown, for Maury's mower and reaper........ 1 00
Jacob Sterner, independent horse rake.......................... 1 00
Powell & Hagenbuch, of Allentown, for a highly finished and well
   made threshing machine and separator........................ 2 00
John Q. Cole, of Allentown, for a very handsome churn and jack, and
   other cedar ware.. 1 00
Powell & Hagenbuch, of Allentown, for the best and greatest display
   of agricultural implements, consisting of five different ploughs, of
   the manufacture of Proutty & Mears, Boston, three corn shellers,
   hand rakes, hay forks, revolving horse rake, grain drill, Moore's
   patent... 5 00
A grain drill, Pennock's patent, no card.....................Diploma.
Stroub & Balliet, of Milton, an iron chopping mill, for feeding stock.. .Diploma.

No. 8.—MANUFACTURED ARTICLES.

The committee allude to the astonishing progress that has been made in the manufacture of carriages in our county. The art has been brought to such perfection that it is extremely difficult for any who are not coach makers to decide which are the best.

Class No. 1.

For the best two horse carriage, made by John Schitz $4 00
For the best two or four horse carriage, made by Lehr & Fried... ... 4 00
For the best one horse carriage, carved work, made by Robert Kramer 3 00
For the second best one horse carriage, carved work, made by John Schitz 1 00
For the best one horse carriage, plain work, made by Thomas Heimbach 2 00
For the best display of finished leather, to W. K. & J. K. Mosser.... 2 00
For the second best display of finished leather, to Abraham H. Wint 1 00
For the best set of double harness, to M. Biedler.................. 2 00
For the best set of single harness, to M. Biedler 2 00
For the best display of boots and shoes, to Young & Leh.......... ·2 00
For the best display of hats, to Weider & Boyer.................. 2 00
For the best display of ready made clothing, to Breinig, Neligh & Breinig.. 2 00
For the best display of segars, to Evan W. Eckert................ 2 00
For the second best display of segars, to Charles H. Ruhe.......... 1 00
For the display of segars, exhibited by John F. Ruhe & Sons.......Diploma·

Class No. 2.

S. H. Price, for the best specimen of cabinet ware, manufactured by him.. $2 00
Solomon Blank... 2 00
Mrs. Ferguson, for the best display of same....................Diploma.
Riess & Seiger, best display of Windsor chairs.................. $2 00
Charles Brader, for a new and very superior pruning shears........ 2 00
David Mertz, best wheat flour................................. 2 00
H. J. Schantz, best rye flour.................................. 2 00
   Do.   do.   corn meal................................. 1 00

No. 9.—GARDEN VEGETABLES.

The committee say that they found many other specimens well worthy of notice and mention, particularly a lot of gold leaf onions exhibited by Mrs. M. Erdman, the egg plant and Mexican pumpkin, of James Weiler, the sweet pumpkins of Stephen Lentz and Jacob Hagenbuch, which were of unusual size, and the cabbage of Mr. Lewis Klumpf.

For best display of vegetables, by Lewis Klumpf.................. $2 00
Second best, Mrs. Albright..................................... 1 00
Tomatoes, (yellow pear,) Joseph Wint.......................... 1 00
Half bushel white onions, J. Slemmer.......................... 1 00
Red beets, William Jacoby..................................... 1 00
Parsnips, J. B. Mosser.. 1 00
Long carrots, Edward Kohler................................... 1 00
Cabbage, Thomas Knecht.. 1 00
Egg plants, John Metzger...................................... 1 00
Squashes, Henry Loudenschlager................................ 1 00
Pumpkins, Robert Oberly....................................... 1.00
Celery, Miss Albright... 1 00
Lima beans, John Metzger...................................... 1 00

No. 10.—POULTRY.

The exhibition in this line was excellent, and all the articles exhibited of a good quality and stock. They awarded the following premiums:

Two pair of Brahma Pootra fowls, Dr. W. Wilson, of Bethlehem.... $1 00
One pair Shanghais, James Weiler, best........................ 1 00
One pair Shanghais, Manassa Beidler, second best...........Fowl Breeder
One pair Shanghais, John F. Ruhe & Sons, third best........Fowl Breeder.
One pair Cochin China, Hiram J. Shantz, best.................. $1 00
One pair Cochin China, Hiram J. Shantz, second best........Fowl Breeder.
Largest and best variety of poultry, John Bortz.............. $1 00
One pair white Dorkings, E. R. Newhard, best.................. 1 00
One pair Irish game, E. W. Eckert, best....................... 1 00
One pair English game, E. R. Newhard, best.................... 1 00
One pair English game, C. Eckert, second best..............Fowl Breeder.
One pair white turkeys, Peter Troxell......................Fowl Breeder.
One pair large white geese, B. Slifer......................Fowl Breeder.
One pair top-knot ducks, (no com.) John Bortz..............Fowl Breeder.
One pair Rowan ducks, George Beisel........................Fowl Breeder.
One pair white Bantams, John Bortz.........................Fowl Breeder.
One pair black Bantams, Lewis Mertz........................Fowl Breeder.
One pair Creole chickens, William W. Weaver, best............. $1 00
One pair Creole chickens, E. W. Eckert, second best........Fowl Breeder.
Lot of Spanish fowls, Henry Laudenschlager.................Fowl Breeder.
Best lot of Rough Neck pigeons, John Bortz.................... $1 00
Second best, Lewis Mertz...................................Fowl Breeder.
Second best variety of poultry, John W. H. Engelman........Fowl Breeder.

No. 11.—Dairy and Honey.

The Committee on this branch of Home Department found a very handsome display of moulded butter, but only one specimen of honey and cheese. They award as follows:

Mrs. Weidner, for the best specimen of butter...................... $2 00
M. D. Everhard, the second best...................................... 1 00
Mary Beisel, the third best...Diploma.

The butter of Mr. Joseph Wint and that of Mrs. Paul Balliet is deserving of meritorious consideration.

Mr. John Moll, for the best specimen of honey..................... $2 00

A sample of potted cheese without name, is deserving of particular notice.

No. 12.—Fruit.

The Committee on Fruit report that they found the exhibition of fruit unexpectedly large and of the first order, considering the unfavorable season we have had; showing an onward progress in fruit-cultivation among our citizens. They examined all the specimens on exhibition, with regard to beauty and quality, comprising the following samples:

Apples.

A good variety of meritorious apples from the garden of John J.
   Krauss, to which is awarded the first premium................. $1 00
The second best variety on exhibition is from the garden of Charles
   Brader, deserving the second premium..........Fruit Garden Companion.
A variety of very good apples were exhibited by Peter Troxell, among
   which was found an apple which he names Main apple, which is
   decidedly the finest and best fall apple for culinary purposes on
   exhibition, deserving the first premium........................ $1 00
A beautiful specimen of apples by Mrs. Dresher, of the quality of
   which we could not judge, it being evidently a late winter variety.
A lot of Follawalter apples, by S. W. Burcaw, the best on exhibition,
   deserving the first premium................................. 1 00
Another fine lot of the same variety, by Nathan Berner, deserving
   second premium...............................Fruit Garden Companion.
A third lot of the variety by Henry Miller, were pronounced good
   considering the unfavorable season.

Pears.

For a lot of Bartlet pears, from the garden of Mr. Charles Keek, we
   award the first premium..................................... $1 00
The specimens being the most perfect and beautiful that we ever saw. We would on this occasion recommend this prime pear for general cultivation; it is a sure and profuse bearer, doing well in all soils, and not to be surpassed for beauty and size.

Specimens of the Duchess de Angouleme from the garden of A. J.
Ritz. This is the largest of all pears, attaining an enormous size.
It is a very good late variety, yet scarce in this neighborhood—deserves a general cultivation, and no fruit garden should be without
it. The specimens on exhibition are of good size and very perfect,
deserving the first premium of............................... $1 00
Dogenne, (so labelled, but doubtful.) Fine specimens of a beautiful
pear from the garden of Dr. Charles A. Martin. Second quality,
second premium...........................Fruit Garden Companion.
Winter pears, (name not known,) from the garden of Mr. John J.
Krause. This pear we would recommend for general cultivation,
it being a very good bearer, the fruit of excellent quality, keeping
till spring. No orchard should be without this variety. We award
it the first premium as a winter pear...... .... $1 00
Winter pears, two varieties, by Mr. Paul Balliet, of the merits of which
the committee was not able to judge, the specimens being too hard
and green.

Peaches.

The exhibitors of this wholesome and delicious fruit are the following per-
sons : John Lawall, J. A. Blumer, Charles Brader, Tilghman Stattler, Edward
Kohler, George Stein, Charles S. Bush. All specimens on exhibition are of
good quality and size, the following deserving the premiums :
Malacatoons, John D. Lawall, first premium.................... $1 00
Malacatoons, Jacob A. Blumer, second premium...Fruit Garden Companion.
Morris White, C. S. Bush, first premium...................... $1 00
Seedlings, Tilgh. Stattler, first premium........................ 1 00
Seedlings, Edward Kohler, second premium.......Fruit Garden Companion.

Plums.

Huling's Superb, from the garden of Mr. Tilghman Stattler, large and beautiful—first premium. No competition. Award Fruit Garden Companion.

Quinces.

The specimens of quinces on exhibition were extraordinarily fine, and the
committee remark, that there being always a deficiency of quinces in the
markets of our larger cities, and our soil being admirably adapted to their
growth, it would be as well a source of profit and accommodation as pleasure
to raise this fruit in greater abundance. As soon as the railroads now in
progress are finished, it will find a ready and good market.
The committee were at a loss how to designate the best lot on exhibition,
there being three or four lots of equal beauty. The exhibitors are Messrs.
William Dech, Edward Kohler, C. S. Bush, Charles Keck, Stephen Lentz,
James W. Wilson, Mrs. Dresher, and Daniel Beisel. We repeat that all the

specimens were extraordinarily fine, and that we would rather plead incompetency, than not do justice to the highest merit.

We award the first premium to Stephen Lentz.................... $1 00

The second best to William Dech..............Fruit Garden Companion.

Grapes.

Catawba, best specimen, Charles Brader, first premium............ $1 00

Isabella, best and finest on exhibition, Dr. C. H. Martin, first premium, 1 00

For the second best, Paul Balliet,................Fruit Garden Companion.

A beautiful lot on exhibition from the garden of Mr. A. L. Ruhe, were not ripe. There are a few more specimens on exhibition, which are, however, rather imperfect, owing to the unfavorable season.

Paw-Paw.

One specimen on exhibition by Mr. John Schantz. This is a very good fruit and deserves a more general cultivation. We award to Mr. Schantz a premium of Fruit Garden Companion.

No. 13.—LADIES' WORK.

The committee remark that in some articles they found a full variety, while in others it was not such as could reasonably have been expected. Of some articles there were but one of the kind, and consequently no competition. They hope, however, that hereafter the deficiency may be supplied.

Class No. 1.

For the best cotton bed quilt, first premium to Miss Susan Balliet, of

North Whitehall... $1 00

Second best, to Mrs. Weidner, of Saucon......................Diploma.

Other quilts placed on exhibition, by Mr. Platz, of South Whitehall, Mrs. Edwin Saeger, of Allentown, and Mrs. Shaffer, of Allentown, were very handsome and entitled to a great deal of credit.

For the best coverlet, the committee award the first premium to Mrs.

Nathen Shaffer, of Allentown................................. $1 00

The second best, to Miss Sabina Balliet, of North Whitehall.......Diploma.

The coverlets presented by Mr. Daniel J. Rhoads, of South Whitehall, Miss Josephine Balliet, of North Whitehall, and a variety of coverlets of Henry Gabriel, of Allentown, were all excellent articles and entitled to favor.

The best pair home made blankets, are those of Mr. Daniel J. Rhoads, of North Whitehall.

For the best display of bed clothing, we award the first premium to

Mr. Henry Gabriel, of Allentown, his display being excellent..... $1 00

For the best rag carpet, we award the first premium to Mrs. Margaret

Erdman, of Bucks county..................................... 1 00

Second best, to Mrs. Paul Balliet, of North Whitehall.............Diploma.

  Other rag carpets, presented by Mr. Daniel Weiss, of Allentown, Mrs. C. A. Ruhe, of Allentown, Mr. David Long, of Allentown, were truly excellent articles, and the committee recommend them to special favor.

For the best domestic flannel, the first premium to Mr. Henry Gabriel,

  of Allentown............:..............................-.............. $1 00

Second best, to Mr. Daniel J. Rhoads, of North Whitehall........Diploma.

  A piece of domestic flannel, presented by Mrs. Paul Balliet, of North White-hall, was a good article and entitled to praise.

For the best chair cover, the first premium to Miss Amanda Yeager,

  of Allentown... $1 00

Class No. 2.

Mrs. Wey, ottoman..Diploma.
Ann Wilson, chair worsted work............................Diploma.
Wilt & Miller, fly brushes................................... $1 00
Wilt & Miller, fan and feathers...............................Diploma.
Mrs. Wey, hair work...Diploma.
Mrs. Metzger, hair work, first premium...................... $1 00
Sarah Ritter, bonnets, first premium........................ 1 00
Sarah Ritter, worked slippers, meritorious.
Amanda Yeager, worsted work, first premium.................. 1 00
Mrs. Dresher, lace veil.
A. Smoyer, sampler, meritorious.
Maria Eberhard, sampler, handsome.
Beisel & Stein, caps...Diploma.
Emma M. Saeger, worsted socks.............................Diploma.
Mary M. Stopp, lamp mat....................................Diploma.
Mary M. Stopp, caps...Diploma.
C. M. Pretz, cake mat..Diploma.
Elemina Balliet, lamp mat....................................Diploma.
Catharine Balliet, lamp mat..................................Diploma.
Mrs. Abele, toilet cushion....................................Diploma.
Mrs. Abele, reception chair cover............................Diploma.
Mrs. Abele, screen stands....................................Diploma.
Amanda Balliet, worked basket...............................Diploma.
R. H. Beisel, needle work....................................Diploma.
R. H. Beisel, darned stockings...............................Diploma.
Mrs. Cushing, embroidery....................................Diploma.
Maria German, needle work.................................. $1 00
Maria German, bureau.......................................Diploma.
Ann Maddern, tidy..Diploma.

No. 4.—Natural and Artificial Flowers.

For the best display of natural flowers and plants, an orange tree, exhibited by W. H. Seip... $1 00

Second best, several Oleanders, exhibited by C. A. Ruhe.........Diploma.

Best display of artificial flowers, two vases of beautiful flowers, Mrs. Walker... $1 00

Second best, a flower basket, Maria Eberhard.....................Diploma.

For the best display of wax flowers, Elizabeth Troxell............. $1 00

Second best, Susanna Weiss......................................Diploma.

For the best collection of dahlias, Mrs. A. Spinner................ $1 00

Second best collection of dahlias, Mrs. Cole.....................Diploma.

For the best collection of roses, a bouquet, no name............... $1 00

The committee mention as worthy of special notice, an Egyptian calico flower, a strange and interesting plant, exhibited by R. Jacoby.

A beautiful variety of ladies' ear-drops, exhibited by Miss Rosensteel.

A neatly arranged collection of sea mosses, exhibited by J. Peabody.

A Palm plant, exhibited by Elizabeth Moll.

A beautiful collection of flowers, by Mrs. Erdman, of Bucks county.

Several roses, exhibited by S. Blank.

No. 65, a pretty collection of flowers, especially an ear-drop.

No. 15.—Home Department.

Two jars of jelly, Peter Troxell................................ $1 00

Two jars of preserved quinces, Mrs. J. Roney.................... 1 00

One jar quince jelly, Mrs. Ruhe................................ 1 00

One jar grape   do.   do...   .... 1 00

Soda cake, Susan Balliet.. 1 00

Lot preserves and pickles, J. W. Wilson........................ 1 00

One bottle white currant wine, J. D. Baring.................... 1 00

One loaf wheat bread, Solomon Blank........................... 1 00

One loaf rye bread, Mrs. Paul Balliet.......................... 1 00

One sponge cake, Emma C. Ruhe................................ 1 00

One bottle red currant wine, A. H. Wint....................... 1 00

One jar preserved peaches, Margaret Erdman.................... 1 00

The committee particularly notice one plate pot cheese, and one plate of rusks, No 65, without name of contributor. Also,

Mrs. Aaron Spinner, loaf of wheat bread.

" Hiram J. Schantz   do.   do.

" Paul Balliet,   do.   do.

" J. D. Barring,   do.   do.

baked by steam.

Mrs. Joseph Wint, rye bread.

" Hiram J. Schantz, rye bread.

13

Mrs. Peter Troxell, sponge cake.
"   Peter Troxell, pickled fruit.
"   Jacob Ruhe, pickled pears.
Miss Elizabeth Moll, pickled fruit.
"   Lydia Moll, sponge cake.
John P. Goundie, blackberry wine.

No. 16.—PLOUGHING MATCH.

Peter Troxell... $5 00
There was no competitor.

No. 17.—NON-ENUMERATED ARTICLES.

The Committee on Non-enumerated articles, respectfully beg leave to report
the following articles, viz:
For an iron pump, by Joseph Shiffert, of Allentown, a very useful
article, a premium of..................................... $2 00
Lewis Wolf, for a patent iron pump, Kase's...................Diploma.
Jacob Ruhe, Jr., for a hog gallows $1 00
T. Stattler, of Allentown, for a handsome set of Rockaway wheels..Diploma.
Joseph Meyer, Saucon Valley, for two carpenter puzzels..........Diploma.
Lewis C. Smith, of Slatington, for two very handsome and highly
wrought slate mantles, manufactured in Lehigh county, the imita-
tion of finest marble, is most perfect....................... $2 00
A. B. Carlin, of Allentown, for a lot of machine-made carriage wheel
spokes...Diploma.
C. Arnold, of Allentown, for a lot of bent carriage fellows........Diploma.
Balliet & Graff, of North Whitehall, lot of roofing slate, Union slate
quarry...Diploma.
Leh & Fryman, lot of roofing slate...........................Diploma.
C. Rose, of Allentown, for two handsome window blinds, from his
factory..Diploma.
Edwin Saeger, of Allentown, for a lot of toys, &c...............Diploma.
C. S. Massey, Joseph Ilko and George Stein, of Allentown, for man-
tle and ornamental clocks, each a...........................Diploma.
T. J. Hoffman, of Trexlertown, for a cage and pair of Java sparrows,
very rare and beautiful.....................................Diploma.
John C. Malthaner, of Bethlehem, for a highly toned and well finished
piano, diploma and... $2 00
Simon Sweitzer, of Allentown, for a handsome piano, diploma and...   1 00
S. Burcaw, of Allentown, for a lot of handsome Daguerreotypes....Diploma.
Mrs. A. Spinner, of Salisbury, for two very handsome shell baskets, Diploma.
Wilt & Miller, of Allentown, for a lot of splendid feather fly fans...Diploma.
H. J. Schantz, of Upper Macungie, exhibited a cage of flying squirrels.
Wm. Hey, of Allentown, a case of very handsomely bound books.

E. Kohler, Esq., of North Whitehall, exhibited a lot of continental money, of all denominations.

Edwin Saeger and A. C. Pretz, both of Allentown, each exhibited a vase of handsome gold fish.

P. Pretz, of Allentown, exhibited a case of well selected minerals.

Henry Steinberger, of Allentown, exhibited a gun one hundred and thirty years old.

Francis Weidner, of Upper Macungie, exhibited an air gun.

The committee found a lot of splendid whip stocks to which no card was attached; also a lot of Indian wrought beed mocassins, reticule, &c.

A petrified turtle was exhibited by O. L. Schreiber, of South Whitehall.

Also a lot of mineral specimens, by a gentleman from Bucks county, name not known.

ADDRESS

Delivered by R. E. Wright, before the Lehigh County Agricultural Society.

When one of England's earliest and most accomplished architects was called to his eternal home, closing in honored peacefulness a long, laborious and most useful life among his fellow men, his host of friends who gloried in the fame he had acquired, and wished to hand it down to after ages in all its greatness, reared it is said, over his last resting place a simple marble tablet, on which, for answer to any that might inquire what he had done while here, was carved the word *circumspice*. No fulsome labored epitaph was written, no long eulogium was needed; for all around, throughout the length and breadth of that renowned and proud old city, the lofty spires, and massive walls of many a noble temple, which his intellect had planned, and his unequalled skill and industry had completed, towered towards the heavens; while close around the spot in which his body was consigned to earth, rose stately pillar, shaft, and architrae of his creation, and high above it, in all its beautiful and gorgeous grandeur, hung the stupenduous dome which he had poised in air, (then and ever since a wonder of the world,) the proudest monument that most unbounded reverence could hope to rear, or wildest love of earthly fame aspire to.

With feelings something akin to those which inspired the simple but expressive word in which this great man's fame is thus recorded, can you ladies and gentlemen in answer to any who may ask this day: What has this association done? reply *"Look around you."* It is not long, not very long, since in answer to a call somewhat extensively promulgated in the county, that a few choice spirits met for a single hour to discuss, not the propriety but the possibility of forming an Agricultural Society in Lehigh county. I remember well how few there were, for it was my fortune to address that meeting and to present as best I could some reasons why it should at least be attempted.

What was then *said* has passed away. The words, the thoughts are doubtless all forgotten. What was then *done* was not so evanescent. The seed then sown has flourished well, and for its fruit *look around you.* This association had no youth.

The change from infancy to maturity was the only one which it experienced.

Springing from an origin as feeble and as humble as can well be imagined, it has with one mighty bound, vaulted into a position that is far beyond the wildest expectations of its most sanguine friends : and, checked by no obstacle, retarded by no thwarting power, it stands to-day beside the best and oldest in the Commonwealth.

This spacious and admirably arranged enclosure—these imposing and attractive structures that have as it were by magic risen up within it—their numerous, varied, and valuable contents, and the vast crowd of admiring spectators that annually grace it with their presence ; all unite in attesting the energy which has guided, and the success which has attended the movements of this association.

The cherished thought of the few, who with such earnest hopeful spirits gathered around the birth of this enterprise, is now the favorite idea of the many. Where there was a single voice to greet its advent, there are thousands to encourage its onward and upward progress, and now, with a past that is darkened by no disaster—a present that is without alloy—and a future that is clear and bright before us, we have assembled here, presenting to the public our third annual exhibition.

Nor is there any lack of encouragement from without the pale of membership. Our best and most influential citizens are with us now. The agriculturalist finds here an appropriate stage on which to exhibit the triumphs of his skill at home. Our merchants and manufacturers surround and sustain it, as an enterprise that is well entitled to their warmest support, ministering, as it does, to their best interests—our merchants and professional men, both clerical and lay see in it a nucleous, around which may flourish in perrenial beauty, the warmest and kindliest feelings and sympathies of our nature—a centre point about which for many, many years to come, may revolve in harmonious interlacing orbits the best and most important interests of this community.

Age with hoary head and ripened judgment, is here to hallow this scene with its venerated presence. Youth with warm and generous impulse is here, to enliven it with its vigorous animation—and women, too, both old and young ; our mothers and our daughters, our sweet-hearts and our sweet wives, are here to brighten it with their loveliness, adorn it with the offerings of their taste and skill—to cheer us with their approving smiles, and as in the days of ancient errantry (happily for the world so long gone by) to decorate the weapons of our social warfare with flower wreaths woven by the hand of beauty.

Here then we stand. On this proud eminence we can pause; and from that which is present, and that which has gone by, see something of that which is to come.

I have said that the future is clear and bright before us. It is so, and it will remain so if we are true to ourselves. If ever clouds and darkness hang on our horizon—they will arise from within this enclosure. If our energies shall ever become paralyzed, our progress ever be impeded, or our usefulness ever impaired, it will be because we have departed from our true course, and forgotten the lessons which we have thus far learned and practiced. And when we do this, we shall deserve our fate, and sink into an oblivion that will be alike merited by us, and advantageous to the community.

But if on the other hand, this association shall continue to be controlled by counsels wise as those by which it has hitherto been guided—if, holding as of little value, the glitter and tinsel with which it is but common to surround the operations of such associations; they in whose hands the destinies of this society are placed, shall aim, in all that they do, at that which is practically useful, it may and undoubtedly will remain, one of the permanent institutions of the county.

But in the midst of this congratulation, and the past and present causes for it, let us not for one moment entertain the thought, that our work is now accomplished, and the day for enjoyment arrived; that because our annual festivals are so brilliant and successful, we have nothing more to do. No error could be more fatal. Much as we have done, much more remains to be accomplished. What this association has learned and taught to others— what we have made our own, or of our own, added to the common stock, is nothing, compared with that which we may yet acquire and impart. We have been active, we have been successful, but we have only "gathered a few shells on the shore while the great ocean" of agricultural knowledge "lies unexplored before us."

Unless therefore we resolve as an association to pursue steadily, and as far as possible, the career on which we have entered—unless, too, each member shall feel, that on him rests the duty of adding to this common stock of agricultural knowledge—that while he is resolved that what is known by his contemporaries he will know, what is successfully done by others in this science, he will do—while he is determined to draw for his own purposes whatever he can, from the great and annually increasing treasury of agricultural wisdom, he will not fail annually to add his mite to this same treasury for the use of others; unless I repeat, this spirit be found among us, we shall maintain our associated existence in vain, and "spend our strength for naught."

For I need not surely say to you that the science of agriculture is one that is growing as well as great—that it is the youngest and most vigorous, as well as the oldest of all the arts, or that while it was the first and chief employment of the rescued remnant of the old world when cheered by the hope inspiring hues of the first rainbow, they descended from their ark upon the

misty mountains and fertile valleys of the new ; it will beyond all doubt occupy
and bless their descendants *"to the last syllable of recorded time."* Nor need I
tell you that it is one which is susceptible of almost endless improvement—
that while the wants of the wildest savage are amply supplied by the application of its simplest principles, it is also capable of ministering to the most
luxurious wants, and of occupying to the fullest extent, the brightest intellects
of the most refined and accomplished of the human race.

For so good is God, and so wisely has he made the world, that while it
may lie, as it doubtless hath lain for ages, useless and unproductive without
decay, it is capable also of supplying the wants of any amount of animal life
that can by any possibility come upon its surface, without exhaustion. Nay,
so profoundly wise is its construction, that its productions ever keep pace
with the advancing civilization and expanding intellect of man, so that just
in proportion as he is wise, will all subordinate animal and vegetable life advance and improve, meeting and supplying most fully and appropriately all
his increasing wants and wishes.

" For the world was made for man, and man for heaven." The three kingdoms of nature are *his* kingdoms, all of which are more or less under his
control and intended for his use. Over the mineral kingdom, his power,
though great, is circumscribed ; over the vegetable world, it is almost unlimited. He may combine, and change, and use the former, almost at will,
but he can neither improve the quality or increase the quantity of its products, because it is the basis of the other two, to one of which he himself
belongs ; and because the nature of its component atoms, and the laws by
which they are combined, are beyond the reach of any thing but creative
power.

But over the vegetable kingdom, which springs from the bosom of the
mineral, for the support of the animal, his control is only limited by his
knowledge of the laws by which it lives, and the wisdom or weakness with
which he uses this knowledge.

The quantity and quality of all vegetable productions depend on what is
called cultivation ; this, in its turn, depends on the knowledge which the
cultivator has of the laws which regulate their existence ; and as all that God
has made partakes of the infinity of his perfections, for the simple reason
that it is his work—an out-birth of himself—and cannot therefore be imperfect, it follows, that the more we know of these laws, and the better we learn
to apply them, the nearer shall we approach that perfection of which they are
susceptible.

That this proposition is true, must on reflection be evident to every one ;
but if proof be wanted, the world is full of it.

The present state of the whole science of agriculture, as compared with
its condition not many years ago, as well as the changes that have been made
in particular instances, proves it. For example, the admirably, highly flavored and annually improving apple of the present time, was once a bitter,

unsightly and disgusting crab. The luscious peach, of which each year seems to produce a new and still more delightful variety, was once a bitter almond, the juice of which was used to poison the arrows used in the warfare of the then savage world. The potato, which now feeds half the civilized world, was once an insignificant root, unfit for the use of man or beast. The changes which have taken place in these and a thousand other things that might be named, is the result of cultivation, which I have before said is nothing more than the rational application of the knowledge which we have acquired (either by accident or experiment) respecting the laws which regulate their life. If such results have been the consequence of what man *now* knows—if the products of the vegetable world have thus far kept pace with the improvements of the human race—who will limit the one more than the other? or who that believes, as I do, that man can never reach his *ne plus ultra* here, or live and yet cease to learn, can at the same time believe that things which have thus far kept side by side, will ever cease to do so?

It follows then, from this, that progress in the art of agriculture, in all its branches, depends almost entirely on ourselves. That we have the power to stand still, to go backward, or to advance—that the only way to advance is to acquire knowledge—and that he who knows and does the most, will always effect the most. To foster and disseminate this kind of knowledge, should be the mission of this association. Toward that perfection of which I have spoken, every individual member of it should direct his steps; until the carelessness that has disgraced us and the ignorance that has hitherto retarded our real progress, shall have been banished from our borders, and our land be filled with model farms and model farmers.

I am not much of a practical agriculturalist. We cannot all be independent. Indeed it is as well, perhaps, that we cannot be so; for, from the very nature of the world, as it is wisely made, there must be a consuming as well as a producing class. Belonging to the former somewhat exclusively, I may not be competent to speak upon the means by which this desired result may best be produced. But I have in my mental eye a portrait of what a model farmer should be—a class of men that grow up rapidly around these associations—which this association should endeavor to create, and which I doubt not will increase most rapidly among us hereafter. Bear with me if my sketch be rude, and pardon me if some lines be drawn too strongly.

A model farmer, then, such an one as agricultural societies create, is one who cares a good deal more for the *quality* than he does for the *quantity* of his land. He does not believe much in spreading his labor over two hundred acres, when, by confining it to half the quantity, he can double the produce. Like a well made plough, he never takes on more than he can turn over. He thinks that the interest of purchase money, and taxes and fences on a farm of a moderate size, are well laid out—because every foot that is fenced and paid for is productive—and that it is folly to pay purchase money, interest, taxes and fencing, for that which he cannot properly use. He thinks more of the *depth* of his farm than he does of its *length* and *breadth;* and while his neighbors spread themselves over a large and profitless surface of the earth, he goes towards the centre, and finds profit in so doing. There is a good deal of the error here indicated, in this part of our State; but thanks to the laws of Pennsylvania, relative to the partition of real estate by the orphans' court, it is rapidly passing away. I know one farm in this county, divided some years ago into four parts, among the heirs of the former owner, each part of which produces now more than the whole tract did when together.

A model farmer is one who will understand thoroughly the nature of the soil he lives on, and will know exactly how to manage it. Soils he knows are of various kinds, in order that the productions of the vegetable world may be various also. Some, even on the same farm, are heavy, others light and sandy; some wet, others dry; some fertile and productive almost to excess, others nearly barren; and he concludes, from this, that the same cultivation must not be applied to all. Every farmer, no matter how ignorant, knows this fact by experience, often very dearly purchased, and, by a kind of guess work, adopts his mode of cultivation to the nature of his soil. But the true agriculturalist knows, with chemical exactness, the peculiar properties of each particular soil on his farm—knows, too, wherein each is deficient, how to make them alike fruitful, and, consequently, has not an unproductive field in his possession. Like Judge Buel, of New York, he can take up a tract of barren sand, on which no man ever saw a weed or blade of grass, and can by analysis find out just what is wanting to make it productive, apply the proper article, and in a year or two convert the sand bank into a garden lovely and fertile as that of Eden.

If the model farmer owns a farm, he owns the whole of it. His lawyer tells him that it is his, down to the centre of the earth, and houses just as much of it in that direction as he can get at. He does not, as is generally the fashion, act as if his farm was only six inches thick.

O, I have seen farmers, and so have you, who, except when they sink a well or cistern, or dig a milk cellar, seem, by their mode of using their farms, as if they thought that all of it below the first six inches belonged to somebody else. Men who would just as soon think of crossing a neighbor's line fence, as of allowing their ploughs to touch the land of this imaginary neighbor, whose valuable farm lay idle and uncultivated just seven inches deeper than their own. One might suppose that this ultra honesty would wear away in time with some of them, especially when the wives and daughters of these men, having no such *shallow* notions, dig down in the kitchen garden usually as deep as the spade will go, and produce, in consequence of it, about ten times as much as their husbands and fathers do on the same extent of surface. But no, all this is of no avail. True to the old rule, no sooner does the plough by accident dip below this point, than up goes the nose of the coulter, as if some sin had been committed, some trespass on another man's ground, until at length the poor tortured surface is worn out and sleeps in death, upon the mass of rich land which lies undisturbed below it.

The "Agricultural Society" farmer does not do this. He uses all that he owns, and goes just as deep into his land as the longest agricultural implement will penetrate.

Again, the real agriculturalist never plants the same thing twice in succession in the same field.

He knows that although some crops fertilize, most of them exhaust the soil. Most farmers know this, but the model farmer knows also that all crops are not alike in this particular, that they neither exhaust the land alike, nor abstract from it the same substances; and that therefore while one kind of plant may completely exhaust the soil of its particular food, enough may remain to produce luxuriantly a plant of a different kind. He knows also that each plant that grows discharges at its root a substance which, while it is food for one of a different kind, is poisonous to those of the same nature. He knows too that every plant has its peculiar tribe of predatory insects, and knowing all this, by a judicious rotation of crops, he avoids that which is such a blot upon the fairest portion of the south, a farm of worn out fields.

The farmer which I have in my mental eye looks also with care to his live stock, and has on his farm, or endeavors to have, the very best breed that can be found. When we reflect on the vast difference that there is between the labor and produce of good and bad stock; while the expense of keeping them is about the same; is it not painful to see so many anatomical horses, so many melancholy consumptive looking cows, such herds of ragged sheep, and "alligator" hogs as we do see scattered up and down the land? There has been a great improvement in this particular here, but the room for improvement is still greater, and one of the principal uses of this association will be to encourage, and aid its members in this most important work. Its funds can be invested in nothing better than the purchase of specimens of the best stock, at almost any price.

In the matter of dairy produce, too, the true agriculturalist is active, and in this item is far in advance of the farmers in this county generally. It is remarkable that in a matter where we might stand *first*, we are nearly *last*. Our splendid streams and rich meadows and low lands fit us eminently for this kind of produce, and yet with a few exceptions what stuff we have.

First quality butter is rarely if ever seen in market—the worst is plentiful enough, all owing to sheer carelessness or neglect. And as for cheese, we make but one kind, and that like ourselves is "Dutch," a very good and pleasant thing, I doubt not, for those who like it, but which it would seem cannot make its way in the world abroad, notwithstanding its *age* and well known *strength*. I hazard the prediction, that if properly attended to, particularly now since we are about to be connected by railroad with the two greatest cities in the country, the revenue that might be derived from this source, would in a few years be equal to that derived from any thing that we produce.

In the matter of fruits, the model farmer is most particular. The love for nature in her artless and uncultivated simplicity and beauty is a very fine thing, but like other fine things it may be carried too far, and it seems to me that there is rather an excess of it here. Our county is very full of orchards, almost every variety of fruit may be found here, for nature has been very kind to us; but with a few exceptions what wretched stuff we have. Apples almost as large and as hard as hickory nuts—peaches whose beauty is but skin deep, being little else than skin and stone—cherries that might pass for huckleberries if they were not so bitter, with other fruit to match—the ragged trees that bear them encumbering the ground on which they grow. This is all very wrong, and is never allowed by any educated farmer. He who plants a tree simply because it is a tree, without caring for its quality and selecting the very best of the kind that can be found, is guilty of a fraud on posterity, is no wiser than his grand-father was, and is in the emphatic but somewhat modified language of the scripture proverb, "planting sour grapes that his children's teeth may be set on edge."

Another matter never fails to receive the attention of the model farmer, to wit: the free use of proper agricultural machinery. I am aware that there is a deep rooted prejudice here against what are called " Yankee Notions," and am not sure that there is no reason for it. A good deal of money has been thrown away on labor saving machinery, that when tried was found to save neither labor, time, nor money. There is scarcely an· old farm in the county, around which you may not see the fossil remains of some curious antediluvian combination of wheels and pinions, cogs and levers, intended as ploughing, or planting, or threshing machines; which were never of use to any one but to the man who made and sold them; and which are carefully hung up and preserved by the "*old man*" as beacons to warn the green and rising generation of the folly of wasting their money on new fangled Yankee inventions.

All this is true, and worth regarding too. But there is a point at which prejudice must stop or the world will leave us behind them. For the man who now sows his grain without a drill—who perfers the sickle and the cradle to the modern reaper, the scythe to the mowing machine, and the eel skin hickory flail to the threshing machine—who true to the old school shells his corn with a fire shovel over a wash tub, instead of using the modern corn sheller, will find out before he is much older, that in the quality and quantity of his crops—the celerity of his harvesting, and the prompt conversion of his produce into money, that he is far behind the man who makes a judicious use of inventions that are really useful. One thing more and I will close. If there be any man in the world who can and ought to live most comfortably, it is in my opinion the farmer; and the model farmer that I have been speaking of does live so. His dwelling house, his home, and the grounds around it are models not of luxury (he has too much sense for that) but of rustic beauty, comfort and convenience. But how few such homes do you find. Farms neatly laid out, fences and fixtures that are perfect—barns and out-houses that are models of neatness are very common every where in Pennsylvania. But houses of the same character are seldom met with. How common a thing is it, as you approach a model farm to see an immense brick barn eighty or an hundred feet long, as large and as fine as a meeting house—furnished with all the skill that rural taste can suggest—a cattle yard close by, with every imaginable convenience in and near it—a well finished comfortable pig and poultry house; with a neat marble slab built in front of the main building on which there is an inscription informing all that read that "John sombody and his wife" have munificently erected all these fine buildings for the accommodation of their horses, cows, and their cattle. While away off by itself, as if ashamed of being seen by the side of its elegant neighbor, stands perhaps a little one story or one and a half story log house, built sometime during the last century; some fifteen or twenty feet square, without a tree, or shrub, or rose bush near it—the ground around it pretty much as it was thrown out when the cellar was dug—with a weather beaten flour barrel for a chimney and a molasses hogshead for a cistern, all of which is kept for the comfort and accommodation of said John and his wife and their growing sons and daughters. And how often as we see such things do we wonder, why here the order of nature should be so completely reversed, and the quadruped fare so much better than the biped; and what a heart full of humanity a man must have who takes better care of his cows than he does of his wife—whose calves and chickens are better accommodated than his children, and who builds a better house for his horse than he does for himself. Thank heaven there is little, if any of this in Lehigh county; and even that little is rapidly passing away. Let this association hasten the movement. But I am growing tedious and will close. In the name of this association I thank you for your attendance and for the attention you have paid to these crude remarks. To you, gentlemen of Lehigh county, this association looks with confidence for that encouragement which is so essential to its existence. While you continue to manifest an interest in its welfare, it cannot fail. From you ladies we expect as heretofore your sweet approval; grant but this and our success is certain.

With this we shall know no such word as fail. In adversity it will sustain, in prosperity reward us. And as in times gone by, the warrior in the tented field, amidst the danger and the din of battle, looked through its mirky canopy on the banner wrought for him by woman's hands, or on the farewell token which her prayer had blessed, or thought upon some happy hour that had been hallowed by her smile; and bore himself all the more nobly as they passed before his vision; so we, in these piping times of peace, when the soldier has laid down his arms, when the sword has no dream of the battle, and the spear no remembrance of blood; assembled in this field nobler in its results than any field of battle—engaged in a war for that which is purer and holier than the poorest "cause of war," will, as we pursue our onward course look upon your annual contributions—recall your looks of approbation—your prayer, for our success, and under their influence press forward with renewed and untiring energy towards the perfection of an art, which though in came upon our race by woman's first transgression, has been changed into a blessing by her smile.

TREASURER'S REPORT.

The account of Owen L. Schreiber, Treasurer of the Lehigh county agricultural society.

DR.

To membership fees.	$165	00
To a loan.	923	81
To receipts at the fair.	2,515	70
To county fund.	100	00
To deficiency.	3,517	66
	7,222	17

CR.

Paid for premiums attending the fair.

Building and other expenses	$3,644	51
Paid interest on fair ground	60	00
Due to sundry creditors	418	85
Due to a lean	923	81
Due to fair ground	2,000	00
Interest due on first of April, 1855	175	00
	7,222	17

Correspondence between Edward Kohler, Esq., and the Hon. G. H. Gundie, United States consul at Zurick, in Switzerland.

[Translated from the German.]

NORTH WHITEHALL, LEHIGH CO., PA., }
July 24th, 1854. }

Hon. G. H. Gundie:

DEAR SIR :—The editors of the American Farmer (German,) have in their paper repeatedly urged the propriety of forming an association in the German counties of Pennsylvania, for the pupose of importing from the continent of Europe, namely from Switzerland, pure blooded cattle, for the purposè of improving the domestic breeds. Please communicate your opinion in relation to Swiss cattle, besides a comparison with the English Durhams and Devons, as well as the prices and probable costs of transportation. I doubt not, if we become better informed on the subject, there will be no difficulty of forming such an association in Lehigh and the adjoining counties.

Respectfully yours, &c.,
EDWARD KOHLER.

—

CONSULATE OF THE U. S. OF AMERICA, AT ZURICH, IN SWITZERLAND,
September 9th, 1854.

To Edward Kohler, President of the agricultural society in Lehigh county, Pennsylvania, U. S. A.

In answer to your desire expressed in a letter of the 24th of July last, I made due inquiry, the result of which I herewith literally communicate.

According to a communication of Mr. Dangely, director of the agricultural school for the canton of Zurich, who may be considered competent, the following are considered the best breeds of cattle in Switzerland :—

1. The Schwytzer breed. This breed of cattle is met with in the Schwytzer district March, and in Gaster, a district in St. Gallen ; also in the county of the Zurich see, and as far as the Wallensteader see, where it is fostered with particular care, namely in relation to pure blood. Masses of this cattle are annually, in autumn, transported to Italy. The most proper time in relation to purchase, may therefore fall in the month of September.

The cow of this breed yields a great quantity of milk. (That for example at the agricultural school,) yields sixteen measures, eight gallons daily. Her meat, in comparison with that of other breeds, is the most delicate ; she is preferred as a milking cow, and in this relation indisputably stands as the best cow in Switzerland.

From spring to autumn she remains on the Alps, (mountain pasture,) where her milk in particular is turned to butter and cheese, its manufacture being the principal branch of industry of a considerable portion of Switzerland.

They come in market, frequently going with calf, in which condition they are higher valued. The average price of a heifer, i. e., a cow, which has not yet cast, amounts to twenty louisd'or, (ninety-five dollars.) It however depends on the amateur ; indeed cows of peculiar properties, be it on account of a rich milk production, or on account of peculiar beauty or symmetry, costs thirty louisd'or, (one hundred and forty dollars.) Nevertheless, one may expect an excellent cow for the first indicated price.

Though this cow in summer eats the most exuberant herbs of the Alps, in winter she is nevertheless very contended and satisfied with inferior hay ; consequently she can be raised wherever the latter can be had.

2. The Erlenbacher breed, from Simmenthale, in Berne. This cow in general, is stronger built than the Schwytzer, and better adapted to fatten.

In relation to breed they are less valued than that of the latter, whose yield of milk is significantly larger.

3. The Freyburger breed, from Romant and Greierz. This cow, in respect of milk production, is inferior to the Schwytzer cow, but on account of her firmness, she is like the Emmenthaler cow, better adapted to fatten.

The prices of the two last breeds are equal to that of the first.

In relation to English cows, such the Swiss follows, because the meat of this is not so tasteful as of that. The Schwytzer breed dare come the English however tolerably near, and in this respect possesses the most similarity to that.

The English cow, in relation to milk production, stands moderately behind the Swiss. This, in general, is more an Alp cattle, and therefore better adapted to a mountainous country than the mostly stable raised English cattle. A Swiss cow climbs with peculiar ease, without haste and without injuring herself, all heights on which grass grows. She is accustomed to heat and cold—to fair and bad weather.

For transportation heifers would be peculiarly adapted, i. e., cows which have not yet calved, but going with calf, at an age of about two years.

Bulls dare not be older than one year, as yet never turned to breeding; on account of providing ten heifers two bulls should be procured.

As regards the transportation, it will be indispensable to send a competent person, perfectly intimate with the treatment of the cattle, along.

The freight from Basel to Havre, per railroad, will probably amount to two hundred francs (forty dollars,) per head. Passage from Havre to New York, per steamer, about five hundred francs (one hundred dollars,) per head, feed extra—the water delivered from the ship. The conducter of the cattle costs two hundred and sixty francs, (fifty dollars,) board on the ship, for the passage from Havre to New York inclusive. The freight for cattle on sail ships would be about one half. The feed, however, should be taken into consideration, which would be about three times as high; therefore the swift voyage per steamer would be advisable.

It becomes joy to me, if I could perform you a service in this affair, for which I am otherwise also always ready.

Your devoted,

G. H. GUNDIE, *Consul.*

N. B. The purchases should be made in the middle of September, at which time the cattle comes in from the Alps, and stands ready for sale, and purchasers arrive from all parts of the world. Later in season the cattle, however, are too much selected, and the best and handsomest are sold.

D. O.

All which is respectfully submitted.

EDWARD KOHLER,
President of the Lehigh County Agricultural Society.

NORTH WHITEHALL, *December 15, 1854.*

NORTHAMPTON COUNTY.

NAZARETH, *March* 3, 1855.

To the President of the Pennsylvania State Agricultural Society :

SIR :—It is impossible for us to make a return satisfactory to you, or even to ourselves, as we are as yet in our infancy as a society. We hope in future we may be able to make a report, more complete in every respect:

Our annual exhibition was held in October, at Nazareth, and was well attended, notwithstanding the lateness of the season, the weather being at the time too cold for delicate fruit, plants and flowers to be exhibited ; and those which were there suffered much from frost, which made them look rather dreary.

All other matters appertaining to the society, were transacted in the regular manner during the past year.

Respectfully submitted.

P. B. STEINMETZ, *President*

CHS. R. HOEBER, *Secretary.*

Officers for 1855.

PRESIDENT—Peter B. Steinmetz, Stockertown, Pa.

RECORDING SECRETARY—C. R. Hoeber, Nazareth, Pa.

CORRESPONDING SECRETARY—William Beitle.

Report of the Committee appointed to award Premiums and Diplomas upon articles exhibited at the Northampton County Agricultural Fair, held at Nazareth on the 17th, 18th and 19th days of October, 1854 :

ON HORSES.

Best stud horse for field and road, J. E. Jones. . . . . .Book and $3 00

Second best do., G. Snyder. . . . . .do. . . 1 00

Best mare, P. Long. . . . . .do. . . 2 00

Second best mare, S. Chamberlin. . . . . .do. . .

Best filly, between two and four years old, A. Heintz. . . . . .do. . . 2 00

Second best do., Samuel Shortz. . . . . .do. . . 1 00

Best horse colt, between one and two years old, Mr. Laubach . . .do. . . 1 00

Second best do., J. H. Keller. . . . . .do. . .

Best filly, between one and two years old, Reuben Dech. . . . . . . .do. . . 1 00

Second best do., Fr. Miksch. . . . . .do. . .

Best gelding, light draught, B. C. Cleckner. . . . . .do. . . 2 00

Best gelding, three years old, George Jones. . . . . .do. . . 1 00

Best pair of farm horses, Samuel Shortz. . . . . .do. . . 2 00

ON CATTLE.

Best Durham bull, three years old, Wm. Firmstone.........Book and $3 00
Best Durham bull, between two and three years old, R. White-
  sell, stewart of Northampton county poor house...............do...   2 00
Best Devon bull, three years old, S. G. Riegel................do...   3 00
Best mixed do., between two and three years old, John Heckman, do.:.   2 00
Best mixed do., between one and two years old, John Agnew...do...   2 00
Best Durham cow, Wm. Riegel..............................do...   2 00
Best Durham heifer, one year old, R. Snyder.................do...   1 00
Best Devon heifer, between two and three years old, H. J. Beck, do...   1 00
Best Durham heifer, between two and three years old, Peter
  Lawall..do...   1 00
Best mixed heifer, between one and two years old, G. L. Beitel, do...   1 00
Second best do., John Agnew...............................do...   1 00
Best native breed, T. Biery................................   1 00
Best Devon cow, Aaron Gold...............................do...   1 00
Best mixed cow, John Agnew,..............................do..   1 00

ON POULTRY.

Brahma Pootras, R. C. Pyle.......................Book and $2 00
Imperial Chinese, R. C. Pyle..............................do...   2 00
Cross Shang. to Dork., Ph. Walter........................do...   2 00
Grey Shanghais, Wm, B. Levan...........................do...   2 00
Red Shanghais, G. H. Bute...............................do...   2 00
Bucks county do., Samuel Hoffman........................do...   2 00
Dominicks, Miss Eliza Michler............................do...   2 00
Yellow Shanghais, Henry Richards.........................do...   2 00
Mixed grey and barn Shanghais, Aaron W. Lymn............do...   2 00
Brood Shanghais, A. B. Steiner...........................do...   2 00
Mixed fowls, J. C. Leifried...............................do...   2 00
Barn yard, Miss Eliza Michler............................do...   2 00
Yellow Malays, Richard Hillman...........................do...   2 00
African chickens, Wm. Trittenbach........................do...   2 00
Poland fowls, W. B. Levan................................do...   1 00
Golden pheasant, W. B. Levan............................do...   1 00
Sumatra fowls, W. B. Levan..............................do...   1 00
Cochin China, Samuel Hoffman...........................do...   1 00
Brood fowls, W. H. Gross.................................do...
Creole fowls, Richard Hillman............................do...   2 00
Seabright bantams, Wm. Yohe............................do...
A pair of geese, G. L. Beitel.............................do...   2 00
Muscovy ducks, Samuel Hoffman.........................do...   2 00
Brood turkey, Fr. Miksch................................do...   2 00

Brown ducks, S. Hoffman..............................Book and $2 00
Peacock, Dr. Rohn...do....
A pair of rabbits, J. R. Reutzheimer................................ 1 00
Maltese cat, John Morey................................ .... 1 00

SHEEP.

Southdown buck, one year old, W. Firmstone.............Book and $2 00
Ewe with three lambs, E. R. Kramer.........................do... 2 00
Buck and ewe, mixed, Peter Lawall...................do... 2 00
   Do........do.....Wm. Rodrock.........................do... 2 00
Best display of sheep, J. O. Beisel.........................do... 2 00

SWINE.

Best boar, one year old, Wm. Firmstone, diploma, book and........ $2 00
Next best, Jacob Bear, diploma, book and 2 00
Best boar pig, between two and six months old, C. Whitesell, book and 2 00
Next do.   do.   A. Gold, book and 2 00
Best five pigs, John Agnew... 2 00
Second best fat hogs, Jacob Beck............................... 2 00
Next best, Michler & Bellisfield............................... Book.

AGRICULTURAL IMPLEMENTS.

Cutting box, Isaac Stocker.....................................Diploma.
Reaper, B. Yeakle.. do.
Seed drill, Charles Lee.. do.
Corn sheller, Lake & Reese..................................... do.
Plough, Edward Knause.. do.
Best display of agricultural implements, F. W. Noble............ do.
Best horse-power, Peter Beachy................................. do.
Corn plough, A. Biery .... do.

AGRICULTURAL PRODUCTS.

Red wheat, Wm. Rodrock... Book.
White wheat, E. Woodring....................................... do.
Rye, C. Seifried... do.
Barley, C. Kichline.. do.
Yellow corn, C. Kichline....................................... do.
White corn, Philip Walter .... do.
Mixed corn, R. Young... do.
Flax seed, C. Kichline... do.
Potatoes, Jacob Heller... do.
Beets, J. C. Leibfried... do.
Wheat flour, J. Luckenbach..................................... do.
Shell bark, Wm. Dech .... do.

14

DOMESTIC AND HOUSEHOLD MANUFACTURES.

Best ten yards flannel, Miss Susan Reigle.......................... $2 00
Best ten yards woollen cloth, L. A. Doster....................... 2 00
Best home made carpet, Sarah Biery 2 00
Best pair of cotton stockings, C. Hoeck.......................... 1 00
Best worsted chair cover, Miss Malthaner.
Best specimen of needle work, Mrs. Philip Johnson.............. 1 00
Best lamp mats, Mrs. Ellen Christ........................'...... 1 00
Best crayon painting, Miss Loesch............................. 1 00
Best crotchet work, Harmonia Roussel......................... 1 00
Best hard soap, S. Hoffman................................... 1 00
Best ribbon work, Mrs. E. Christ.............................. 1 00
Best wheat bread, Mrs. M. Reigel.............................. 1 00
Best rye bread, Miss Rebecca Kram............................ 1 00
Best honey, C. Kichline....................................... 1 00
Best net work, Mrs. E. Christ................................. 1 00
Best bead work, Mrs. Doct. G. J. Shool........................ 1 00
Best fancy basket, Eliza Heckman............................. 1 00
Best quilt, by a child six years old ....: 1 00

A large variety of other articles were exhibited which deserve particular notice, viz:

Preserves by Mrs. Wetherell, apple and quince by C. Jones, and a large variety of quilts, amongst which was a silk quilt, by Miss E. Frankenfield, and a number of others which reflect the highest credit upon those who manufactured them.

Worsted work was also exhibited by Miss E. A. Scholl and Catharine Hoeck, which deserves honorable mention.

MANUFACTURED ARTICLES.

One two seated carriage, John Sheetz...........................Diploma.
One one seated buggy, John Albright .... do.
One one seated buggy, John Albright........................... do.
Display of cedar work, John Q. Cole........................... do.
Display of furniture, David Garis............................. do.
Display of leather, Fr. Lorenz................................ do.
Display of harness, C. M. Hooper.............................. do.
Display of woollen goods, Levi Dasher......................... do.
Display of hats, C. M. Bodder................................ do.
Best pair of boots, Syl. Billing .... do.
A bonnet, Eliz. Steckel....................................... do.
A display of locks and brass articles, F. W. Hebinger........... do.
A display of fancy confectionary, W. F. Rauch................. do.
A box white zink paint, Penn's & Lehigh zink works............ do.
One piano, J. C. Malthaner................................... do.

MISCELLANEOUS.

Chapman & Short, first quality slate... Book.
C. B. Daniel, second quality slate... do.
J. O. Beitel, Daguerreotype...................................... do.
J. O. Beitel, clocks.. do.
R. A. Grider, first quality paintings.............................. do.
Em. Doster, water col'd paintings................................ do.
Gilbert & Wetherill, minerals...................................... do.
S. W. Stein, silver ware... do.
Nazareth Hall, a variety of curiosities............................ do.
Josiah Bower, imitation of wood.................................... do.
Wm. Kumman, imitation of wood.................................... do.
Wm. Kumman, paper hangings....................................... do.
Benj. Clewell, tobacco... do.
Amos Rogers, horse shoes.. do.

NEWSPAPERS.

E. H. Rauch, Lehigh Valley Times...........................Diploma.
Josiah Cole, a German paper.. do.
A draft of law, by E. Leibert...................................... do.

DAIRY.

Mrs. E. Miksch, for the best five lbs. of butter...A pair of silver butter knives.
Mrs. H. Kemmerer, for the best Dutch cheese........... Book and $1 00
There were other lots of butter, but on account of the quantity cannot award a premium.

PLOUGHING.

John Agnew, best ploughman.. $5 00
Stephen Billheimer, plough boy.................................... 2 50

ORCHARD AND GARDEN.

Ed. Ricksecker, best cabbage...................................... Book.
J. P. Beisel, largest pumpkins.................................... do.
Wm. Christ, six best sweet pumpkins............................... do.
Th. Kemmerer, six field pumpkins.................................. do.
Th. H. Kemmerer, best turnips..................................... do.
J. S Haman, stalk celery.. do.
Saml. Wetherell, best display of vegetables....................... do.
Mrs. A. D. Beitle, design of natural flowers...................... do.
Simon Johnson, quinces.. do.
Ed. Ricksecker, grapes.. do.

Daniel Wilhelm, tomatoes..................................... Book.
Chs. R. Hoeber, citrons...................................... do.
Fr. Miksch, apples... do.
Ell. Sellers, best arranged boquets.......................... do.

Some very fine peaches were exhibited by Ed. Ricksecker, but not a sufficient quantity to entitle a premium. Dr. Bute exhibited some very fine lemons and Smyrna fig trees. C. G. Beitel, Chs. Sellers and E. Ricksecker exhibited an extensive and beautiful variety of evergreens, flowers and plants—each three dollars and a book.

The receipts of the year, from different sources, amounted to.... $1,674 69
Expenses amount to.. 1,105 61

Owing partly to the circumstance that our fair has not been permanent till now, so that the hauling of the timber and erection of the building were a very considerable item.

CAS. R. HOEBER, Secretary.

PHILADELPHIA COUNTY.

To the President of the Pennsylvania State Agricultural Society :

The Philadelphia Society for promoting Agriculture, with its auxiliary, "The Farmers' Club," constitutes the only agricultural society in the county. It is not, however, properly speaking, a county society. Having been organized in 1785, and being then, and for some time thereafter, the only agricultural society in the Union, its field of usefulness was widely extended, and it included among its members most of the prominent American and many of the European agriculturists of the day. As, under the auspices of those who participated in its deliberations, new societies sprang up in this and in other States, it lost its national character; and when, mainly through the exertions of its members, the Pennsylvania State Society was organized, the circle of its immediate influence became further contracted. It still has upon its roll, members in Maryland, Delaware and New Jersey, and in Bucks, Montgomery, Chester and Delaware counties, in this State ; but the great majority of its actual supporters reside within the limits of the county of Philadelphia. Its functions are, therefore, chiefly those of a local institution. Every farmer in the land will find a source of pride and exultation in the fact, that the prolific mother of American agricultural organizations, although now on the verge of three score years and ten, enjoys an active and vigorous existence.

The room of the society contains a library of choice agricultural works, and is provided with the principal agricultural periodicals of the United States and Great Britain. The number of members is over two hundred. Exhibitions are held annually. That of 1854 was omitted, in order that the weight and influence of the society might be thrown in favor of the State Fair. Meetings are held regularly on the first Wednesday in every month. The following is an abstract of the proceedings :

PHILADELPHIA SOCIETY FOR PROMOTING AGRICULTURE.

Stated meeting at room in Masonic Hall, South Third street, Wednesday, January 4, 1854. President, Dr A. L. Elwyn, in the chair. Minutes of preceding meeting read and approved.

The following gentlemen, proposed at the preceding meeting, were elected members:

Anthony L. Anderson, of Lower Merion, Montgomery county, Pa.; Robt. Patterson, of Philadelphia; Joseph Swift, of Philadelphia; Matthew W. Baldwin, of Philadelphia.

Three nominations for resident membership were received.

Mr. Landreth, in behalf of the Executive Committee, recommended that the debt of the society be funded for the present, and that a note, signed by the President and Treasurer, be given for the amount, bearing interest from date.

H. Ingersoll, Esq., offered the following resolution, which was adopted:

Resolved, That the Executive Committee be requested to report, at the meeting in April, the financial condition of the society, specifying the reliable annual revenue from each source, and in the aggregate, and the probable ordinary annual expenditure, in detail.

On motion of Mr. A. S. Roberts, a new roll of the members, and their residences, was ordered to be prepared.

The annual election being held, resulted as follows:

PRESIDENT—Alfred L. Elwyn, M. D.

VICE PRESIDENTS—Anthony T. Newbold, Aaron Clement.

CORRESPONDING SECRETARY—Sydney G. Fisher.

RECORDING SECRETARY—Alfred L. Kennedy, M. D.

ASSISTANT RECORDING SECRETARY—Philip R. Freas.

TREASURER—George Blight.

EXECUTIVE COMMITTEE—David Landreth, Anthony T. Newbold, Samuel C. Ford, Chas. W. Harrison, Dennis Kelly, Algernon S. Roberts.

The Treasurer presented his annual report, showing balance in his hands on 1st instant, seventy-three dollars and sixty-five cents, which report was on motion referred to the proper auditing committee. Adjourned.

———

Stated meeting held at the rooms, Washington Hall, Wednesday morning, February 1, 1854. President, Dr. A. L. Elwyn, in the chair. Present, thirty members. Minutes of the previous meeting read and approved. Three candidates for membership elected, and three propositions presented.

Mr. Elliot Cresson called attention to the vast importance of the cultivation of flax. He had learned from reliable data, that the total value of the seed and fibre produced annually in the United States, was quite equal to thirty-six millions of dollars. As the cultivation was in this country conducted chiefly for the seed, the most valuable portion of the yield was wasted. A friend of Mr. Cresson's had traveled ten miles over a road which was, so to speak, turn-piked with the stems of flax. Thirty-six thousand tons of seed were import-ed into the United States annually from India duty free, while our products paid, on being admitted into that country, a duty of 400 per cent. Such is the reciprocity to be expected from England. It was now seriously proposed in Congress, to remove the duty on linens altogether, and thus blast the pros-pects of a rising and highly important branch of national industry. He thought it the duty of this society to prepare an address to Congress on the subject, protesting against a proposition fraught with so much evil to existing and growing interests.

Mr. David Landreth inquired if any of the newly invented processes of preparing flax, had been found fully to realize the hopes of the inventors.—Claussen's method had been highly lauded. A so-called improvement on that method had been stated in general terms to the society about a year since, but he had recently heard nothing of it. Mr. Ellsworth, formerly commissioner of patents, had embarked extensively in flax-growing. He (Mr. L.) would be pleased to hear with what success. He agreed with Mr. Cresson as to the propriety of our society taking action on this subject, and would suggest that the President correspond with societies and others interested in it.

Mr. Cresson thought that a great national question, now agitating the coun-try, was in some measure involved in the extension of the growth of flax.—He deemed it inexpedient to attack slavery directly. The evil could be reach-ed as certainly by a less objectionable means, viz: by producing a rival to cotton. Such was to be found in flax, which was more durable and capable of applications, even more varied. In the west, Claussen's method was gen-erally confided in.

Mr. Algernon S. Roberts had more than a year ago, called the attention of the society to this subject, and at his suggestion liberal premiums for the growth of flax had been offered by the society. These premiums had not been competed for. The members would remember the beautiful specimens of so-called flax-cotton, and flax-silk, exhibited at a meeting twelve or fifteen months since, proving the great beauty and fineness of the fibre and its adapt-edness to receive the most delicate tints. He (Mr. R.) did not fear a reduc-tion of duty on linens; he thought it would more likely be increased, espe-cially if this manufacture was valuable to the west. The west had great influence in the National councils—she knew it, and would take care of her-self.

Mr. James Gowen thought that Pennsylvania had a great interest in the growth of flax. The climate and soil was admirably adapted to it, and her German citizens had cultivated the plant very successfully. Flax did very well with carrots, springing up, keeping the ground clear, and when the flax was pulled, the ground was left finely divided, ready for the heaviest growth of the root crop.

Mr. Cresson said that any attempt to manufacture flax into a substance resembling cotton, injured the staple of the former. He felt that he had not over estimated the importance of the matter before the society, and moved—That the Corresponding Secretary be and he is hereby requested to prepare a memorial, setting forth the important interests involved in the cultivation of flax in the United States. The memorial to be signed by the President and Corresponding Secretary of this society, and sent to the Governors of this and the western States, and the chairmen of the Congressional Committees on Manufactures. Which motion was unanimously adopted.

Mr. P. R. Freas moved, that a committee of ten, of which the President of the society shall be the chairman, be appointed, to take suitable measures to secure the holding of the next State Fair at Philadelphia. Mr. Freas urged the necessity of decisive action at this time. The subject was of importance not only to the society, but to the county, and the whole eastern section of the State.

Mr. A. S. Roberts had attended the recent meeting of the State Society at Harrisburg. That society desired to receive proposals for suitable grounds on which to hold its great annual exhibition, and he believed was favorable to Philadelphia. The committee would require time to select a site and raise subscriptions. Last year and every previous year, the State Society had paid rent for its grounds. At Pittsburg $250 had been paid. Ground near Harrisburg had been offered the society this year without charge. He hoped the citizens here would be liberal and the committee active, as the Executive Committee of the State Society would meet early in April to receive proposals.

Mr. Freas' motion was adopted, and the following gentlemen appointed to constitute the committee: Dr. A L. Elwyn, Gen. Robert Patterson, Harry Ingersoll, A. T. Newbold, Isaac Pearson, A. S. Roberts, P. R. Freas, John Lardner, W. C. Rudman, C. W. Harrison. On motion of A. S. Roberts, Gen. George Cadwalader was added to the committee.

A communication was received from a sub-committee of city councils on the subject of the sanitary influence of the *Ailanthus tree*, which was, on motion, referred to a committee of three, consisting of Dr. A. L. Kennedy, Dr. G. Emerson, and C. W. Harrison.

On motion, that delegates be appointed to the U. S. Agricultural Society, at the rate of one for every ten members of the society, which was so ordered, and the following gentlemen appointed by the chair: A. T. Newbold, A. S. Roberts, David Landreth, John Lardner, Owen Sheridan, Harry Ingersoll, Gen. R. Patterson, Dr. A. L. Kennedy, C. W. Harrison, Elliott Cresson, John M'Gowen, Isaac Pearson, S. C. Ford, C. W. Sharpless, W. C. Rudman and Aaron Clement.

Mr. James Gowen announced to the society, the death of one of its members, Dr. James Smith, of Chestnut Hill, and submitted the following resolution:

Resolved, That this society has heard with much regret of the death of one of its members, Dr. James Smith, and deeply sympathises with his family in this painful bereavement.

Mr. Aaron Clement announced to the society the death of Mr. John R. Suplee, recently a member, and submitted the following resolution :

Resolved, That in the death of Mr. John R. Suplee, our society having lost an active and useful member, sympathises with his family in their sudden and severe affliction.

Which resolutions were unanimously adopted, and the society adjourned.

———

Stated meeting held at the room of the Masonic Hall, South Third street, Wednesday, March 1, 1854. President Dr. A. L. Elwyn in the chair. A letter from the Secretary, then absent at Harrisburg, was read requesting Mr. Clement to act for him, which was so ordered. The minutes of preceding meeting were read and approved.

The following gentlemen, proposed at preceding meeting, were duly elected, viz : Major Hagner, of Bridesburg ; Matthew Haas, of Chestnut Hill ; Peter Maison and Jeremiah L. Harrison, of Philadelphia.

Eight propositions for resident membership were presented.

The committee appointed to investigate the sanitary influences of the Ailanthus tree, presented a report, which, after a protracted discussion, was amended by the substitution of the following resolutions offered by S. G. Fisher, Esq., and adopted :

Resolved, That this society, after investigation through a committee, have found no evidence of the insalubrious qualities of the Ailanthus tree.

Resolved, That this society, nevertheless, does not desire by this expression of its opinion to encourage the propagation of this tree, but would discourage it, as there are others far preferable in all respects both for town and country.

Resolved, That a copy of these resolutions be sent to the city councils.

Mr. Landreth read a letter from Mr. Thomas P. James of this city, stating that he had presented to this society by request of Ellis Yarnall, Esq., a large package of seeds, and other agricultural products, which had been exhibited at the World's Fair, London, and were from Dr. J. Forbes Royle, of the Royal Botanic Garden, Calcutta.

The thanks of the society were tendered to the above named gentlemen.

S. G. Fisher, Esq., read a letter from a gentleman in Kent county, Delaware, on the trade and monopoly in guano by the Peruvian Government.

H. Ingersoll, Esq., moved that a committee be appointed to inquire to what agricultural society the late Mr. Elliot Cresson left the legacy of five thousand dollars, which was adopted, and Messrs. Ingersoll and S. G. Fisher were appointed the committee.

The following resolutions on the demise of Elliot Cresson, Esq., were offered by S. G. Fisher, Esq., and unanimously adopted :

Resolved, That the society has learned with sincere regret of the death of their associate, Elliot Cresson.

Resolved, That this society hereby expresses and records its high sense of his private worth and useful life, and especially of the disinterested enthusiasm with which he devoted time, energy and money to the advancement of scientific knowledge, and the promotion of enlightened schemes for the public good.

Resolved, That these resolutions be communicated by the Secretary to the family of the deceased. Adjourned.

Stated meeting at room in Masonic Hall, South Third street, Wednesday April 5, 1854. President Elwyn in the chair. Present, twenty-five members. Minutes of preceding meeting read and approved.

The following gentlemen, proposed at preceding meeting, were elected resident members, viz: Job R. Tyson, Yeaman Gillingham, John Clark, Andrew Coates, Charles F. Hupfeldt, Redman Abbott and David S. Brown, of Philadelphia ; Harnden Corson, of Germantown, and George Oldmixon, of West Caln township, Chester county.   •

Five propositions for resident membership were submitted. Dr. Charles Willing, Spruce street, and W. H. Gatzmer, Tacony, by Dr. Elwyn ; M. A. Kellogg, Race street, by A. T. Newbold; T. T. Lea, Philadelphia, by A. Clement; W. R. Morris, Philadelphia, by I. Newton.

Mr. C. W. Harrison, from the Executive Committee, presented an elaborate report on the finances of the society from December 31, 1850, to the present time.

At the last exhibition the society offered premiums amounting to,	$1,101 00
Of this amount there was awarded..........................	739 00
Other expenses of exhibition.............................	364 00
Room rent, periodicals and other expenses for the year.........	368 00
Total...	1,471 00
Receipts from all sources for last year......................	1,681 00
Balance in favor of society for year..................	210 00

On motion the report was accepted.

The committee appointed at preceding meeting, to inquire to what agricultural society the late Elliot Cresson, Esq., had left the legacy of five thousand dollars, reported through their chairman, Harry Ingersoll, Esq., that they had attended to that duty and asked to be discharged, which request, on motion, was granted.

Sidney G. Fisher, Esq., Corresponding Secretary, to whom was referred the motion of the late Elliot Cresson, Esq., that a memorial on the importance of the flax culture be prepared and sent to the Federal and the State Executives and Legislatures, and agriculturists generally, reported, that all apprehensions lest Government should lessen the duty on linen fabrics were groundless. To do so had at first been seriously intended, and hence the motion for a memorial, but those interested in the growth of flax had made such strong representations to the proper authorities at Washington, that the disposition was rather to increase than to decrease the duty. There being no necessity for the preparation of a memorial, the Corresponding Secretary was, on motion, excused from the further consideration of the subject.

The President presented a number of blanks from the Smithsonian Institution, to be filled with notes of observations on the occurrence of certain natural appearances, such as the budding and flowering of plants, the return of birds, etc. The blanks were distributed among the members, with a request that the notes should be made throughout the season and sent to the Institution at Washington.

Mr. David Landreth introduced to the society Mr. Myron Finch, editor of the "Plough, Loom & Anvil," who addressed the society in support of a proposition to erest a suitable monument to the memory of the late Jno. S. Skinner, Esq., and to provide a fund for his widow.

The President presented a letter from P. B. Savery, a member, on the subject of life memberships in the Penn'a State Agricultural Society, which was read by the Secretary. Mr. Savery urges the immediate purchase of a number of life memberships in the State Society, in order to enable it more fully to carry out the objects of its organization.

Mr. Isaac Newton called attention to an article in the Farm Journal for March, by Mr. James Gowen, in which the author criticises the conduct of Mr. Newton and others. Several members, objecting to the introduction of personal matters on the floor, the chair sustained the objection, but stated, if any portion of the article reflected on the society, it might be introduced, when a motion obtained, that the article so far as it referred to the acts of the society, be read by the secretary, which was done. On a motion that he be allowed to explain, Mr. Gowen disclaimed all intention of disrespect to the society, but maintained, that the manner of appointment of a committee in December, 1852, to examine the merits of Guenon's method of determining the milking properties of cows, was informal, and that the report of said committee, submitted at a subsequent meeting, was oral, and that it was adopted without due reflection. Several gentlemen, who had been present at the adoption of the report, affirmed that it had been presented in writing, and properly considered. On motion that the minutes of the two meetings aforesaid be read, which was so ordered, when it appeared on the record that the report had been read, adopted, and ordered to be printed, if its authors so approved.

Dr. Kennedy presented the following resolution:

ℱ *Resolved*, That the action had at a meeting of the society, held December, 1852, appointing a committee on the subject of Guenon's method of determining the value of milch cows, was perfectly regular, and that the report of said committee at the following meeting, was regularly made, read and approved. After some remarks in favor of the resolution, by Mr. J. C Montgomery, and in opposition by Mr. Gowen, it was adopted unanimously.

On motion, adjourned.

———

Stated meeting at Masonic Hall, South Third street, Wednesday morning, May 3, 1854.

Dr. Elwyn, President, in the chair.

Minutes of preceding meeting read and approved.

The following gentlemen, proposed at previous meeting, were elected resident members: Mr. W. H. Gatzmer, of Tacony, and Dr. Charles Willing, and Messrs. M. A. Kellogg, T. T. Lea, and W. R. Morris, of Philadelphia.

A proposition for resident membership was received.

The committee appointed to secure, by subscriptions from citizens generally, the holding of the next State Agricultural Fair at Philadelphia, reported subscriptions amounting to two thousand eight hundred and thirty-five dollars, which amount would be increased several hundred dollars when full returns were received. The committee had not yet waited on retail dealers. It was so obviously the interest of that class, that the State Fair should be added to the business attractions of Philadelphia, that any deficiency in the required amount would doubtless be speedily supplied.

The President stated that little or no doubt existed that Philadelphia would be selected by the Executive Committee of the State Society, for the next grand autumnal display. He inquired if the committee had visited the grounds liberally offered for the purpose by the Pennsylvania railroad company.

Mr. A. T. Newbold had visited the grounds, in company with Mr. A. S. Roberts, and examined their suitableness for the State Fair. It has been objected that the locality was too near the city, and not well watered. Were such found to be the case, no difficulty could arise, as Mr. O. Jones' grounds, eligibly situated, one and a half miles from the bridge, were also at the disposal of the Executive Committee.

Th Peresident requested Mr. Cook, an English farmer present, to inform the society of the estimation in which the Italian Rye grass was held in England. The grass had been sown on Mr. Reybold's farm, in Delaware, and was much approved there.

Mr. Cook had sown the Italian Rye grass alone, two bushels to the acre—or better with eight lbs. red clover, late in the sason. He had mowed four times a season—others five times, when used for soiling purposes. He knew no grass preferable to the Italian Rye grass.

Dr. Emerson called attention to the preference of the English farmer for imported seed, and thought that the American would do well to imitate his example.

Mr. Cook gave as a reason, that seed raised at home was generally mixed with that of other grass seeds. The yield of Rye grass was three tons per acre at first cutting, and one and a half tons at second. The best hay was worth five pounds per ton—ordinary, four pounds per ton. The Rye grass sprang early. He had seen it one and a half yards high in April. It was eaten by cattle at all seasons, and did not purge. For soiling purposes in England, he had seen it mowed on first of April. The orchard grass, extensively sown in America, was not approved of in England. A few pounds were sometimes sown at seeding time.

Mr. A. Clement did not regard the Italian Rye grass as affording good pasture. He acknowledged that it had an early start. He had seen it this season a foot high in patches in the city.

Mr. H. Ingersoll reminded the society that the value of hay differed in the two countries. Our timothy had not met with much favor at the London stables. Here it brought the highest price. When it sold at twenty dollars a ton alone, mixed with half clover, it was rated at fifteen dollars.

Mr. C. W. Harrison inquired if cattle fed on Rye grass hay, second cutting, slobbered or were salivated; other grasses caused the affection in this country.

Mr. Cook stated that such salivation was unknown in England.

Dr. Emerson remarked that the disease, if so it might be called, was ascribed, not to the grass, but to certain milky weeds. He felt more disposed to attribute it to the clover seed, which produced salivation in the human subject, when given in decoction.

Dr. King had not observed cows salivated by the after-grass.

Mr. I. Newton's observations so far from agreeing with those of Dr. King, had taught him that cows were so affected.

Mr. Newbold mentioned that the Rye grass on Mr. Reybold's farm, had been brought from England about fifteen years ago, by a Mr. Blandon.

Mr. Cook thought that the plant had been unknown in England until about that time.

Dr. A. L. Kennedy, in reply to a question from the chair, mentioned that there were three species of Lolium growing in this country. The Italian rye or Rag grass was the *Lolium multiflorum*.

The president said there was no doubt that the Italian Rye grass thrived in this climate. It furnished pasture several weeks earlier than the Poa family. It was less exhausting than timothy. He invited an expression of opinion on the subject of subsoiling. He believed that in England the practice was not regarded with as much favor as formerly.

Mr. Cook said, that with shallow draining, say one to two feet deep, subsoiling possessed value; but the present method of draining, three to four feet in depth, superseded the necessity for subsoiling. He had abandoned the practice entirely since he began to drain deeply.

Mr. Gustavus Engle had a neighbor who had subsoiled for corn, with great success. The surface soil was light—the subsoil a yellow loam, not tenacious. The first ploughing was four inches deep—the second nine. Mr. E. had never seen finer corn.

Dr. King had experimented in subsoiling land previously drained. He did not think that draining superseded the necessity for subsoiling. Land which, with drains two feet deep, had yielded in 1852, but ten bushels of corn per acre, was sown with oats the following year, after a portion had been subsoiled. On this, although the whole was otherwise similarly treated, both head and straw were much fuller. The present season the wheat on the part subsoiled, looks far better than that on the portion which had been merely drained. His subsoil is a stratum of clay four feet thick.

The President admitted that root crops required a loose soil, but questioned if herbaceous plants sought food very far beneath the surface.

Dr. Emerson had seen the roots of wheat three feet long. He would inquire what root crops were preferred in England.

Mr. Gook.—The purple-top Swedish turnip, which on land impoverished by continuous grain cropping, will, with three to four cwt. of guano per acre, yield thirty to forty tons of roots, tops off. These turnips are fed whole to stock. A large ox will fatten on a weekly ration of ten to fifteen cwt. of Swedish turnips and barley straw. The white turnip is seldom used. The average weekly allowance of a bullock may be twelve cwt. turnips and sixty lbs. straw, equal to two cwt. hay and three bushels corn. The corn being taken at seventy lbs. to the bushel.

Mr. Newton preferred a mixture of turnips and Indian meal. Bullocks would fatten half as fast again on a mixture, say half and half, than on either alone.

Mr. Ingersoll insisted that we forgot differences in climate. Our turnips, as food, are not equal to the English. Our cattle would not fatten on them alone, although cows might be kept in condition.

Mr. Harrison thought that root crops were overrated in America. Grain was certainly cheaper in the end.

Mr. Cook hoped that members would not lose sight of the fact that grain impoverished the soil, while roots enriched it and left it in fine order.

Mr. Newton specified two bushels of corn and one and a half bushels turnips per week for a bullock of a thousand weight. Sheep fed on roots alone yielded mutton of an inferior quality, by no means comparable in flavor to that from sheep fed on a mixed dish.

On motion of Mr. Ingersoll, that the further discussion of the subject be postponed until next meeting; which was so ordered.

A communication was received from Marshall P. Wilder, president of the American Pomological Society, inviting the election of delegates to the next annual meeting of the Pomological society to be held in Boston.

Dr. Kennedy submitted for action at next meeting, a resolution, providing that new members, on the payment of one dollar, be furnished with a framed certificate of membership.

On motion, adjourned.

A stated meeting of the Philadelphia Society for promoting Agriculture, was held at the room, Masonic Hall, South Third street, Philadelphia, on Wednesday, June 7th, 1854, at eleven o'clock, A. M., President, Dr. A. L. Elwyn, in the chair.

The minutes of the preceding meeting were read and approved.

Five propositions for resident membership were received. Mr. T. W. Fisher, previously proposed, was balloted for and duly elected.

The Secretary inquired of the chair, if the place for holding the next annual State Fair had been definitely fixed. He regretted that, at this advanced period, so little had been decided on in regard to an event so important to the State and city. He would ask if a local committee of arrangement had been appointed by the State Society, or if the Philadelphia Society was expected to act in that capacity.

The President stated that a committee of three, of which he was one, had been appointed by the Executive Committee of the State Society, to visit grounds suitable for the exhibition. In company with Messrs. A. T. Newbold and A. S. Roberts, he had visited Powelton; there was a fine lot of twenty-five or thirty acres, twenty of which could be enclosed for the purposes of the Fair. The same gentleman had also examined the grounds of Mr. Owen Jones, referred to at last meeting, and were decidedly in favor of Powelton. Mr. D. Landreth agreed with the Secretary as to the importance of deciding on the place as soon as possible, and submitted the following resolution:

Resolved, That a committee of five, of which the President shall be one, be appointed, for the purpose of reporting forthwith to the State Society, on the adaptedness of Powelton for exhibition purposes.

Mr. O. Sheridan thought that we were neglecting the business of our own society, in order to attend to that which properly belonged to the State organization. It had not yet been decided whether or not our society would hold an exhibition next fall.

S. G. Fisher, Esq. disapproved of holding the State Fair so near the city as Powelton. A few miles distance was a check to the introduction of unpleasant and disorderly persons, who felt no interest in agriculture, but who would congregate around and within any show in the suburbs.

Mr. A. Clement thought such apprehensions groundless. In New York they were not entertained; for there the State Fair was to be held next autumn, within the thickly built portions of the city.

The question being taken on Mr. Landreth's resolution, it was adopted, and the following gentlemen appointed the committee, viz: Messrs. A. T. Newbold, A. S. Roberts, H. Ingersoll, D. Landreth and A. L. Elwyn.

Dr. Kennedy renewed his inquiry as to the appointment of a local committee of arrangement for the State Fair. Its success mainly depended on the activity and efficiency of such a committee. We had a committee of sixteen to raise subscriptions. Was it expected that they would also act as a committee of arrangements?

Mr. A. S. Roberts thought not. Any delay in the appointment of a committee of arrangement, was attributable to the State Executive Committee, to which the power belonged.

Mr. S. V. Merrick considered that the society should lend every possible assistance in forwarding the objects contemplated by the State Society, in holding its next exhibition in this city, and submitted the following resolution, which was unanimously adopted:

Resolved, That the President be authorized to tender to the State Executive Committee the services of this society, as local committee of arrangement.

On motion of Mr. A. S. Roberts, the committee to solicit subscriptions towards rendering Philadelphia the site of the next State Fair, be instructed to collect the amount subscribed, without delay, which was so ordered.

The President inquired if, within the observation of members, the fungous excrescences on the grasses had been found to produce abortion in cows.

Several members stated, in reply, that they had observed nothing confirmatory of such a suspicion. The season at which these fungi appeared, rendered it improbable.

Mr. A. Clement, in answer to an inquiry from the chair, regretted to say that the annual county subscription to the society, continued uninterruptedly for so many years, had been lost for this year, through the neglect of the Legislature to pass the necessary act of appropriation.

Mr. A. S. Roberts read several letters on the subject, which he had received from members of the Legislature. He and the Secretary had visited Harrisburg several times during the winter, and had had frequent interviews with members, both of the Senate and House. A bill had been reported, and its provisions agreed upon by a majority of the County Board; but, chiefly through the opposition of one member of that body, it had not been properly brought before the House.

The President submitted several autograph letters of General Washington to Samuel Powel, Esq., formerly President of this society, which letters were the property of Mr. Powel, one of our members, who had politely permitted their perusal at this meeting. On motion, the letters were read by the Secretary, and ordered to be copied into the minutes, and the thanks of the society were tendered to the owner.

Dr. Hare stated briefly his method of preventing rapid decay in animal substances, and of converting bones and city refuse into manure.

⁺On motion, Dr. Hare was requested to write out his remarks for publication in the minutes.

The President presented the published edition of the minutes of the society, from 1785 to 1810, which, as a member of the committee appointed for the purpose, he had had printed.

On motion, the thanks of the society were tendered to the President, for the service rendered, and an order was drawn in his favor, for the amount of the bill of printing.

On motion, adjourned.

A. S. KENNEDY, *Recording Secretary.*

PHILADELPHIA, 2d *August*, 1791.

The President of the United States has received a letter from Arthur Young, Esq., from which the following is an extract: " You will receive the annals continued, two sets; one of which I take the liberty of requesting your presenting to the Agricultural society, as before." In compliance with Mr. Young's wishes, the President sends herewith the annals from No. 61, to No. 86, both inclusive, to Mr. Powel, requesting him to be so good as to present them to the society.

SAMUEL POWEL, ESQ.,

President of the Philadelphia society for promoting agriculture.

DEAR SIR:—At the moment you proposed, half after eleven to-morrow, to see the operation of Col. Anderson's machine, it did not occur to me, that at two o'clock I must be at home. Quere—Is there full time between these hours to perform the ride and have full proof of the utility of the threshing machine? If you answer in the affirmative, let the hour remain—if in the negative, I am under the necessity of postponing my attendance until the next day, or some other time. Your solution of this question, will much oblige

Your obedient and affectionate humble servant,

GEORGE WASHINGTON.

Wednesday, 17th August, 1791.

DEAR SIR:—By one of the late ships from London, I have received from Mr. Arthur Young, two sets of his annals, numbered from 93 to 108, inclusively. Although no direction is given concerning them, I take it for granted that one set is intended as usual, for the Agricultural society of this city, and to you as President thereof, I send them accordingly.

With esteem and regard,

I am, dear sir,

Your obedient servant,

GEO. WASHINGTON.

Mr. Powel.

—

. New York, *December* 15, 1789.

Dear Sir :—I am sorry to find from your favor of the, 9th., that you have had cause to recall the report made to Major Jackson, relative to the Hessian fly. I have not written to Mr. Young yet on this subject ; perhaps it may be some time before I shall. In my late tour through the Eastern States, I was informed, (particularly in Connecticut,) that this destructive insect had also appeared in their fields of wheat. What an error it is, and how much to be regretted, that the farmers do not confine themselves to the yellow bearded wheat, if, from experience, it is found capable of resisting the ravages of this otherwise all conquering foe.

Mrs. Washington and myself are very much obliged by Mrs. Powel's kind remembrances of us, and offer our best respects and sincerest good wishes in return to her and to yourself.

I have the honor to be, dear sir,

Your most obedient servant,

GEO. WASHINGTON.

—

. New York, *February* 21, 1790.

Dear Sir :—I have the pleasure to acknowledge the receipt of a letter, which you have been so good as to write to me by the direction of the Philadelphia society for promoting agriculture, and I beg leave to request your communication of my thanks to the society for their polite attention in the present which accompanied it.

Among the advantages resulting from this institution, it is particularly pleasing to observe that a spirit of emulation has been excited by the rewards offered to excellence in the several branches of rural economy, and I think there is every reason to hope the continuance of these beneficial consequences, from such well judged liberality. As no one delights more than I do in the objects of your institution, so no one experiences more real pleasure, from every proof of their progress, among which it marks the discernment of the society, to have distinguished Mr. Matthewson's improvement in the useful

Your most obedient servant,

GEO. WASHINGTON.

SAMUEL POWEL, Esq.,

Prerident of the Philadelphia society for promoting agriculture.

—

Letter comprising the substance of a verbal communication on the conversion of offal flesh into manure, by Robert Hare, M. D.

291, CHESNUT STREET, PHILADELPHIA, June 9.

MY DEAR SIR :—My object this morning in making a verbal communication to the agricultural society, was to suggest that the carcuses of dogs killed under the "dog law," so called, might be employed to carry out upon a large scale, some experiments of which I made mention to the society some years since, in which fish or flesh was converted into a pulverizable mass, equivalent to guano. It would only be necessary to steep the animals in a solution of about three parts of sulphuric acid, four parts of salt and about thirty of water for from six to twelve hours, and subsequently to dry them under a shed, protected from rain, or by an anthracite fire, as meat is smoked.

Preferably, the skin should be removed before the steeping, and the abdomen opened. The animals might, however, be stunned by a blow and thrown into the solution, or they might be injected by the solution by the jugular artery, and also through the gullet or rectum.

Hydrostatic pressure might be used by placing the solution in any elevated position, in an upper story, for instance, of any building resorted to, and bringing it down by a leaden pipe. When the deseccation is effected by heat as above suggested, it may be carried to the temperature of melting tin, nearly, say 400 degrees, without diminishing the ammoniacal elements.—When this heat is used the whole mass becomes freable and easy to reduce to powder. The bones as well as the flesh slugs roasted to this point, becomes as brittle as glass. This fact was verified on a pretty large scale by the liberal assistance of Robert Gilmore, Esq., of Maryland, who wrote a most favorable account of the success of the resulting manure. When animal matter, such as slugs or bones, are heated in a close vessel, the first escape of ammoniacal elements may be detected by a feather dipped in muriatic acid, or by a very weak and almost colorless solution of blue vitriol or sulphate of copper. Fetor is corrected by wood tar or rosin, which may be made more active by mingling with oil of turpentine.

Sincerely the well-wisher of yourself and of the society,

Truly yours,   ROBERT HARE.

DR. A. L. ELWYN,

President of the Philadelphia society for promoting agriculture.

Stated meeting at rooms, Masonic Hall, South Third street, on Wednesday, July 5, 1854. President, A. L. Elwyn, M. D. in the chair. Minutes of preceding meeting were read and approved.

The following gentlemen proposed for membership at previous meeting, were balloted for and declared duly elected:

Dr. Charles Noble, Philadelphia.

· Dr. J. E. Fox,   do.

Mr. Marmaduke Watson,   do.

Dr. Wm. V. Keating,   do.

Dr. Edward Peace,   do.

Two propositions for resident membership were received.

The committee of five appointed at the last meeting, to report to the Executive Committee of the State Society, the adaptedness of Powelton for the purposes of the State Fair, reported that the necessity for their acting had been superseded by the visit of the President and Secretary of the State Society to the grounds. On motion that the committee be discharged, which was so ordered.

The President reported that agreeably to resolution, he had tendered to the State Society, the services of the society as local committee of arrangement for the exhibition, and that the offer had been accepted.

Voted on motion, that a sub-committee of nine be appointed to execute the duties devolving on this society as local committee of arrangements for the State Fair; whereupon Messrs. A. J. Newbold, John M'Gowan, Aaron Clement, C. W. Harrison, S. C. Willits, David George, George Blight, D. Landreth and L. H. Twaddell, were appointed by the chair.

It having been intimated that grounds for the ploughing match would be required in addition to Powelton, several members gave the assurance that from adjoining or neighboring property, every accommodation could be obtained.

The President reported that he had just returned from a highly satisfactory trial of Adkin's reaper. He invited members to relate their experience with the various mowing and reaping machines; whereupon an animated and prolonged discussion ensued, wherein Messrs. G. Blight, C. W. Harrison, D. Landreth, J. Pearson, O. Sheridan, D. Kelly, S. C. Willitts and others participated, and during which the superiority of Ketchum's, Hussey's, M'Cormick's, Allen's and Adkin's reapers was respectively affirmed and denied. The great advantage to the farmer of this application of power was generally recognized. Failures were attributed rather to defective construction than to error in design. The identical machines which had succeeded perfectly with some, had failed with others, success being ascribed to greater evenness of ground, erectness of crops or experience on the part of the farm hands.

Dr. Kennedy submitted the following resolution:

Resolved, That the Secretary be and he is hereby authorized to advertise the meetings of the society, and to invite the proprietors of new and improved implements, machines and other objects of agricultural interest to send specimens and models to the meetings.

The resolution was adopted unanimously, and the society adjourned.

———

Stated meeting, August, 1854.   President, Dr. A. L. Elwyn, in the chair.
Minutes of preceding meeting read and approved.

Dr. William Shippen and Mr. J. C. Cresson, proposed as resident members at last meeting, were balloted for and duly elected.

Two propositions for resident membership were received.

Mr. David George tendered his resignation from the Joint Committee of Arrangement on the State Agricultural Fair.   On motion, the resignation was accepted, and Mr. John Rice appointed in his stead.

Mr. Harrison, from the same committee, reported that the grounds at Powelton had been enclosed for the purposes of the fair, and that a proposition had been made to the Pennsylvania Horticultural Society, to adopt their premium list, and the awards of their judges, provided the society would waive their usual exhibition and throw their influence in behalf of the Horticultural department of the State Fair.

The President inquired concerning the result of the late exhibition of implements at Mr. Stavely's, in Bucks county.

Mr. Landreth had understood that, owing to the great diversity of opinion which prevailed, awards had been made to several of the competitors.

On motion of Mr. Landreth, that the Secretary be and he is hereby authorized to send a copy of the published minutes of the society recently prepared in pamphlet form, to every kindred society in the Union.   Which was so ordered.

Dr. Kennedy hoped that the discussion on reaping and mowing machines, postponed from last meeting, would be resumed.   Hitherto our society had devoted too little attention to agricultural machinery, a department in which our countrymen would probably attain to the highest excellence.   In the improvement of stock, in irrigation, in drainage, in the cultivation of soils and the application of concentrated manures, we competed with Europe unequally.   There labor was cheaper, and wealth more concentrated.   The high price of labor, while it prevented expensive experiments in agriculture, stimulated to the invention and perfection of labor-saving machinery.   Reaping and mowing machines were cases in point.   American agriculture had received no greater boon for many years, and agricultural societies could do no greater service to the cause, than by increasing the list of their premiums for improved implements and newly invented machinery.   In England, where such inventions were less needed, their production was vastly more stimulated by prizes. M'Cormick's reaper was the great feature of the Agricultural Department of the World's Fair at London.   Yet the speaker had there seen a drain-laying machine which dug the trench, laid the tiles and covered them up by power applied to a windlass at a remote part of the field! Tile-making machines came properly within the province of the agriculturist. Tiles were now made in Europe in a continuous tube, the clay being forced through proper orifices in steel plates, by the pressure of a piston, (as in the manufacture of macca-roni,) or by friction of rollers. The tubes as they are formed are cut into appropriate lengths. Dr. K. had failed to find such tile machines in Albany, where he had been on the preceding Saturday. He farther explained their action, and also that of the tile-laying machine, above cited.

Mr. Sheridan contended that drain-laying machines might do in a light, well-worked soil, in Europe, but not in the refractory, stony soils of America. He could not imagine a subsoil plow which could cut a drain without leaving a wide, open trench.

Mr. Samuel Williams had seen such ploughs. They burrowed, as it were, the lower part, not improperly called a shoe, connected with the frame of the plough, by means of a thin, strong piece of iron, which, like a coulter, pre-sented its edge to the sod. The peculiarity of the machine described by Dr. Kennedy, did not consist so much in that it made a trench, as that it laid the tiles evenly immediately following the plough, and closed in the soil over them.

Mr. Landreth was pleased to hear the amount of agricultural machinery at the World's Fair, and coincided in the opinion that the subject of agricultural machines had not received sufficient attention and encouragement. He re-sumed the debate on the reaper and mower, and was followed by Messrs. Har-rison, Willits, Newton, Geo. R. Engle, Gustavus Engle, Sheridan and others. Adjourned.

Stated meeting at room in Masonic Hall, South Third street, on Wednes-day, August 3, 1854. Dr. Elwyn, President, in the chair.

The minutes of preceding meeting were read and approved.

Professor J. C. Cresson, Dr. Wm. Shippen and Mr. T. C. James, proposed at previous meeting, were elected resident members.

Mr. A. T. Newbold, in behalf of sub-committee on State Fair, reported having met the members of the joint committee appointed by the State So-ciety. A proposition inviting the co-operation of the Pennsylvania Horti-cultural Society had been passed, and there was reason to believe that it would be accepted by that society.

The chair inquired as to the result of the exhibition of implements recently held at Mr. Stavely's, in Bucks county. Mr. Landreth had understood that the exhibition was well attended, and that the equality of merit of the im-plements tried, was so marked, that much diversity of opinion prevailed as to them. Awards were made to several, especially to the mowers and reapers.

Mr. Landreth moved to authorize the Secretary to send copies of the pub-lished minutes of the society, from 1785 to 1810, to kindred societies in the United States, which have libraries and hold regular meetings. Agreed to.

The discussion [on mowing and reaping machines, commenced at the preceding meeting, was then resumed and continued by Messrs. Newton, Gustavus Engle, Landreth, Harrison, Sheridan and others, pending which the society adjourned.

———

September meeting, 1854. Dr. A. L. Elwyn, President, in the chair. Minutes of the preceding meeting read and approved. Dr. Pepper and Mr. Wm. P. Walter, both of Philadelphia, were elected members. Four propositions for resident membership were presented.

The sub-committee of arrangement for the State Fair, through their chairman, Mr. A. T. Newbold, reported the condition of the grounds and the progress made in the arrangements.

A communication was received from Lieut. Jas. S. Biddle, light-house inspector, offering to furnish members of the society with seeds of several varieties of colza or rape, which had recently been imported, with a view to its extensive growth in this country, as a source of oil for purposes of light-house and other illuminations.

Mr. Landreth, in reply to a question from the chair, stated that the seed was already well known in this county. It was of easy cultivation, and could be sown in any corner, at the same time as ruta baga. The plant was some time used for green soiling. He had eight acres sown with the seed, and designed the plants for cattle in the autumn. The habit of the colza was precisely that of ruta baga, and it was cultivated in the same manner, the young plants being set out in the spring. He did not raise the seed because of the plant hybridizing, with other species of Brassica.

On motion, that the communication be filed and its receipt acknowledged, which was so ordered.

Mr. Ford called attention to the importance of the potato crop and the means of preserving potatoes throughout the season. He thought that the time of taking them up, and the kind of place required for storing them, were not properly regarded. He believed that the cold dews and hot sun had destroyed large quantities in 1849. He had taken his up early, and with the adhering soil had placed them in a heap in a close cellar, merely leaving the door open occasionally, to change the air. His loss had been comparatively light, both in that year and in 1851, when he repeated the process. He was satisfied that potatoes planted late were in most danger, and that early planting and early digging up were sure means of safety.

Mr. Sheridan attributed the loss of the potato crop to careless cultivation.

The chair inquired of Mr. Ford if his potatoes were now sufficiently advanced to be dug?

Mr. Ford. Certainly—and already the largest and oldest, if any, will be found diseased. Potatoes should be planted early in April. I would even recommend fall planting. Potatoes left in the ground, are often found sprouting vigorously in the spring.

Mr. Landreth had generally succeeded in planting potatoes in the fall for table use early in the spring. Last winter, however, was known to be the most severe for many years, and he had lost his winter planting. His practice was, to plant deep, put manure on the potato, and heap the soil well up. His potatoes are up at the usual time of planting in the spring. He thinks fall planting generally practicable; and there is a gain in time, at a season when there is not much to do.

Dr. King corroborated Mr. Landreth's statements as to the loss of the crop by the severity of last winter.

Mr. Ingersoll suggested that a slight mulching would give additional security against cold.

Mr. Landreth had tried it, but the weeds had gained the advantage under the plan.

Mr. Willets, when near the sea shore recently, had seen potatoes green and flourishing amid the general barrenness, in consequence of their having been mulched with salt grass. They were quite clean of weeds. He had found the advantage of fall planting in a row accidentally left undug in one of his fields. The potatoes came up in the spring, and in June were large and fine, and three weeks earlier than those planted at the usual time.

Mr. Pearson's experience favored the views of Mr. Ford. Spread on a dry barn floor many of his potatoes had decayed; but in a cellar stored with the soil adhering, they had kept well. Two great care in cleaning potatoes was the cause of disease. Dirt kept them dry.

Mr. G. W. Holmes used a well ventilated cellar, in which he had stored seven hundred bushels with soil attached; but fifteen bushels had rotted. The top of the heap became at first wet, but this soon dried. He had found no difficulty with his crop, either before, during or since the appearance of the rot.

Mr. Ingersoll approved of close packing. He thought highly of the effects of charcoal dust. He had taken a diseased potato, sprinkled it with such dust, put it in an exposed place, and the disease went no further.

On motion, adjourned.

Stated meeting, October 4, 1854. Vice President, A. T. Newbold, in the chair. Minutes of preceding meeting read and approved.

Messrs. Edward Armstrong, B. H. Brewster, Wm. Blight and Jos. Glenat, were elected resident members.

The sub-committee of arrangement of the State Fair, reported that the exhibition as a whole had never been equalled in the Union. The sub-committee, however, were unable to make any statement of the amount of the receipts and expenses.

A free conversation ensued on the general subject of the management of the Fair, after which the society adjourned.

Stated meeting, November 1, 1854, at usual place. President, Dr. Elwyn, in the chair. Minutes of preceding meeting read and approved.

Mr. Henry C. Pratt, of Frankford, was proposed for membership by Mr. John M'Gowan.

The resolution previously proposed by Mr. A. T. Newbold, "that the Recording Secretary be ex-officio a member of all Standing Committees," was called up and discussed.

Dr. C. R. King moved to amend by striking out the words, "member of all Standing Committees," and inserting "Secretary of Committee on Exhibition," which amendment prevailed, and the resolution as amended was then agreed to.

Mr. A. M. Spangler, on a call from the chair, stated, that he had attended the recent exhibition of the Lancaster County Society, and found the attendance slim, and the display poor, both of implements and cattle. This he attributed in part to the late severe visitation of the cholera in that county. The jealousy on the subject of the exhibition, between the towns of Lancaster and Columbia, each being anxious to secure the holding of it, was injuring the society as well as the county exhibitions.

Mr. Sheridan moved, that the advertising of the meetings of the Society, in the newspapers, be discontinued; which motion was not agreed to.

Adjourned.

A stated meeting of the Philadelphia Society for promoting Agriculture, was held at the room, South Third street, on Wednesday morning, December, 1854. President, Dr. A. L. Elwyn, in the chair.

The minutes of the preceding meeting were read and approved. Mr. Henry C. Pratt, of Frankford, was unanimously elected a resident member.

The President stated that Vice President Clement had recently visited agricultural fairs in Maryland and Virginia, and called upon him for an account of his visit.

Mr. Clement responded, by describing the fair at Richmond as exceedingly successful. The grounds, twenty-five acres in extent, were superior, the attendance large, and the display fine. The society has a fund of fifty thousand dollars, permanently invested.

The society exhibiting at Petersburg, is composed of members in North Carolina as well as in Virginia. The grounds are near the town, and comprise fifteen acres, and were beautifully arranged and decorated, and good accommodations for objects exhibited were afforded. The subject of purchasing an experimental farm was proposed, and met with so much favor that ten thousand dollars were subscribed on the spot.

The exhibition at Baltimore was by no means equal to those formerly held.

Mr. Waring, of Connecticut, was present, and at the request of the chair described the cattle show of the United States Agricultural Society, at

Springfield. The best cattle there were impórted; their quality was excellent, but the number small. The award of prizes was liberal and caused much competition.

Mr. Harrison moved that a committee be appointed to nominate officers for the ensuing year. Adopted, and Messrs. Harrison, J. Lardner, M'Gowan, Williams and Newbold were appointed the committee.

On motion of Dr. Kennedy, that a committee be appointed to correspond with the agricultural societies in the State, and obtain statistics of their condition, organization, meetings, exhibitions, etc., which was so ordered, and Drs. Kennedy and M'Crea, and Mr. C. W. Harrison, were appointed the committee.

Mr. Tyson suggested that the fact of the existence of societies might be learned by addressing the President Judges of the county courts.

The chair having requested Vice President Clement to give an account of the first introduction of Durhams into this country, that gentleman made a most interesting statement, during which he said that the first animal in this country of the stock in question, was a cow, called the Kilton cow, which had been sent from England about 1805, on speculation. She was valued at two hundred guineas, but at that price found no purchaser, and was sent back. She was with young when she arrived, and while here she had a bull calf, which was given to Jacob Serrill, of Darby, Delaware county, Pa., for the trouble he had had in keeping the cow. From this calf, by crossing with our so called native cows, very fine cattle had been obtained—steers weighing from fourteen to sixteen hundred pounds.

The committee on nominations reported the requisite number of nominees. Adjourned.

SCHUYLKILL COUNTY.

OFFICE OF THE SCHUYLKILL COUNTY AGRICULTURAL SOCIETY, }
Orwigsburg, February 15, 1855. }

To the President of the Pennsylvania State Agricultural Society :

SIR:—In compliance with your circular, I herewith transmit you a brief report of this society. It was organized on the 22d of February, 1851, held no exhibition the first year, but held its third annual exhibition at Orwigsburg on the 17th, 18th and 19th days of October, 1854. The society is in a prosperous condition, although it counts only about three hundred members, regular and irregular.

The amount of premiums awarded at our last exhibition was three hundred and twenty dollars.

The annual address was delivered by Gen. George M. Keim, of Reading, a copy of which I will transmit for publication in the transactions of the State Society.

The officers elected on the first of January, 1855, are:

PRESIDENT—Hon. Jacob Hammer.

VICE PRESIDENTS—Joshua Bock and J. J. Paxson.

RECORDING SECRETARY AND LIBRARIAN—Joshua S. Keller.

CORRESPONDING SECRETARY—Samuel H. Madden.

TREASURER—Joseph Hammer.

CURATORS—Dr. J. F. Treichler and Rubens Peal.

The regular meetings of the society are held on the last Saturday of each month.

J. S. KELLER, Recording Secretary.

ADDRESS.

MR. PRESIDENT AND GENTLEMEN:—

That nation whose agriculture is prosperous, is foremost in civilization, whilst an inability to supply food betokens a weak government, in constant dread of famine, and a total lack of independence. Of old, agriculture was known as the nursing mother of the arts, for Xenophon has shown that "where it prospers, the arts thrive; but where the earth is uncultivated, there the other arts are destroyed."

It may justly be termed a school of industry, which teaches a reliance upon our own efforts for reward, and dignifies labor by the noble enterprise of subduing even the elements to the purpose of human subsistence. The palmiest days of Rome were distinguished for their reverence to this worthy employment; Cincinnatus, on his return from conquest, was more impatient to retire to his little villa, than to be greeted in triumph by the whole Roman people. The hand of Regulus fitted the plough as well as the sword. Whilst he was absent in Africa, the Senate attended to his crops, and sent him word that they would continue to do so, as long as he remained at the head of their armies.

Julius Agricola has the merit of being one of the earliest benefactors of Great Britain, in inculcating the art of culture, which afforded abundant supplies not only to the army but large quantities of grain were exported from the Island. After the Roman power declined, the constant predatory incursions of the numerous clans upon each others' possessions, rendered the tillage of the ground a precarious pursuit. The spirit of the warrior seemed humbled in the exercise of works so pacific and bloodless. Hence on such grounds must we infer those laws were founded which treated the cultivation of land as unworthy the notice of men, and prevented it from being followed except by women and slaves. There is in the character of the North American Indians a similar disregard for any occupation of industry. They leave all that is to be done by handicraft, to women and slaves. The attractions of the chase are more congenial with their pleasures, than those which of necessity are more sedentary and tedious. What is the Red Man with such antecedents but a wanderer upon the face of the earth? Vainly have efforts been made to instruct him in the arts of civilization; he becomes an adept only to such as administer to his untamed passions, and his mission is closed wherever the stroke of the axe opens a path through the forest, and invites the fostering hand of industry to awaken the latent virtues of the soil. In a political as well as moral view there is much to be acquired from a permanent investiture of the soil. The principal charm of life is identified with it. Not only is it promotive of the right of property and a consequent dependence upon the safety and security of the State, but the cottage reared by our forefathers, and the old oak that overshadows it, impress us with pleasing recollections. The associations of youth, of middle age, or of declining years, cluster around the heart in memory of the old homestead. The family altar is there—there, the first letters of instruction have been inculcated, and character has been formed, to mark the progress of life with good or evil. The spirit of good is peculiarly the invocation of the husbandman. His daily observations of physical changes astonish his senses, and lead him onward to a study of the source from whence they emanate. The truths of Revelation become manifest before him, without which civilization itself were but half accomplished. Just as well might we hope for bountiful crops from a parched and sterile desert, as that the best fruits of human knowledge could be gleaned without the salvo of some guiding principle, to renovate the mind and establish its future destiny. Advantages arising from the influences of agriculture upon the character of nations are palpable and of easy discernment.— Wherever labor is degraded and luxury, idleness and pride predominate, nations or individuals sink into insignificance and reproach, but where industry lends its vigorous features to civilization, the blessings of peace, prosperity and happiness enure as well to the people as the State.

The prosperity of a nation is also augmented when the domain is apportioned into such divisions as may increase the number of landed porprietors, thus to insure not only a better appreciation of every acre, by making it thoroughly productive, but also to rear a permanent yeomanry as ready to pay her taxes as to fight her battles. In this view the progressive spirit of the age points to the homestead bill as a rational measure by which humanity is elevated beyond the common vicissitudes of fortune in assuring a home for the homeless. By such means the burdens of taxation will be lessened, and as small farms afford the largest profits, the value of productive wealth must be largely increased.

The quiet serenity and composure of rural districts, compared with the noise and turbulence incident to cities, would indicate that whilst commerce feeds the passions, agriculture calms them. The agitations of trade are not congenial to the enlargement of human knowledge or to the improvment of that preception of pleasure which makes contentment the principal object of human happiness. Districts and sections of country occur in which that happiness is a reality.

Imagine if you please an area of three hundred square miles with a population of four hundred persons. The inhabitants reside in numerous small hamlets neatly elevated by the hill side, and by common consent their local government is patriarchal. The aged of the village are generally the ancestors of the rest, and all seem to be united as one family. Their occupations are various, for none are idle. Some are agricultural, some pastoral, some fell the forest, and some penetrate the thickets in the chase, or perchance lure with gilded bait the lithesome trout. They spin and weave the fleece of their own flocks, and color their clothes with native hues that vie in lustre with the Tyrian dye. Their fields afford them bread, and their own herds present rich rashers of beef, redolent with the fragrance of sweet pastures and fresh air, that would bring tears of delight to the admirers of "England's staple," and make even a monk of La Trappe solicit temporary absolution. The wide spreading maple renders the tribute of sugar, and the wild bee brings them its casements of honey. Their trysting times are constant and not periodical.— Hospitality to the stranger is their ruling virtue. On such occasions the tables are laden with the choicest viands. Water, sparkling and bright, fresh as from the rock of Horeb, graces the festival, fit emblem of innocence and purity that adds new charms to every repast. There was but one fellow-being whom they could not encourage—he was the physician, and old age was the only disease, for which Materia Medica suggested no remedy. The tax gatherer was provided for, and beside him, they owed no man any thing. Their every want was supplied and their every wish gratified, whilst care, the constant companion of mortals, seemed not yet to have discovered this little nook of Paradise. This is a truthful description of a township in this Commonwealth, whose virtues may well be imitated. There are doubtless many political theorists who would object to the unproductive character and apparent lethargy of a community, whose commerce is complete without any foreign import, and whose requirements are supplied without the need of money. To such as desire to enlarge the area of exchanges, and believe in the importance of increasing the mutual relations of nations by commercial intercourse, there may be gleaned but a sorry consolation from these statistics. Yet on the other hand, if the object of government is the alleviation of human suffering, and the assurance of man's highest happiness, it may be well to inquire whether these objects are not better obtained in this simple manner, than by those ingenious devices of art which constrain an increase of exertion to attain an end already accomplished. If we are independent of foreign nations and have within ourselves all the resources of abundance to supply our wants, the danger of war is not to be dreaded, because without an object of gain it is unfashionable to provoke it. The wealth of the government in our system of liberty, is rather an evidence of misrule than of good fortune, for whatever may be the wealth of individuals, that can only be maintained and protected by the most simple and economical administration of public affairs. With us, excessive accumulations in the treasury are a nucleous, around which disasters cluster like moths around the glare of a lamp; it beguiles them from their better instincts, and draws them into a vortex of ruin that never can be retrieved. Schemes and projects however impracticable and speculative, are induced into plausible shape, and exhibit a disgusting picture of peculation and artifice, in which not only our law-givers participate, but the very Ministers of the Constitution have been willing to lend their superior service. A desertion of gradual means for a sudden and alluring prospect of gain, has degraded nations in the scale of power. Our own California with all her fascinations, has cost us more than she has yet paid; Spain like a spider, sits crouching upon the ruins of her former grandeur, and the celebrated cities of the Hanseatic league present a melancholy contrast to their once formidable power. The strength of our national prosperity consists in the even tenor, the energy and firmness of our agricultural population, who seek not by sudden exertions to obviate the necessity of future labor, but rely on their own efforts for the supply of every want, and for a resource under every emergency. The husbandman in a free country occupies the first rank amongst men. Instead of soliciting the favor, accommodating himself to the caprice, or administering to the vanities of mankind, he enters upon an equable and uniform career. The changes of the seasons and the operations of the elements, are subjects whose nature he studies and to whose variations he conforms his practice. His vigilance never slumbers, but inspires a shrewd caution without that despicable cunning, which is acquired by bending to the humor of the times, and speculating on the changes of the fashions. Thus the art to which he is devoted, as far as it tends to elevate the mind and create a dignity of sentiment, must be allowed to rank among the pursuits of life, as higher and more worthy of his being. Look, if you please, for a moment at his present condition. In what dilemma is now the farming interests of the country? Where is its indebtedness? With what wild adventure has it become involved? Commerce, confused and precarious, ideal projects of vast extent, commenced upon groundless promises, are fast sinking into that insignificance to which a want of means consigns them. But this confusion presents to him no alarm, he has relied upon the bountiful resources of his well tilled soil, and invested in no adventure than that which long experience has sanctioned, and sound judgment approved. Almost all the classical authors whether statesmen, philosophers or poets, have left some memento upon this art. What Hesiod, Xenophon, Cato, Columella and Cicero deemed worthy of their regard, remained for Virgil to adorn with the eloquence of his poetic genius. The whole theory of farming is found in the instructions left us by Cato, that "the first thing to be done is to plough well, the second to plough, and the third to manure." In 1534 the first book on English husbandry, by Judge Fitzherbert, was published. After him, Gabriel Plattes published a dissertation, which invites attention only for its quaintness of style. His directions how to discover a coal mine is part of his subject, and may afford some amusement if nothing else.   He remarks, " When I consider the great number of treasures and riches which lyeth hidden in the belly of the earth, and doth no good at all, and when I consider that the most part of the mines hitherto discovered have come by mere accident, I thought that I could not be better employed than to give rules and directions for the same, for though it is not impossible that if two men be sent to seek a thing that is lost, and one of them be hoodwinked and the other have the use and benefit of his eyes, yet the person hoodwinked may casually stumble upon it, nevertheless it is twenty to one that the other should have found it before him.   So in this case, I dare hazard a wager of twenty to one, that there will be more good mines discovered within seven years by these rules and directions than have been in twenty-seven years before.   Though the pit coals be of small value, yet if a good mine thereof shall be discovered, herein is a receipt for the purpose.— About the middle of May, when the subterrannean vapors are strong, which may be discovered by the fern which about that time will suddenly grow out of the earth in a night or two, almost a handful in length, then take a pure white piece of tiffany and wet it in the dew of the grass which is all of that spring's growth, and not soiled with cattle nor no other thing, then wring out the dew from it, and do so five or six times; and if there be coals, the tiffany will be a little blacked and made foul with the sooty vapors arising through the coals and condensed among the dew.   I admonish him that shall try with the tiffany upon the dew, to let his hands be washed before with soap and hot water, and wiped with a pure white cloth till they will not foul the cloth at all, else if they spend their money in digging and find nothing they may thank their foul fingers for that misfortune."

Sir Wm. Temple, in 1680, thus treats upon gardening : "That which makes the care of gardening more necessary, or at least more excusable, is, that all men eat fruit that can get it.   So as the choice is only whether one will eat good or ill, and between these the difference is not greater in point of taste and delicacy, than it is of health, for whoever is used to eat good fruit, will do very great penance when he comes to ill.   Now whoever will be sure to eat good fruit, must do it out of a garden of his own, for there is something very nice in gathering them and choosing the best, even from the same tree. The best fruit that is bought, has no more of the master's care than how to raise the greatest gains.   His business is to have as much fruit as he can upon as few trees, whereas, the way to have it excellent, is to have but little upon many trees.   So that for all things out of a garden, either of sallad or fruits, a poor man will eat better that has one of his own, than a rich man that has none."

It was left for Jethro Tull to suggest the wonderful advantages of drill culture, by which an impulse was given to the better construction of the tools and implements of husbandry.   The primitive instruments of the days of Gideon and Saul, when iron was unknown, and ploughs made of crooked roots pointed with ox horns, were now no longer used to torture the rugged earth into obedience. Mathematical precision and accuracy, and a goodly stirring up of the earth, were accomplished by the drill invention of Jethro Tull. Although it was to the improvements of the present day, as Franklin's kite compared with the electric telegraph; yet, the conception once achieved, the thought indurated and spread abroad, becoming a new incentive to additional efforts in saving labor and perfecting the mechanical machinery of culture. Whitney's cotton gin sprang from this source, and created a staple commodity for this country, that otherwise, from the high rate of labor, could not have been made available. The hoe, harrow, the plough, the roller, the clod crusher, the rake, the corn plough, the mower, the reaper and thresher, with daily accessions to their number, are constantly being rendered more effective and useful. The application of chemistry to agriculture is comparatively of modern date. To Doctor Priestley are we indebted for the first experiments that demonstrated the decomposition of the carbonic acid of the atmosphere, by leaves of vegetables giving out oxygen and assimilating carbon. Sir Humphrey Davy, taking this initiative, occupied himself with every philosophical inquiry in the application of chemistry to the growth of plants and organic processes.

Liebig, professing to follow in the train of Davy, by minute research and devoted study, has applied the physical sciences to agriculture, until the laws of vitality, which govern the functions of plants, are fast ceasing to be a mystery.

The necessity for some means of renovation and rendering fertile, worn out and exhausted lands, is of the greatest importance. The work of destruction is going on to so great an extent, that in after time, what now is a smiling prairie, may become a desolate waste. The sugar and cotton planter deem the refuse of their crops so great an impediment to their present convenience, that they either erect high chimneys in order to burn them, or else cast them into the neighboring streams as a nuisance. The corn growers of the west have similar troubles, whilst the grain growers of the north are being admonished by the diminution of results, and the reduced average of product per acre. That the earlier cultivators had better have hoarded those resources with more care, is the sad experience of their descendants. Science has been providentially and wisely directed to these investigations, in determining the various ingredients of the soil and their relative qualities, in ascertaining their combination, and in the application thereof to plants; not to plants only can this research be limited, but animals, birds and insects, their structure, habits and manners, are features indispensably necessary to be known. Science also teaches us that the laws of nature are unchangeable, and that all the phenomena which matter evolves, are the result of these laws. Thus, to gather causes from effects, to assign to each agency its share in the growth of plants, becomes an object of instruction and profit. Many of the conclusions of physical science are as yet upon the threshold of their subject, among the intricacies of which, the greatest point to be understood, is the existence of an universal power that governs organic structure.

To ask that every farmer should become a chemist, is requesting more than his arduous duties would permit; but that he should avail himself of the advantages arising therefrom, would be an evidence of knowing his best interests and minding his own business.

He would learn that the principal property of a potato is potash; that of wheat, rye, corn and buckwheat, is phosphoric acid; of corn stalks, soda; of meadow hay, silica; and of clover, lime. The food that plants obtain from the air are oxygen and hydrogen, although nitrogen composes four-fifths of the atmosphere, yet, it is said, that plants do not receive it directly from this source, but from its compounds, as in rain water, and as ammonia, which consists of nitrogen and hydrogen. Carbon, which is also contained in the atmosphere, enters largely into and forms the greatest constituent of all plants; it is but 1-500 part of the atmosphere. The inquiry may be made, as nature supplies such an excess of nitrogen, and requires so little, whilst carbon is so small a constituent and yet so much required, whether these are not among the impenitrabilia of nature, into which science has not yet been permitted to enter? The organic food is from the air, and the inorganic from the soil, composed chiefly of soda, potash, magnesia, sulphuric acid, phosphoric acid, chlorine, silica and lime. This, then, is the theory of agricultural chemistry. It proposes to define the component parts of the soil and atmosphere, and by an analysis of the products which are cultivated, it supplies by artificial means to the soil again, those properties of which the crops deprived it. It is true, that the processes by which plants absorb the different elements are not yet understood, and it has been questioned whether mineral manure, or ammonia, is the most advantageous to those processes. Experiments in the field can alone determine the fact, although it is safe to say, that great benefits result from the use of both. This is emphatically an age in which there seems to be a perfect epidemic for books on every subject, and agriculture comes in for a large share. Too frequently, however, more is claimed for a discovery or invention than it deserves; as of yore, the alchemits professed to make gold by means of a refined and mystical powder, applied to the inferior metals, so the pretensions of the bibliopole promise many more advantages than can be realized; where so much is doing, some new theme of agitation is constantly invoked, so as to afford interest and variety, and thus insure a sale of the book itself, or the patent fertilizer it may recommend. It has become a reproach to us, that our attachment to old customs prevents any attempt at the introduction of improvements. This is an unjust imputation. If you cast your eye upon the counties of Lancaster, Berks, Lehigh, Northampton and York, and compare the refreshing aspect they present with any other agricultural region in the Commonwealth, you will find the sycle of crops as well understood and practiced, as in any part of the world, wherever wages rule at the same rate. They seek to learn the truth of an experiment before it is adopted, and whilst they are conscious that many operations upon the farm may be more effectual in results, yet the question of expense is often an evidence of the inutility arising from it. What avails the increase of products, if the cost thereof exceeds the profit? Men of unlimited means may amuse themselves by every suggestion that theory presents, but the soil is expected to remunerate the husbandman, or else his labor is bestowed in vain. Let it not be said that there is an aversion to improvement, since so much is expected by inventors and patentees, that it would require more than a farm is worth to yield a trial to all the projects they choose to offer.

In agricultural pursuits it is better to be cautious of innovations than to be led away too hastily by every suggestion that finds its way in print, from an irresponsible source. If the cardinal virtues of the husbandman, industry, temperance, economy and prudence are wanting, he looks in vain for success or prosperity from any quarter, experimental or practical. The sooner he closes his account current with our good and benign Mother Earth, the better it will be for him and posterity, for men cannot "gather grapes of thorns, or figs of thistles." Usages, honored in memory, have mostly answered a good purpose, as the custom of looking into the almanac for a propitious sign, at least establishes a time and a season for work, if even the moon has no influence upon the operation. Too much attention to the mechanical labor cannot well be exerted upon land. Every stone that can be removed, adds to the facility of working it; and if it could be afforded, spade culture is known to be more perfect and successful than any other, because the regular pulverization of the whole is more complete than by any other method. The fertility of a soil must be repaired, not only by proper ploughing and hoeing, that it may be subjected to atmospheric influences, but it must also be fed with such substances as afford nutriment to vegetation. This is done by manure. Whilst science has shown that there are many sources from which the manure heaps may be replenished, there has as yet been no denial of the value, nor has any substitute been preferred to the old fashioned modicum, commonly known as barn-yard manure. This has been, heretofore, the main reliance of farmers, and when applied abundantly, has never been known to fail. Yet, the inventions of concentrated manures, such as can be purchased at a reasonable price, and possess fertilizing qualities, is a powerful aid to those who have not the opportunity of procuring a better restorative to a worn-out soil.

The water or moisture in barn-yard manure is generally four-fifths of the whole, so that the expense of labor for every twenty tons upon the field, embraces the item, sixteen tons of water. These twenty tons, it is contended, are not more efficacious than five hundred pounds of super-phosphate of lime. It is an excellent excitement to the growth of clover, which in this part of the country has always been considered the chief support of a good system of husbandry. Various other chemical inventions are found in the market, but the super-phosphate of lime, made of bones dissolved in sulphuric acid, to which is added ammonia, seems to bear the palm of merit. Another recent invention of adding dried blood to super-phosphate of lime, in order to nitrogenate it, is spoken of. Whether the potash, ammonia, lime, magnesia, chlorine, phosphorus, sulphur and soda, which may be wanted, can be thus supplied, is questionable. From my own experience, the super-phosphate of lime, although an excellent renovator, induces the growth of smut and ergot, in the excess of free phosphoric acid. Public attention for some time has been directed to guano, as likely to prove an invaluable adjunct to revive fertility. The interest of the national debt of Peru is paid by the sale of this article alone. Such is its wonderful effect, that they have a proverb, "although guano is no Saint, it performs many miracles." It is supposed in the present year the exports of guano to all ports, may reach three hundred thousand tons, paying to the government of Peru twenty dollars per ton, or six millions of dollars profit. Of this amount, the United States receives about one hundred thousand tons, being an increase of ninety-five thousand tons over the first shipment in 1845. There are other guano deposits elsewhere, but of inferior quality. Owing to the great demand for this article, English and American merchants, ever on the alert, by advances and loans to Peru, have obtained peculiar privileges in the trade, until at length the price has reached the exorbitant sum of fifty-four dollars per ton. At such rate it ceases to be remunerative to the farmer, as the crop will be absorbed by the expenses incident to it. Efforts are making by the United States to have the price reduced, but thus far negotiations have failed. Peru owns the islands from whence it is taken, and which in fact are but the roosts of sea birds. As it never rains there, the dung accumulates, which, together with the spray of the sea, and the refuse of dead birds and garbage, form this invaluable compost. The States of Maryland and Virginia have chemists specially authorized to investigate every lot that arrives, so that purchasers are assured of the quality they acquire.

The following very valuable compound, or artificial guano, has met with great favor in Virginia, and may be prepared at a cost of fifteen dollars per ton:

Poultry dung	10	bushels.
Mould from pine woods	10	do.
Fine bone dust	3	do.
Ground gypsum	3	do.
Nitrate of soda	40	pounds.
Sal ammoniac	22	do.
Carb. ammonia	11	do.
Sulphate of soda	20	do.
Sulphate of magnesia	10	do.
Common salt	10	do.

Dissolve No. 5, 6, 7, 8, 9 and 10 in water sufficient therefor, and then add the whole together as if making mortar, putting in the gypsum last. Keep in a dry place, covered so as to exclude the air until used. This will answer for six aces of land.

In this region, the abundance of anthracite coal dust may be considered an excellent means of assisting the fertility of the soil, particularly when composed of clay. Owing to its black color, it absorbs heat to a greater extent than clay, and acts mechanically, in rendering the soil arable, loose, and permeable to the air. It contains ninety per cent. of carbon, and frequently traces of sulphur; the latter is always subject to the action of the atmosphere. Although the carbonic element may be too concrete to be soluble in water, yet the usual action of the weather tends to promote decay, which is also hastened by the coal being a large absorbent of water. What is mineral anthracite, was once living plants, that abstracted carbon from the air, which, by burning, or the slower atmospheric decomposition, is returned again to be appropriated to the uses of vegetation.

To rely upon artificial manures as a universal remedy for wasted soils, is to elongate the suggestion with the same enthusiam that Homeopathy asks its followers to take occasional doses from the fragrance of an empty vial.

To deny the value of mineral manures, as lime and gypsum, would run counter to the judgment of every practical observer; and in view of their admitted efficacy, are there not other minerals that might be advantageously applied to the soil? Phosphorus, that enters largely into the material of crops, is equally important with lime and gypsum. Every one hundred bushels of wheat contains sixty pounds of phosphoric acid. It occurs in the fossiliferous rocks below the coal formation, yet, as a component part of minerals, it is rare. From its scarcity among minerals, and the great requirement that some plants have for it, the phosphate of lime deserves a fair trial. The reason that guano answers so good a purpose, is, that like barn yard manure, it contains all the elements that promote the growth of plants.

One of the most powerful and simple means of saturating the ammonia of manure, or of fecal substances, is sulphate of iron, which is abundantly found in every coal mine of your county. What is commonly known as *sour water*, so deleterious to steam boilers, is the diluted mixture of sulphuric acid, iron and water, which, if evaporated to dryness, would form the copperas of commerce, an article of great use in coloring processes. If applied to the dunghill, it will combine with the ammonia and convert it into a fixed salt, that would thus be saved. The numerous topics to which the husbandman yields his attention, such as ploughing, rotation of crops, selection and treatment of seeds, soiling and fattening cattle, harvesting, irrigating and draining, are constantly subject to his closest investigation. There is no department of his pursuit that can be neglected, and every day's experience teaches him the truth of poor Richard's maxim, that

"He who by the plough would thrive,
Himself must either hold or drive."

Although it seems a paradox, yet he will find the art of draining has at last been applied, as well to dry lands to induce moisture, as it was at first supposed to be beneficial only to such as are wet. He must also establish such rules of discipline as will be most profitable, and by which his economy is regulated. If it takes more than five pounds of corn meal to make one pound of beef, or three and a half pounds to make one pound of pork, the cost is greater than the profit. The choice of live stock, their habits and qualities, require earnest consideration. The Devon or Middle horned cattle, essentially the same with those of Sussex, Wales and Scotland, are deemed to be the native breeds of Great Britain. Time and care have brought them to such perfection, that they are standard models throughout the world. Our common stock originated from thence, and may, by similar care, add greatly to the value of domestic herds. Choose, for instance, from your alpine districts the best cow that can be found, and place her in the pastures of your valleys; assume as a guide to her selection that seven quarts of milk make one quart of cream, or twenty-one pounds of milk produce one pound of butter, and you will then have good ground upon which to base your most sanguine endeavors. The supply of food, and the best form in which it is given, are of primary consideration, and it is scarcely necessary to add, that poor stock well attended may excel the best that is neglected. From wool culture in this part of Pennsylvania but little profit can be realized. It takes one ton of hay to make fourteen pounds of wool, in addition to which the losses from disease and accidents are numerous, because of all animals the sheep is the most defencelss and inoffensive. Sheep require clear ranges, that the wool may not be disturbed by the undergrowth and thicket. In Schuylkill county such ranges are rare, but all the mountainous and uncleared portions, would be well adapted to the rearing of that most despised animal, the goat. It is so singularly constituted, that it prefers the neglected wild to the most cultivated fields, and delights in browsing upon the boughs and barks of trees, whilst in winter it is contented with the dried leaves of the forest. Its milk has more consistency than cow's milk, keeps sweet a longer period, and is also richer in caseous matter. Its flesh, properly prepared, is not inferior to venison, and whilst its hair possesses but little value, its skin is known everywhere in the shape of kid gloves and morocco shoes.

The fact that the goat will thrive where sheep will not, entitles this animal to more notice than it has hitherto received. With all the attractions of interest that surround the farmer, the most skillful efforts remain unfruitful without favorable seasons. Besides the rust and smut, new enemies of the insect species are becoming formidable. For rust and smut there appears to be no certain prevention, it being a parasitic fungus which insinuates itself into, and diseases the plant, but for the ravages of insects there should be some remedy. The wheat midge has been destroyed in a degree by burning Orpiment, a mixture of sulphur and arsenic, before sunrise, or after sunset when the plant commences to flower. Care must be taken not to inhale the fumes. A simple remedy, is to carry strong lights around the field when the night is dark. A greater cure for this evil would be, to stop the war of extermination now constantly being waged against the feathered tribe. If this amusement were confined to mere birds of prey, or to those which inhabit the sedgy margins of our lakes and rivers, or delight in sporting their graceful forms upon the summit of our rock-bound mountains, it is probable that the order of nature which assigns them food in their secluded haunts, would keep them from being considered of great consequence. But the wanton and indiscriminate slaughter of the minutest warbler that nestles in the cottage eaves, of the numerous and innocent birds that guard your orchards, and watch the destroyers of your grain crops, is a barbarity unworthy the dignity of a sportsman. What a trophy it is, for a stalwart specimen of humanity to while away all the antecedents of his moral and social qualities, in exchange for the life of a harmless sparrow. There is a sympathy in every heart, which renders us feelingly alive to the pains and sufferings of the humblest object of animated nature. It was this sympathy that caused an act of Parliament in the days of Charles I, "against the cruelty of plough- ing by the tayle, and pulling wool off living sheep." Now every act of cruelty has a tendency to extinguish the sentiment of sympathy, and stifle the feelings of tenderness and benevolence. If a child be early trained to such exhibitions, the vicious propensity grows into a habit, and his sensibility even to human suffering, will be proportionally diminished. The torturer of a kitten, or the murderer of a bird, will, by degrees, become unrestained from positive acts of violence towards his own species, whenever goaded thereto by the influence of interest or passion. Upon this foundation crimes are soon erected, until at length, grown callous to every social and moral im- pression, he closes his profligate career by the prepetration of a deliberate murder. Is it a wonder that the corn worm revels, or the wheat midge swarms, or the caterpillar clusters, in untold myriads, when the race of birds that feeds upon them is almost extinct ?

The emulation which societies, like yours, inspire, is conducive to the public good, and in all your public exhibitions there is something to be learned, for which those who promote them may be congratulated. Knowledge is becoming so universal, that the complications of civil government vanish before it, and what were once known as the learned professions, will be less distinguished through the general diffusion of public education. What nobler pursuit remains than agriculture, as a source of study and employment! The day cannot be far distant, when the plough will be the first instrument with which the scholar may diversify his exercises, as it surely must become the only reliable basis upon which a free government can be maintained. It is a vast field of con- templation, in which all are interested to ascertain whether we can keep up the proper condition of the soil to afford sufficient food for the wants of an increasing population around us. Let this inquiry be fairly investigated. The fate of empires may be read in its detail, and memorials of former gran- deur be gleaned from crumbling relics upon a desert waste.

SOMERSET COUNTY.

*First Annual Report of the transactions of the Somerset County Agricultural
Society, made March 26th, 1855.*

The Somerset County Agricultural Society was organized in April, 1851,
but did not succeed in holding a fair until October 13th, 1853, which continued three days. The utility of a fair was doubted by many, but it met
with unexpected success, and greatly encouraged its friends to persevere in
their efforts. We would only remark, that this enterprise, the first of the
kind in this county, perhaps like many others elsewhere, had to encounter
serious difficulties. Indeed, it was pronounced an experiment, and many
stood aloof from an active participation, quite confident of witnessing a failure.
The clear and satisfactory result of this experiment, to such was a great
wonder. But these difficulties have been measurably overcome, and the establishment of an Agricultural Society in Somerset county can no longer be
considered an experiment ; our farmers and mechanics will awaken to a just
and comprehensive view of its general importance, as well as to their unquestionable personal interest in its final success.

The officers for the year 1854, were,

PRESIDENT—David Husband.
VICE PRESIDENTS—Peter Meyers and Isaac Kaffman.
TREASURER—John O. Kimmel.
CORRESPONDING SECRETARY—Christian C. Musselman.
RECORDING SECRETARY—Alexander Stutzman.

A Concise Statement of the Proceedings of the Society during the past year.

The society have purchased for fair grounds about four acres of ground, for
the sum of four hundred and fifty dollars. It is located in the borough of
Somerset ; it has been enclosed with a substantial board fence seven feet high.
Three very convenient and comfortable buildings have been erected on the
ground, together with a music stand, one office, one refreshment tent, a sufficient
number of stalls and pens built for stock on exhibition, together with a course
or horse ring for exhibiting horses, with a stand in the centre for the judges.
A good well has also been dug. All these improvements, together with the
cost of the ground, have been made at a cost of about one thousand three hundred and sixty-one dollars. Our second fair was held on these premises on
the 5th, 6th and 7th days of October last.

The address was delivered in the Court House on the evening of the first
day of the fair by J. S. BLACK, the Chief Justice of Pennsylvania, and is herewith presented :

ADDRESS.

Gentlemen of the Agricultural Society:

Of course I am not expected to give you any instructions in the details of practical agriculture. If I were competent to such a task, this is not the occasion to execute it. An essay on the breeds of cattle, or the genealogy of horses—on the process of making butter, the composition of manures, or the cultivation of particular crops—would, at present, be out of place and out of time. My purpose is broader, if not better, and more general, if not more useful. The duty assigned to me will be done if I lay before you a few of the facts and reasons which tend to establish one most important truth, namely: That the art which you profess is in a condition which needs, and will most amply repay, a vigorous effort to improve it.

When those who belong to a particular profession hear themselves addressed by one whose life has been devoted to a different pursuit, they take his advice reluctantly, or not at all. They believe as far as they please. It is so much easier to *talk* than to *do*, that an outsider can never speak as one having authority. But I do not know why you should not take a suggestion, or listen to a remonstrance, let it come from whom it may. There is nothing at all suspicious in the fact, that a merchant or mechanic, a physician, minister, lawyer or judge, takes a deep interest in your business. It is their misfortune that they do not follow it; for most of them would if they could. The taste for agricultural employments and rural scenery is almost universal. The cultivation of the earth is the only trade which God ever commanded any man to exercise; and it seems to have been a part of the divine economy to surround it with attractions. Our natural organization is fitted for the country, and not for the town. The human eye is so formed, that it rests with pleasure on green and blue, and cannot indeed, endure any other color for a long time without injury. Our sense of sight is never so much delighted, because never employed in a manner so congenial to the nature of its organ, as when we look upward into the clear blue of the heavens, or abroad upon the green earth. When man was entirely blessed he was placed in a garden—not merely a patch for cabbage and potatoes, three perches square and closed in by a paling fence—but comprehending grounds of vast extent and boundless magnificence, adorned with flowers and enriched with fruits. Hill and dale, forest and fountain, shady walks and sunny slopes, rich fields and verdant meadows, with four great rivers rolling through them, made a landscape, such as no eye has ever seen since the fall. It was here, that Heaven and all happy constellations shed their selectest influence on the marriage of our first parents. Imagination has never painted a scene of perfect happiness without similar surroundings. Scenes of idyllian beauty form the principal feature in the heaven of every religion, whether true or false. The Elysian fields of the Greek mythology, and the Paradise of Mahomet, are ready examples. The land which flowed with milk and honey was, to the Jew, a type of that better country, to which he should go after his journey through the wilderness of life was closed. And many a Christian, when his soul recoiled from the dark stream of death, has felt his courage revived by the assurance, that

> "Sweet fields beyond this swelling flood
> Stand dress'd in living green."

Other occupations are followed for the wealth and fame they produce, but agriculture is crowded with amateurs, who pursue it for its own sake; and thousands feel the same desire, whose narrow means forbid them to indulge their wishes. When Cincinnatus abandoned the leadership of the mightiest empire in the world, to hurry home and finish his ploughing before it got too late in the season, and when Washington retired from the Presidency, to cultivate his farm, they both yielded to an inclination as common as it was natural. The praise they have received for it, is a thousand times greater than they deserved. The passion for fame, for wealth, or for power, does undoubtedly predominate in some persons; but love for the simple pleasures of a county life is seldom extinguished in any sane man's mind.

These natural tastes, however, do not account for all the solicitude, which is felt for the prosperity of agriculture. Our interest in it is marvelously quickened by the fact that our bread depends on it. It is the art preservative of all arts. Its success lies at the foundation of the general welfare.— The fruits of the farmer's labor supports the industry of all other classes. The ultimate reward for every species of toil must come directly or indirectly from the earth, that common mother,

> "Whose womb immeasurable, and infinite breast,
> Teems and feeds all."

But though it be true that agriculture is the most useful, as well as the most attractive, of all pursuits, it is equally undeniable, that it has advanced more slowly than any other towards the perfection of which it is believed to be capable. Speaking comparatively, it can scarcely be said to have advanced at all. In every thing that aids commerce and manufactures, improvements are made, which have changed the whole face of human society. Those interests are projected forward into the future, with a force which overleaps centuries, while agriculture creeps on with the slow pace of the hours. In other departments ingenuity and skill have supplied the place of labor, but the hard toil of the husbandman has not been perceptibly lessened, nor his profits in any striking manner increased. Even the useful improvements that have been invented are slowly and suspiciously accepted. No class of people in the world, except lawyers, are more reluctant, than farmers, to change an old mode of procedure for a better one.

This has been seen and felt, as a great misfortune, by those who are determined to mend it if they can. They do not believe that there is any inherent difficulty in the nature of the subject, which should make the progress of agriculture less than that of other branches of industry. Scientific men and practical men—men who think, and men who work—are every where giving their attention to this, as the greatest of human concerns. If the effort be successful, those who aid in it will earn a title to public gratitude, such as no conqueror ever won with his sword.

One of the forms which this movement has taken, is that of Industrial Exhibitions. The great shows at the Crystal Palaces of New York and London may have done some good. It is certain that the State Fairs have been exceedingly beneficial. But county exhibitions, when they become general, will be fairly worth all others put together; because their effect and influence come directly home to the business and bosoms of the very persons, by whom alone the cause must be carried through. It is on the local societies that the chief reliance is placed. I trust, that the day when an Agricultural Society was formed here, will be an era, on which your memories, and those of your children, will love to linger.

To make the society useful, it is necessary that we should be as nearly unanimous as possible. We must disarm hostility wherever we find it, and rouse the indifferent to active exertion. We may reasonably hope, that what we see and hear on this occasion will contribute something to that end.

I do not see how any man can withhold his assistance from you—much less how any one can oppose you—unless he belongs to one or other of the four classes, which I am about to enumerate.

1. There are men who think that agriculture is wholly incapable of any improvement whatsoever. With them farming is farming, and nothing more; knowledge cannot do it better, nor ignorance worse; the business is now, and was when Adam left the garden of Eden, in as perfect a condition as it ever can be.

2. Others believe that though much more might be known, it is not best that they should know too much, especially about their own business. In their opinion the tree of knowledge continues to bear a forbidden fruit, and no man can make himself a perfect fool except in one way, and that is by being wiser than his father.

3. Those who belong to the third class assert, that agricultural societies are not the fit and proper means of spreading among the people the knowledge which they admit might, and ought to be communicated in some way.

4. The fourth set are almost too contemptible to be mentioned. They bear to the country the same relation that hardened sinners do to the church. They don't care. You may convince them that this cause is a good one, and still its success would give them no pleasure, its failure no pain. Such people never regard any thing beyond their own most immediate and most selfish interests.

It would be an insult to this assembly to suppose that it contains a single person of the description last mentioned. I do not believe it does. It will be sufficient therefore for all present purposes to show, that great and very desirable improvements may be made in agriculture by means of agricultural societies.

Improvement—what do we mean by that word? An art is improved simply by the use of more science in the practice of it. I know very well that the mention of scientific farming suggests to many minds the idea of a *model farm*, conducted on fanciful principles, by some soft-handed gentleman, with plenty of money and not much common sense—a place pleasant enough to look upon, but very expensive—absorbing annually from other sources of the owner's income, three or four times as much as it produces. But this is not what I mean. The improvements I speak of are those which will lighten labor and swell the profits; improvements which can be measured by the increased value of your land, and the additional number of dollars in your purse at the end of each year.

The earth is a machine with certain powers, which are in constant motion during the summer season, carrying on the process of vegetation. Like other machines, it is liable to get out of order. It also resembles other machines in the fact, that the value of its products depend mainly on the skill and care of those who attend it. Badly managed, it turns out bad work, in small quantities, and its powers are speedily exhausted. With more skill it will yield larger and better products, with less labor and expense, while its capabilities will become greater by use. The knowledge necessary to keep this grain and fruit making machine running to the best advantage, is agricultural science.

If you relied for a living on a water mill or a steam engine, you would not be content without knowing as much about its structure, and the laws of its motion, as would enable you to get the most out of it with the least wear and tear. This would be mechanical science.

Science is the handmaid of art. The latter cannot exist, even in a rude state, without the former. I do not say that every artisan is bound to comprehend the whole theory of his trade. But he should know—or, at least, he should not refuse to know, the practical results of other people's experience as well as his own. Very little is done in this world by mere force. Blind labor swells its muscles, and strains its nerves to no purpose. The miner digs in vain, until geology tells him the position of the treasure he seeks. The dyer cannot make his colors adhere, unless chemistry furnishes him a mordant. Optics must teach the painter the law of perspective, before his picture will stand out on the canvass. The vessel of the mariner will float at random, until he learns from natural philosophy that the magnetic needle points to the pole.

It is thus that science aids us in the commonest business of life, and scarcely claims the work as her own. Star-eyed and glorious as she is, she disdains not the humblest employments. She comes to you with benevolence and truth beaming from her face, and offers her service, not only to decorate your houses and train the flowers in your garden plots, but to fashion your implements, to compound your manures, to sow and gather your crops—to relieve you, in short, from a whole world of drudgery, and to scatter plenty all over the smiling land. She will put time and space under your command, and pour out uncounted heaps of treasure at your feet. It was of her that Solomon spoke, when he said: "Her merchandize is richer than the merchandize of silver, and the gain thereof greater than fine gold. She is more precious than rubies, and all thou canst desire is not to be compared unto her. Length of days is in her right hand, and in her left hand riches and honor."

Without science, man, the ruler of this world, would be the most helpless of all animated beings. His Creator made him the monarch of the earth, and gave him dominion over it, to govern and control it; to levy unlimited contributions upon it, and convert every thing in it to his own use. But he found himself at the head of a revolted empire. All its physical forces were in a state of insurrection against his lawful authority. The inferior animals were his enemies. The storms poured their fury on his unsheltered head. He was terrified by the roar of the thunder, and the lightning seared his eyeballs. He was parched under the hot sun of summer, and in winter he was pierced by the cold. The soil, cursed for his sake, produced thorns and thistles. The food that might sustain his life grew beside the poison that would destroy it, and he knew not how to distinguish the one from the other. The earth hid her minerals deep in her bosom, and guarded them with a rampart of thick-ribbed rocks. The rivers obstructed his passage; the mountains frowned their defiance upon him; and the forest spread its gloom around him, breathing a browner horror upon the dangers that beset his way. If he left the dry land and trusted himself to the ocean, the waters yawned to engulph him, and the tempest came howling on his track. He seemed an exile and an outcast in the world of which he was made to be the sovereign. But Science comes to rescue the powerless king from his misery and degradation. Gradually he learns from her the laws of his empire, and the means by which his rebel subjects may be conquered. From age to age he accumulates the knowledge that clothes him with power and fills his heart with courage. Step after step he mounts upward to the throne which God commissioned him to fill. He holds a barren sceptre in his hand no longer. Creation bends to do him homage. The subjugated elements own him for their lord, yield him their fealty, and become the servants of his will. The mine surrenders its treasures; the wilderness blooms around him like a new Eden; the rivers and the sea bear his wealth upon their bosom; the winds waft his navies round the globe; steam, the joint product of fire and water, becomes his obedient and powerful slave; the sunbeams are trained to do his painting; the lightning leaps away to carry his messages; and the earth works with ceaseless activity to bring forth whatever can minister to his gratification.

But the whole of his empire has not yet been entirely subdued. The richest portion of it—the agricultural region—has been much neglected; and there he has won but a partial supremacy. Science is organizing an "army of occupation" to march into it—to take complete possession—to tame the rebellion of Nature, and to bring all her powers under the absolute sway of man, their imperial master. You will volunteer for the war, when you think how much has been effected in other departments by similar expeditions. The fight is not to be dangerous, nor the result doubtful. At the worst, you will only be annoyed for a while by Ignorance and Error, these savage, but not very formidable bush-fighters, who will hang upon your flank and rear. The victory, which must come, will crown you with laurels, bloodless, but green with an everlasting verdure, and load you with spoils to enrich you and your children in all coming generations.

Every one knows that this is an age of progress. No one is so ignorant as not to know, that in modern times the laws of nature have been revealed with a fullness, and defined with a precision, unparalleled at any former period. It is equally well known, that these discoveries have been used, with prodigious effect, in all the arts, except agriculture, to which they are applicable. The facts and figures, which mark some of the capital points of this progress, will not be inappropriate; for I repeat, that Science stands ready to do for you all that she has done and is doing for others.

A single steam engine now carries, at the rate of five hundred miles a day, the same quantity of goods which, forty years ago, it required seven hundred and fifty horses to haul, at the rate of fifteen miles a day.

In the business of weaving, one man now does, with ease, what it taxed the hard labor of twelve hundred to perform before the invention of the power-loom.

All sorts of manufactures are carried on in ways so much superior to those which were used, even one generation ago, that goods of every description are furnished to the consumer very much cheaper, and many of them at less than one-tenth of their former price; and this, although the demand has been enormously increased, and the profits of the manufacturer are much greater than ever.

Macaulay says, that in the reign of Charles II—not farther back than twice the length of an old man's life—a letter sent by mail from London to one of the midland counties of England, where it would go now, in four or five hours, was as long in reaching its destination as it would be at this day in going from London to the interior of Kentucky.

A man may start from here, cross the Atlantic, visit every capital city in Europe, and return home again, in less time than used to be required for a trip to St. Louis.

The means by which those who "go down to the great sea in ships," have brought their art to its present state, is an illustration, as striking as any that could be given, of the practical use which has been made of scientific discoveries. It is an old tradition, that the first idea of navigation was suggested to the mind of an ingenious savage, by seeing a hollow reed, which had been split longitudinally, floating on the water. He took the hint, and made himself what, in western phrase, would be called a "dug out." In process of time, oars were added. Then came a more complicated vessel, with sails to more and a rudder to guide her. In this, a bold navigator would venture from headland to headland, keeping one eye carefully on the shore and the other on the clouds. At length they learned, from the old Chaldean shepherds, how to steer by the stars. With this little knowledge of astronomy they went far away from land, though it became wholly useless just at the time it was most needed—when the skies were over-clouded and the tempest came out on the deep. Navigation stood still at that point for thousands of years, because it was believed (as some farmers now believe of *their* art,) that it was already too perfect to be improved. But see what modern discoveries have brought it to. The mariner now leaves the port of his departure, with a serene and steady confidence in his resources. Astronomy, natural philosophy, optics, magnetism—the whole circle of the physical sciences—and numerous instruments, contrived with the most exquisite mechanical skill, are all at his command. He can measure his rate of sailing exactly, and knows the course he is on with absolute certainty. When he is a thousand miles out, if he doubts the accuracy of his reckoning, he is able to correct it. He lifts to his eye a tube, fitted with glasses, through which he can see far out into illimitable space—many millions of miles beyond the reach of his unassisted vision. He ascertains the relative position of some awfully distant world; and thence, with the help of his chronometer and his nautical almanac, he calculates his longitude. Another observation with a different instrument, upon another celestial body, gives him the means of finding his distance from the equator. Combining these two results, he puts his finger upon a spot in the chart, and says, with undoubting confidence, "I am precisely there." Geography tells him where to steer his vessel for the port of her destination, and how to avoid all the dangers that lie between. He holds her head to the true course, and fearlessly stretches away over the dark blue waters, and they bear him onward like the horse that knoweth his rider. When to this is added the power of steam to propel him, it may well be said that he has conquered both wind and wave. Fire may consume his vessel, or an iceburg may shatter it; but the ordinary perils of the sea are reduced almost to nothing.

Our all-wise Creator has endowed us with no faculty in vain. He permits us to discover no useless truth. Some, which appeared the most unpromising and barren, have borne the richest fruit. A nameless philosopher, somewhat more than three thousand years ago, was handling a piece of amber, called in his language *electron*. He saw, that when it was briskly rubbed, it had the power of attracting and holding to it certain light substances. He thought it was endued with some kind of animal life. This satisfied him, and no better explanation of the marvel was given for several centuries. Yet there was the germ of that science, out of which arose the Voltaic pile, and the Galvanic battery, whose powerful interrogations of nature have compelled her to yield up the most important secrets of chemistry. Still no one dreamed of the identity of lightning and electricity; and Franklin's letter suggesting it, was read in the Royal Society at London amid roars of laughter. Neither philosophers nor unlearned men could believe that the crackling noise, produced by rubbing a cat's back, was caused by the same agent which "splits the unwedgeable and gnarled oak." But Franklin quietly drew it down from the cloud along the string of his kite, and he knew that his name was linked forever with the grandest discovery of the age. It was immediately turned to practical account. In every part of the civilized world iron rods arose above the houses, and pointed towards Heaven, to catch the lightning and lead it away. Franklin had accomplished for all timid people, what Macbeth desired for himself, when he wished, that he might

> --Tell pale hearted fear it lies,
> *And sleep in spite of thunder.*

But the end was not yet. The great triumph of the amber science was still to be achieved. You see it now in the vast system of electric wires distributed all through the country, along which the "sulphurous and thought-executing fires," go flashing with intelligence, wherever they are sent by the will that controls them—bearing the news of life and death over mountain, and lake, and river, and valley—clearing thousands of miles at a single bound. By means of this amazing instrument, the eloquence of the statesman thrills in the nerves of the people at each extremity of the nation, almost as soon as it is uttered at the capitol; the friend at one side of the continent takes counsel with his friend at the other, as if they stood face to face; and the greeting of the far off husband leaps in an instant to the heart of his wife, and makes the fireside of his distant home glad with the knowledge of his safety.

Science has extended her dominion even over regions which seemed to be entirely ruled by the fickle sceptre of Chance. Life is proverbially uncertain; yet nothing can be truer than the life tables of an insurance company, when its officers desire to make them so. The destiny of each human individual is hid in deep obscurity—shadows, clouds, and darkness rest upon it, and conceal it from every eye except the All-seeing One. But disease and mortality do their work on large communities by general laws. The average duration of life, and the average amount of sickness, in a nation, can be counted beforehand with perfect accuracy. Thus, while the individual man is a mystery to be solved by Omniscience alone, man in the aggregate is reduced by his brother man to a mathematical problem.

We dare not boast of much improvement in law or politics. Indeed, they seem to be growing worse. While other things are rising, they have a fatal proclivity for the downward track. They darken with error in the full blaze of surrounding truth. But medicine has advanced with magnificent strides. Life is much longer, and health far better, than it used to be. When the cholera came to London in a form so frightful that every one was appalled by the report of its ravages, the mortality was not greater than it had been at the healthiest times a hundred and fifty years earlier. Truly did Solomon say, that wisdom has length of days in her right hand.

What the trade of the Mississippi and the Hudson was before steamboats—what the manufacture of cotton was before the days of Arkwright or Whitney—what ocean navigation was before the invention of the compass—what land traveling was before railroads—what medicine was when a patient was steamed for the small-pox—such is agriculture in the present stage of its progress. It will not have its due until it is up, at least, to their present condition. There is a certain amount of skill and science applied, every day, to the working of this machine, which we call the earth. It would be as wise to forget all that, as to learn no more. He, who has a race to run, is not surer of losing the prize, when he turns upon his tracks, than when he stands still in the midst of his career. To look back, over the ground already traversed, will be an incentive to the work, which is yet to be accomplished. If something has been done in the dark time, that is long since past, what may we not hope for with the sun-light of modern civilization beaming on our path? It may startle some of you, and sound in your ears like a slander to tell you, that you are all scientific farmers. It is true, nevertheless. That knowledge, whether it be much or little, which comes from experience, remembered and arranged so as to be ready for use when wanted, is science.— There was a time when it did not exist at all, in any degree. When we reflect how high we are placed by the little we have, above those who had none, and what a struggle it must have cost somebody to introduce it at the beginning, we shall appreciate its value, and, perhaps, make an effort to get more.

Let your imaginations carry you back to the time when agriculture was in its infancy—before the earliest dawn of Greek civilization. In those days men depended principally upon the chase for a living. They ate the flesh, and clothed themselves with the skins of wild beasts. Fruits and other vegetables of spontaneous growth added to their luxuries, in summer. They were not long in discovering one fundamental law of nature, namely: that seeds deposited in the ground would grow, and produce similar seeds in larger quantities. But they knew nothing of the difference between one soil and another. They preferred the poorest, because it was easiest cleared and, lying higher up on the ridges, it needed no draining. Here they made holes in the ground with sticks, and dropped the seeds a few inches below the surface. The rest was left to nature. If such cultivation gave them a two or three fold crop, they were lucky. It happened much oftener that its growth was choked with weeds, or that it met with some other evil chance, by which

"The green corn perished e'er his youth attained a beard."

The planting and gathering were left to women and children; the men despised such work, as being inconsistent with their honor and dignity. Hunting and fighting were the employments, in which they found pleasure and glory, as well as food and clothing. But there was one man among them more thoughtful and observant than all the rest. He had watched the unfolding vegetation, from the sprouting of the seed to the maturity of the fruit, with a keen perception of the whole marvelous and beautiful process; and he devoted his attention to the rearing of useful grains, with a pleasure, which he had never felt in the excitement of the chase. He discovered the proper season for planting; he noticed that weeds were unfriendly to the growth of his crops; he found that mixing certain substances, such as ashes and decomposed leaves, with the soil, would increase its productiveness; he learned that stirring the ground about the roots of a plant would make it thrive more rapidly; he even got himself a kind of hoe made, by some cunning worker in iron. Here was a philosopher, whose intellectual stature rose high above that of his fellows. Being a patriot also, and willing to do good for his countrymen, he conceived the thought of persuading them to quit hunting and win a surer living from the earth. At his request, they assembled under the spreading oaks, to hear his plans; and this was the first agricultural meeting—1 will not say the first on record, for I do not know that it is recorded—but certainly the earliest you ever heard of. The sage unfolded his new science to them, proving it, as he went along, by the facts of his own experience. The chase, he said, was a precarious business at best, while agriculture would be a sure and steadfast reliance. He told them that he himself, with the moderate labor of his own hands, had gained in a single season, what would sustain life longer and better, than all the spoils taken, during the same time, by the best ten of their hunters. This, he asserted, was true of an ordinary season, but sometimes the game disappeared entirely. His voice grew deeper, and its tones had a melancholy impressiveness, as he described the sufferings endured by them all, when they, the strong sons of the wilderness, with their wives and children, became the prey of gaunt famine and wide wasting pestilence. He concluded by promising that long lives of wealth and contentment should repay them for a general devotion of their labor to the cultivation of the earth.

No cheers followed the speech, but, on the contrary, hoarse murmurs of disapprobation came up from the multitude, swelling by degrees into loud opposition. The new measure was attacked with all those shallow sophistries—those miserable fallacies, so hollow and truthless—with which conservatism arms her ignorant votaries. That solitary defender of truth was overwhelmed by the sort of arguments which are sometimes re-produced in modern political meetings and legislative bodies. Some accused him of a deep design upon their liberties. Some declared that he had opposed the nation in its last quarrel, and was, in fact, no better than a traitor. One set knew him to be unsound in his religious faith, and brought all the prejudices of superstition into the field against him. Others charged down upon him with a whole army of "illustrious ancestors," whose opinions, they said, were not like his. Others still there were, who could see no objection to the man or the measure; but this was not the proper occasion—the time was out of joint. A portion of the crowd saw, in their much wisdom, that to quit hunting would enervate their frames and make them a race of cowards. Most powerful of all, and most profoundly wise in their own conceit, was the party who declared they would never consent to the enormous sacrifice of property required by such an innovation. They had invested a large capital in bows, and arrows, and spears, and traps, and knives, and these would all be useless if their future occupation was to consist in tilling the ground. There was one mighty man there, a blacksmith, who had gained great consequence, and earned innumerable skins, by making the weapons which were used in killing the beasts of the forest. He thought his *craft* was in danger, and he objected to agriculture for the same reason that Demetrius, the silversmith, afterwards opposed Christianity. He put an end to all discussion by uttering a catchword, with just enough of no meaning in it to make his friends unanimous. He lifted up his big voice and cried out, " Great is Diana, the goddess of the bow and the patroness of hunters." The whole assembly in full chorus echoed the cry, and there was a great uproar. They would have stoned their prophet, for the sight of his meek countenance and the recollection of his blameless life exasperated their wrath ; but no one proposed it, and he was suffered to escape.

This primitive apostle of agricultural science was defeated. He died in the melancholy belief that his people were destined to remain forever in barbarism. But not so. A truth had been spoken; and truth can never die. It had gone down in the shock of the first encounter with falsehood, but it was not crushed. Agriculture found an efficient champion where such a thing could least have been expected. At the great meeting under the trees there was a little girl, whose parents had both died of starvation, and her two brothers had perished in the pestilence which followed the famine. Hunger and its concomitants had carried away every relative she ever had. She was gifted by nature with a quick intellect and a kind heart, and her lonely condition had made her thoughtful and wise above her years. She listened to the words of the sage with beaming eye, and flushed cheek, and lips parted in breathless interest. When she heard a proposal to furnish bread in abundance—bread at all times—bread which would always stay the ravages of famine, whether game was plenty or scarce—it roused every faculty of her mind. She knew the whole subject by heart, as soon as she heard it explained. Henceforth she had neither eye nor ear for anything else. She gave herself up entirely to the one great task of spreading agricultural science. Every day added to her own knowledge and to the irresistible power with which she impressed it on other minds. She grew up with a lustrous beauty, which seemed more than mortal. Her elocution, though gentle and persuasive, had all the vigor which springs from enthusiasm. She swayed those rude men with an influence they had never felt before. One after the other her countrymen threw away their bows and spears, and, with hoes in their hands, came and placed themselves under her tutelage. What she was unable to teach, they learned from their own experiences mutually communicated. Soon all the hill sides were covered with rich crops of waving grain, and the heavy timber began to disappear from the bottom lands. Stately

17

houses took the place of the mean hovels which the hunters had occupied. All the beasts of the forest which could be made useful to man, were domesticated. The wild boar was captured and tamed for the sake of his flesh; the sheep submitted to the shearer; the ox bowed his shoulder to the yoke; and the mouth of the horse became acquainted with the bridle bit. The wild fruits were transplanted into gardens and orchards, and were totally changed under the influence of a careful culture. The sour grape became a delicate luxury; the useless crab grew to be an apple; the sloe expanded into a delicious plum; and a nameless fruit, resembling the bitter almond, swelled out into a peach, with surpassing richness of flavor. New implements of husbandry were successively invented. The plough, the harrow, the sickle and the scythe, each had its share in making the general prosperity greater.

Agriculture once established, became the parent of other arts. Navigation, commerce and manufactures added to their wealth. Cities rose up, filled with a refined population. The nation grew strong and powerful, and spread its dominion far and wide. The name of a Greek became synonymous with all that was great among men. Their descendants were painters and sculptors, who furnished the models for every succeeding generation: poets, whose sublime strains have been feebly imitated ever since; philosophers and statesmen, whose words of wisdom will be heard with reverence to the end of time; warriors, whose deeds made Thermopylæ and Marathon the watchwords of the free; and orators,

"Who wielded the fierce democratie at will,
Shook the arsenal, and fulmined over Greece."

They were not unmindful of the benefactress, who had given the first impulse to their high career. They assigned her a celestial parentage. Temples were erected to honor her. They believed that though her home had long been fixed among the stars, she still presided over their affairs and pleaded their cause in the Senate of the Gods. They painted her figure, as they imagined it, all radiant with supernatural beauty—her hand bearing the horn of plenty, and her head garlanded with ears of wheat. They worshipped her with all the fervor of idolatrous veneration, and for a long lapse of centuries they knew not that the labors of the farm were blessed and rewarded by a greater deity than Ceres. To this day we keep her memory alive by calling the most useful of agricultural products after her name—the *cereal* grains.

Such, we may suppose, was the transition state of agriculture—the passage from ignorance, barbarism, sloth and hunger, to systematic industry, refinement and plenty. It was only a beginning. It has been advancing somewhat ever since, though the arts which sprang from it have outgrown their parent. Numberless instruments for the saving of labor and time have been invented. Preparing the ground, sowing, harvesting and threshing may all be done now with machinery vastly improved. The character, nature and value of many products are better understood. New breeds of stock are introduced. Chemistry analyses every soil, and shows precisely what elements it needs to increase its fertility. Highly concentrated manures are imported from the most distant parts of the world, and others are manufactured at home, out of substances, which, once, were not only wasted, but suffered to reek their offensive odors on the atmosphere, and poison the health of the people.

In the days of Augustus the fields of Italy, (then the centre of civilization,) were cultivated with an instrument resembling what we call a shovel plough, only it seems to have had no shovel. The immediate predecessor of the patent plough, in use at the present time, was not much better. Most of you remember it—"a low, long, rakish looking craft," whose wooden mouldboard had to be cleaned every ten rods, and its wrought iron share and coulter taken to the blacksmith shop at least once a week.

The most important improvements yet made in agriculture have never been adopted here. A simple fact will show how much they have done for another country. Mr. Malthus, one of the profoundest thinkers of his day, calculated that the population of England would increase so rapidly, supposing its natural growth to be unchecked, that at the end of a certain time the soil would not yield a subsistence for the half of the people. For the other half starvation was the only prospect, unless a merciful Providence would kindly send war, pestilence and plague, to thin them out, and reduce their numbers to a level with the quantity of food, which they could produce. This dismal theory was believed by the foremost men in the world; and it would have been true, if the land had not afterwards been cultivated with greater skill, than before. But it turned out to be a total mistake. The population of England did increase, as rapidly as Malthus predicted; but the agricultural products of the country have increased in a ratio two hundred and fifty per cent. greater than the population. The people, who were to have been starved long ago, or else prematurely cut off by millions at a blow, are living better than ever, with two and a half times as much food for each individual, as they had when the theory was announced.

With the system of cultivation practiced now in some parts of Europe, the soil of Pennsylvania could be made to support fifteen millions of persons. There are large regions in Scotland, naturally poorer than any land we have in this county, and under a sky far less genial than ours, covered all over with crops, which the richest valleys in the west would not be ashamed of; and wheat is produced, bushel for bushel, at a less expense than it is here.

This is but the beginning of the end. All that has yet been done, is as nothing, compared to what may yet come. Hitherto agriculture has been traveling over rough roads, in an old-fashioned slow coach. She is about to take the railroad, and, with a mighty train of her sister arts, she will go sweeping along. Not being either a prophet, or the son of a prophet, I have no right to predict anything. But one of these days we may be startled by some grand discovery, which will burst upon the world like the light of a new sun. Very sober-minded men live in the hope of seeing such things. One of the most successful farmers in this State has declared his conviction, that, before long, manures will be so concentrated, that a man may carry out in his pocket handkerchief, what will enrich the land as much as a hundred wagon loads would now. This is very extravagant, no doubt, and quite as foolish as it would have been thirty years ago to prophesy of railroads, telegraphs, or Daguerreotypes. About fifteen years since a person, whose name I have forgotten, said that he knew how any plant, from the tallest forest tree to the tiniest blade of grass, could be made to grow four times as fast as it does naturally, and with almost no additional trouble. The government refused to buy his secret, though the most distinguished men at Washington, to whom it was confidentially revealed, certified their belief in it. If it be really true, it will be heard of again. It would be something to raise four crops a year, instead of one. Actual experiments have repeatedly shewn, that a plant may be made to germinate, rise above the ground, unfold its leaves, and grow to maturity so rapidly, that it seems to the beholder like magic. Electricity, I believe, is the stimulus used. A gentleman in England laid a wager, that he could raise a dish of salad, fit for use, in less than three quarters of an hour from the moment when the seeds were deposited in the ground. He tried it and won the bet. Professor Espy has proved, in a manner which admits of no denial, that even the weather may be controlled, and extensive rains be produced by artificial means. It has been done more than once, in our own State. In Florida, where the materials can be easily had, it is no uncommon thing, in a dry time, for persons to get up showers, at an hour's notice, on their own private account. Perhaps such facts as these are more curious than important. I mention them merely to show that there is something to hope for in the future, not from these things only, but others, as yet not dreamed of in your philosophy. These are but the shadows which coming events have cast before them. The wave which will bear us onward, has not reached us. But we feel it swelling beneath us, and see its lofty crest in the distance. In a little while it will lift us nearer to the stars than we ever expected to be in this life.

But how are agricultural societies to help this cause? I answer, much, every way. No great change has ever been wrought in the habits of any people without a united effort. Political principles, moral reforms, religion itself, are spread only by societies. As a bundle of sticks, tied together, is stronger than any separate stick, so is the united effort of an organized body of men, more powerful than any separate efforts which can be made by the individual members. When you have a building to raise, you do not invite your neighbors to come at different times, and request each one to take a lift by himself. In that way they might break their backs without doing you any good. The building will never go up, unless they all lift together. If agriculture is to be elevated, it can only be done by a simultaneous lift. At such a raising you can well afford to spend all the time that is required.

The emulation excited by such a society, though very important and useful in its effects, is the least of its advantages. The county societies are in communication with the State Society, and with one another. A good thought might be made to travel among them almost as fast as the telegraph could carry it, and a humbug exposed by one, need never trouble the rest. All the societies in the State are, in fact, but one; and you have the multiplied strength of all to aid you in any enterprise you wish to carry. But the great purpose they serve, is seen in these periodical exhibitions. They are the best means ever yet invented, of collecting the evidences, and satisfying the people, on the whole subject. The world is full of imposture. No man but a fool would change his mode of cultivation, or throw away his old implements for others, unless he knew that he was doing so for the better. How can he know, unless he has an opportunity of examining? Seeing is believing.— Here, all the successful experiments made in the whole county, (and many of those made elsewhere,) are annually brought together, and subjected to public inspection; and for each one of them, you have the sensible and true avouch of your own eyes. It was well said, in an address delivered here about six months ago, that we come here not to hear arguments, but to see facts, and look at demonstrations.

I ought to remind you, that the State Society is not a mere voluntary association of private individuals, but a public institution, established, protected and guarded by law. Some of you may not know, that the profits of its exhibitions have already made it rich. One of its officers told me, a few weeks ago, that it had about thirty thousand dollars in its treasury. Forty thousand more were probably added last week, at Philadelphia. It is proposed to invest this fund, or a portion of it, in the purchase of a large farm, and to establish a school there, at which scientific and practical agriculture will be fully taught; and I presume without any expense to the pupil, except the labor he bestows on the farm. Half a dozen such schools may be established, in the course of the next ten years, and it will, perhaps, be your fault, if you do not have one in this part of the State.

Every citizen has an interest in this institution—I mean the State Society. You have a legal right to be represented in its councils, and should see that you are. I do not know, or believe, that it has yet been touched by any man who is not perfectly honest. Its active members are certainly far above suspicion. But its funds are swelling rapidly, and it seems very difficult in these times, to have much treasure deposited any where, so safely that thieves will not break through and steal. Somerset county—and every son that claims her for his birth-place, or his abode, may speak it with honest pride—has never produced a public defaulter, and her people never knowingly sanctioned an act of bad faith. From the highest to the lowest of her officers, every one, for sixty years, has settled a clean account. In the glory of this enviable distinction she stands almost alone. It is fit that such a county should be well represented, wherever there is a common fund, that needs watching.

There are some other topics which ought not to be overlooked on such an occasion as this. But I have already taxed your patience more than I intended.

The future of this great country is full of exciting hope. But it depends entirely on the tillers of the soil, whether that hope shall be realized, or not. The neglect to improve our agriculture will be followed by the decay of all else that we ought to cherish, in morals and government, as well as in the arts. Mexico has gone all to pieces—the property of her people is the spoil of robbers, and their liberty the plaything of a tyrant—simply because her agriculture is half a century behind the age. But for this she would have had an independent and stable government to-day, and might have laughed to scorn the force we sent against her in the late war. A well cultivated soil produces not only grains, grasses and fruits, but another, and far more precious crop—men—men who know their rights, and dare maintain them—a bold, honest, and intelligent people—the just pride, and the sure defence of every nation.

On the other hand it startles the imagination to think what we may become in a few years, if we adopt the improvements already made, and keep pace with those which are yet to be. We have the grandest field to work upon that was ever opened to the industry of man. A territory is ours, stretching through every variety of climate and soil, from the wheat lands of New England, lying, for half the year, four feet deep in snow, to the orange groves of Texas and New Mexico, where winter never comes—valleys of unbounded fertility—mountains filled with inexhaustible wealth—lakes that spread out with a sea-like expanse—rivers, which make those of Europe seem like brooklets in comparison—everything, in short, made on a scale of magnificent grandeur. The child may now be born, whose old age will look upon the American people and see them three hundred millions strong. Suppose such a population, doubling itself every twenty-two years and a half—living under a government of equal laws—moving onward and upward, with the energy which freedom alone can inspire—and aided by the highest science in making the most of their natural advantages. Who shall curb the career of such a country, or set a limit to its deep founded strength? Milton himself never dreamed of a power so boundless, or a people so blest, even in that enrapturing vision, when he saw, "a mighty and puissant nation, rousing herself like a strong man after sleep, and shaking her invincible locks," or like an eagle "muing her mighty youth, and kindling her undazzled eye at the full blaze of the mid-day beam; purging and unscaling her sight at the fountain itself of heavenly radiance." The man, who, with his senses open to the truth, would thwart such a destiny, or refuse his aid to accomplish it, is a traitor—not to his country alone, but to the best interests, and highest hopes of the human race.

The present number of members is five hundred and sixty-eight. Very few satisfactory reports were handed in by competitors. We will only say that a great variety of stock was on hand, and some very fine specimens. The array of agricultural implements was good, and the departments of domestic manufactures and fancy articles, together with fruit and vegetables, would compare favorably with many of the older societies. Indeed, in every branch of industry, the representation was most creditable, and the admirable spirit which seems to be infused among the farmers and mechanics of Somerset county, bids fair to place our agricultural society and our exhibitions at once in the very front rank of such associations in Pennsylvania.

All of which is respectfully submitted.

CHRISTIAN C. MUSSELMAN,

Corresponding Secretary of the Somerset County Agricultural Society.

SULLIVAN COUNTY.

CAMPBELLSVILLE, SULLIVAN COUNTY, }
January 9th 1855.

To the President of the Pennsylvania State Agricultural Society:

DEAR SIR :—The friends of agriculture in this county, being desirous to have some connection and correspondence with the State Society, I embrace this opportunity to forward some of our documents.

Our county is new and small, and a great many take little or no interest in our cause. We have had three fairs, each succeeding one has been better than its predecessor.

Our annual meeting, which was held on Monday of last week, presented an encouraging scene; three or four times as many assembled from all parts of the county, than ever attended before.

Most respectfully,

RICHARD BEDFORD.

The Agricultural Fair which was held at this place on the 8th instant, was well attended. The large building on S. E. of the public square, and the grounds adjoining, were used for the purpose of exhibition. Quite a number of horses, cows, oxen, bulls, sheep and hogs were placed upon the ground, and were favorable specimens of the stock raised in the county. The weather was so unfavorable as to interfere very much with bringing in animals or looking at them. A number of large Chittagong chickens were exhibited by Dr. Taggert, and fine Shanghais, Polanders, and common fowls by B. L. Cheney, A. J. Deitrick, Chapman Baldwin and others.

The display of vegetables was extremely good. We do not remember to have seen better potatoes than those exhibited. Beets, turnips, rutta bagas, squashes, pumpkins, onions, vegetable oysters, &c., &c., were there in large quantities. Some excellent fruit was also there; but not in as large quantities as the capabilities of the county should properly supply. Honey, sugar, bread, butter, dried fruit and preserves, and many other articles of the kind were exhibited; also, flour, corn meal, grain, horse shoes, &c. We shall not undertake to enumerate the articles, but among other things were noticed a patent horse rake, that seemed well adapted for use in this county; a churn worthy of the notice of butter makers; a couple of wooden horses easily made, and acceptable, no doubt, to little boys taking their first lesson in horsemanship; and a centre-table with a standard supported by buck horns.

The room was handsomely decorated with evergreens and a large variety of flowers. Quilts of various patterns and neat work-*woman*-ship were suspended around the walls, with chair tidies, babies' sacks, needle work, carpets, cloths and the like.

Altogether, considering that it was a rainy day, the fair exceeded the expectations of the most sanguine members, and gave bright promise of the future prosperity of the society.

AGRICULTURAL FAIR.

Awards of premiums made by the Judges at the "Sullivan County Agricultural Fair," held at Laporte, on Monday, the 3d of October, 1854:

CATTLE.

Best bull, James Taylor	$2 00
Best cow, Wm. Meylert	2 00
Second best, Thomas Corothers	F. Journal.
Best yearling, Enoch Howell	$1 00
Second best, Elon Wilcox	G. Farmer.
Best bull calf, Elon Wilcox	$1 00
Best heifer calf, Lewis Zaner	1 00
Second best, Wm. A. Mason	G. Farmer.
Best yoke of working cattle, M. Meylert	$2 00
Best two years old cow, Lewis Zaner	1 00
Second best, Thomas Corothers	1,00

HORSES.

Best stallion, Thomas Anderson	2 00
Second best, John A. Hiddleson	1 00
Best pair of matched geldings, George Edkin	2 00
Second best, A. J. Dietrick	1 00
Best brood mare, John A. Hiddleson	2 00
Best pair of matched mares, James Taylor	2 00
Best two years old mare colt, Henry Bennett	1 00
Best sucking colt, John Sones	1 00
Second best, John Sones	Certificate.
Best three years old horse colt, C. H. Dana	$1 00
Best gelding for all work, M. Meylert	50

SHEEP.

Best buck, E. T. Fargo.. $1 00
Best ewes, E. T. Fargo... 1 00

HOGS.

Best boar, James Taylor... 1 00
Best sow, James Taylor.. 1 00
Second best, A. J. Dietrick....................................F. Journal.
Best four pigs, A. J. Dietrick...................................... 50

POULTRY.

Best pair Chittagongs, Dr. J. P. Taggart........................... 50
Best Shanghais, A. J. Dietrick..................................... 50
Second best, B. L. Cheney....................................Certificate.
Best pair Poland fowls, B. L. Cheney............................... 50
Best pair common fowls, C. Baldwin................................. 50
Second best...Certificate.
Largest and best collection of fowls, Chapman Baldwin............. $1 00
Second best, B. L. Cheney.. 50
Fifty-four fowls on exhibition, all of a very fine quality.

VEGETABLES.

Best peck of early potatoes, J. N. Messenger....................... 50
Second best, J. B. Hiddleson.................................G. Farmer.
Best peck of late potatoes, Lewis Zaner............................ 50
Second best, Daniel Reynolds................................G. Farmer.
Best half dozen blood beets, Wm. Reeser............................ 50
Second best, Dr. C. H. Dana..................................Certificate.
Best half dozen white beets, R. Bedford............................ 50
Second best, Wm. Meylert....................................Certificate.
Best three heads of cabbage, A. J. Dietrick........................ 50
Second best, James Taylor...................................Certificate.
Best half dozen carrots, Wm. Meylert........................G. Farmer.
Second best, Richard Bedford................................Certificate.
Best half dozen onions, Michael Meylert............................ 50
Second best, Mr. Baldwin....................................Certificate.
Best half dozen parsnips, Michael Meylert...................G. Farmer.
Best winter squashes..F. Journal.
Second best, Mr. Finch......................................Certificate.
Best summer squash, Wm. Meylert.............................G. Farmer.
Second best, Mr. Baldwin....................................Certificate.
Best sweet pumpkin, Wm. Meylert.................................... 50
Best field pumpkin, Wm. Meylert.............................F. Journal.

Second best, J. N. Messenger..................................Certificate.
Best half dozen white turnips, John Sones........................ 50
Second best, Richard Bedford...............................Certificate.
Best half dozen ruta bagas, M. Meylert....................F. Journal.
Second best, A. J. Dietrick................................Certificate.
Best half dozen tomatoes, Dr. Dana.............................. 50
Second best, J. B. Little...................................... 50
Best half dozen winter radishes, M. Meylert..............G. Farmer.
Best vegetable oysters, Dr. Dana............................... 25
Best cucumber, Richard Bedford................................. 25
Seed cucumber, James Taylor.................................... 25
Best sugar beet, Michael Meylert............................... 25
Best turnip beet, Michael Meylert.............................. 25
Sweet peppers, Enoch Howell.................................... 25
Red peppers, R. E. Shipmon..................................... 25
Best artichokes, Wm. Pryor..................................... 50
Choicest and largest variety of table vegetables, Michael Meylert..... 1 00
Second best, Richard Bedford............................F. Journal.

FRUIT.

Best peck of fall apples, John A. Speaker...................... 50
Second best, George Edkin, 2d..............................Certificate.
Best winter apples, John A. Speaker............................ 50
Second best, George Edkin, 2d..............................Certificate.
Best pears, George Edkin, 2d................................... 50
Choicest and largest variety of fruit, Geo. Edkin, 2d.......... 1 00
Second best, John A. Speaker................................F. Journal.

FLOWERS.

Choicest and largest variety of flowers, Mrs. E. Howell........ 50

DRIED FRUIT, PRESERVES, ETC.

Best peck dried apples, Lewis Zaner............................ 50
Best peck dried peaches, Mrs. Geo. Edkin....................... 60
Tomato catsup, Mrs. M. Meylert................................. 37
Apple jelly, Messrs. M. Meylert................................ 37
Currant jelly, Mrs. J. C. Wilson............................... 33
                                                              37
Cider vinegar, Wm. Reeser..................................G. Farmer.
Preserved peaches, Mrs. M. Meylert............................. 37
Preserved strawberries, Mrs. W. Meylert........................ 37
                                                              37

DAIRY, MAPLE SUGAR AND HONEY.

Best tub of roll butter, Mrs. R. Bedford.................................... $ 75
Best honey in the comb, Lewis Zaner....................................... 75
Strained honey, Wm. Reeser... 75

GRAIN, SEEDS, FLOUR AND CORN MEAL.

Best half bushel of winter wheat, L. Zaner.............................. 1 00
Second best, E. Gower,...G. Farmer
Best half bushel of rye, Lewis Zaner..................................... 75
Best half bushel of oats, Wm. Reeser.................................... 75
Best half bushel of buckwheat, Lewis Zaner............................. 75
Best flour from one bushel wheat, A. J. Dietrick....................... 75
Corn meal........................do........................... 75
Rye flour........................do........................... 75
Corn in the ear, Lewis Zaner... 75

AGRICULTURAL IMPLEMENTS.

Lumber wagon, A. C. Wilber... 1 00
Churn, H. E. Shipman... 75
Horse shoe, David Parmeter... 50
Ox shoe........do... 50
Willow basket, Frederick Smith... 37
Summer horse shoe, J. H. Shell... 50

The committee also report one horse rake, exhibited by Peter Steriger, a non-resident of the county, as a very fine implement for the use intended.

HOUSEHOLD MANUFACTURES.

Best rag carpet, Mrs. A. C. Wilber....................................... 75
Best quilt, (pieced) Mrs. A. C. Wilber.................................. 75
Second best, Mrs. H. E. Shipman... 50
Best coverlet, Mrs. A. C. Wilber.. 75
Best pair woollen socks, Mrs. J. B. Little.............................. 37
Best pair cotton socks, Mrs. J. B. Little............................... 37
Best pair woollen mittens, Mrs. M. Rogers............................... 25
Best pair woollen gloves, Mrs. J. B. Little............................. 25
Best linen thread, Mrs. James Taylor.................................... 37
Best worsted ottoman, Mrs. M. Meylert................................... 50
Best worsted head dress, Hannah Armstrong............................... 50
Best worsted shawl, Mrs. J. B. Little................................... 37
Best worsted sampler........do.. 25
Best emery ball............do.. 25
Best silk embroidered baby blanket, Mrs. A. J. Dietrick................. 25
Second best do. Miss Maria Meylert...................................... 25

Best white woollen yarn, Mrs. L. Zaner........................... $ 25
Second best, J. C. Wilson..Certificate.
Best mixed woollen yarn, J. C. Wilson...........................   25
Best chair tidy, Mrs. M. Meylert   25
Second best, Mrs. Wm. Meylert...............................Certificate.
Best boy's shirt body, Mrs. M. Meylert..........................   25
Best silk embroidered baby skirt dress, Mrs. Wm. Meylert..........   50
Best centre table, Wm. Pryor...................................   50
Best loaf wheat bread, Wm. Reeser.............................   25
Best beeswax, John Mullen......................................   25
Best soft soap, Mrs. J. B. Little...............................   25

Amount received and disbursements of Sullivan County Agricultural Society.

Amount received from members, 1852.......................... $29 50
Amount received from county tax, 1852....................... 29 50

                                                             59 00
Amount paid on premiums....................................   3 00

Balance in the treasury..................................... 56 00

Amount received from members, 1853........................... $31 50
Amount received from county, 1853........................... 31 50

                                                             63 00
Amount paid on premiums...................................   56 00

                                                              7 00
Incidental expenses..   50

Balance in the treasury.....................................   6 50

Amount received from members, 1854.......................... $27 50
Amount received from county commissioners.................... 26 00

                                                             53 50
Amount paid on premiums...................................   78 55

        The above I received from the Secretary.

                              R. BEDFORD, *President.*

ADDRESS

Of Benjamin S. Bentley, Esq., before the Sullivan County Agricultural Exhibition, October 3, 1854.

FRIENDS AND FELLOW CITIZENS :—I am here by invitation to address you to-day, and I thank you for the honor conferred upon me. I do not intend to trespass long upon your time, or go particularly into the science of agriculture, or attempt to show the best methods of cultivating particular soils, or what crops should be put upon them, or into any analytical view of the subject, though it might be pleasant for me to do so; but I will content myself by making a few practical suggestions—and if by so doing, I can present to your minds any new views, or can induce you to a more vigorous prosecution of the ones you already have, I shall be indeed happy in so doing. I feel a deep interest in the cultivation of the soil for many reasons. I spent the earlier part of my life in it. I cut down the timber, burned the fallow, piled the logs, picked up the brush, burned the log heaps, harrowed among the stumps and roots, harvested the crops, hauled stone, made stone wall as well as brush fence, ploughed the ground, burned the stumps, and in short went through with all the various processes of farming, which you all understand, and with which many pleasant reminiscences are connected. It is the most independent of all the occupations known to man, and it has seemed to me that the curse that was pronounced upon our first parents, upon their expulsion from the Garden of Eden, that they and their posterity should eat their bread by the sweat of their brow, was almost, if not altogether, a blessing in disguise. Every other occupation in the world is one of comparative dependence upon the whims and caprices of mankind. If a man don't want to go to law, he will not employ the lawyer, and he is the better off for not doing it. If a man does not like a newspaper he won't take it, even though the printer starve. If a man choose to have his wife and daughters spin and weave the wool and flax that grow upon his own sheep and upon his own soil, the manufacturers of silks and laces and broad cloths, must surrender. His occupation, like Othello's, is gone. And if he choose to show the independence of his calling by home industry, by raising and manufacturing for home consumption all that he needs, the ships of commerce might moulder away at their docks, and the sails that now whiten every part of the great waters, would disappear, no more to be filled with the favoring breezes of Heaven

I would by no means speak disparagingly of commerce and manufactures, or of any of the great and beneficial enterprises of man, or of any of the thousand lawful and praiseworthy occupations and professions in which he may be engaged. Far be it from me to do so. My object only is to show the pre-eminent independence of him who cultivates the soil. Every other man depends upon him. Every other branch of business must be suspended if he stop. He may help others and others may help him. He can live without them, but they cannot live without him. God has so designed it. He has in his wisdom and goodness impressed the stamp of honor, honesty and independence, indelibly upon the business of cultivating the earth, and drawing from her rich stores that which sustains and supports the whole human family. Nor is she fickle or unfaithful to him. If he cast into her bosom, in seed time, in due time she will yield to him the rich harvest.

I thus mention these matters, from the fact that persons, and particularly young persons, get the notion into their heads that farming is rather a small business; that in order to be respectable it is necessary for them to be a lawyer, or clerk in a store, or a merchant, or a doctor, or may be a pedler of some kind, or some kind of agent. There never was a greater mistake, and experience will most fully teach it to them. Not that there is anything disrespectable in these callings, but because the business of farming is as respectable as the best of them, and by far the more independent to man.

But there is a deep and interesting science in agriculture, and the young man who wishes to study and discipline his mind can find a wide field for its pursuits. I may make this proposition, that the science of agriculture consists, in that whereby any man's farm may legitimately be made to produce the largest of profit amount during a series of years. Not one, but many years. No universal system or infallible rule can be laid down for the cultivation of the different soils. They are various almost as the faces of men, with which we meet, and what would be good in the cultivation of one might be decidedly bad in another. And yet there are certain general rules, the application of which will not be without benefit to the farmer. Every farmer ought to know something of chemistry. It has been said to be handmaid of all sciences, and it certainly is of agriculture. Whether the farmer knows it or ever thinks of it, the earth and the atmosphere are a great natural laboratory in which a chemical process is constantly going on.

If a distiller wish to make alcohol he takes his grain and submits it to a certain process, by which some of the component parts are thrown off and others united in certain proportions and the result is an article poisonous in its nature, and instead of being like its original, wholesome and nutritious, it maddens the brain and sets on fire the blood of man. If a man wish to make putty he does not mix butter and flour together, but white lead and oil. If a woman wish to make a loaf of bread or a pudding she certainly would not mix saw-dust and water, nor even flour and water, and make the composition and let it go at that. If she were to do so her husband would certainly get the reputation of being a cross man when he should come to eat it. No, the house-keeper understands her business better than that. When she wishes to make a loaf of bread, she selects those articles that she knows will make good bread, when put together in certain proportions and in a certain manner. She takes her flour, puts in her yeast in a proper proportion, submits it to a proper degree of heat, lets it ferment to a certain extent, then bakes it. She must have everything about it right or she won't have good bread—that's certain. If she don't have good yeast or leaven enough in it, it won't rise. If she gets too much in it she will have sour or sticky bread. If she is to make the different kinds of cake or of puddings, she must take different kinds of articles to make them of and put them together in different ways or she won't succeed. She don't make apple-dumplings from turnips nor plumb-puddings from squashes. She might call them such, if she pleased, but her husband might be so inconsiderate as to fret some, and to think (if he did not speak it aloud) that she didn't know anything about her business, and that he had made a great mistake, in getting such a person to make bread and puddings for his use. But this is not so, our mothers and sisters and wives are not guilty of such folly as this. They have learned chemistry, if not from books, they have from their mothers or from nature. They have learned that certain means produce certain ends. They know that neither grease nor lie will wash well separately, and they would not think of using either of them for that purpose, and yet when they are united in certain proportions, they constitute soap, a very cleansing and health-giving article. The air we breathe is formed of two principal gases combined in proper proportions. If they were separated, as they easily can be, one of them would instantly extinguish all life, and all the fire in the world. The other would cause the least spark of fire to ignite whatever should be next to it as to soon burn up and destroy every thing in the world, not sparing the earth nor the solid metals in its very bosom, and would so exhilerate our spirits as to cause us to live years in so many hours! and yet when the two are combined they form the blessed atmosphere of Heaven, in which we live and breathe, and in which the fires do not rage and destroy, but become the useful and necessary servant of man.— I refer briefly to these things as matters of illustration. Every kernel of wheat and of corn and of every kind of grain, has its regular and well defined component parts, all put together in due and proper proportions. If you analyze fifty kernels of wheat, you will find that each one has precisely the same constituent parts, and put together in exactly the same proportions. The same in regard to every thing that grows, whether animal or vegetable; and whence do vegetables derive their component parts? From earth, air and water! The process by which they are put together, we call growing. If you wish to make leather, you feed the hides with liquor from tan-bark. You would not expect to raise corn and wheat in tan-bark. Why not? Because, although it may have that within it that will feed hides and make leather, it won't furnish the necessary food for corn or wheat.

Intuitively man, knows but little. By experiment, observation and reflection he can learn much. Why is it that New York and other cities are not now lighted with tallow candles and oil lamps as formerly? It is because men tried experiments, and in trying those experiments they found out that by combining certain articles a gas was thrown off, which would burn with a clear and transparent light, and thus at a comparatively small expense, darkness was driven from the streets and dwellings of our cities.

About one hundred years ago our own Benjamin Franklin, by a simple experiment with a kite, drew down and confined the lightnings of Heaven, and discovered and settled the great fact, that lightning and electricity are the same. Since then it has been controlled and has become the messenger of man; has annihilated space and time in conveying messages from one part of the world to others. The telegraph, steam, and a thousand other discoveries of the present age, astonish us as we think of them. And yet they are no new principles. They have existed since the world began—we only discover them—we only reach results by experiment and different combinations of simple principles. As I have said before, oil and white lead mixed make putty. How was it discovered? By experiment. We owe almost all that we have under God, to experiment. It is the great railway car, if we may so express it, that has carried the present age so far in advance of all preceding ages—that has removed the civilized and enlightened world so far in advance of the barbarian and savage state. And does not this principle apply to agriculture and the mechanic arts as well as to every thing else? How do you know, my friends, that when you plant an apple seed, that it will not produce a thorn tree?—or a beet seed, that it will not produce a turnip? Because you have learned by observation that there are certain laws of nature, that under certain circumstances will produce certain results. Why don't you plough up some poor, miserable, worn out sorrel or mullen patch, and sow it with wheat? Because you would not get any if you did. And why not? You answer that the land is worn out—it is too poor—worn out and too poor. How so, is there not soil enough there for the grain to root in? Certainly so. Have you not ploughed and harrowed it till it is smooth and mellow as an ash heap? Certainly. Then why will not the wheat grow? As I have already stated, chemical experiments have shown that every kernel of grain, every beet, every turnip, and every other vegetable that grows, is formed of definite, distinct, and proportionate parts—alike in each kind of vegetable, but differing in different ones to a considerable extent. The earth, air and water hold in them the constituent parts of these vegetables. You plant in your garden a little, rough and apparently dried up beet seed. Soon it begins to swell; presently a little root or germ starts out from it. Life is there. It begins to appropriate to itself whatever is necessary to make a beet, not a turnip, nor a hill of corn, but simply a beet; and if it does not make a large beet of itself, it will be because there is scarcity of the right kind of food within its reach. It will have its own kind, and won't take any other. If it can't have that it won't grow. If it can have it in abundance, it will grow enormously. Some beets have been known to grow to the weight of some fifty or sixty pounds each. So of all other vegetables. They all want their own kind of food, similar it may be but in different proportions. I have been told by one of your citizens, since I came here, that he had a squash vine that grew by actual measurement some twelve inches in about fifteen hours. It is very evident that that vine had an abundance of squash food within its reach, so that it could appropriate to itself just as much as it wanted, and as fast as it could eat and digest it; or in other words, compound it and form it into squash vine.

We often hear it remarked that such a country or such a piece of land is not adapted to wheat or corn. What do we mean by it? Simply this, that naturally in the soil those properties are wanting that predominate in wheat or corn, and consequently a want of that food that they require, and without which you cannot make them grow. As well can you make fire burn without fuel, as crops without their natural and necessary food. If the soil has not naturally the properties for any particular crop, you must find out what they are, and put them there, or put in some other crop. These things we learn by the looks of the soil, by experience, experiment and observation.

In this consists one of the great secrets of successful agriculture. As I have already remarked, we learn these things by observation and experiment. Without these we should make a sorry business at farming. When I was a boy at work on my father's farm, a gentleman from England purchased a farm near by. He had never been engaged in that business, and yet, he had an idea that he was going to show the farmers in the neighborhood, that they did not know much about their business. He was going to show them how to raise wheat. He summer fallowed a very nice piece of pasture, and after ploughing up the sward, he took every bit of it off, and left nothing but the soil below. He sowed his grain, harrowed it, and rolled the ground very nicely; it looked very smooth, and he was very proud of it; but when the grain began to grow, it soon showed itself to be of the small yellow kind. The life of the soil was gone in taking off the sod, and he could not cheat the crop, by giving the ground good looks. Take a Philadelphia merchant, who has always been behind the counter, and who has no knowledge of the different kinds of soils and crops, and he would be as likely to sow wheat in hemlock muck as any where else.

A strong prejudice has existed in many persons, (I hope much less now,) against what is called book farming. Now my opinion is, that the best kind of farming in the world is that which is done upon the *soil itself* by the man who " either holds himself or drives;" yet I have no doubt that great benefits have been derived from agricultural books and publications; not so much perhaps from the theories that they contain, as from their being a record of the experience and experiments of others. They may be great aid to the farmer, in making suggestions to him, and in giving him the results of many years' experience. One man don't know everything, whether about farming or any thing else; and when he thinks he has got so wise that he can learn nothing from any body else, in the language of the wise man, there is more hope for a fool than of him, for he has become *wise in his own conceit.*

But there is one mode of getting information upon this subject, which, to my mind, is beyond all others in *practical importance.* It is that which brings you together to-day, the County Agricultural Society. Its importance to my mind cannot be over-rated. I will not attempt to detail the many advantages connected with it. Neither time nor ability will permit. Each one has the benefit of his own knowledge and experience, and gives it ungrudgingly to others, while in time he appropriates that of all others to himself. The pleasure derived from meeting once a year on such an occasion as this—of congratulating each other—of renewing old acquaintances and forming new ones—is of itself ample compensation for all it costs.

But beyond this, the meeting of the society at its annual fair, is a living report of the agricultural interests of the county for the current year.

Men are learning the simple yet important fact, that it costs as much to keep a poor horse, ox, cow or sheep, as it does a good one, and that a poor fruit tree shades as much ground as a good one. They are learning that there is really a difference in the breed of animals, and that if one man can sell a cow for fifty dollars, when his neighbor can get but twenty or twenty-five dollars for his, that has cost him just as much, he begins to think that there is something more than fancy in the different kinds of stock. The quickest and most effectual way to make us learn and understand our interests, is to touch our pockets; and when one man finds out how much butter his neighbor has made from one cow, how much corn or wheat he has raised from one acre, how much wool he has taken from one sheep and how much he sold it for; when he sees the nice looking stock of his neighbor, the nice, plump and easily fattened hog, the noble plough, carriage or fast horse, he begins to reason with himself why is it that he keeps such poor animals himself, so unprofitable and so unsaleable—why his lands are so unproductive, and why he has half a crop when his neighbor, who has no better farm than he has, gets whole ones. A laudable ambition is at once aroused in him, or should be, and if there is any better stock of fruit in the county than he has, he wants to get hold of some of it; and if any body raises better crops than he does, he wants to know why. If he has any life or ambition about him, he will attempt to improve by what he sees and hears; and let me say to that man, that every thing he spends in thus doing, will be an investment that will, sooner or later, repay him the principal, with compound interest.

The society has a claim upon every member of community, upon every man and woman in your county. Make it what it ought to be. You all have a deep and abiding interest in its prosperity. Contribute to its fund; it is yet in its infancy, and needs your support and fostering care. Let ten or fifteen years roll round, and the expenses you are at in sustaining it will be but a drop in the bucket, compared with the many benefits it will be to your county. If properly conducted, the most unbelieving will have to admit the advancement of the agricultural interests, under its auspices and operations. Let no sectional interests arise, and no unpleasant rivalries be fostered; but let the good of the *whole be the earnest desire of each.* Let knowledge increase; take and read the publications devoted to the cause of agriculture; apply the principles that you glean from them to your own soil and circumstances; get knowledge from all; impart your own to all. I cannot say a more important thing to you, than to recommend your own society to you.

I had often heard of your county as being new and rough, and not inviting in surface or soil. I never visited it till now. I can truly say, that I am happily disappointed in its appearance. It is true that it is a new section and most of it, so far as I have seen, heavily timbered. The question came to my mind, why has a section of country, capable of becoming so good, remained so long in a wild state. The answer as readily came. It is because it is so far from other settlements. It has not been easily accessible from sections around you. Had a railroad, a canal or a river passed through it, instead of the wilderness, it would have been before this, converted into good farms, well covered with herds of cattle and sheep, and waving grain. But this day is not far distant. The settlements around are crowding in, the centre of the forest is broken, a settlement is commenced there, and soon from aggressions without and aggressions within, the forest must yield, and give way to the building up of churches and school houses and happy fire-sides.— It will cost labor and toil to accomplish this change, but who is happier than he who participates in doing it? I believe there is no happier people on earth than those who go into the wilderness as pioneers to chop down the trees, clear up the fallows, and change the forest into fine villages and farms. If I can judge aright, a great proportion of the lands of your county, will make fine farms, many of them the very best; some of them may have rather more stones upon them than will be convenient at first, while there is an abundance of timber for fencing. But I believe they will all be wanted. Be not frightened at them, often is it the case that the most forbidding country, in its first view, becomes the most wealthy and desirable. Look at old Massachusetts, many portions of her are stonier and rougher than any thing you have in your county, and yet she is rich, her soil could almost be covered with silver dollars by her inhabitants, and her sons are the most enterprising and happy people in the world. You have a great many natural advantages in this county. It is unnecessary for me to enumerate them, as you know them.

A thickly populated country is north and south of you, and soon you will be closed in upon, and when the day comes, which I presume is not distant many years, that a railroad shall run through some of your valleys, then what shall prevent your becoming one of the best counties in the State? I cannot see, your soil is good, your water good and abundant; and you are as pure and healthy as can be found, and you will be but a day or less from the great metropolis of the State. These things should encourage every man who has located himself within your boundaries. It is no place for idlers, but industry will surely be rewarded. There is aggression in every thing, good or evil. If a man clear up his land and then permit the bushes and briars to crowd in upon him from the outside, they will after a while drive him out, but if he keeps up an aggression upon them he will continue to drive them back into the woods till there be no longer any woods to drive them into, and he will have a fine cultivated farm. Go on and clear up your fields, draw off the stone and make good stone wall, rear your buildings, get the best stock that you can find and keep it well when you have got it, get all the knowledge you can of the nature of the different soils, and of the best means of raising the best crops thereon, interest yourselves in all the operations of your society, and give it life and vigor. How can a man be lazy and idle in a new county when there is so much to be done, and so much pleasure and profit in doing it? Where land is at so low a price, that any man may purchase sufficient to make him a farm, and which with industry will soon rise in value till it will make its owner independent. I have known many such and so have you.— But the man who is willing to idle away his hours and his days, who will let the bushes and briars hem him in, who will for years plough over the loose stones upon a small piece of ground instead of putting them into good wall, who is willing to half cultivate his land and get poor crops, who has no pride in getting good stock, who is afraid of book knowledge or of any other kind, lest he depart from the ways of his fathers, who takes no interest in the agricultural society, who is always talking about the county in which he lives, as being a hard one, and how hard he has to work, and how much better luck others have than he has, and who is always looking for some opening somewhere else, such a man is no benefit to a new county, he ought not to be in it, he is not entitled to its blessings and enjoyments. The men that are wanted are men of integrity, industry, economy and energy. There are such in every community and they ought to become living epistles and examples to all others, and be rid of them. I might go on and detail to you the many improvements of the present day in the different kinds of stock, fowls, fruit, farming utensils, implements of husbandry, &c., and the great advantages that have been derived therefrom, to individuals and communities, and the value and use of manuring, &c. But I must forbear. I have already trespassed too long upon your time and attention.

If you will interest yourselves in these matters, if you will attend your own county fair, and those of your neighboring counties, and even the State Fair, when you can and see what is to be seen, and hear what is to be heard, and compare notes with your brethren, that are engaged in the same great enterprise with yourselves, of giving to the world, the manifold comforts and luxuries she enjoys from your hands, you will soon learn the secret of agricultural success, you will soon learn that knowledge, to the farmer, is as important and as advantageous to him, as it is to the statesman, the lawyer, physician or any other class of citizens. Discipline and expand your mind, by reading, observation and experiment, and with all, be industrious and economical of your time. He that is careless and wasteful of his hours, will be of his days, and no man has ever yet accumulated his pounds, when he was careless of his shillings. It is an old and true maxim, that if we take care of our pennies, the pounds will take care of themselves. The farmer is the hope of our country, civilly, politically and necessarily. There is no station of honor or of profit in our broad land, but what is open to him and the poor boy, who may now be attending school in the log school house, in the dense forest, and who is acquiring knowledge by the light of the pitch-pine knot, by his father's fire-side. Knowledge is power, the world over, get it, and exercise it, in whatever you do. Our greatest statesmen have been our best farmers, and when they have retired from public life, like Cincinnatus of old, they have returned with pleasure to the plough. But there is one other class of our audience, to which I must briefly refer before I close. I mean the ladies. We always find them engaged in the good, if ever in the bad, it is an exception to a female rule. Their presence always cheers us, their handiwork furnishes to us a thousand things, necessary for our comfort and enjoyment. Heaven designed them to ornament beauty, adorn and bless the world. Who can select and arrange from the great "Floral Hall" of nature the beautiful bouquet, and make it an emblem of herself, but her own fair hand. In whatever is beautiful and ornamental she always excels. But this is not all, while she excels in these, she is not wanting in whatever is useful. We can often judge of the value of a blessing, by looking at the opposite and by seeing what we would be without it. Apply this rule to the case before us. Without the kindly aid and influence of woman we should soon be a nation of unshaven barbarians. What a spectacle would be presented to the world by a community of old bachelors, unblessed by the smiles and influence of woman. They would make a sorry business of living could they prosper in any thing that makes life desirable or even endurable. As well might vegetation grow and prosper without the genial influence of showers. No it cannot be, we owe our nations prosperity under God, to them. The patriotic fires that burned in the breasts of our sires of our revolution, were kindled and fanned by their noble mothers. We cannot too highly prize their aid in any of our undertakings. If we do not appreciate them in their endeavors to strew the pathway of life for us with every thing that is useful and lovely, we throw contempt upon Heaven's best gift to man. In prosperity she gladdens us with her smiles, in adversity, she is a sympathizing friend, and encourages our hearts. Upon the sick and dying bed she is always as a ministering angel to us; her devotion knows no end, she knows no fatigue, no want of rest, but the brow of the dying husband, son, brother or friend, is moistened with her tears, and his pillow is smoothed by her untiring hand. Such is woman, our co-helper in all that is good, in all that is lovely. May Heaven bless her, and man appreciate her in all her attempts to bless the world, till time shall be no more.

SUSQUEHANNA COUNTY.

To the President of the Pennsylvania State Agricultural Society:

The report of the President of the Society for the advancement of Agriculture and the Mechanic Arts, in Susquehanna county, respectfully represents:

That, while little has been done in this county, to arrest the attention, or excite the interest of farmers in other parts of the State, a steady and gradual, as well as sound and healthy improvement in almost every branch of industry, which our society was intended to foster, has been plainly manifest. Notwithstanding the severity of the drought felt by the western and north-western parts of the State, partially diminishing the fall crops in this county, several instances are reported of corn reaching seventy, and one as high as seventy-three bushels per acre. The wheat crop has been diminished by the insect "*cecidomyia tritici,*" but the Hessian fly, or "*cecidomyia destructor,*" has done comparatively little injury. We cannot say, as was reported some years since, that the latter has never been found in Susquehanna county, but it has been by no means as destructive as in less elevated regions, and many of our farmers have never yet seen it. We believe the largest crop of wheat reported to the society this season, is twenty-seven bushels per acre, and several others are stated by our members to have yielded twenty-five bushels; these were all spring wheat. A general impression appears to prevail, that we have lost the seed of the genuine Italian spring wheat. During the period when that variety was generally used, our crops were reported better than they have been within the last few years. Our oats and buckwheat have been unusually light crops, both in measure and weight, but a large surplus of both has been sent to market. Our hay crop, potato crop; our butter, pork and beef, have all yielded satisfactorily, and we have had much cause to be thankful, that in common with the south-eastern portion of the State, we have in a great measure escaped the calamity that blighted the hopes of the husbandman elsewhere. We have had an unusual proportion of fruit, and this branch of rural economy is not only rapidly advancing and obtaining more than ordinary care, but we have good reason to believe, from this year's experience, that our county is becoming gradually fitted for its production, and that its culture will soon be profitable. We have long been considered by a greatly mistaken public opinion, as excluded and debarred from fruit culture, by the peculiarities of our soil and climate, but peaches and grapes, owing perhaps to the intensity of the heat, were unusually fine, and melons of various descriptions have, with the sweet potatoes of the south, come to maturity in due season; and our root crops generally have been highly productive. We have every reason to believe, that our success in these particulars has been in a great degree owing to our better mode of culture, to increased interest in our occupations and pursuits, and to a greater degree of perfection in our machinery; but we have long felt, that unless active and energetic efforts were made by farmers generally, to introduce, perfect, and use machinery more extensively, their lives must remain what they have ever been—lives of unmitigated and unrequited toil. No portion of the masses of human society have profited less by improvements of this nature, and that portion of them who commenced the settlement of a rough and wooded country, are the longest subject to this inconvenience. We hope and believe that a change is approaching, that will relieve us more or less from this unnecessary toil, and at the same time invigorate and improve our mental energies; and while the laboratory of the chemist and the analyst can neither supercede the laboratory of nature, nor supply the place of labor and care; the discoveries of science and the inventions of art are constantly offering useful and efficient aids to our branch of human pursuits. Deep and subsoil ploughing are some of the results of improved machinery, and are constantly adding an increased and increasing interest to our business, while at the same time they increase our crops. Our ploughing match, held the day preceding our annual exhibition, has justified the opinion, that in this first and most important art of the husbandman, we are on an equality with the most favored portion of the State; and while it can hardly be expected in a new country, where stumps and rocks, until within a few years occupied three-fourths, if not nine-tenths of the surface, that perfection in ploughing should be promptly attained. We know that the northern and eastern States, from whence the bulk of our population is obtained, are as prolific in these inventions as any portion of the earth, and where the genius of our country is encouraged to offer new designs for agricultural machinery, there can be little doubt that such inventions will soon obtain a proper place, wherever the improvements of the surface justify the use of them. Nearly every improvement in the ploughs of the country has been seized upon with eager avidity, and were exhibited in great numbers on the ground; and very few farmers among us hesitate at making the expenditure necessary to test all such as they think adapted to our soil and circumstances. Our subsoil is composed, in a great degree, of what in New York is called "hard-pan," a kind of indurated clay, that most of us consider, when not too near the surface, a great and essential advantage, preventing the waste and escape of manures, and retaining moisture to an extent unknown in the south. In some localities it has prevented farmers from subsoiling their land, and this inconvenience is increased by the negligence so manifest with regard to under-draining. It is truly incredible, when the vast difference in productiveness between dry and wet land is so evident to the most superficial observer, that farmers so generally neglect this simple process. We have found however, by analysis, that this subsoil possesses a larger proportion of the carbonate of lime than the surface soil, and that when slightly mixed with the latter, and exposed for a season to atmospheric influences, it increases its fertility—it becomes more absorbent, and in every respect better fitted for the growth of cereal plants, and especially wheat. The active members of our society have accordingly strove, by both example and precept, to inculcate deep ploughing, subsoiling and draining; but in doing so, have done more to improve and ameliorate their own land, than to make an impression upon the old and less productive system of practice.

One of the means that has largely contributed to an improved culture, is the great increase of root and hoed crops. The railroads and canals have brought us gypsum and other fertilizers; gypsum has brought a vast increase in corn; corn and corn-fodder have increased our stock, and an increase of stock has of course not only increased the fertility of the land, but has added largely to the produce of the dairy, and to the production of beef for the New York market. This again leads to the sowing of turnips, beets, mangel-wurtzel, and carrots, and I feel perfectly safe in saying, that a greater breadth of land has been applied to produce these crops, in a single township, within the last year, than was to be found applied to those purposes in the whole county, ten years since. Our butter is raising both in quantity, reputation and quality, by the influx of settlers from Orange, Dutchess, and Westchester counties, in New York, and is now competing successfully with the butter of those counties, in the market where they have heretofore had a monopoly. The county is particularly adapted by the hand of nature, to the purposes of the dairyman and grazier; and when these are associated extensively with the feeding of cattle, which we hope will soon be the case, it will add greatly to the prac-tice of preparing, by higher pulverisation, and more perfect culture, for better ploughing and tillage; it increases the quantity and quality of manure, as well as the crops that may be raised with it; and it may not be amiss, in connection with these facts, to notice, that a single farmer, near the western line of the county, has this season had thirty-six head of fat bullocks, supposed to average one thousand eight hundred pounds each, from which he has partly realized, and expects fully to realize, eighty-five dollars per head. We regard this not only as an indication of improved farming, but of an improvement in the quality of our stock. Twenty-five or thirty years since the best cows in the county could be bought in the fall, for a price from twelve to eighteen dollars. There are many men now residents of the county, who own cows that could hardly be purchased for one hundred dollars each; and many in-stances could be quoted where *grade* cows have brought fifty dollars each, and two years old steers have been sold at forty dollars each. It may be that these prices are not entirely the result of an improvement in stock, but we think we can with confidence say to our young men having farms here, that emigration westward, with a view of increasing the facilities of obtaining a livelihood by feeding stock, or of enhancing the comforts of a farmer's life, by dairying, is at least a problem to be solved by much risk, if not by actual loss · Our exhibition in this department of a farmer's business, has been far in advance of that of any previous season, and we greatly doubt whether any county in the State, with an equal amount of capital, has been able to exhibit a more rapid progress.

We may, under all these circumstances, safely conclude, that our farmers are not only progressing in their system of culture, in improving the appearance and the value of their farms, and their stock, but are exhibiting more taste, and a higher sense of the advantages of combining the useful and the beautiful—the needful with the pleasing enjoyments of life, than can generally be found in new and uncultivated countries. All the mountain ranges of Pennsylvania have once exhibited a hard and forbidding aspect, enough to discourage the most enterprising and the boldest spirits; but the tenacity with which men cling to their native hills, has seldom been more manifest than within her borders. If this feeling and this spirit can be continued and increased—if an attachment to the land they have redeemed from the forest and the wilderness, can be cherished and enlarged, it may still be a prejudice, but it will be a salutary prejudice, gradually leading to horticultural as well as agricultural improvement. It is perhaps a truism that fruit can never be produced without flowers, and we may safely conclude, that when all these are judiciously combined, nature offers no higher objects for the employment of opulence—nothing better calculated to increase the *amor patria*, or to make our mountains and our valleys ring with our own glorious motto of "*Virtue, Liberty and Independence.*"

Respectfully submitted.

CALEB CARMALT,

President Susquehanna County Agricultural Society.

FRIENDSVILLE, 1 *Mo.* 1, 1853.

TIOGA COUNTY.

To the President of the Pennsylvania State Agricultural Society:

SIR:—I make herein, in brief, the first annual report of the Tioga County Agricultural Society. This society was organized September 12, A. D. 1853, by adopting a constitution and electing officers under the same. Nothing was done during the year 1853, except to organize and prepare for the coming year. In May, 1854, the Executive Committee offered and published a list of premiums, amounting to four hundred dollars, to be awarded to successful competitors in the various departments of mechanical and agricultural labor, at the first annual fair of the society, to be held at Tioga village, on the 4th and 5th days of October ensuing. The idea of a fair was almost entirely new, and much hesitancy and doubt were manifest; but the first day of the fair came around, and, to the surprise and gratification of the officers, a large concourse of people were in attendance. The articles offered for exhibition were not numerous, but were very excellent in quality. Hundreds had come to see what was to be done, and how the thing was to be managed; and when they saw, they were highly pleased, and regretted that they, too, had not become competitors. Owing to ignorance of, and inattention to our published rules, there were no written descriptions of the process of raising crops and cattle, or of the manufacture of the articles on exhibition. Our society have adopted more stringent rules for the future, in this respect, and in our next annual report we hope to furnish some interesting and valuable details. Our society have established a system of lectures or addresses, to be delivered before the members on the first Monday of May of each year, and at the annual fair to be held each year. A very able address was pronounced before the society, on the first Monday of May last, by the Hon. Andrew B. Dickenson, of Steuben county, New York; and on the 5th day of October last, at the first annual fair of the society, by the Rev. David Murdock, D. D., of Elmira, New York, printed copies of which I transmit herewith. The society anticipate a flourishing condition for the coming year, and wish to distribute, in premiums, six hundred dollars, a portion of which will be in agricultural books and periodicals. I annex the condensed reports of the Committee on Premiums.

All of which is respectfully submitted.

F. E. SMITH,
Corresponding Secretary.

Tioga, *December*, 1854.

REPORTS OF COMMITTEES.

ON FARMS.

For best cultivated farm, B. C. Wickham	$8 00
For second best cultivated farm, Ira Buckley	6 00
For best farming utensils, Ira Buckley	5 00

FIELD CROPS.

For best average wheat, twelve and twenty-seven bushels per acre, Ira Buckley	3 00
For second best, ten and twenty two bushels per acre, Richard Videan, Sr	2 00
For best one acre of corn, eighty-five bushels, I. Buckley	2 00
For best half acre of potatoes, eighty-five bushels per half acre, Benj. Van Deusen	2 00

HORSES.

Best stallion, four years old and over, Smith Stevens	3 00
For second best do., M. D. Bozzard	2 00
For third best do., P. C. Hoig	Diploma.
For best stud colt, two years old, H. W. Caulking	$2 00
For best brood mare and colt, M. S. Baldwin	2 00
For second best do., Lewis E. Cook	1 00

For third best brood mare and colt, H. W. Caulking............Diploma.

For best sucking colt, H. W. Caulking.......................... $2 00

For second do., M. S. Baldwin.................................. 1 00

For third do., Lewis E. Cook.................................Diploma.

For best yearling colt, H. W. Caulking......................... $2 00

For second do., E. J. Stevens................................. 1 00

For third do., Homer Elliott.................................Diploma.

For best three years old gelding, Thomas J. Berry............... $2 00

For second best, John Prutsman................................ 1 00

For third do., Alexander Haining............................Diploma.

For best three years old mare, D. C. Edwards................... $2 00

For second best, Abram Prutsman............................... 1 00

For third do., Joseph Aiken.................................Diploma.

For best two years old gelding, T. E. Arnold, diploma and........ $1 00

For second best, Homer Elliott................................ 1 00

For third do., John V. Swan.................................Diploma.

For best two years old mare, Horace Roff, diploma and........... $1 00

For second best, Alexander Haining............................ 1 00

For best matched horses, Joseph Fish.......................... 3 00

For second best, John Dickinson............................... 2 00

For third do., John C. French................................. 1 00

For best single horse, T. J. Berry............................. 2 00

For best single mare, Vine De Pui............................. 2 00

For second best, H. G Harrower............................... 1 00

CATTLE.

For best Durham bull, two years old and over, Ira Buckley......... 3 00

For best native bull, do., R. B. Bailey......................... 3 00

For best Durham cow, Julius Clark.............................. 2 00

For second best, Ira Buckley.................................. 1 00

For third do., B. C. Wickham...............................Diploma.

For best do., three years old, Ira Buckley...................... $2 00

For second best do., Ira Buckley............................... 1 00

For best heifer do., two years old, Ira Buckley.................. 1 00

For second do. do., C. F. Miller.............................Diploma.

For best Durham yearling heifer, J. Aiken....................... $1 00

For second best native do., A. E. Niles......................Diploma.

For best pair of matched calves, Ira Buckley, diploma and......... $1 00

For best yearling steers, B. C. Wickham, diploma and............. 1 00

For best Devonshire yearling bull, J. P. Wilcox, diploma and....... 1 00

For second best, Charles Blanchard..........................Diploma.

For best Durham bull calf, Ira Buckley, diploma and............. $1 00

For second best, B. C. Wickham............................... 1 00

For third do., Thomas Mitchell..............................Diploma.

For best native do., H. W. Caulking, diploma and............. $1 00
For best fat oxen, Wm. E. Crane............................... 3 00
For best working oxen, Henry Oldroyd........................ 3 00
For second do., Lewis E. Cook.................................. 2 00

SHEEP.

For best Merino sheep, two pair, E. T. Bently................ 2 00
For best Leicester, one pair, Ira Buckley...................... 2 00

SWINE.

For best boar, no competitor, T. L. Baldwin...................Diploma.
For good sow and pigs, no competitor, T. L. Baldwin...........Diploma.
For best sow, J. W. Guernsey.................................. $1 00
For second best, Abram Prutsman..............................Diploma.
For best litter of pigs, no competitor, D. M. Shaw.............Diploma.

POULTRY.

For pair Shanghai fowls, D. Walker...........................Diploma.
For best pair Dorking fowls, D. Walker....................... $1 00
For second best, J. Sutton....................................Diploma.
For best pair Bantams, J. Sutton............................. $1 00
For best pair Pheasants, J. Sutton........................... 1 00
For best pair Polands, J. Sutton............................. 1 00
For best pair Irish Greys, J. Sutton......................... 1 00
For best pair geese, Jefferson Sherman....................... 1 00

DOMESTIC MANUFACTURES.

For specimen of quilting, quilt four years old, Mary Whitney......Diploma.
For one pair stockings, Abram Walker ....Diploma.
For best rag carpet, H. W. Caulkings......................... $1 00
For second best, Wm. Garretson...............................Diploma.
For best quilt, C. Osmun.....................................Diploma.
For best coverlet, C. Osmun..................................Diploma.
For cradle quilt, Mrs. E. C. Goodrich ....Diploma.
For wool carpet, Miss Rachel Prutsman........................Diploma.
For wool and linen carpet, Miss Julia Elliott.................Diploma.

MECHANICAL DEPARTMENT.

For best two horse buggy, Henry Petrie....................... $1 00
For best lumber wagon, S. M. Gear, diploma and.............. 1 00
For best specimen of horse shoeing, S. M. Gear, diploma and....... 1 00
For best specimen of cabinet ware, F. Fuller, diploma and......... 1 00
For best specimen of tailoring, C. Osmun, diploma and............ 1 00
For best two horse harness, John Alexander, diploma and.......... 1 00

For best single harness, Horace Peck, diploma and............... $1 00
For best specimen of marble engraving, C. H. Fitch, diploma and... 1 00
For best churn, patent applied for, A. Sanderson, diploma and....... 1 00
For best saw and arber, L. Tabor, diploma and..,............. 1 00

FRUITS AND ROOTS.

For best peck Irish potatoes. Thaddeus Mitchell..................Diploma.
For best six heads cabbage, J. S. Bush......................Diploma.
For best six blood beets, Vine De Pui.......................Diploma.
For best six white beets, J. S. Bush........................Diploma.
For best six celery, blanched, L. Bigelow...................Diploma.
For best peck tomatoes, L. Bigelow.........................Diploma.
For best six turnips, F. Russell...........................Diploma.
For best three bunches Isabella grapes, B. C. Wickham...........Diploma.
For best three bunches Madeira grapes, Miss Julia Elliett........Diploma.
For best variety native grapes, Miss Julia Elliott................. $1 00
For best twelve autum apples, John F. Donaldson................. 1 00
For second best twelve do., J. Duryes......................Diploma.
For best twelve winter do., E. T. Bentley...................... $1 00
For second do., B. C. Wickham.........................Diploma.
For best variety of apples, three of each kind, E. T. Bentley, diplo-
    ma and.. $1 00
For second best do. do., Ira Buckley........................Diploma.
For best six Preston peaches, R. J. Guernsey................. $1 00
For best two dozen plums, Mrs. T. L. Baldwin................. 1 00
For best twelve quinces, Miss Rachel Prutsman.................. 1 00
For best two watermelons, J. Sutton........................Diploma.
For lot pumpkins, very fine, B. J. Guernsey..................Diploma.

PLOUGHING MATCH.

First premium, one quarter acre, forty-one minutes, Sim. Prutsman $5 00
Second premium, one quarter acre, forty minutes, Isaac Aspenwall 3 00

BUTTER, CHEESE AND HONEY.

For pot of butter, Mrs. Vine De Pui.......................Diploma.
For rolls do., Mrs. B. C. Wickham........................Diploma.
For kettle do., M. B. Metcalf........................... $1 00
Pot firkin do., R. Toles................................ 2 00
For best cheese, A. E. Niles............................ 1 00
For second best, Miss Julia Elliott........................Diploma.
For best specimen of honey, Davis' patent hive, C. W. Bailey...... $1 00
For second best do., Stodard's hive, N. Whitney................Diploma.

LADIES' DISCRETIONARY COMMITTEE.

Best bed quilt, Mrs. S. B. Hathaway............................. $1 00
Second best do., Miss Mary E. Purple......................... 1 00
Best specimen worsted embroidery, Mrs. C. Robinson............. 1 00
Best specimen tapestry, Mrs. C. Robinson....................... 1 00
Second best do. do., Miss Ellen A. Goodrich..................Diploma.
Best do. muslin do., Miss L. N. Lonmagnd.................... $1 00
Second best do. do., Mrs. Mecajah La Bar.....................Diploma.
Second do. do., as good as above, Miss Ellen M. Tuttle............Diploma.
Best made knit slippers, Mrs. T. L. Baldwin...................Diploma.
Best taste, Miss Ellen M. Tuttle...............................Diploma.
Best ottomans, Mrs. Henry Sherwood........................... $1 00
Best piercing, Mrs. George M'Leod..........................Diploma.
Best sewing, Miss Ellen Tuttle.............................Diploma.
Best dress hat, Miss Julia Knapp..............................Diploma.
Best preserves, pickles and catchup, Mrs. J. W. Guernsey.......Diploma.
Best two knit, two net and two crochet tidies, Mrs. F. E. Smith....Diploma.
Best worsted lamp mat, Mrs. C. Robinson....................... $1 00
Best paper lamp mat, Mrs. F. E. Smith........................Diploma.
Best plain sewing, Mrs. J. S. Bush............................Diploma.
Best needle book, Miss Sophia Guernsey.......................Diploma.
Best book mark, Miss Anna Guernsey.......................... Diploma.

A good many other other articles were offered under this class, but the persons not being members of the society were not entitled to premiums.

GENTLEMEN'S DISCRETIONARY COMMITTEE.

Four bird cages, two birds in each, Mrs. L. Bigelow..........Work on birds.
Horse net, Mrs. F. E. Smith.................................. $1 00
Two silk chair bottoms, diamond squares, Mrs. F. E. Smith........ 1 00
Single squash, weighing 65½ pounds, Mrs. Isaac Tucker........... 1 00
Specimen of drawing, Miss E. Lowrey.........................Diploma.
Specimen of drawing, James W. Morris........................Diploma.
Specimen of oil painting, J. F. Robinson....................... $1 00
Do. leather frame, J. F. Robinson............................Diploma.
Do. leather box, Miss N. A. Robinson........................Diploma.
Introducing a new variety of spring wheat, N. Whitney, of East
     Charleston.. $3 00
Model of Stodard's patent bee hive, Wm. Rose.
Bees and bee hive and honey, Davis' hive, C. W. Bailey.
Bees and bee hive and honey, N. Whitney.

AN ADDRESS

Delivered at the first Annual Fair of the Agricultural Society of Tioga county, October 5, 1854, by the Rev. Dr. Murdoch, of Elmira, N. Y.

OFFICE TIOGA COUNTY AGRICULTURAL SOCIETY,
Tioga, October 5, 1854.

At a meeting of the Tioga County Agricultural Society, held October 5, 1854, the following, among other proceedings, were had:

"On motion of John W. Guernsey, Esq., it was unanimously

"*Resolved,* That the thanks of the society be tendered to the Rev. David Murdoch, D. D., for the very able and interesting address delivered by him this day before said society, at its first annual fair, and that the President appoint a committee of three to solicit a copy of the same for publication by the society. Whereupon the President appointed Messrs. John W. Guernsey, Benjamin C. Wickham and F. E. Smith such committee."

Extract from the minutes.

F. E. SMITH, *Rec. Secretary.*

———

OFFICE TIOGA COUNTY AGRICULTURAL SOCIETY,
Tioga, Pa., October 5, 1854.

REV. DAVID MURDOCH, D. D:

SIR :—The undersigned were appointed by the Tioga County Agricultural Society, to solicit from you, for publication by the society, a copy of the "very able and interesting address this day delivered by you before said society, at its first annual fair, at Tioga, Pennsylvania."

If agreeable to you, will you please favor us with the manuscript at your earliest convenience. Yours, &c.,

JOHN W. GUERNSEY,
BENJAMIN C. WICKHAM,
FREDERIC E. SMITH,
Committee.

———

ELMIRA, *November* 1, 1854.

John W. Guernsey, Benjamin C. Wickham, Frederic E. Smith:

GENTLEMEN :—I have received yours requesting a copy of my address before the Tioga County Agricultural Society; and send it to you since you think it was calculated to promote the end for which it was delivered.

Yours, &c.,

DAVID MURDOCH

ADDRESS.

Mr. President and Fellow Citizens :—Having been in many parts of the world, and seen numerous exhibitions of the same kind as this, which has gathered such a vast company together, I consider myself somewhat qualified to express an opinion on the merits of this first agricultural fair in your county. It is therefore with sincere pleasure that I say here, that in no other county have I seen any thing superior, as a whole, to what has been shown to-day. In one chief element of utility and pleasure, I am confident none has come before you—enthusiasm. But it is not in that only, as the fruits of your fields, your gardens und your orchards, brought hither, will prove. To my judgment, the produce of your dairies is not surpassed by the far famed butter and cheese of some New York counties, while your improved breeds of imported and native stock would equal some who live more in the wide world east of you. Nor can I pass by the articles of domestic use, and ornaments, so creditable to the wives and daughters of Tioga, evincing alike their taste and industry in producing those things which add to the comfort of home, while, at the same time, a higher degree of improvement in mind and morals is promoted, by having what is useful made up in the forms of elegance, and adorned with needle work. This being the first display you have made, it certainly bids well for your industry and taste, promising fair for the future advancement of this whole region what constitutes the only real prosperity of a country.

It is not beneath the care of even a fine lady, that she puts forth her energies in adorning man and horse. " The virtuous woman seeketh wool and flax, and worketh willingly with her hands. Her husband is known in the street where he sitteth among the elders of the land. She maketh fine linen and selleth it, and delivereth girdles to the merchant. She looketh well to her household, and eateth not the bread of idleness."

These annual exhibitions, whether of a county or of a State, are indicative of progress in civilization, and therefore deserving of special encouragement. Fairs during the feudal ages were granted as privileges to certain places, as marks of royal favor, to which the merchant and the trader from distant regions came with their various wares, enriching themselves and the place where the mart was held. But an assemblage like this here to-day, was entirely unknown till the present century. In fact, there never could be an agricultural fair, as we understand that phrase, except where the people have reached a high state of cultivation, and of entire freedom.

The state of agriculture in a county, is a sure and certain sign of the condition of that people. Mental cultivation is not a more direct indication of the condition of the individual, than the cultivation of the soil is the sign of genuine progress in the possessors of that soil : others would regard an advancing commerce, the discoveries in science, or the perfection of art as the more certain signs ; but if civilization means the highest notions of living in a sodial state, the basis must be something else than commerce, or of the fine arts, without fear of successful competition. We affirm, that where the land is not generally cultivated in a country, equal to the progress made in other departments of political economy, there are no substantial grounds on which to rest our opinion concerning the real progress of the people in the art of living well. Taking our Declaration of Independence as an incontrovertible authority, where it says that "life, liberty and the pursuit of happiness are inalienable rights," then whatever advances those pursuits is what every nation should seek after most assiduously. If it can be shown that agricultural pursuits tend more than any other to the attainment of those ends, it will follow that legislation should always give a prominence to that interest over any other. No class of men should take the precedence of the farmer. No law should interfere with his pursuits, but every encouragement should be given to him, so that he *may produce the greatest amount of food from the least portion of land*, in the *shortest time* and with the *smallest injury* to the soil.

To do all that, he must have the greatest facilities in bringing his produce to the market; and new markets must be continually opening to him so that he may be incited to increasing improvement, and be bound in a community of interest with other classes who invest and speculate, and trade and carry, and legislate for the general good. The highest condition of man in society is when the whole machine goes on without jarring; each part performing its own work, and all tending to the one great end of social existence, life, liberty and the pursuit of happiness.

The farmer is not the only man in the country, but he is so essential to its interest, that as he rises or falls, so we judge of all other classes of citizens. We ask then if he holds his own in the legislative Hall, at the ballot box, in the town meeting? What place does he take in education, in religion and philanthropy? We are not so anxious as some are concerning his general appreciation of the fine arts, nor even of their general acceptance as the sure sign of advancement. We see that in countries where the most of that peculiar cultivation exists, that the people are trodden down by tyranny and priestcraft; and while we do hear, from American travelers, of the great ease, gracefulness and merry manners of some nations, we do not look upon such things as the evidence of superior cultivation, nor of greater enjoyment, than we see where stiffness and clumsiness, care and earnestness prevail. Indeed, we prefer the last to the first, where these are the result of that thoughtfulness and soberness which a responsible being should always discover. We hold that an intelligent, earnest man is higher in the scale of civilization, than a merry, thoughtless one. Still we allow that on the character of the thinker, who cultivates the soil, may be engrafted a true refinement of mind and a genuine refinement of manners. Is it not possible to cultivate both the soil and the mind of your children, so that the one shall be a support and an ornament to the other? As things are in the world, we fear that public opinion is against the idea of a man being a laborer and a refined gentleman;

19

and until that influence be removed, we fear that those things which God
hath joined together, shall still be kept asunder—the skill of the head and
the labor of the hand. All ought to work, all ought to think, if they would
enjoy a healthy body and a reasonable soul.

This is orthodox in book, and in theory, but in practice we see a different
principle put in motion. One might suppose that working with the hands was
regarded by many, and by some farmers' sons and daughters, and with others
as a sign of barbarism. See how unpopular working on a farm has become,
when all the young people of the household want to get into genteel society,
to do something else than labor on the soil. The sons want to be traders or
students, doctors or lawyers, counter tenders, or even bar tenders. Something in a village perhaps, or on a railroad; anything rather than work on
the old farm. For this reason, we see so many good farms sold after they
have been in the family for generations. The old people have no more sons
at home, and cannot work it themselves, so they sell and retire to the village
where they rust out the rest of their days; their sons off on business which
is uncertain, and their daughters trying to live in genteel society.

The regard paid for labor, and especially to agricultural labor, is a sure
sign, not only of common sense, but of the highest order of intellect, surveying the whole pyramid of society, from its base to its crowning ornaments.—
It will ever be the first inquiry of the political economist—what does this
produce? In what condition is the land? You may trace the progress of
agriculture along side of civilization. They have kept pace with each other.
The hunter's state is a condition of barbarism. Our Indian squaws did all the
farming before the Saxon race came hither, and that was but a patch of maize,
pumpkins and beans. Perhaps a small orchard here and there, but whether
these last which were most plentiful, in what is now western New York, were
imported from France or a previous cultivation cannot be affirmed. But these
wandering habits prevented their cultivation of the soil, and hence, to this
day it is with difficulty they can be trained morally, or taught the principles
of the gospel; could they become fixed in mind they would become stationary
in their abode, and that would re-act upon their mental and moral habits. A
striking instance of this is seen in the South Seas where less than a hundred
years ago Cook found them on the Sandwich Islands in the lowest state of
savage life; but now these same people are rising in the scale of moral culture; and as one of the most evident proofs, we are told that New Zealand
already exports wheat to Australia. How remarkable that the same people
who in the year 1820 were cannibals, have risen so as to live on the rich
fruits of the earth. It is also noted as an evidence of the advancement of the
Sandwich Islands that in this present year they will raise wheat sufficient for
themselves. They trusted before to the richness of their native fruits, and
having a supply for their hunger it was all they desired; but now as their
wants are increased with their increasing knowledge, they are having recourse
to the soil for a further supply.

The natural progress of agriculture is easily traced in this country. The first settlers were from older countries, and expected to till the soil; but you will perceive that the generation which immediately followed the first comers were apt to become hunters, depending on nature for their support. Daniel Boone and others like him, did nor cultivate the land, and their children sank back one step towards barbarism, being less instructed and less refined than their predecessors. They were inexperienced, and had to commence society upon a new basis, and with new implements. They girdled a few trees, scattered a few seeds, drawing over them the surface soil in the easiest manner : a heavy branch of a tree their plough and their harrow. Nor were they disappointed, for kind mother nature helped them with her showers and her smiling sun, bidding them to go on, hoping for a harvest. The first crop was abundant, and enough fell from the ears of that year to become seed for the next, and the rude farmer went on becoming comparatively well off; but he soon exhausted the rich vegetable matter that lay on the top; so he must go deeper. He must turn up the ground beneath to the air and to the light if he would reap any more fine crops. So he ploughed and had abundance for years to come ; until he exhausted all the nourishing qualities of his field. Then what must he do ? Remove to another farm which he has been preparing in some other region, leaving his first to return back to nature for resuscitation. He knows that he has been acting unjustly to the first field; but he has no time nor taste to put out labor upon the same since he can with less expense, remove to some virgin soil farther to the west. Such was the course of agriculture on all this continent till within a few years. People were few—land plenty—instruments rude, live stock thinly scattered, and manure not cared for. The choice being made of land, light in its quality because easily stirred, was as easily exhausted. Such will be the case so long as land is plenty.— When it becomes scarce in one place, or the whole country—annexation is the cry.

Such is not the cultivation of the soil. It is not doing justice to the earth, nor is it the best state for moral improvement. The people who toil and live in such a country have not yet reached that highest point which a free people may attain—shall attain in a more advanced state of cultivation. See Russia and Poland on rich grain soils half worked upon, and themselves but half civilized. They know nothing of renewing the soil. On the shores of the Walga and its tributary streams, they may be seen removing their dung heaps to the ice, so that when winter breaks up the floods may carry it away out of their sight. The same thing may be seen in Lower Canada among the French, who are so far behind their neighbors, as if they had slept two hundred years.

That the productive qualities of land in the older States of the Union are deteriorating can be known by the census taken lately. The number of acres in any one State is laid down, and the number of bushels to the acre is ascertained, and it falls short of the same production in the new States by at least one-third. The average of each acre of wheat is not over fifteen bushels in the State of New York. There was a time when it was twenty-five. Even Ohio has come down from its primitive condition. Pennsylvania occupies a place somewhat between these two States.

Such being the state of things, there is an evident demand upon the intelligent citizens of all classes; but especially on the farmer for help to the land. It would be more clamorous, only that we have such large tracts of land unoccupied; and those who have no feelings concerning the old homestead, will pull up stakes and leave for new soil. There are, however, some, we wish there were more, who have a feeling of living and dying where their fathers are buried; and they are asking what is to be done. Should this decrease continue on for years to come, till we have as dense a population as in old countries, how are all these mouths to be fed? These questions are now engaging the attention of the thinkers in the old world. Germany, France and Great Britain are inquiring how shall the productiveness of the soil be increased? What means can be employed for obtaining the largest crop in the least possible time at the cheapest rate, and with increasing benefit to the land?

This is then a most important stage in the progress of a nation, for these very inquiries concerning the means of obtaining a large amount of food for the people is making inroads upon the prejudices and customs of by-gone times. It is calling upon the great mass of men to let go their hold of past idolatries, and take a step forward on improvement. Get their attention fixed upon improving their outward condition, and you rouse up their thoughtful consideration on more important matters. As an example, take that old and general opinion concerning the necessity of all land lying fallow some time every four years, so as to recruit itself, and place beside it that notion of modern discovery, that the land may be kept in use all the time, and be getting better every year, and you startle a fixed farmer out of his slumber. Let him begin to try the art himself, and you have overcome his prejudices on many things.

Perhaps this plan of keeping the land in use all the time, and yet improving it, is the greatest discovery in agricultural knowledge in this age. We are indebted for this chiefly to the British farmer, just as he is indebted to the American farmer for improvements in his implements. The English and Scotch cultivator, instead of naked fallows, has what he calls green crops grown on the land which would be otherwise idle. To eat these green crops cattle are kept, and so manure is made. Turnips in Britain have been the great means of turning the whole of that country into its present rich condition. These do not exhaust the land like such as perfect their seed in the same year; and besides having large leaves they shade the soil, preserving it from the scorching influence of the heat, while they derive all the nourishment from the air themselves. How far the American farmer may profit from these improvements, it is for himself to say. He must consider the expense of labor, the price of land, and the difference of climate, before he can decide. One thing may be asserted here, that there is not a finer field for reform in this country than in matters connected with the farming interests; and if every town could have a model farm, where experiments could be made without injury to the individual it would enhance not only the value of real estate, but improve proportionably the moral condition of that section of country. The man of means could not do better than try new plans for the general good. For what we want chiefly is a model of farming on a more exact and systematic manner; and this cannot be till we have it in a more scientific form. This, however, like all other things, must be the result of necessity rather than of preordination. We have too much land now to require it. It is only the intelligent farmer who will look beyond the immediate wants of his family, and of his country. Let us hope that these exhibitions are indications of a general intelligence, which will put itself forward in this good work, so that the farmers of this country will look beyond the present year, using their land so as not to abuse it, endeavoring to obtain constant production without exhaustion of the soil.

The last dry summer has been severe on many parts of our country, and will naturally excite in all inquiring minds a fear lest these summer droughts become more frequent, through the changes which naturally take place in a country clearing up of its forests; the consequent drying up of those marshes, which did remain full of water on to midsummer, supplying streams, and even the air with moisture through the scorching seasons. Will these droughts become longer and more general as the land becomes bare? The only one thing we can see as a remedy for these scourges is, that the land be well and deeply tilled. Science will teach any man that the looser the particles of earth, the better the soil is pulverised, the more freely the moisture from beneath will ascend to the surface of the ground, upon the principle of capillary attraction. A piece of lump sugar put into a vessel half filled with water, will be saturated far above the water line, and let a glass be placed over a vegetable on the hottest day, and in the dryest time on a well cultivated bed in your garden, and you will see beads of dew upon it; while on the same kind of soil in your half tilled field there will be little or none. This arises from two causes; first, there is a moisture from beneath, which finds its way through a rich soil well turned up, and also because that soil is cooler on the surface than the air above, which is changed into moisture; as the hot air becomes dew on the sides of a cool pitcher on the dinner table. But leave the surface of the ground hard, it will neither let the moisture from the nether springs pass through, nor convert the hot air into dew, being itself hard and hot. This is argument enough for subsoil ploughing, and continually stirring of the ground at all seasons, except when it is so moist as to make it cohere and bake. And it is equally a telling argument in favor of draining the land in all places where the water lies underneath. How many fine meadows are all but lost to the possessor, through his allowing large spots of sour grass and unwholesome weeds to luxuriate in abundance near his door, from which they spread all over his farm; or he suffers some bog marsh to send up its unwholesome miasma, very hot, to the danger of health, when the plough drawn a few times through it each spring, would clear the whole and give him the richest field on his farm in a few years. It is a maxim well known, a little farm well tilled "is better than a large domain half gone over." This would be practiced upon more than it is, were there not so much land to the west of us. The Hollanders understand the art of draining well, and have made their own country out of the sea at vast expense; and other instances, both in the old country and in this new land, could be produced as examples of how labor has been remunerated when a little skill has been used in the exercise.

Upon this point of frequent drought in our summers, we may say that attention should be directed to irrigating of the land in valleys and on side hills by conveying the upland springs along the higher ground that the water may dribble over the meadows or cultivated fields, so as to preserve the roots alive and renew the fading leaf of the plant. This has long been known in different parts of the world. The overflowing of the Nile was but the natural irrigating of a land dry through the season. You may read in the words of the wise King who could talk upon this subject of agriculture, or of horticulture, or of live stock with the most practical of men, for he spake of trees, from the cedar tree that is in Lebanon, even unto the hyssop that springeth out of the wall. He spake also of "beasts and of fowl." He had "vineyards and gardens, and orchards," and he "made him pools of waters to water therewith the wood that bringeth forth trees." Thus antiquity furnishes us with lessons concerning the means of watering our lands in dry seasons; and these have been improved, even in countries where it is less needed than with us. Mr. Webster, who understood agriculture well, and who had great taste and pleasure in carrying out valuable experiments, watched every new improvement with enthusiasm. He saw among other things which pleased him while he was in England, a plan of irrigation which might be successfully followed here among these hills of Tioga. A little rivulet running down a valley which lay in a sloping direction so that the water could be kept in a reservoir near the top, and turned along the brim of the hill so that it trickled down on the sides. These are called water meadows; one of them which Mr. Webster saw had been ten years before so useless that the whole land could have been bought for a trifle; but though it had not been manured it became so valuable from its productive qualities that the owner would not part with it on any account. Could not the same method be used here where there are so many springs high up running through these valleys, on whose sides there are rich lands which might be made so as in a measure to be independent of all drought?

These are considerations thrown out to the intelligent farmer; all others will laugh at them, because they are either too remote from their usual methods, or because they require too much thinking and hard work to put into use.

But there is one thing which all men can understand, and which none but the most indolent practice in some degree—manuring their land. There is much yet to be learned on this subject, both as regards its real value and the best means of increasing the amount. It is not every farmer who understands that plants have to be fed as well as their cattle, and that more of it could be made were they only to take more pains. There ought to be the greatest economy used in this department. Mr. Webster says that he learned while in England, that the value of manure alone was more in amount than the profit of all the export trade of that country. We can understand from this fact alone how it is that the harvest in wheat and other grains of the past season there, has exceeded twenty millions sterling more than other years. It is to be attributed not merely to a favorable season, but also to the high feeding of the field; the extraordinary care which they bestow upon their manures, and their manner of apportioning them to the different kinds of soil. In these two branches consists a great part of a farmer's education—how to increase manure, and how to apply it. He must remember that every thing around him of a vegetable and animal nature is good for land, and he must also know that all lands have *first* a proportion of organic matter which can be dissolved or destroyed so far as it is useful to him. *Second*, that all naturally fertile soils contain eleven different mineral substances. *Third*, that where one of these is wanting, his crops will not be good. *Fourth*, that through his knowledge these differences may be added by skillful manuring; and *Fifth*, that where there is an excess of any of these eleven substances, it becomes noxious to the plant and should be in some way removed.

These results of science should be pondered over by every willing scholar on a farm; and though we do not expect much from the present generation, we hope a great deal from the young men just entering on the stage of action. Fathers and mothers must help here, by giving their children, sons and daughters, a farmer's education. Insist upon teachers giving the young a knowledge of the nature of the land on which they are to work, so that they may do justice to the soil, using it all the time, taking the largest crop off of it and making it all the time better. Chemistry, geology and botany are as easily understood as common grammar, and as useful as Latin in exercising the intellect, while they give a vast amount of useful information upon the business which the young man is to follow. To do these parts well, there ought to be experiments made before the eyes of the scholar, so that he may see for himself what makes vegetable matter—what makes an ox fat—what kind of grass makes the best butter and cheese—what kind of manure is best for corn—why lime on pasture should be put on one field and not on another. County societies ought to have a travelling professor going from town to town, during the winter months, giving lectures on these topics; and every State should have a grand agricultural college, where the highest kind of knowledge in this department might be obtained.

Does any one ask what good all this increase of trouble would be to the farmer himself, or to the country? It would be difficult to inform the man who is so ignorant of things, who would put such a question. Two objects would be gained: first an increase of food. The country would become richer in the best kind of wealth, and then the inhabitants would be better off, having, along with a sufficiency of food, time to improve their minds and their morals. Such has been the result of those discoveries in chemical science, by Leibeg in Germany, Johnston in Scotland, and Norton in Connecticut. The time is past for men now to despise book farming, as it has contemptuously been styled. The call you have made to-day upon one of another profession to address you, shows that you are willing to receive whatever science may furnish, with the view of putting book knowledge into practice.

As an example of the hints which may be furnished through the researches of the agricultural chemist, hear what he could say to the question why certain plants once grew abundantly on fields which are now barren. One of the substances essential to their growth has been exhausted, and you must supply it in some way; or there is too much of another kind, and you must counteract it by some means. The blue grass which once grew luxuriantly on clay soil, has worn out on old land; and one class of trees is succeeded by another, because the necessary substance which a pine forest required is not to be found any more on that same hill side; so the silex necessary for the corn stalk must be renewed even on rich soil; or lime must be supplied on some other field which has become exhausted of alkaline substances. A very limited knowledge of chemistry, which every boy may obtain at the common school, will show the value of a correct and systematic mode of farming.

The influence of scientific agriculture upon the welfare and civilization of a nation, must be apparent to the watchful statesman as well as to the reflecting citizen. The main pillar of the State must be here, and the moment that seems to give way the others must crumble and fall. See the present condition of commerce, and suppose that a famine had come along with the scarcity of money, and what would have been our condition? Or if Great Britain, together with her present war, had had short crops? We would have felt the effects of that even here. But Providence has saved us from a famine of bread, and given England abundance; and we hope to weather the storm of a commercial panic brought on by neglecting the land and dealing in railroad stocks; investing money in western lands instead of cultivating that which is nearer home; buying silks and velvets, brandies and fancies abroad, instead of making good home-spun to wear and home-brewed to drink. I am bound to say that if every farmer would set about making and applying the manure he could make, that it would be more valuable than all the wild land bought for ten years past, and certainly more valuable, at a price, than all the foreign trade of the United States. Thousands who are running wild after the uncertain gold of California, have neglected the real treasure to be found in a good dung heap, at their barn door.

Let farmers see in all this the folly of encouraging their sons entering into trade and merchandize. Leaving the good homestead, where so much labor has been put out and so many associations connected with it of a pleasing nature, for the chance and success of being rich and harassed to death, with the still greater probability of dying in a miserable condition. It is a fact, proved by actual calculation, that only *four out of the hundred* ever succeed in the business; and yet young men leave a certainty for such uncertainty; and sometimes fathers and mothers, out of a false notion of giving their children an easier life than they have had themselves, sell their property and invest their hard earned savings in a store, that is blown up by the next panic that comes over the commercial sky. Look round the world at the present time, and see who are the most secure in their property. Men who held their heads high, lived in fine houses, dressed in all the fine things of the foreign market, are now sunk in their own esteem and in that of the public, while the honest, industrious farmer is sitting under his own roof and at ease of mind. One year since there could be found, in almost all prosperous places, those who thought themselves rich, through some speculation, who find that their wealth has now collapsed into—nothing. His wife's velvets and furs, his daughter's piano and his son's pony, have all vanished, while the little farm of the homely farmer is there still, though his lumber wagon is all the coach he ever rode in, and his wife's spinning wheel all the musical instrument she ever had in the house, of use, except the baby's cradle; but then his ducks paddle in their own pond, and his hen's cackle in their own yard. When the once swelling merchant comes to his house, he finds that the sheriff has been there before him, while the hard fisted farmer has a home of his own, where all his happiness and his wealth are his own, and the fruit of a kind Providence who smiles upon labor and well directed industry.

It is the duty of that same farmer, however, to render his own condition and that of his family such that they will have nothing to envy when they go abroad. It is not enough that he gives his children an education which will fit them for any station in out-door life; he must make their home like the best, and up to the times in the way of comfort and refinement. The house and furniture, the field and the garden should not be merely for saving and for profit, but also for pleasure; since he is cultivating in the educating of his children a taste for the beautiful, he must allow them the chance of making their own home beautiful, and then the desire for going abroad will be less. Farmers must not live only to make rich, but to be useful citizens; and since they cannot live here always it should be their ambition to see their sons and their daughters at the head of their profession. Until we see the agricultural interest taking its high stand as one of the noblest professions in the world, there is no hope of its holding its own against the power which all other professions will bring to bear in sustaining themselves. If the farmer be not the first man in the country, it is because he is not true to himself. The ignorant farmer has ever been and will ever be the slave of the community where he lives.

WELLSBOROUGH, May 2, 1854.

Hon. A. B. Dickinson:

DEAR SIR :—Under a resolution of the Tioga County Agricultural Society, who listened with much pleasure to your very interesting address, before the society and public last evening, we are requested to solicit from you a copy for publication.

Could you consent so to favor us, you would confer a great favor upon the society and farming interests of our county.

By order of the Executive Committee.

Very respectfully, I remain,
Your obedient servant,
JOHN W. GUERNSEY.

—

WELLSBOROUGH, May 2, 1854.

DEAR SIR :—At the request of the committee, communicated in your note this morning, I cheerfully place at your disposal a copy of my address. If, in any manner, I advance the interests of the farming community, it will afford me much pleasure.

Agricultural societies are doing much good. Persevere in your efforts, and your county will soon derive great benefits from your association. With my best wishes for the success of your society, and for the welfare of the farmers of Tioga,

I am very respectfully,
Your obedient servant,
A. B. DICKINSON.

JOHN W. GUERNSEY, Esq.

———

ADDRESS

Of Hon. A. B. Dickinson, of New York, delivered before the Tioga County Agricultural Society, Monday evening, May 1, 1854.

MR. PRESIDENT, LADIES AND GENTLEMEN :—I am here by your kind invitation to address you on the important subject of agriculture, and the practical tilling of the soil. Honorable as our vocation is and as much as has been said and done, there is room for more, without falling back on stale and threadbare topics of ancient or modern times.

The inventive powers of man are only equalled by his ingenuity in constructing and bringing into requisition useful implements to cultivate the earth, and bring forth her hidden treasures to contribute to the benefit, the wants and luxuries of mankind; and to this end every farmer should study well, and know to what his soil is best adapted, and for what the God of Nature intended it, without endeavoring to change the organic law of nature itself, by laboring to raise crops which neither the soil nor climate of the country is calculated to produce. As the difference in the price of any of the staple products is small, except in the vicinity of cities for marketing, it will not as a general rule, pay any considerable portion of the expense consequent upon quarreling with the unerring and fixed laws of nature.

There are, Mr. President, many kinds of farming—fancy and practical, profitable and unprofitable, importing and exporting, of every shade and grade, all aiming at the same great end; industry, accumulation and intelligence:— And to this end New York sends to Virginia for her profoundest statesman to deliver the annual State Fair Address; 'and Indiana sends to New York for her living Encyclopedia to speak to the farmers of Indiana. Although these addresses did great credit to both the distinguished gentlemen, for the learning which they evinced and the general useful information which they imparted, yet the former never attempted to tell to what the soil in the vicinity of Saratoga is best adapted, and the latter failed to portray, with his usual eloquence, the peculiarities of the soil of Lafayette and its adaptation to congenial products, for the reason that neither knew the peculiar, natural, germinating qualities of the soil on which they stood. And here permit me to say I much fear I shall find myself at fault, or at least my hearers will find me so; but Mr. President, with your permission, I will make the attempt, although I am well aware that many, very many of the farmers of Pennsylvania whom I see around me, could much better perform this task than myself.

The soil of Wellsboro' and vicinity is better adapted to grazing than to anything else; and here let me remark that all grass countries grow rich, while all exclusively grain growing countries become poor and finally run out, unless so adapted to grasses that the soil can be renewed by their cultivation. For instance, in portions of Monmouth county, N. J., where wheat formerly grew on the original soil as well as in the best wheat growing counties of western New York, former wheat fields are thrown out to the common, and now produce nothing but fifinger and poverty grass. And yet in the impoverished state, land can be-reclaimed with lime, and made to produce good crops of wheat again, but soon runs out; in short, it costs more to renovate the land than it is worth, while so much cheap land lies idle at the west.

Although this vicinity is emphatically a grass country, it is not so certain for wheat. The system of grazing can be pursued to most advantage to the husbandman, and that after all is just the information the farmer needs, to know well the soil he cultivates. Your pastures, in my humble judgment, are best adapted to making butter and the growing of wool, more particularly butter. As the quantity of land in the United States is much less that will make good butter than that which will grow sheep and wool, there is less competition in the production of the former than in the latter, and the farmer should always choose that branch of business in which there is likely to be the least competition, other things being equal.

The first quality of butter-land is confined to portions of the New England States, New Jersey, Pennsylvania and New York, while cheese can be made and sheep grown wherever grass grows, as I will endeavor to show hereafter. First quality of butter has been worth, on an average, for the last twenty years, twenty-five cents per pound. Last year it brought, in the New York market, thirty-one; this season twenty-five cents; and when I speak of these prices I mean the very best quality that can be made which is very small, but might be very much increased. You have here all the elements for making just that kind of butter. To begin with, you must have in your pastures timothy, white clover, blue grass, red top or fowl meadow grass, which I think is one and the same thing, only differing as it grows on different soils, pure soft water, and a rolling or hilly country. All these things you have, or may have, as these different grasses will all grow well, if sowed and properly cared for; and I have never seen the first pound of good butter made, where the cow did not feed on some or all of these grasses; and it cannot be made from these until they have been sown long enough to have the soil swarded over, to protect it from the sun, frost, rain and drought. There will be then, and not till then, a solidity and sweetness to the grass that will give to the butter, that rich, sweet flavor which makes it so desirable. Butter partakes not only of everything the cow eats and drinks, but of everything offensive within its reach after it is made; as for instance, if a cow be fed on ruta bagas, her butter and milk partakes of that flavor. If she feeds in pastures where leeks, garlicks and wild onions grow, there will be a still more offensive flavor. If she feeds in pastures where she can get a bite of briar leaves, beach or apple-tree leaves, or anything of the kind, it injuriously affects the flavor of the butter, though not to the same extent, and would scarcely be perceptible for immediate use. So with red clover. Butter made from cows fed on red clover is good when first made, but when laid down in packages six months or a year, it seems to have lost all its flavor, and generally becomes more or less rancid, as the clover was of rank and rapid growth on which the cow fed. The water the cow drinks must not only be soft, but clear, living, wholesome water, fit for the use of man. If she drinks from stagnant, filthy water, it will knock off three or four cents the pound from butter, all other things being right.

In the western country, on plain or prairie, the most of the water, in dry seasons of the year, is in stagnant streams, or pools covered with a green blanket, and just in the same proportion as it is offensive to the smell or taste of man, it will exhibit itself in butter, when laid down and kept for any length of time; and yet none nor all of these things on which the cow feeds injuriously, affects the making of cheese, for the reason that the rennet necessary to form the curd, gives so sharp and different a taste, that all others are neutralized. The work of making butter is not completed when you have every thing necessary for the cow to feed on; you must provide a good spring-house where every breeze is as sweet as that wafted from the rose itself, and every thing not only cleanly, but the butter must be worked at the right time, and every particle of butter-milk must be worked out; and when that is done the working must cease. A little too much working spoils the grain and it becomes oily, and is only a second or third rate article. Salt must only be used in sufficient quantities to make it palatable, as salt is not necessary to preserve butter any more than it is to keep lard. Be sure to use Liverpool or Turks Island, as no other salt has stood the test, although Onondaga saves pork just as well, and beef and butter reasonably well for immediate use; but for keeping until the next spring, it is not so good, as its flavor is lost. Great care should be taken in selecting salt, as the manufacturers at Syracuse, have become very expert in grinding and putting up their salt in imitation of the Turks Island and Liverpool, and yet the butter when salted with Onondaga salt, after lying six months in packages, never fails to disclose the fact by a loss of two or three cents on the pound to the manufacturer.

The reason rolling land is better for pasturing than level is simply this. In the rainy weather in May and June, on the flat land the water does not drain off so soon, and the wet with the warm weather, sours, and in some instances mildews the grass, and it becomes flashy and loses its flavor, and the butter is insipid and the price falls correspondingly. The difference between first quality of butter and a common article, is eight or ten cents per pound; on a very common article, one half. I desire it to be borne in mind, the better the butter the greater the yield. It is just like brewing or distilling, the sweeter and cleaner every thing is kept, the better the yield. And now let us count up the profit of keeping cows. A first-rate cow well cared for, will make two hundred pounds of butter in a season—that is one pound a day for two hundred days, and that at twenty-five cents per pound, is fifty dollars. Her milk will make one hundred pounds of pork, worth six dollars more. We will call three acres sufficient to keep one cow a year, which is a large estimate for good grass land. This is a better business than can be done on the best wheat-land in the country, with this advantage, that every year the farmer uses his farm for grazing it is improving; if like these grass-lands in sight, they will improve at least five per cent. a year in productiveness, if properly used. I do not want to hear a farmer say that on such land his meadows or pastures are running out. I can only say to that farmer, he does not understand his business; and if he will sow one bushel of plaster on each acre of land, every year, and not pasture his meadows after mowing, neither in the fall nor in the spring, nor turn into his pastures until there is something for his cattle to eat, he will in a very few years have meadows that will average two and a half tons of hay to the acre; and one acre and a half will pasture a cow through the season, and two and a half acres keep a cow the year. In twenty years, by this system of farming, dairy lands now, would become fatting lands. And what I mean by fatting lands is where pasture is so nutritious that steers will fat in pasture, from the 10th of May until frost affects the pasture in the fall, as fast as the most skillful feeder could fatten them, on the best of hay and as much grain of all kinds as he chose to feed them. That I call fatting land. Of this quality of land there is far less than of dairy lands, and it is more scattered, yet they are the best dairy lands in the world, where the water and climate is good, and no offensive vegetable grows with the grasses.

The leek or wild onion which spoils butter, does not hurt the beef; that is to say, cannot be detected in the live animal. There is considerable fatting land in Virginia and in Kentucky, from Louisville to the base of the Blue Ridge; very little at present in Ohio, more in Indiana, a very small proportion in New England and New Jersey. In New York it is principally confined to Orange, Putnam, Dutchess, Madison, Jefferson, Tioga, Chemung, Steuben and Livingston. The limestone water is not detriment in fatting, and may be a benefit, as your State has some of the best fatting lands in the Union. Chester county stands pre-eminently high, and Philadelphia meadows are number one. They rent for the interest of three hundred dollars per acre, annually, on long leases, the occupant paying all taxes; without a building on the premises—the highest rental paid on the continent for broad acres for agricultural purposes. There, meadows and pastures were never ploughed, and they have improved in the last thirty years, as I have no doubt they will continue to do for all time to come, so as to be perceptible in the life-time of man, if used as they should be; and the time will soon come when the plough will in a measure cease to be used on the most of the uplands of this county, except for raising oats, root-crops, and corn where the land has been highly manured. Your cattle will cease to be grazing late in the fall and early in the spring, and running at large. In the winter they will be kept in the stable at night, and in the yard during the day, instead of laboring hard all day to pick up a trifle to sustain nature, destroying ten times as much by tramping up the meadows, as all they get does them good. There is nothing more destructive to your soil than cattle running over it when the frost is coming out of the ground, and yet there are some soils which this kind of treatment, so injurious to yours, would really improve. And just as with regard to the kinds of grasses you grow, those that are the very best, and I might say, indespensable for your use, would be almost as pernicious to the wheat-grower as the Canada thistle—that is blue-grass, which is, of all others the best for butter-making and fattening, not only for its nutritious qualities, but for keeping fresh throughout the season, and is less affected by frost than any other.

The red clover is the only kind of grass the wheat grower should cultivate; and that is the very kind the grazier does not want, except to sow mixed with his blue grass, timothy and red top. All these are slow to start and mature, while the clover starts quick and protects not only the soil, but the other grasses until they mature and spread, and run the clover out. But one word on the importance of having all the different kinds of good grasses mixed which grow well on your soil. We all know, when any kind is green and fresh, cattle do much better than when ripe and dried up. The kinds I have named come forward in order. Timothy is first and blue grass last to mature, and by having these mixtures you have fresh pasture through the season. One word on the subject of preparing your field for sowing the grass seed. Though ordinarily you have not much trouble in this respect, in this immediate vicinity, there are occasionally some fields or parts of fields which do not catch. The remedy for all this is, your dry land where your seed would not be as likely to grow, have your soil well prepared early in the spring, and sow it with spring rye. On the first dragging let a man follow the drag with four quarts to the acre, of each, of white clover and blue grass, rolled in plaster; then drag it all in well. Then put on a good heavy roller; and a failure will never happen if the seed is good. Sow one bushel of plaster to the acre when the rye is a few inches high. This course is only necessary in extreme cases. The reason that rye is better to seed after than any other crops that I have tried, is, it grows tall and without leaves at the bottom, while oats and other spring crops grow thick at the bottom and smother the young grass.

Your soil is well adapted to the growing of sheep and wool as it is to dairying. The growing of wool is as different a business from that of growing sheep, as dairying is from that of raising cattle. The farmer who lives near a market town, with pasture adapted to growing sheep, should keep a large sized animal; first, for the purpose of selling lambs, which, if good at ten or twelve weeks old, bring in the New York market from three to six dollars: I have sold one at nine dollars. The carcases of the dams are usually disposed of the same season, as the lambs are taken off early, and ewes get fat and are sold at an advance of two or three dollars above what they cost the year previous; therefore, wool is but a secondary consideration with the sheep grower. The Southdown is one of the best breeds for marketing. The same farmer, with precisely the same kind of land, two or three hundred miles from market, without a railroad communication to send forth his lambs and fat sheep, would keep and grow an entirely different sheep, for the reason that wool would be his object. The large sized Southdown say would weigh one hundred pounds; a common sized Saxony ewe would weigh fifty pounds; the Saxony ewe, if well kept, would shear three pounds, which would bring, if of the best quality, seventy cents a pound. The Southdown would bring forty cents the pound. The Southdown would eat twice as much as the Saxony, which would make just twice the difference in quantity. For keeping the hundred pounds of Southdown, he would receive for his wool one dollar and twenty cents; while for keeping one hundred pounds of Saxony sheep, he would receive for his wool four dollars and twenty cents—more than three times as much. It may be said by some, that large sheep will not eat twice as much as the small ones. I have only to say, that whoever will take the trouble to weigh his sheep and hay, will find the rule holds good with sheep, and the same is true of neat cattle, not with horses any more than with man.

Small sheep of the same breed shear more wool, according to their size, than the larger ones, as two small sheep have more surface than one that weighs twice as much; and therefore the smallest healthy sheep, of any breed, gives more wool, according to what it consumes, than a large one; and another great difference between the Southdown and the Saxony is, the one has a thick, tight fleece, while the other has a loose, open one. Your soil here is, I have no doubt, as well adapted to raising the best and finest grades of wool as any in the United States. The same sheep kept here, will produce finer wool, though not as much of it, than it would if kept on limestone land. The difference would be so perceptible, that a good assorter of wool could pick out and divide accurately nearly every fleece, should you divide a flock and keep one half on your soil and the other on a soil highly charged with lime.

The difference between the limestone and soft water land is very great, even in the trees of the forest. A sugar maple standing on the former will make more sugar, and of a coarser grain, than on the latter.

And with all your advantage for growing fine wool, I would not advise the keeping of the Saxony over the heavy fleece Merino, unless I know my man. In the first place, I should want to know that his horses were not shod in winter. In the next place, that he was a very industrious man, one who would rather work than play, and withal a patient man, with a wife that prefers her own fireside in winter to that of her neighbors—one who would rather receive company than visit.

If you have such a man or set of men, they can make more money by growing the finest and best wool than in any other way.

For the man that does not keep his horses shod, cannot very well spend much time sleigh-riding; and if a patient man, if one of his sheep gets poor and weak, he will feed in such small quantities as not to kill it by over-feeding, which is usually done; and if an industrious man he will see his flock at least three times a day. Every grazier should keep more or less sheep to destroy briars and bushes, and sweeten portions of his farm that needs it; and for those farmers who raise wheat, nothing is so good as sheep to prepare the field for the crop.

The breed of cows best adapted to making butter, I regard as a matter of no consequence, only that they have been bred from the best of milkers, and are the right shape, with small necks and horns, broad and straight backs, wide on the hip, with thin thighs to make room for a large bag. The same formed animal for a good milker, would, as a general rule, be the best shape for fatting.

For beef cattle, those that give the most pounds of choice meat to the quantity of poor or coarse pieces, are the best; and yet there are some cows of the very best form, that are poor milkers and worse butter makers. Every cow's milk should be tested, which is very easily done, by straining it in a perpendicular glass vessel, and letting it stand in a cool place until the cream rises. By this rule, the measurement of both cream and milk is easily made. The cow must always give a large mess of milk to be a first-rate butter maker, although some cows that give but small messes will make more butter than others that give a large mess. The first-rate dairy cow must give a large mess and be rich with cream. A cow must be well wintered and well lined with tallow, to make rich milk. A cow will make more milk and butter by feeding her back her milk after it is churned, with bran or meal; but the butter is not so good, and will not command the highest price.

I have made forty-four and one-half pounds of butter from two cows in seven days; more than three pounds each, per day. They were well wintered and were fed back not only their own, but as much other milk, as they would drink. Their average weights of milk per day, was over fifty-four pounds. They were the best out of a lot of more than two hundred dairy cows.

I think I did not add more than one half of a pound per day each in the quantity of butter, by feeding back the milk, and it was at the time when the pasture was at the very best. This extra feed would have kept this large quantity up, when the grass was not so good.

The butter was good—but not first quality, not so solid nor as highly flavored as that made on pure grass. I am thoroughly convinced that nothing that has ever been tried will make the very best of butter, except the grasses which I have mentioned. The butter made on the sweet scented vernal grass is as good as any when first made, but like that made from red clover when laid down in packages looses its flavor.

If the first quality of butter could be made from any or all kinds of roots, the Dutch would have succeeded in this, as they are, to say the least, as neat and untiring in their pains to accomplish this great object as any people on earth. Although their butter is good and brings the highest price in the London market, yet it is not of the best quality, and never brings within five or six cents the pound of the highest price of our very best butter, nor do I believe they make much, if any, of the very best butter in England. Of this however I do not pretend to know, and only speak from facts that I have witnessed in the market as a dealer and maker of butter. Last season when butter was very high, there were large quantities imported. At that time nearly all the steam vessels, purchased in the New York market, of our best butter for their own use, not only for their out, but return voyages—whilst we are exporting Southern Ohio, Indiana and Illinois butter, not worth more than lard in our markets. If the English made the best of butter, the Holland butter would not bring the very highest price in the London market, any more than in New York.

The Holland butter brings in our southern market the highest price, as one of the very dairies are shipped to Charleston, Savannah or New Orleans; as there is a great demand in New York for all the best quality of butter made, and room for more. To make this butter you must churn all the milk as well as cream, and churn it before it sours, as the sour and rancid taste in the cream can never be eradicated from the butter. A horse is the best of all animals to churn, and no matter if he churns six hours, as the milk should be churned sufficiently cool, which should be tested by a thermometer, to have the butter come solid.

Firkins, before butter is put into them, should be soaked in strong brine, then filled with sweet hay and hot water, and be allowed to stand until the water is cooled. When the firkin is filled, put a cloth all over the top, cover it over and keep it well covered with a brine made of salt, salt-petre and loaf sugar, until it is sent to market. When you have done all this, procure a tryer, and before sending to market, try every package, and if, at any time, your cows have eaten any roots, cabbage, or anything else they should not, you will find it in the butter. Go to market with your butter, and sell it yourself, and take your wife along, as she is the best judge; as ladies rarely smoke or chew tobacco, and no man that does either, can detect the finer flavor of the nicer qualities. Thousands of men and women have lived and died in good dairy countries, and never tasted a first-rate article of butter in their lives.

I said, go to market with your butter yourselves, and secure a customer; if your butter stands the test, you will not have to go the next season. The factor who handled it the last year, will be anxious to buy your butter again, as he has his customers who do not regard the price, if the butter exactly suits; and the last year's butter, if good, establishes your character as a butter-maker, and will enable you to obtain a penny or two a pound over last year's prices.

I have said the plough would nearly cease to be used on good grass lands. The older the meadows and pastures, of the better quality will be the grass, and the day is not far distant when you will mow and pasture in the same field. As soon as the stumps are out, and the stone picked up, and the fields smoothed down, that operation will be commenced. The mowing machine and reaper are destined to work a great revolution in the agricultural, as did the spinning Jenny and power loom, in the manufacturing world. By mowing and pasturing in the same field, you improve the quality as well as the quantity, your grass all becomes thick and fine, the best of which the cattle pick out, and what is left is much better than coarse hay, mown on newly seeded meadows. As pastures grow older the thicker and finer the grass.— On newly seeded timothy and clover, the stalks are hollow and coarse, and if cut ripe have but little more substance than straw. On the other hand, on old pastures treated as they should be, the sod becomes four or five inches thick; neither heat nor cold, wet nor dry, can easily prevent a fair crop.— The stalks of the different kinds of grass have nearly or quite grown solid, the red-top and blue-grass can be cut any time before a heavy frost. There is a great diversity of opinion with farmers as to the proper time for cutting hay. My experience is that coarse clover and timothy should be cut very early, for horned cattle and sheep. If permitted to stand until the seed ripens and the stalk dies, it becomes nearly worthless, while the fine grasses acquire solidity and sweetness by maturing, and becomes so thick that they rarely if ever seed, consequently no man can tell without a critical examination of his meadow, at what time it should be cut. I will only add that coarse clover and timothy without bottom, can hardly be cut too green, while timothy mixed with fine grasses which have become so thick that the timothy does not head, should stand so long as the bottom is improving more than the top is loosing. Hay should be cured well for horses and sheep, so much as not to have a particle of dust. For horned cattle, if cut as it should be, when there is no dew nor rain on the grass, it can hardly be housed too soon, and if it moulds a little so much the better.

Good hay is not only the basis of fatting, if you feed in winter, but all you need for wintering stock which is in good order in the fall. A skillful farmer can make healthy cattle grow all winter by taxing his ingenuity to see how much good hay he can manage to get them to eat; and this is the great secret of keeping stock. He who attempts the experiment as very many do, of trying to winter cattle on the least possible quantity of hay, will find himself in the end, in very much the condition of the economist who tried to see with how little salt he could winter his pork. When warm weather came, however, to his great astonishment he had not only lost his salt, but his pork. The farmer, above all others, should practice economy, but he should not starve, or even pinch his stock, or his farm, but should feed both on that which will give the best return. Grass and hay are cheapest and best for stock, and plaster is the cheapest and best renovator of your soil. One bushel of plaster to the acre would increase your pasture and hay at least twenty per cent. The higher the land the more good the plaster will do; more on the west side of your hills, than on the east, for the reason that the lands that descend in the direction from which the winds generally blow, will receive the greatest benefit from the use of plaster, which is conclusive to me that it extracts growing qualities from the atmosphere.

The skillful farmer, with a practiced eye, traveling in a country where plaster does much good, could tell from what direction the winds generally blow, with the same certainty that he could from the leaning of the tops of the trees in the forest, which is an indication that never fails. Place an Indian in the midst of your forests, in a cloudy day and he could point to the pole, with as much accuracy as if the sun was blazing forth in the heavens.

Mr. President, I have said your soil was better adapted to grazing than grain growing. I do not mean to be understood that wheat could not be raised on your soil to advantage. The dryest of your lands will grow fair wheat; but I do not regard yours as a natural wheat soil.

The farmer who raises wheat here should spare no pains or expense to secure his seed from the best wheat growing district, every year. Perfect seed sown here, of the whitest kind, would, in a very few years, if continued to be raised here, become red as hemlock tanned sole-leather, and in the middle of the head some of the berries would be of good size, and much larger than the berries at each end of the head; the berries would continue to grow less, with a larger and deeper crease in them. While wheat raised on the best of wheat lands in Monroe, Livingston, Yates and Seneca counties, would produce kernels of the same size top, bottom and centre, if well cultivated; should they sow this imperfect wheat, it would take no longer time to restore it to its original perfectness, than it did to deteriorate from its perrect state on less congenial soils; and hence the importance of using our lands for what they are best adapted, and trying to improve them so as to increase the natural crops to the largest capacity. Nothing but practical observation will give a thorough knowledge of these important truths, though science has done much in aiding, and is continuing to do, and is destined to do more.

Every farmer should take at least one good paper devoted to agriculture, of which there are many, and I know of none better than the *Genesee Farmer*, though many others are equally good. The most intelligent farmer can find much to interest, and many things which instruct, and will enable him to improve his crops and give a much richer reward for his labors. As farmers, we must read and think for ourselves, and when we are told that science can unfold the latent or germinating qualities of the earth, great care must be taken that we comprehend the chemical operation or process by which these developments are demonstrated and brought to our aid. The best chemist on earth could not tell you, if you should go to yonder wood and bring him a box of the surface earth, what germinating qualities it contained, and yet the experienced, practical farmer, could generally tell by the timber, soil and climate; and I have no doubt should that forest be cut down in February or March next, and burned in June or July, in less than ten days after it was burned, fire-weeds would be up all over, as thick as the hair on a dog, and the first frost would kill them though they had grown as high as the ceiling, and the next year, most likely, sorrel would make its appearance, and the year after, white clover; and yet neither the chemist or the practical man can find one seed of either, or tell why it is so.

There are some hidden mysteries which nature has chosen not to divulge, which have thus far baffled science and the closest observation. And now let the chemists and practical men unite in one common cause, to unlock the secrets of nature, and unfold her mysterious workings, that her gods may proclaim to an astonished world, that if man will only persevere, he shall "go on conquering and to conquer," until the hidden shall be made manifest, and the mysterious made plain to the most common understanding.

To the President of the Pennsylvania State Agricultural Society:

The second exhibition of this association, at Lewisburg, on Thursday and Friday, the 12th and 13th of October, was very encouraging, both as respects the number in attendance and the animals and products of the soil exhibited. The weather was fine, the ground and rooms were commodious, and several thousand people visited the premises, of whom from one-third to one-half, we judge, were from adjoining counties on the West Branch. Chillisquaque and Milton furnished several contributors, and very many spectators. We regret to add that our friends at Selinsgrove contributed not a thing to the exhibition; our Mifflinburg neighbors nothing also. New Berlin, where one year ago hundreds went from Lewisburg and vicinity, had *two* contributors only; and from all " Snyder county" there was but *one* contribution! Excepting, perhaps, twenty competitors, the fair was wholly a mirror of the wealth and productiveness of Buffaloe and Dry valleys, and as such was a proud day for her people.

The number of spectators, and of strictly agricultural contributions, was probably double that of last year, at New Berlin. In the departments of household and domestic manufactures, although respectable, there was perhaps no improvement over the first exhibition—a deficiency for which we cannot and will not attempt to excuse our ladies and mechanics; but in horses, cattle, grain, vegetables, fruit and dairy products, there was a most cheering advance. After the rich, large and abundant fruits we saw last week, we no longer deem Buffaloe valley deficient in at least some appreciators of the value and the facility of fruit raising.

The cabinet of the University was thrown open to public inspection, and was visited by most of those present. With a little more time devoted to arranging the various rooms of the building, it is doubtless the most commodious and attractive edifice to be found for such purposes outside of the cities.

The yard comprised two acres, enclosed by a board fence seven feet high, with hitching posts, stalls, pens, &c., conveniently arranged, and all securely guarded by two watchmen at night. The expense to the citizens of the borough for these arrangements, and the furnishing of hay, &c., for the cattle, was about one hundred dollars.

The receipts for admittance were something like two hundred dollars, and with the cash on hand and other receipts, place the society in a condition to meet every demand promptly, with ample means to enlarge her premium list materially for another year. (We may mention, that several liberal gentlemen of Lewisburg offered the society (to admit all without charge) a sum equal to the probable amount she would receive by charging for admittance; but the officers declined altering the published regulations, generally believing that the substantial interests of those most interested would, in the long run,

be best promoted by requiring from those pleased and benefitted by the exhibition, some share in defraying its expenses, instead of giving them all its
advantages, and throwing all its burdens upon a few.) The sound policy of
requiring an admission fee having prevailed, we hope may not be again waived,
however strong the plea.

On Thursday, the fair was visited by *The Continentals*, a military company
from Tamaqua, who dress in the costume of the American army of '76, and,
marching to the music of the fife and drum, they excited most stirring
thoughts of the noble men of other days.

Unfortunately, although repeatedly published, most of our citizens had
forgotten the address by Prof. Bliss, on Thursday evening, and but a small
number heard it. His remarks were entirely practical, and we wish could
have been heard by every farmer in the two counties. His points were:
deep ploughing, a guard against the evils of drought, and also against too
much moisture—the preservation of manures—and the philosophy of draining
all arable lands by means of porous pipes five feet below the surface. We
will mention one fact, to show the benefits of deep ploughing. Prof. Mapes,
near Newark, N. J., ploughs seventeen inches deep, and follows that with an
instrument which stirs the earth seventeen inches deeper still. During the
recent uncommon dry season, while the corn of Prof. Mapes' neighbors was
shrunk, dry, and the shrivelled leaves rustling in the wind, his corn, on precisely the same ground, was green, thriving, erect, and producing an abundant harvest! The philosophy of these modes of guarding against the ex-
tremes of wet and dry, was plainly but forcibly expressed; and if generally
understood and practiced, would add millions yearly to the productive wealth
of the farmers.

Considering the dryness of the past season, the prevailing sickness, and
the small circle of country from which most of the animals and products
were drawn, we confess we were agreeably surprised with the effort. Indeed,
it is looked upon with almost unallowed pleasure by all, mingled with a hope
that another fair, at the same place, and that soon, may tend to bring out
still more general contributions, and from a wider circuit.

Our position for two years past has precluded us from much personal
knowledge of the materials contributed, and we are therefore unable to add
any thing of importance to the official reports of the judges, to be found
below. These judges may, in the eyes of partial friends, have committed
errors in various cases; but they no doubt acted with a sincere desire to
favor all as much as possible, and their decisions should be frankly acqui-
esced in by the less successful, with a determination not to be discouraged;
for it is this very resolution to excel, which excites inquiry and investigation, stimulates exertion, creates improvements, and thus benefits the competitors in various ways, whether they be successful or unsuccessful in obtaining premiums. Were no premiums ever paid, the very sight of improved

breeds and products, once a year, would more than pay all trouble and costs incurred in maintaining these associations.

Among the curiosities we noticed, were silk cocoons and a cotton pod in close proximity, the former the result of the labors of Mrs. Nevius, and the latter raised by Geo. M'Collum; mammoth sweet potatoes and egg plants; a pin cushion, sixty years old, brought by Sarah Sholl, of Lewisburg; and the spectacles and spectacle box of Col. Craig, of the Revolution, in the possession of Hugh Wilson, Buffaloe.

REPORTS OF JUDGES.

No. 1—Horses.

Daniel Rengler, Sr., Buffaloe, dark brown, best stallion, "Superior" breed.. $5 00

Daniel Rengler, Jr., Buffaloe, dapple gray stallion, seven years old, Canadian, second best.................................... 3 00

Thomas Hoff, White Deer, exhibited a dark brown stallion, four years old, which the committee regard as a fine horse, but rather under the size required in our country.

Thomas Wilson, Kelly, for the best breeding mare................ 3 00

Wm. Wilson, Kelly, for second best do......................... 2 00

John Rengler, of Buffaloe, for best gelding not over seven years old, a strawberry roan, saddle and light draught.................. 3 00

D. A. Barber, Columbia county, second best do.................. 2 00

[Mr. Barber not having entered, not entitled to draw premium. *Ex. Comm.*]

John Alexander, Kelly, for sorrel stallion colt, three years old...... $2 00

Robert H. Laird, East Buffaloe, two years old sorrel gelding........ 2 00

Wm. Wilson, best sucking horse colt............................ 1 50

Andrew Ruhl, Buffaloe, second best do......................... 1 00

Jacob Hartman, Kelly, for best sucking mare colt................ 1 50

Jacob G. Brown, East Buffaloe, second best do.................. 1 00

Wm. Wilson, best span of working horses....................... 4 00

Isaac Eyer, Union, second best do............................. 2 00

Wm. Heinen, Milton, best pair of matched horses................ 3 00

Wm. Frick, Lewisburg, for a horse of the greatest speed.......... 1 00

The committee would also particularly mention a horse of A. J. Weidensaul, Lewisburg, an animal of fine speed and action.

Wm. Moore, Lewisburg, a horse of good speed and bottom, and with training will make a superior traveler.

The committee also recommend the following discretionary premiums:

John Alexander, for the largest stock of horses, best quality and blood, $3 00

Jackson Wolfe, Buffaloe, for pair of matched three years old colts, black... 2 00

D. A. Barber, for a span of fine carriage horses..................... $2 00

Dr. T. A. H. Thornton, Lewisburg, for a pair of Canadian matched

horses.. 1 00

A. M. Lawshe, Lewisburg, for pair matched two years colts, well broke 1 50

The committee also take particular notice of a beautiful fancy colt, cream colored, exhibited by Wm. Eilert, of Hartleton.

John Wilson, of Kelly, exhibited a two years old black colt, very handsome and spirited.

Ellis F. Gundy, of East Buffaloe, also a filly, two years old, of remarkable size and development for that age.

Charles Sleer, East Buffaloe, exhibited two fine colts, two years old.

John Rengler, a filly two years old, a very beautiful and gay colt.

John Roland, Buffaloe, also a three years old colt, of remarkable action and strength for that age.

Paul Lohr, Chillisquaque, a three years old cream colored filly, that deserves particular mention for her beauty and action.

There were many single horses, exhibited under the saddle and in harness, nearly all of which performed well, but the committee cannot enumerate them particularly, as it would swell this report to too great a length.

The exhibition of horses was a most admirable and splendid one, and between so much blood, merit and action, we have sometimes had great difficulty in coming to a conclusion, but have done the very best we could, being much pressed for time in the examinations as well as in making up this report.

> DANIEL RENGLER,
> GEORGE GEBHART,
> THOMAS PENNY,
> MARK HALFPENNY,
> R. V. B. LINCOLN,
> JOS. GREEN,
> JOS. CASEY.

No. 2.—Ploughing Match.

The ploughing was all well done, but if there was any difference we would report:

Jacob Dieffenderfer, of Buffaloe, best................................ $3 00

George Rengler, of Buffaloe, second best............................. 2 00

Martin Guyer, of Chillisquaque, best ploughman under twenty years

of age.. 2 00

George Wensel, East Buffaloe, ploughed so well that if the funds of the society will allow it, we would recommend a premium of $1 50.

> FLAVEL CLINGAN,
> ADAM GUNDY,
> ABRAHAM FREDERICK,
> ABRAHAM BROWN,
> BENJAMIN LOHR.

No. 3.—Neat Cattle.

Browns & Gundy, East Buffaloe, best bull between two and five years
  old $3 00
Paul Lohr, Chillisquaque, second best.......................... 2 00
David Grove, Kelly, best bull calf............................. 2 00
Jacob Gundy, best cow for all purposes, two calves shown, including
  dairy qualities, making thirteen and a quarter pounds butter per
  week... 3 00
Isaac Eyer, Jr., second best................................... 2 00
Jonathan Wolf, Lewisburg, best stock cow, three of her calves at two
  births having been sold for two hundred and sixty dollars....... 2 00
Joseph Green, Lewisburg, two best dairy cows kept by one person, J.
  or R. and..$1 or 2 00
Ellis Brown, East Buffaloe, best two years old heifer, J. or R. and $1 or 2 00
Martin D. Reed, East Buffaloe, best cow for butter, yielding sixteen
  and a quarter pounds butter per week....................... 2 00
Peter Hagenbuch, Kelly, best year old heifer................... 1 50
Daniel Rengler, best heifer calf............................... 1 00

The committee further report that no one person exhibited ten head of cattle. There was a number of very fine cattle exhibited by numerous persons, to whom we would be glad to award premiums if in our power to do so; but as there is no provision made by the Executive Committee, we cannot take the responsibility of going beyond our authority.

> JAMES MARSHALL,
> JACOB HUMMEL,
> WILLIAM S. CLINGAN,
> CHARLES S. YODER,
> JOHN S. SCHRACK,
> CHRISTIAN GEMBERLING,
> JOHN NOLL.

No. 4.—Sheep and Swine.

John Alexander, best boar, five months old.................. $2 00
John Alexander, best sow and pigs............................ 2 00
John Alexander, five or more pigs, between two and ten weeks old, J.
  or R. and... 1 00
T. & J. Wilson, four best pigs, five months old............... 1 00
John A. Gundy, East Buffaloe, six best lambs.................. 2 00
Andrew Ruhl, six best ewe sheep.............................. 2 00

> J. D. DIEFFENDERFER,
> J. F. PONTIUS,
> R. M. MUSSER.

No. 5.—Oxen and Steers.

David Grove, Kelly, best working oxen.......................... $3 00
Wm. Cameron, Lewisburg, best match steers................... 3 00
R. M. Mussor, Lewisburg, best Durham steers.................... 1 00
R. M. Mussor, Lewisburg, second best Devon steers.............. 1 00

> FREDERICK KREMER,
> GEORGE MEIXELL,
> GIDEON BIEHL,
> WILLIAM WILSON,
> PHILIP RUHL.

No. 6.—Poultry.

After a careful examination of all the poultry brought upon the fair ground, in pursuance to the rules and regulations of the society, we award the following premiums, viz:

James Kelley, Lewisburg, best pair Shanghais.................. $ 75
Solomon Ritter, Lewisburg, second best pair Shanghais.......... 25
Abraham Hubler, Lewisburg, best pair Chittagongs.............. 75
Augustus Stoughton, Lewisburg, best Cochin China............. 75
Augustus Stoughton, Lewisburg, best common kind.............. 25
Paul Lohr, Chillisquaque, best speckled Creoles................ 75

Messrs. H. C. Pardoe, Joel Kelly, A. M. Lawshe and A. Stoughton also exhibited Shanghai chickens of this year's raising, all being very fine and large specimens of the kind, and received the united approbation of the committee.

Joseph Moore, second, East Buffaloe, exhibited a pair of domesticated Canvass Back ducks of a dark brown color, and well deserves a premium for his efforts in taming this excellent kind of the feathered tribe, but no provision has been made for that purpose.

Thomas Meckley, Milton, exhibited one cock and three hens, full grown Java Bantams, of a dark brown color, being about the size of our quails—a fine specimen of the kind, for which he has the good opinion and thanks of the committee, but no provision being made for this case we can only award a premium of merit.

> SAMUEL WEIRICK,
> HENRY GIBSON,
> DANIEL NOLL,
> JOHN H. GOODMAN,
> JOHN LINN,
> W. A. SHREYER,
> S. J. HILBISH.

No. 7.—FIELD CROPS.

There were ten excellent specimens of white wheat exhibited. We award

John S. Schrack, East Buffaloe, best five acres white wheat, thirty-eight bushels per acre.. $5 00

R. V. B. Lincoln, Hartley, second best, white, twenty-three and a half bushels per acre.. 3 00

John Alexander, third best Mediterranean, twenty-seven and a half bushels per acre.. 2 00

J. & T. Wilson, best bushel wheat.. 1 00

Joseph Kelly, second best Mediterranean.. 50

J. M. Nesbit, P. Lohr, A. Eyer, E. F. Gundy and J. Guier, for samples of white wheat, received premium each........................ 50

J. S. Schrack, best bushel rye, received.. 1 00

Peter Smith, Hartley, best lot clover seed, received........................ 1 00

Paul Lohr, Chillisq. best bushel corn.. 1 00

John Locke, Lewisburg, second best.. 50

J. M. Nesbit, Jacob Gundy, A. Frederick, James Kelly, specimens of corn, received each.. 50

Benjamin Lohr, Buffaloe, best bushel oats.. 50

Philip Sipley, West Buffaloe, one bushel black oats, received........ 50

John Alexander, best half acre potatoes, (140 bushels)................ 3 00

H. W. Fries, Lewisburg, second best ¼ acre potatoes (132 bushels)... 2 00

Martin Dunkel, Jackson, best bushel sweet potatoes.................... 1 00

William Nagle, Kelly, second best, received.. 50

William Ketcham, Kelly, best bushel potatoes........................ 50

J. Chamberlin, W. Wilson, for specimen potatoes, received each.... 50

Robert Lyon, Chillisq. best bushel turnips.. 50

Mrs. M. Taylor, Lewisburg, best bushel beets........................ 50

William Frick, Norman Ball, John Locke, for beets, received each.. 50

N. Ball, for best peck Lima beans.. 50

James D. Chamberlin, Buffaloe, beans, received........................ 50

Do.   best peck peas.. 50

Robert Lyon, best lot of cabbage.. 50

F. B. Sterner, Lewisburg, lot cabbage, received........................ 50

Joel Kelly, Lewisburg, best pumpkins.. 1 00

J. H. Beale, N. Ball and R. Lyons, second best pumpkins, received each 50

G. R. Bliss, Lewisburg, for best egg plant and broccoli, received.... 50

J. D. Chamberlin, best half bushel tomatoes, received................ 50

THOMAS HAYES,
GEORGE SLEER,
PHILIP SIPLEY,
JOHN C. WATSON,
JOHN HAUCK,
JOHN WILT.

No. 8—Fruit.

The committee report that the display in this department is uncommonly fine, and would, in their opinion, do credit to the oldest county agricultural society in the State. In several cases they found great difficulty in selecting, from among samples of nearly equal excellence, those which should be entitled to the highest rank.

We award the premium for the best lot of winter apples, to David Heiser, of Buffaloe, who exhibits the seven following varieties: London Lady, French Pippin, Bellefleur, Rambo, Pound, Sweet Russet and Golden Pippin J. or R. and $1 00

For the second best, to John Glick, of Buffaloe, who exhibits one peck of each of the following kinds: Bellefleur, (very fine,) Rambo, Smokehouse, (very fine,) Pound, Romanite, Long Island Red Streak, and Pennock....................................... J. or R.

They also award diplomas to J. Eyer, of Union, M. J. Laird, of East Buffaloe, and Francis Wilson, of Buffaloe, for very fine displays of apples.

The premium for the best variety of apples is awarded to James D. Chamberlin, of Buffalo. He exhibits specimens of twelve varieties, most of which were grown on trees set out in 1852, viz: Swaar, Smokehouse, French Pippin, Roxbury Russet, Fallenwalder, Rambo, Winter Sweet, Red Spice, Gunshahocka Pippin, Golden Pippin, Sweet Rambo, Black Apple, J. or R. and................. $1 00

The best half bushel of apples is exhibited by P. S. Sipley; he calls them Shellenberger 1 00

Diplomas are awarded to J. M. Goodell, of Buffaloe, and John Wilt, of Hartley, for lots of choice apples.

A special premium of $1 and Journal is recommended to be given to James Adams, of White Deer, Union county, for a new and choice variety of apples, named, by Mr. Noll, the Adams seedling.

A special premium of $1 00 is recommended to A. M. Lawshe, for specimens of very fine Magnum Bonum plums.

The premium for the best specimens of pears is awarded to James D. Chamberlin. He exhibits the Dengler, Chambers, Garden, Ulster, and Winter pear.. $1 00

For the best peck of peaches, to Mrs. Nicely, Lewisburg; variety, Heath cling.. . 1 00

A special premium of $1 is recommended to D. Moore, Buffaloe, and a like premium of $1 to S. Ritter, of Lewisburg, for their very fine Seedling peaches.

For best peck quinces, A. M. Lawshe........................ $1 00

For best lot grapes, P. Nevius, Lewisburg..................... 1 00

JOHN W. SIMONTON,
WILLIAM HAYES,
MICHAEL BROWN,
CHARLES S. JAMES.

No. 9—DAIRY PRODUCTS.

The committee have examined various lots of butter exhibited by Mrs. M. D. Reed, Mrs. J. F. Pontius, Mrs. R. H. Laird, Mrs. J. Alexander, Miss Mary Mertz, Miss Maria C. Guier, Mrs. John Gundy, Mrs. Jacob Gundy, Mrs. J. Rengler, Jr., Mrs. I. Eyer, Jr., Mrs. Sarah Gundy, Miss Eliza Wilson. A majority have come to the conclusion that the best lot is that of Mrs. Sarah Gundy, and therefore award her a premium of silver butter knife and $2 00

The second best lot was that of Eliza Gundy, and we would award her the second premium, if the order awards such.

Although it is beyond our power to award a premium to any other lot, yet they cannot omit saying that the others were highly creditable to the exhibitors, and especially the lots of Miss Wilson, Mrs. Eyer, Mrs. Reed, two rolls, Rachel Gundy.

There was but one cheese, exhibited by Mrs. John Gundy, and that coming within the order of the society as to weight, we award to her the premium of.. $2 00
Robert Kelly, of Kelly, exhibited the only lot of honey—a splendid lot—for which we award the premium of..................... 1 00

Mrs. SARAH S. CLARK,
" HENRIETTA RAWN,
" MARIA MOORE,
" ELIZABETH CHAMBERLIN,
" SARAH L. SLIFER.

No. 10—FLOUR AND BREAD.

Your committee award Danl. Rengler, for best barrel wheat flour, a premium of... $1 00
Mrs. D. Reber, Lewisburg, best specimen flour bread, with written statement of manner of making........................... 1 00

MICHAEL BROWN,
JOHN W. SIMONTON,
WILLIAM HAYES,
CHARLES S. JAMES.

No. 11—HOUSEHOLD MANUFACTURES.

Your committee award the following premiums:
Statten, Marr & Co., best fulled cloth.......................... $2 00
Miss Lucretia Wilson, best ten yards woollen flannel............. 1 00
Mrs. Maria Laird, second best do................................ 50
Benj. Angstadt, best wool carpet................................ 2 00

Samuel Wilyard, second best wool carpet........................ $1 00
S. K. Driesbach, best rag carpet................................ 1 00
Benj. Angstadt, second best do................................. 50
Mrs. M. Laird, best half dozen pairs woollen hose.............. 50
Mrs. M. Laird, best pair mittens............................... 50
S. K. Driesbach, best woollen shawl............................ 1 00
S. K. Driesbach, second best do................................ . 50
Benj. Angstadt, best pound woollen yarn........................ 50
Miss Elizabeth Wilson, best quilt.............................. 2 00
Miss S. A. Wilson, second best do.............................. 1 00
Mrs. G. Deck, best bed-spread.................................. 1 00
Miss H. Meixell, second best do................................ 50
Mrs. E. D. Wilson, best specimen needle-work................... 1 00
Mrs. Sarah Cook, second best do................................ 50
Miss Marietta Morison, best specimen raised worsted work....... 50
Mrs. Amanda Miller, best canvass worsted work.................. 50
Miss Lucretia Wilson, best specimen domestic soap.............. 1 00

The committee would also make honorable mention of, and recommend premiums if funds sufficient, to Mrs. M. D. Reed, Mrs. Sarah L. Penny, Miss Ellen Flannigan, Miss M. Morison, for exceeding fine specimens of needle-work; to Miss Louisa Wilson and Mrs. Deck, for handsome bead and worsted wrought pin cushions; to Miss E. Wilson for bead purse; to Mrs. Sarah Gundy for quilt; and to Miss Matilda Gundy for a fine specimen of canvass worsted work.

The committee regret that a large variety of articles came in too late to be entered, and consequently could not come in competition with articles of the same class which were entered for exhibition within the prescribed time. Had all been in, in time, the awards of the committee would, no doubt, have been different in a number of instances.

They would say to all, be sure to be in time next year.

JAMES HAYES,
C. W. SCHAFFLE,
SOLOMON RITTER,
AUGUSTUS SCHREYER,
DAVID BEBER.

No. 12.—DOMESTIC MANUFACTURES.

Josiah Girton, Lewisburg, best buggy.......................... $2 00
F. A. Donachy, Lewisburg, cabinet work........................ 2 00
J. H. Beale, Lewisburg, best dress coat....................... 1 00
J. H. Beale, Lewisburg, best dress vest....................... 50
George B. Eckert, Lewisburg, buggy harness.................... 1 00
Weidman & Hess, Adamsburg, best half-dozen calf skins......... 1 00

L. Sterner, Lewisburg, best half dozen kip skins................ $1 00
Fries & Deck, West Buffaloe, best half dozen sides sole-leather..... 1 00
John Seebold, New Berlin, best lot harness leather.............., 1 00
Nelson Polk, Lewisburg, riding bridle,......................   50

HUGH WILSON,
JACOB HORLACHER,
WEIDLER ROLAND,
JOHN ROLAND.

No. 13.—Agricultural Implements.

The committee, after examining the different articles submitted to their in-spection, do award the following premiums :

George A. Frick, Lewisburg, for the best sward plough............,.. $3 00
John Kinkead, Chillisquaque, second best....................... 1 00
Charles S. James, Lewisburg, best subsoil plough, only one entered 1 00
J. M. Nesbit, Chillisquaque, best cultivator.................... 1 00
F. Liechtenthaler, Montour county, for corn plough and cultivator... 1 00
Abraham Frederick, East Buffaloe, for churn operated by dog power 1 00

The committee have to regret the apathy exhibited by the farmers in bringing forward their implements, as they are confident a much better display might have been made.

EPHRAIM LONG,
MICHAEL DUNKEL,
SAMUEL ZELLERS,
JOHN CHAMBERLIN,
JOSEPH M. NESBIT,
CYRUS BROWN.

No. 14.—Manures and Farm Accounts.

Charles S. James deposited specimens of ammoniated super-phosphate of lime ; and John Wilt, specimens of home-made manure, and a farm account. No report received from the committee.

No. 15.—Unenumerated Articles.

For a lot of domestic silk, raised and manufactured by Mrs. Eliza Ne-vius, of Lewisburg, we recommend premium................... $1 00
Beautiful flower basket, by Mrs. Susanna Bengler, of Buffaloe :.....   50

Dr. Jacob Horlacher, New Berlin, a specimen of universal salve, manufactured by himself, an excellent article........................ $1 00

Henry W. Crotzer, plan of the borough of Lewisburg, drawn by himself, well done.. 1 00

S. D. Munson, Lewisburg, a bottle of excellent currant wine....... 50

Henry Heitzman, Buffaloe, horizontal pump, made by himself....... 1 00

Henry Heitzman, Buffaloe, steel trap.............................. 50

Solomon Ritter, Lewisburg, a specimen of sculpture, neatly got up
for durability and workmanship.............................. 1 00

Karl Volkmar, Lewisburg, lithographic printing, highly recommended to
the public for neatness and workmanship.

O. N. Worden, Lewisburg, letter press printing, done with neatness, and
deserves praise.

Col. Eli Slifer, Lewisburg, a case of stuffed birds, beautifully got up, and
deserves notice as an ornament.

Spyker & Hawn, Lewisburg, specimens of Daguerreotypes, elegantly got
up, and for neatness and workmanship the committee recommend a diploma.

J. L. Yoder, Lewisburg, a case of jewelry, beautiful specimens of silver-
ware, &c.

B. C. Taylor, Lewisburg, a very neat view of Ohio State Fair, got up at
Cincinnati.

George A. Frick, Lewisburg, six specimens of stoves got up by himself,
show a good workmanship, taste and durability. The committee would especially notice the Globe cooking stove, and recommend it as in their opinion
as good if not better than any now in use, and for merit would recommend a
diploma.

L. STERNER,
JOHN G. BROWN,
THOMAS H. CORNELIUS,
J. SEEBOLD.

At an election held on the second day, the following persons were elected:

PRESIDENT—Jacob Gundy.

VICE PRESIDENTS—John Chamberlin, David Watson, J. S. Sterner, Isaac
Eyer, G. R. Bliss, James M'Creight.

CORRESPONDING SECRETARY—R. V. B. Lincoln.

RECORDING SECRETARY—David Reber.

TREASURER—R. H. Laird.

LIBRARIAN—Samuel Weirick.

EXECUTIVE COMMITTEE—H. W. Snyder, James P. Ross, J. Slenker.

The Treasurer's report stands as follows:

To cash on hand from last year.............................. $100 22
To cash for memberships and admittance fees................. 241 19
To county appropriation.................................... 100 00

441 41

By amount of premiums paid....................... $209 25
By amount paid door and gate keepers, printing, stationery, postage, &c.................................. 29 25

238 50

Amount of balance in treasury............................. 202 91

DAVID REBER, *Rec. Secretary of*
Union County Agricultural Society.

WARREN COUNTY.

To the President of the Pennsylvania State Agricultural Society:

This society was organized in 1851, and has steadily increased in influence and members ever since. The society has purchased a large tent for the purpose of accommodating visitors at their annual fairs.

Receipts for the current year, 1854......................... $246 25
Disbursements   do.   do. 168 63

Balance on hand....................................... 77 62

The beneficial influence of the society is already visibly seen throughout the agricultural sections of the county, but owing to the severe drought few entries were made for premiums on field crops. The yield, however, in corn, for our county, was unusually large.

First premium on corn was for 266 bushels of ears per acre.
Second   do.   do.   179   do.   do.
First premium on potatoes was for 300   do.   do.

Officers for 1855.

PRESIDENT—John Mahan, Farmington.
SECRETARY—Isaac H. Hiller, Sugargrove.
TREASURER—Andrew Low, Lottsville.

In addition to these, there is one Vice President in each township, annually elected.

DANIEL LOTT, *President.*

21

WAYNE COUNTY.

To the President of the Pennsylvania State Agricultural Society :

The Recording Secretary of the Wayne County Agricultural and Mechanics' Art Society, respectfully submits the following reports of the various committees appointed for the purpose of awarding the premiums at the annual fair held in Honesdale, on the 4th inst.

Arrangements were made for a ploughing match, but we regret to be obliged to say that no entries were made.

The Committee on Neat Stock, class 1, submitted the following report :

For best short horned bull, from one to three years old, to No. 18, Capt. A. Flowers	$2 00
For best short horned bull calf, do., Wm. Rockwell	1 00
For best short horned cow, over three years old, R. Henwood	2 00
For best short horned heifer, from one to three years old, R. Henwood,	2 00
Second best do. do. do., C. P. Waller	1 00
Best do. Devon bull, one to two years old, Z. M. P. Bunnell	2 00
Second best do. do. do., R. Henwood	1 00
Best do. cow, over three years old, L. L. Deming	2 00
Second best do. do. do., L. L. Deming	1 00
Best do. heifer, from one to three years old, L. L. Deming	1 00
Best native or grade bull, under three years old, A. Winton	1 00
Best do. do. cow, over three years old, H. Tamblyn	2 00
Best do. do. heifer, under three years old, H. Tamblyn	1 00
Second best do. do. do. do., Thos. Stevens	50
Best yoke work oxen, over five years, H. Bishop	3 00
Second best do. do. do., H. Bishop	3 00
Best yoke steers, three to four years old, N. A. Monroe	2 00
Second best do. do. do., Major Brooks	1 00
Best do. do., two to three years old, N. A. Monroe	2 00
Best do. yearlings, C. B. Reed	1 50
Second best do. do., Sam'l Sander	75

These are all the premiums which the committee saw fit to award.

Respectfully submitted, by

E. G. WOOD,

W. S. FERGUSON,

Acting Committee.

Horses—Class No. 3.

The Committee on Horses submitted the following report :

Best stallion, over five years old, C. B. Reed	$3 00
Second best do. do., C. P. Waller	2 00

Best do. from two to five years old, R. P. Patterson................. $2 00

Best yearling do., C. B. Reed....................................... 1 50

Best brood mare, over five years old, W. L. Ferguson............. 3 00

Second best do. do., A. Winton.................................... 2 00

Best mare colt, Wm. Stevens....................................... 1 00

Best pair carriage horses, G. Knapp......................... 2 50

Best single mare of gelding, Samuel Allen....................... 2 00

Second best do. do., L. L. Deming................................ 1 00

The committee noticed with pleasure some very fine two and three years old colts, and would call particular attention to a three years old colt, entered by Clayton Yale; also, one two years old, entered by Henry Bishop; and another, two years old, entered by Z. M. P. Bunnell; but no premiums being advertised, they hardly think the funds of the society will justify the award of discretionary premiums.

U. V. WHEELER,

WM. H. FOSTER,

HENRY BUNNEL,

Committee.

SHEEP AND SWINE—CLASS No. 2.

Your Committee on Sheep and Swine respectfully submit the following as their report:

Best long wool buck, first premium, A. Winton.................. $1 00

Second best do. ewes, three or more, first premium, A. Winton..... 1 00

Second best do., second premium, Jno. D. Frity................... 1 00

Best native or mixed buck, Jno. D. Frity......................... 1 00

Second best do., second premium, A. Winton...................... 1 00

Best lot of lambs, four or more, first premium, R. Webb........... 2 00

Second best do., second premium, John D. Frity.................. 1 00

Best sow, first premium, T. Stephens............................ 1 00

Best sow, under one year old, first premium, T. Stephens......... 50

Best litter of pigs, first premium, T. Stephens 1 50

POPE BUSHNELL,

EDWIN PIERCE,

E. H. CLARK,

Committee.

FARM IMPLEMENTS—CLASS No. 4.

The Committee on Farm Implements beg leave to report, that they have attended to the duties assigned them, which were light, but few farm implements being entered for exhibition. They award the following premiums:

Best cultivator, first premium, Hand & Kirtland.................... $1 00
Best seed planter, first premium, Thomas Stevens.................. 1 00
Best plough clevis, first premium, Knapp & Neal.................. 50
Best railroad power for churn, first premium, Rob't J. Knapp....... 1 00
Best plough, first premium, Hand & Kirtland.................... 1 00
Second best plough, third premium, Knapp & Neal................ 50
Best model hay-rigging, S. V. Niles............................ 50
Best farm wagon, first premium, Z. M. P. Bunnell................ 2 00
Best fanning mill, first premium, Z. M. P. Bunnell............... 1 00

The committee noticed a butter firkin exhibited by Henry Michter, as the best ; also, a meat tub exhibited by the same. Notice is also made of a dozen axes, not numbered.

All of which is respectfully submitted.

D. M. ENO,
H. JENNINGS,
E. K. NORTON,
Committee.

MECHANICAL DEPARTMENT—CLASS No. 5.

The Committee on the Mechanical Department respectfully submit the following report :

Best morticing machine, No. 1.

The committee were highly gratified with the operations of the above machine, and believe it to be superior to any other yet invented.

No. 2. Best covered one horse buggy wagon, E. Patmor......... $2 00

The above wagon is a very fine specimen of home manufacture, and will compare favorably with those from any quarter.

No. 3. Best pump, A. Barker.............. .... $1 50

The above pump is too well known to require any recommendation from us. Many of our citizens have tested the superiority.

No. 4. A. Barker, is a centrifugal pump, with which the committee are not acquainted.

No 5. Best specimen of Daguerreotypes, by J. A. Griswold....... $1 00

The above were very fine specimens, which we would recommend to the attention of the public.

Parlor and cooking stoves—a quantity of choice patterns on exhibition in the hall, without any number.

S. E. NORTH,
C. F. YOUNG,
ORREN HALL,
Committee.

The stoves mentioned above were entered by Knapp & Neal, of this place, for *exhibition*, and not for a premium ; consequently, no numbers were attached thereto, but the names of the exhibitors. They are deserving of especial commendation for their beauty of pattern, and also as an index of the desire of Messrs. Knapp & Neal to add to the interest of our annual fairs.

———

DOMESTIC MANUFACTURES—CLASS No. 6.

The Committee on Domestic Manufactures respectfully make the following report:

Best ten yards flannel, N. M'Collum............................	$ 75
Best rag carpet, Hannah E. Rundlett............................	1 00
Best pair woollen blankets, Mrs. W. L. Ferguson.................	1 00
Best knit woollen hose, Mrs. W. L. Ferguson....................	50
Best knit cotton hose, Mrs. W. L. Ferguson.....................	25
Best knit woollen mittens, Mrs. W. L. Ferguson.................	25
Best worsted worked lamp mat, Mrs. A. W. Nichols..............	50
Best exhibition of ornamented needle-work, Miss Lydia Stevens.....	1 00
Best do. general needle-work, Nos. 13 and 15, Misses Mary Penniman and Isabella Barker..........................	1 00
Best crotchet work, Miss Henrietta Hamlin.....................	50
Best half hose, N. M'Collum...................................	50
Best worked handkerchief exhibited by Miss E. Watson.	
Best infant's hood by Miss Sarah E. Carr.	
Best artificial flowers, Miss L. Stevens........................	50
Best quilt, Mrs. David Ross...................................	50

The committee would call attention to a beautiful card basket, exhibited by George Gustin; and also two crayon drawings by Dr. Rowland, which they consider the best on exhibition. They were unable to decide upon the best pellis work, as there were many varieties exhibited of much beauty and in excellence of workmanship so nearly equal. The committee found entered in their department, the following articles, which properly belong in the mechanical:

Best pair boots, John Broad..................................	$1 00
A very fine pair was exhibited by P. Beeler.	
Best exhibition of jewelry, Peterson & Brother..................	1 00

They would call attention to a fine exhibition of brooms, manufactured by T. S. Brown, of this place; a small broom by the same gentleman, is worthy of a discretionary premium, and we would recommend a premium of one dollar if the same is sanctioned by the Executive Committee.

Mrs. C. F. YOUNG,
" O. STEVENSON,
" C. S. MINOR,
Committee.

BUTTER AND CHEESE—CLASS No. 7.

The Committee on Butter and Cheese respectfully report :

Best pot June butter, August Loomis.................................. $2 00
Second best pot June butter, John Carr............................... 1 00
Best pot fall butter, Homer Brooks.................................. 2 00
Second best pot fall butter, John Carr.............................. 1 00
Best cheese, L. L. Deming.. 2 00
Second best cheese, S. E. North.................................... 1 00

G. A. STARKWEATHER,
Mrs. JOHN BUNNELL,
Miss H. T. KING,
Mrs. T. H. R. TRACY,
" O. STEVENSON.
Committee.

FRUIT—CLASS No. 8.

The committee would respectfully submit the following report :

Best variety winter apples, E. K. Norton............................ $2 00

They would also notice a handsome variety of winter apples, consisting of thirteen kinds, exhibited by E. Jennings ; another of twelve kinds, very nice, by S. J. Saunders, for which they would recommend a discretionary premium.

Best half bushel winter apples, E. K. Norton....................... $1 00
Second best half bushel winter apples, E. K. Norton................ 75
Best half bushel fall apples, E. K. Norton......................... 1 00
Best cooking apples, E. K. Norton.................................. 50
Best quinces, Z. M. P. Bunnell..................................... 50

We would call attention to a basket of quinces exhibited by John Carr, as very fine, and if we had the power, to award of a discretionary premium.

Best peck of peaches, Walter Spry................................. 50
Best peck of pears, only specimen exhibited, E. K. Norton.......... 75

G. A. STARKWEATHER,
W. R. STONE,
Mrs. C. C. GRAVES,
" C. P. WALLER,
Committee.

FIELD CROPS—CLASS No. 9.

The Committee on Field Crops would report, that they will report on the first Monday in December next, agreable to a resolution passed in 1852. Any statement left with the Secretary, E. O. Hamlin, before that time, will be then acted upon.

O. STEVENSON, *Chairman.*

VEGETABLES—CLASS No. 10.

The Committee on Vegetables respectfully submit the following as their report :

Best peck onions, John S. Eno............. .... $ 50
Best beet, (discretionary) Charles Eldred..................... 25

R. HENWOOD,
T. C. WHITE,
Committee.

No entries were made in class 11.

———

POULTRY—CLASS No. 12.

The Committee on Poultry report :

Best pair Dorkings, Luther Ledyard............................ $1 00
Best pair turkeys, Wm. Stephens 1 00
Best pair ducks, Thomas Stephens............................. 1 00
Best lot of poultry, R. F. Lord................................ 1 50
Best pair Shanghais, William Stephens......................... 1 00
Best pair Bantems, J. F. Lord................................. 1 00

The committee would call attention to a fine Chittagong, exhibited by Dr. Rowland.

The committee believe the display in this department far exceeds any thing of the kind previously presented at our agricultural fair, but think the variety should be very much extended in 1855.

T. H. R. TRACY, *Chairman.*

———

The society was called to order about one o'clock, P. M., by the President, C. P. Waller, Esq., and the following gentlemen appointed a committee to nominate officers for the ensuing year, viz: T. H. R. Tracy, E. K. Norton, W. R. Stone, John Carr, and N. A. Monroe. They reported as follows :

PRESIDENT—Capt. A. Flowers.
VICE PRESIDENTS—Hon. N. B. Eldred and Samuel Allen.
CORRESPONDING SECRETARY—Chas. Avery.
RECORDING SECRETARY—E. O. Hamlin.
TREASURER AND GENERAL AGENT—A. Winton.
MANAGERS—George Waller, Esq., Wm. R. Stone, John Carr, Platt Darling and Gabriel Howel.

The above gentlemen were then elected by the society as officers for the ensuing year.

The committee also "recommended the appointment of E. O. Hamlin, Esq., to publish an address to the citizens of Wayne county, upon the importance of the Agricultural Society to them ;" which appointment was confirmed by the society. William H. Dimmick, Esq., was invited to deliver the annual address in 1855.

The society was very agreeable entertained, after the reports of the various committees, by able addresses from E. F. Stewart, Esq., of Easton, Pa., and J. W. Fowler of Poughkeepsie, N. Y.

The Secretary regrets that during the whole day, his time was so occupied in the duties of his office as to entirely preclude him from taking that general survey of the cattle ground, the mechanical department, and articles exhibited, which would qualify him to speak understandingly of the comparative character of this fair. And, however little he may be able to prophesy in regard to the next, it is his hope, and shall be his earnest endeavor to so digest and arrange the operation of his department, that there may be greater facility in the entering of articles, and in the examination by committees.

The efficient co-operation of officers, and the faithful discharge of their duties by them, will do much to improve the annual exhibitions of our society. But intent and faithful *they* may be, if the members of the society generally, are interested in its operations and will not labor for its success, its annual fairs must deteriorate. In the number of articles entered, the last is, undoubtedly the largest fair ever held in our county, while in many respects, especially in the cattle show, so far as my observation went, it fell far short of last year. It will be observed that the committees reporting are in many instances changed from those advertised previous to the fair. This was necessary for two reasons—first, the absence of many of the persons originally appointed—second, because of the by-laws: That no person can be allowed to sit upon the committee to award premiums in the same department in which he has entered articles for competition.

The Secretary regrets to see, in the last week's Herald, an editorial censure upon "*the Secretaries*," for not having this report ready for the press in time for the last week's papers.

So far as the duties of the Corresponding Secretary are concerned, every one knows, or *ought to know*, that his duties are entirely disconnected with the making up of the annual report.

To any one *acquainted* with the onerous duties of the Recording Secretary of the agricultural society, immediately subsequent to the annual fair, he respectfully submits the question, whether nine days is any too long a time, in the midst of professional engagements and miscellaneous business, to arrange and re-write the reports of the various committees, and perform all the other drudgery of making up the annual report? To have had this report ready for the press last week, it would have been necessary to have handed it in by Monday of last week, leaving only three days for its preparation. To have prepared it in that time would have involved a neglect of other duties, of which, much as he loves the science of agriculture and the advancement of the interests of the Wayne County Agricultural Society, he never could be guilty.

The office has come to him unsought; its labor is not light, and however the Herald's censure may have appeared to others, to him it appears as unkind as it is unjust.

In conclusion, the Secretary begs leave to express his appreciation of the very efficient aid rendered him upon the day of the Fair, by Miles Tracy, Thos. J. Ham, Wm. Ham, Jason Torrey, Robert Torrey and Henry Stone, and also to Dr. Chas. Avery, Corresponding Secretary, for his services, both on the day of the Fair and also in preparing the foregoing report of committees for publication.

EDWARD O. HAMLIN, *Secretary.*

N. B. No person, unless they have become members of the society, by paying one dollar, will be entitled to receive the foregoing premiums.

October 14, 1854.

APPENDIX.

APPENDIX.

APPENDIX.

PLAN OF BARN BUILDINGS.

BY LEWIS F. ALLEN, BLACK ROCK, NEW YORK.

To the Executive Committee of the New York State Agricultural Society:

I present you a plan of barn and stabling, with explanatory drawings, in requirement with your premium list, inviting plans of this kind for your annual meeting in February, 1854. The buildings presented are the plans of structures now in course of erection on my own farm on Grand-Island, in the county of Erie. I do not present them as *new* and untried in merit, therefore theoretical and speculative merely, but as the *reconstruction*, on an enlarged and more durable plan, of a barn establishment, first built by me twenty years ago, and which I have used ever since, for both grain and stock purposes, in all their variety and branches. My experience in their use, together with a very considerable observation of buildings of like character in different parts of the country, has confirmed me in the belief that I cannot suggest so good a plan and arrangement as this now presented to you. I therefore offer them to the consideration of your committee, for such judgment as in their opinion their merits may be entitled.

LEWIS F. ALLEN.

DESCRIPTION.

The body of the main barn is 100 feet long by 50 feet wide; the posts 18 feet high above the sill, and 12½ feet apart, making nine bents. The roof has a pitch of 17 feet, being a trifle over what would be termed a third pitch. The advantages of a steep roof over a flat one, in durability and affording storage beneath it, will not, by experienced men, be questioned. The beams of the barn are 14 feet above the sills, which is the height of the inner posts. It is not necessary, however, to have more than two of these beams, aside from those at the ends, extend across the whole width of the building, as a beam inserted across the entire width at the fourth post from each end, thus leaving a space of 37½ feet at each end, and of 25 feet in the middle section without beams, will tie the building sufficiently strong to prevent spreading, and interfere less with the storage of hay and grain over the main floor. The perloin posts are 12½ feet long, and stand 12½ feet inside the main outer posts. These perloin posts are connected by girts 25 feet long, 3 feet below the perloin plate. The lower rafters are one foot longer than the upper ones, allowing that measure for projection over the main plates; the upper and lower rafters thus being 15 and 16 feet long, respectively.

The barn is divided, lengthwise, into three sections, viz: the main floor in the centre, extending throughout, and a section on each side, accommodating the hay and grain bays, horse power and machinery. This floor is fourteen feet wide; it may be contracted to twelve feet, for hay purposes only; but for the uses required in grain storage, fourteen feet is none too much. On each side of the floor, at the front end of the building, is an open area, 25 feet in length, extending to the sides, or outer posts, 18 feet. On one side is located the threshing machine, corn sheller, grain crusher, straw cutter, and such other machinery, driven by horse power, as may be required; and on the other side is the circular track for the stationary horse power, where the horse walks round the circle like an old fashioned bark-mill. Such an arrangement for *stationary* power I believe to be better, in its simplicity, cheapness and convenience, than any other yet invented. In this arrangement, a perpendicular shaft, with arms, at the extremities of which the horses are attached, is the moving power. A cog-wheel is placed near the upper end of the shaft, over the horses, with segments of iron cogs on its upper side, which play into the cogs of a small wheel or pinion, on a line of shaft which runs across the main floor and through the opposite area. On this line of shaft are placed drums or pulleys, of suitable size to carry the various machinery which may be attached. Next to the end of the barn, at the entrance front, is a passage on either side, four feet wide, leading to the stables, hereafter described. The horse power and track occupies 18 feet beyond, on its own side; and next to that, beyond, is a flight of stairs leading up to the granary and store room, which extends over the horse track and passage before decribed, and eight feet above the floor, being 22 by 18 feet, and as high as the demand for storage may require, if up to the plate: or, this granary or store room may be dispensed with, and the room occupied for hay or grain in sheaf storage purposes, like that over the machinery, on the opposite side. In such case the stairs will not be necessary, and the room occupied by them may go into the bay. The balance of the room on each side of the floor is devoted to bays for hay and grain, being 18 feet wide, and extending 71 feet, to within four feet of the further end, which is reserved on each side for a passage to the stables. These passages should be eight feet high, and over them the hay or grain may be extended from the main bays. On each side the main floor, and 10 feet above it, from post to post, should be extended and framed in, a line of girts, on which, when the bays are filled, poles may be laid over and across the floor, resting upon the girts, and on the poles loose boards or slabs, by way of scaffold, to receive other hay and grain which the bays will not hold. In this manner, taken in, in sections over the floor, the forage may be piled to the peak of the roof, thus holding quite as much as one of the bays. Stored in this manner, the barn will hold over 100 tons of hay, after deduct-ing the large areas for the granary, horse power and machinery. The inner posts and beams are marked in the elevation of the plan, so as to be seen.

In the plan submitted, the barn stands four feet above the ground. The purpose of this is twofold: If the underground room is wanted for stabling stock of any kind, an excavation of three to four feet will give ample room for that purpose, and permit the stables to be light and dry—two indispensa-ble requisites for the health and proper keeping of stock. If not required for stabling, the bays can drop near to the ground, thus giving a large additional quantity of storage for hay: or, if preferred, the earth may be excavated to a sufficient depth beneath the proposed space to accommodate it, and the horse power be stationed below; thus saving for storage the room occupied by it on the main floor. In such disposition of it, however, a driver would be neces-sary with the horses below, as they would be out of sight of the men at work above; whereas, in ordinary labor, with but a single horse, or two, at work, a driver for such work alone would not be necessary. Another object in placing the floor of the barn so high is, that the stables which are attached to it may have storage lofts over the cattle, with a sufficient slope of roof. Still, the barn may be set within two feet of the ground, and the stables be as they now are, in height of posts and storage room, if the barn posts be carried up three feet higher—21 feet instead of 18; or, the outside stable posts may be shortened, so as to give sufficient pitch to the roof; but this will cut short the loft room over them. A consideration of all these will commend itself to the circumstances of the farm and its proprietor.

On each side, adjoining the barn, is a line of stables, 16 feet wide, dropping three feet below the sills of the barn, and standing one foot above the ground. The posts of the stables are 12 feet high; the roof has a quarter or eight feet pitch. One foot below the plates of the barn, and parallel with them, a girt is framed from post to post, its whole length, as a support for the upper ends of the stable rafters. These rafters are 20 feet long, leaving two feet to pro-ject over the sides, and carry the water entirely away from the sills. The beams which connect the outer posts of the stables with those of the barn, and tie the buildings snugly together, are 7½ feet above the floor. For the purpose of further security, every rafter should be spiked at its foot on to the stable plate, and at its head, into the girt on which it rests, between the main posts of the barn, that there may be no spreading apart. The beams over the stables are floored to receive hay, straw, corn-stalks or litter for the cattle, of which the lofts will hold a large amount, and hay doors should be made in every second bent, under the roof, outside, to receive it from the carts or wagons.

The floor plan of the stables, by reference to the drawings, will be readily understood. A passage way extends the whole length next to the barn, four feet in width. A short flight of steps accommodates the descent from the passages at the ends of the barn to those in the stables. This is tightly floored over, and receives the hay from the adjoining bays and loft. Next to this is the line of mangers, two feet wide, into which, from the passage beside them, is thrown the hay. The space beyond is divided into double stalls, from 6 to 7 feet wide, and of course will contain more or less of them, according to their width, which will be determined somewhat by the size and kind of cattle kept in them. In the middle of every bent in the stables, which will of course be 12½ feet apart, except in that bent where is a door, is inserted a dung window, 18 inches long and 15 inches high, closed by a sliding shutter inside. These stables have each two doors, one at the front end and one as above named, in the centre bent on the sides. The doors are 4 feet wide and run up 7½ feet, to the level of the girt supporting the floor above.

The stalls are partitioned from the passage or alley way before described, back 7 feet, with two inch plank, or inch boards if double, and 5 feet high, to prevent the cattle interfering with each other. These stalls are framed by laying two light sticks of timber, say six inches square, parallel, the whole length of the stables, upon the beams connecting the stables and barn posts together. One of these parallel sticks is exactly over the side of the manger next the alley; the other 7 feet from it, into the stable. Either pin or spike these pieces strongly on to the beams. Then frame small posts, say 3 by 6 inches, (the thin sides in the partitions,) from the floor, perpendicularly, into them; and on to these posts nail the partition planks. These posts and planks should be sound, strong wood, as the heaving, and rubbing and wrenching upon them by the cattle, will be severe. The bottom of the mangers should be about 18 inches above the floor, for cattle, and 2½ feet for horses. They may be either perpendicular in the sides or flaring towards the top next the animal; this last is the better way. Bottom supports and side cleats should be well spiked on to the sides of the partition planks to hold them. Planks 18 inches high in front, and 2 feet next the alley, will be high enough to enclose the forage for the cattle. On the alley side a continuous line of one inch boards, nailed on to the partition posts for the stalls, will enclose that side of the mangers, and be stout enough, while 1½ or 2 inch planks should be used next the cattle. A partition between the mangers should be made, so that each should have its own separate allowance, where the cattle stand together. This should be of stout plank also, and as high as the front plank. The partitions of the stalls of course keep the other sides of the mangers separate. The centre of the plank of the manger next the cattle, should be slightly cut out, like a new moon, to let the neck of the animal down while feeding. On each side of the stall, next the manger, a staple and ring should be inserted, into which to secure the rope or chain which holds the animal. By this course, the two cattle standing in the same stall are kept as much apart, so far as interfering with each other's food and goring is concerned, as if in separate stalls, while they occupy less room, are more comfortable and warmer in winter than if each had a stall by itself. If upright stancheons, which shut in on each side of the neck, are used, this will vary the manger arrangement altogether; but as I disapprove that plan, I shall not further allude to it. Now, to prevent the cattle climbing their feet into the mangers, which they are very apt to do, spike a piece of scantling or a flatted pole over the top of the partitions, lengthwise, and perpendicularly over the front of the manger, and the mangers are complete. A passage of three feet at each end of the stable, for access from the like passage in the barn, is necessary, and the outside of the outer stall should be set that distance within. The comfort and cleanliness of the cattle will be enhanced by sinking the floor two inches, seven feet back from the mangers, so as to allow the *stale* to pass off, and the dung to drop below the floor they occupy; and this accomplished, the stable is finished.

The adjoining sheds, attached by a section to the rear of the barn, will be readily understood. A leanto, like the stables just described, and on the same floor-level, is attached to the rear end of the barn, and extends indefinitely, according to the wants of the proprietor. I have made these extensions, on the ground plan submitted, 64 feet between the barn stables and the outer corner section. This leanto, next the barn, has a passage of 14 feet wide, from the main floor through it, *declining* 3 feet in the 16 feet width—a sharp inclination to be sure, but down which an empty cart or wagon can be managed with an ordinary horse or ox-team, by cleeting the floor with strips of plank. A double door, corresponding with the main doors at the other end of the barn, is hung at the outer side. On each side of this floor-way is a room 34 by 16 feet. It may be divided into separate rooms, or mangered off into stables, as required, and the passages at the ends of the bays of the main barn and stables will accommodate the passage of their food to the animals within them. One of these rooms may be used as a calf-house, always a necessary appendage to a stock barn; the other may be fitted up as a hospital, another important adjunct. A cow about to calve, or a sick animal, can always be accommodated in this; and for such purposes, a room apart from other cattle is really necessary, and pays well for its construction. On a line with this leanto extend, each side, a shed of the same dimensions in height, and width 64 feet; thence turning at right angles, extends 116 feet, to the front line of the barn. This is put up in six bents of 16 feet each, and two of 10 feet each, forming the stables at the front ends. The sides next the barn are open for eight feet above the ground; the remaining 12 feet being boarded, and enclosing hay or straw lofts, with hay doors in every other bent. A room, 16 feet square, is made in each corner, (two of them,) which can be used for housing weak ewes, lambs, a bull stable, or any pur-

22

pose required. The stables at each end will be convenient for teams of horses or oxen, or, they may be used for wagon houses, tool houses, or other objects. Racks or mangers may be fitted up in those open sheds for feeding sheep or young cattle, and yards may be built adjoining, on the rear, six or eight in number, into which they may run, and be kept separate. Indeed, I cannot devise any better mode of keeping sheep than this. They may all come into the sheds to eat. Barred partitions may separate the different flocks. Bars may also enclose the opening in front, or they may, by tight boarding, be shut in altogether.

Eave troughs and conductors should take the water from the roofs into cisterns for the cattle. By underground pipes these cisterns can all be connected, if necessary, and the water of them all drawn from one alone, by a power pump. By thus collecting the water from the roofs, the yards will be kept dry, and a large quantity of water be constantly stored for the stock in all weathers. It may be objected that *shed*, or one-sided roofs are given to the outer sheds attached to the barn instead of the common double-sided roof, which may be a trifle less expensive. The object of the one-sided roof is to throw the water falling upon them *out*-side, instead of *in*-side the yards, thus keeping them drier and cleaner.

OBSERVATIONS.

Now, with the continued experience of twenty years, and a large stock of cattle, horses and sheep, for the greater share of that time under my own immediate charge, and with a knowledge of the every day wants of a mixed stock, I cannot conceive of a plan affording more conveniences at so cheap a cost. For a stock breeding farm, a milk, butter or cheese dairy, for stall feeding cattle this arrangement is equally convenient. Cows should be tied up to milk; these stables are just fitted for it. They want extra and separate feeding; these mangers will accommodate it. Bullocks are to be stall fed; here are stalls, and ample preparation, and storage for all manner of food required. Is a sheep barn wanted; here is abundant storage for their fodder, and the sheds, which may be extended indefinitely, are at hand to house and protect them perfectly. If grain be the object of the farmer, and little stock is kept, the main barn is the thing for it, and the sheds can be left off.

A great merit I consider this plan to have over others is, that it contains a *fixed principle* of construction for a barn of any size, larger or smaller. It may be built on a small scale, or it may be much larger than the one submitted. I can see no important objection to so extensive a range of building in connection, except that of fire. In case any part of it should burn, the whole would probably be destroyed. Few clusters of farm buildings, indeed, are otherwise, and I know of no way to remedy this objection but to *insure*; and no man not able to lose his buildings without inconvenience, should neglect insurance. Besides this, the saving in labor and forage, with such a barn as this, will twice pay the insurance every year.

The economy of labor in feeding stock in this barn will be seen, in the immediate proximity of the forage to the mangers. The long passage down the two sides and at the end, between the main barn and the stables, is used to throw the hay into from the bays, and then it can be forked over at once into the mangers. Girts are to be framed into the barn posts next the alley, to keep the hay in place as it is mowed in from the fields. When the bays are full up to the eaves, a well hole is to be cut with the hay knife, from the top, outside, next to the stables, and longitudinally near the centre of the bay, far enough down to push the hay into the alley for feeding. This hole is of course to be enlarged as the hay is fed out, and in a little time the whole side will be open. For cutting feed, the area adjoining the main floor, where the cutting box stands, is convenient to the bays on either side. The granary over the horse power will hold all the *ground* feed for mixing with the cut forage.

The lofts over the sheds will hold a large quantity of forage for the cattle or sheep, which may be fed and sheltered there; and as forage of every kind is enough better, when sheltered from the weather, to pay for such shelter, it should always be stored; and then, in all weathers, the cattle or sheep, dry and comfortable, can eat at their leisure. Step-ladders can be built at convenient places under the sheds to ascend into the lofts.

It may be objected to putting the stables on to the *side* of the barn, when so frequent a plan is to have them in the body of it, under the bays. The objection to this latter mode is, that the *stale* of the cattle soon rots the sills, and exposes the whole structure to infirmity, whereas, if the stable sills decay, they may be readily replaced, at less expense than the others. Besides this, the convenience of low storage in the bays is great, in the saving of labor, over that of pitching every thing so high over head. To this may be added, the whole concern is much warmer, contradicting, in this case at least, the old adage, "as cold as a barn;" and still, perfect ventilation is given through the long ranges of alley all round, and the stable windows.

PROTECTION AND PRESERVATION OF MANURE.

Believing that the best application of barn yard manure on the farm is to get it on to the fields where it is required, with the least possible delay after dropped from the cattle, I should require but little shelter for it at the yard. But as both theory and practice differ in this regard, I can suggest no more economical method of protection to it, from the weather, than to run sections of the stable roof back sufficiently far to protect, as they are thrown from the windows, the dung heaps, from the storms. This may be cheaply done by rafters, say 6 to 10 feet long, according to the extent of protection required, running out just above the dung windows of the stables, and supported by braces from the sills, or posts set in the ground at their outer extremities, and covered with boards or shingles. Such expense, however, is hardly worth while, if the dung is to be applied in its raw state to the land, as strict economy demands that it be taken, unfermented, on to the ground, where its gases and ammonia may at once be appropriated to the growing crop; and if composting it be the object, a covered stercorary in the yard, or under the sheds, where it would be already sheltered, is the better plan. In this very place the theory of composting manures may, in the manner in which it is usually done, in the economy of its preparation, and in the efficacy of its benefits, be seriously questioned. Composts are, as the name implies, compositions of various fertilizing matter, mixed in mass, and each acting upon the other, by the aid of water and atmospheric air, assisted by turning up and mixing, by hand labor, at sundry times. They thus decompose, and amalgamate their various materials, each into the other, so as to become assimilated into one uniform quality of substance. Now, if the same material, in quality and quantity were thrown broadcast upon the soil, and ploughed or harrowed in, according to the requirement of the crop in hand, where the elements would dislodge its ammonia and gases, while the soil and the growing crop appropriated them as they passed off, instead of permitting all this fertilizing matter to escape into the atmosphere, as is the case in the workings of the compost heap, and leaving a mass of effete matter, by gardeners pre-eminently called *rotted manure*, the benefits of such process, to my mind, can admit of little question. The destruction of noxious seeds I conceive to be its chief merit, as that is the first virtue always claimed for it by its advocates. But as this is only incidental to the subject of protecting manures, in connection with the plan of barn and stabling before you, and partly explanatory of this branch of the accommodation required in a complete barn establishment, I will not pursue the discussion. It will be seen that abundant conveniences exist for the housing and protection of manures.

To sum up the various merits claimed for a barn so comprehensive as this in its accommodation, and justify the expense of its construction, larger or smaller, as the circumstances of the farm may require, more is scarcely necessary than to say, that all kinds of forage and farm products should be stored under shelter, for economical preservation and use. All kinds of stock, within the climate of the State of New York, should be sheltered. These are quite as important as to cultivate and grow the crops, either for market or which the stock are to consume, in the best manner, or to produce and care for the life of the stock at the first. The saving in expenditure of the crops, and the greatest possible benefit to the stock in feeding them, together with due provision for their warmth and comfort, is a part of the system of good husbandry, and without these the' system is imperfect. To effect this, a full and complete barn establishment is necessary—as much so as good fences, clean fields, a fertile soil, and a thorough understanding of his vocation, is to the prosperity of the farmer himself.

CONSTRUCTION.

This barn and attachments are built of wood. The sills are of white oak, that being the most durable timber in this region. Chestnut, black walnut, pine or locust will do as well. The other frame timbers may be of any kind of wood, as being dry they are not liable to decay. The sills may stand upon blocks of durable timber, set endwise in the ground, two feet below the surface, and the outside planked up to keep out the cold; or they may be underpinned with stone, laid dry or in mortar—the last plan altogether the best, but the first will do for several years, and the stone work laid afterwards. The sides are covered with pine boards, laid on vertically; the seams or joints battened with strips three inches wide, and the doors and the windows hung and fastened in a substantial manner. Thus the whole building is dry, warm, convenient, and comfortable, to man and to beast.

COST.

The cost of this structure, on the plan submitted, it is difficult to state, depending much on the price of lumber, which varies to the extent of fifty per cent.—even more in different sections of the country; and as hewn timber, scantling, planks, boards and shingles, are the bulk of the material, the expense must vary accordingly as these articles are cheap or dear. Labor, iron work and nails differ little in prices all over the country. If stone underpinning be laid, it will add $500 to the cost over wooden blocks. With the latter, in a lumber country the whole establishment may be built for $2,000. It will be cheap at that. With stone underpinning, complete, and boards at $12 to $15 per 1,000 feet, and other lumber in proportion, it may cost $3,000 to $3,500, depending somewhat on the finish given to it, which may be either increased or curtailed at pleasure. In the essentials, however, no part of the construction should be neglected.

After so fully describing the various parts of the structure, and their different accommodation to the numerous purposes demanded, it may appear superfluous to make a formal array of *claims* to its superiority over other structures of the kind. These may, however, be condensed into: compactness of arrangement and storage; accommodation to all the varieties of crop on the farm; economy in feeding out the forage; saving of labor in that department, by the convenient and compact lodgment of the stock, in connection with the food which they are to consume; the convenience and cheapness in the arrangement of the machinery, driven by either hand or horse power; exceeding convenience of the yards to all kinds of farm stock. In all these a great amount of manual labor is saved—a most important item with the farmer. And last of all, in the appearance of this group of buildings there is a comfort, a fitness and a corresponding character with the farm itself, which should commend itself to the consideration of every husbandman requiring buildings of the kind.

LEWIS F. ALLEN.

BUFFALO, *Jan'y* 30, 1854.

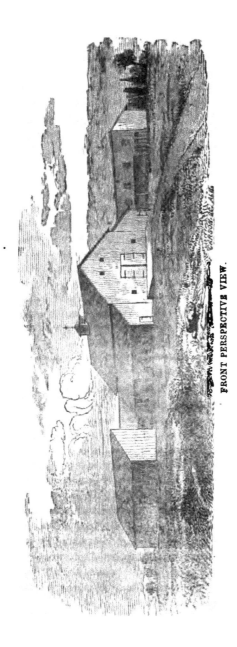

FRONT PERSPECTIVE VIEW.

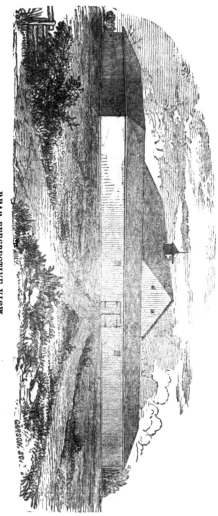

REAR PERSPECTIVE VIEW.

FRONT ELEVATION OF PLAN, SHOWING THE MAIN TIMBERS IN FRAMES.

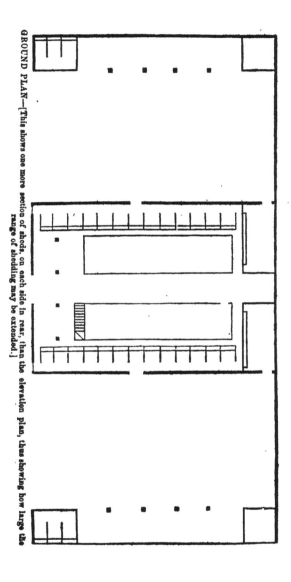

GROUND PLAN—[This shows one more section of sheds, on each side in rear, than the elevation plan, thus showing how large the range of shedding may be extended.]

Having completed the barn arrangement and its connected structures, it now remains to look into the administration of its stores, after the summer and autumn harvests have been gathered within its ample enclosures.

It is related of a distinguished capitalist of our State, that when a young man went to him with the question "how he should go to work to make a fortune?" the reply was, "Why the easiest thing in the world! Put a hundred thousand dollars at interest, and add the annual accumulation to the principal, which also place on interest. Follow it for thirty years, and you will be a rich man." "Very true," replied the inquirer, "but where am I to get the hundred thousand dollars to start with?" "Ah, that is another matter!" said the man of millions. "If you have not the capital to begin upon, I can not advise you." So the first suggestion towards perfect barn management which I would name, is, provide competent buildings to give perfect shelter to all the crops and stock on the farm requiring protection; for without this important item an imperfect administration of barn affairs must be the consequence; and like the rich man's reply, without this prerequisite, any certain course of direction must be at fault. As, however, theoretically, the buildings are provided, the course of procedure will be detailed.

In the first place it is premised that the barn is accommodated with a horse power, which is to drive a thrashing machine and cleaning apparatus for grain, a cutting-box for straw, hay and stalks, and possibly, if a really good one can be found, a crushing machine for coarse grains. In an adjoining building, perhaps, is a steaming apparatus for cooking and softening the food for a portion of the stock. These are all necessary for the perfection of stock keeping in the winter. The hay and grain should be stored in the barn, in such a manner that it may be accessible, each by itself, whenever it may be wanted, without removing a mass of superincumbent forage which covers it; as every removal of the kind, to some extent, wastes and injures it, besides the loss of labor it involves. When the grain is thrashed, the straw should still be kept under cover, if there be room for it; for the moment it goes out of doors, let it be ever so well stacked, more or less waste and depreciation in quality is the consequence. If it is to be *cut up* for stock feeding, its storage inside is certainly an advantage; and if to be fed *long*, under the sheds to outside cattle, if carried out to them direct from the barn, or thrown down from the lofts over head, it comes out clean, bright and palatable. In whatever light, therefore, storage is viewed, it is beneficial to the straw of all cereal grains, and even to that of buckwheat, peas and beans. Indian corn stalks are also included, together with all the hay that is intended to be fed on the farm.

Having stable room enough, every neat animal, or creature larger than a sheep, should be tied up in a stall by itself, excepting perhaps, calves, which may run, to the extent of ten or a dozen, or even up to twenty, in number, in a stable or building, loose by themselves. They should have ample room under cover, and an open yard besides. The advantage of having each creature stabled apart, by itself, that it may have its own proper food, in proper time, quantity and quality, is greater than is usually supposed, as stock, even in the same herd, differ much in their appetites and habits. Sheep may run in very considerable flocks, with sheds to go in and out at pleasure, with feeding racks, or mangers beneath, that storms shall not affect them while feeding, nor injure their food by falling upon it. Any number of sheep, not exceeding two or three hundred, dependent much upon the size of the enclosure, may be wintered together. Even a greater number may be safely kept in a single flock, provided they be not crowded, and are of equal size and age, so that portions of them be not thrust out of the way by the others when feeding, and exposed to storms, when they should be at rest. It is all-important that sheep should be thoroughly assorted when going into winter quarters—the old ones by themselves, and the lambs separate from all others, as each of these require warmer shelter, choicer food and closer attention than the others. Dryness under foot, particularly, is every thing to a sheep, next to food; and shelter over head, although not indispensable in our climate, will pay in their increased fleece and the lessened quantity of food they consume.

WINTER FEEDING.

The stock being brought into winter quarters, if the large animals are stabled, each one should have its own stall, where it is to remain throughout the foddering season, and not be changed. After being wonted, they will find their own stalls, when returning to the stables, with perfect ease; they feed more quietly, and are every way better contented than when changed about, and have no permanent abiding place of their own. Their places once arranged, all the stock should be fed, so far as is possible, by the same hands, and at the same hours. To one who has obverved them, it is surprising to find how animals are affected by subjection to a strict system in all things. The herdsman, if he be a fit man for his business, gets to know the habit and appetite of every animal under his charge, and treats them accordingly. He will save ten to twenty per cent. of food in a winter's keeping, over what irregular attendants would do, and the cattle be better in temper and condition· So with sheep. They are the quietest and most docile creatures in the world, or the shyest and most timid, as they are treated by those who look after them. Shepherds and herdsmen should always love those creatures with whose care they are entrusted. Coarse fodder may sometimes advantageously be fed out, under sheds, in racks or mangers, to stabled cattle, after being let out in the morning and watered. But this should be chiefly 'in severe and dry weather. As with sheep, cattle thus let out should be so assorted that the strong may not overrun the weak; or, where the climate is not too severe, and the shelters good, young cattle may run out in the yard, or under sheds, at will. To pursue this system economically, however, the yard and floor of the sheds should be well drained and the animals properly bedded.

The price of hay, straw and other coarse forage, will much govern the policy of cutting it for stock. The convenience and cost of coarse grains, ground into meal, must also be consulted. All these should be made a matter of strict calculation, together with the cost of increased labor to do the work, which is about double to that of feeding long forage. So far as the hay itself is concerned, the cutting it better' prepares it for the stomach of the animal, saving much labor in mastication. It is quicker eaten and easier digested. Even if no meal is put upon good English hay, it is much better cut than uncut, for any animal, and moistened, with a trifle of salt in the water, they will eat it more readily; so also with coarser forage—but with bran, common mill feed, ground oats, corn, rye or buckwheat upon it, cut and moistened, the coarsest straw of all kinds is eaten up clean, and according to the quantity of meal upon it, with greater economy than hay alone. Sheep, as well as cattle and horses, are very partial to it. Laboring oxen and horses should, when kept up, always have plenty of cut food, when it is possible to provide it for them. There is a saving of at least twenty-five per cent. in using cut feed and meal, over long hay and whole grain, besides enabling the animals to eat it in half the time. As applied to other stock, it must be a matter of calculation and convenience which method to pursue.

Water is one of the chief essentials in the stock yard. Where it is not available by a near stream or spring, or cannot be thrown into the yards by a water ram, pipes, or pumped from a well, cisterns should be constructed and the roof water conducted into them. The horse power will work the pumps, to which they can be cheaply attached. In good cisterns, water will keep all summer. It is computed that every ten feet square, or a hundred square feet of roof will yield five hogsheads of water per annum. An estimate may thus be very accurately formed of the size which cisterns must be made to hold the annual drainage of the roofs. When it is not necessary for cattle to remain in the yards for feeding, after watering, the sooner they are secured back in their stables the better. They are more content there than elsewhere, and lie snug and warm out of harm's way. If there be plenty of straw, the cattle should be liberally bedded; it keeps them clean and warm, and the litter becomes thus better fitted for manure. The stables should be cleaned at night as well as in the morning. Cleanliness is indispensable to the health and comfort of all descriptions of farm stock.

As to the manure, the sooner it is on the land after it is out of the stable, the better; therefore I should not get up expensive compost accommodations in the yards for its manufacture. Yet, if such preparation be necessary, a rough circular shed may be constructed centrally in the chief yard, where the drainage of the buildings may centre—a scooped depression being made for that purpose—and underneath it the manure may be daily brought in wheelbarrows, direct from the stables. As composting manures is a trade by itself, it need not receive further notice here. A deposit thus formed, where the runnings of the yard may converge, and the coarse litter, and all absorbent matter may be thrown to take it up, will probably furnish as valuable and economical a muck heap as can be invented, and it may remain thus sheltered until the necessities or convenience of the farm requires its removal.

A general summing up of the best barn management may be thus: Ample and convenient barn and stable accommodations for all the grain, forage and stock of the farm; horse power machinery to aid in bringing every product into marketable or consumable condition, with the least delay and at the least expense; thorough regularity in feeding every kind of stock on the farm with that food most suitable to their growth, or their milking or fattening developments; an habitual economy and system in every department, regarding time, forage, litter and manure. Let nothing be lost—waste enriches none, but impoverishes all.

LEWIS F. ALLEN

BUFFALO, *February*, 1854.

STATISTICAL TABLES

OF THE AGRICULTURAL PRODUCTS OF PENNSYLVANIA.

———

The tables following are prepared from official returns at the Census office in Washington, and are valuable for the sake of reference as to the actual state of our Agriculture in 1850; and also, to show what an immense surface yet remains to be developed in the State.

AGRICULTURE—FARMS AND IMPLEMENTS, STOCK, PRODUCTS, HOME MANUFACTURES, &c.

COUNTIES.	ACRES OF LAND IN FARMS.		VALUE OF FARMS AND IMPLEMENTS.		LIVE STOCK.				
	Improved.	Unimproved.	Cash value of Farms.	Value of Farming Implements and Machinery.	Horses.	Asses and Mules.	Milch Cows.	Working Oxen.	Other Cattle.
Adams	183,009	72,106	$6,890,066	$228,755	6,408	24	8,408	4	6,063
Allegheny	286,292	147,709	17,952,830	856,588	10,979	27	16,065	281	10,410
Armstrong	188,601	191,196	3,668,908	168,527	7,844	188	8,410	409	11,768
Beaver	124,748	97,251	5,831,172	177,359	5,608	4	6,844	419	6,368
Bedford	148,299	199,262	8,962,047	168,220	6,811	22	7,296	85	7,954
Berks	320,190	92,211	21,429,502	788,998	14,818	99	23,887	48	14,492
Blair	80,088	55,150	8,869,205	129,778	8,612	89	8,768	67	5,830
Bradford	284,029	278,250	8,298,689	892,220	7,288	11	17,067	6,069	20,570
Bucks	298,631	84,810	18,555,583	858,402	12,998	256	25,258	292	9,948
Butler	179,612	107,749	5,014,491	892,266	7,946	16	11,748	1,559	17,171
Cambria	51,021		1,352,348	76,788	8,104	4	4,551	252	5,750
Carbon	14,489	28,678	488,200	28,951	560	40	807	58	687
Centre	114,215	118,510	5,024,568	165,174	5,101	81	5,757	78	11,176
Chester	383,572	82,718	26,425,957	809,863	11,880	76	19,604	5,228	80,244
Clarion	107,817	111,604	2,779,988	160,202	4,167	16	6,122	1,098	7,228
Clearfield	61,116	117,488	1,718,869	94,289	2,601	82	8,426	1,064	8,765
Clinton	44,982	88,229	2,028,610	78,555	1,796	2	2,418	203	8,092
Columbia	90,185	61,298	8,254,346	766	8,592	11	8,886	828	2,601
Crawford	187,451	205,609	5,058,629	269,461	7,477	12	16,912	5,641	28,310
Cumberland	187,931	51,067	8,748,183	802,976	7,207	181	8,901	31	9,890
Dauphin	150,402	71,285	7,175,872	215,341	6,170	47	8,222	25	7,497
Delaware	..,746	16,773	8,873,456	193,626	8,713	10	11,190	789	5,651
Elk	9,7..	57,87.	206,752	14,091	381	2	763	399	729
Erie	179,089	116,490	5,785,638	294,726	7,014	18	16,575	8,994	21,871
Fayette	178,897	153,143	7,3..,.75	249,644	8,108		8,735	896	14,364
Franklin	248,557	98,583	11,911,072	855,940	8,867	18	9,781	11	11,884
Fulton	60,618	68,267	1,146,960	46,726	1,479	8	1,841	51	8,070
Greene	151,612	148,862	6,447,781	125,982	6,102	10	6,481	1,166	10,196

County									
Huntingdon	146,863	156,226	5,147,006	165,849	5,388	2	6,227	182	9,287
India	157,655	189,246	3,118,954	195,698	8,112	177	8,998	685	15,488
Jefferson	56,860	122,900	1,807,095	83,785	2,261	17	8,388	1,817	4,995
Juniata	78,412	42,790	2,617,450	89,820	3,054	......	8,415	66	5,654
...ller	402,480	116,058	85,454,482	939,246	18,777	298	25,434	1,781	27,870
...ne	108,886	68,899	3,042,890	130,665	5,004	44	6,275	1,011	7,958
Lebanon	119,846	46,268	7,085,000	198,415	5,829	15	6,808	4	8,179
Lehigh	141,935	87,099	9,918,608	404,648	6,565	16	9,818	8	5,208
Luzerne	184,580	147,889	6,100,255	236,108	4,050	4	7,902	2,347	8,548
Lycoming	118,264	90,997	4,110,234	164,611	4,066	2	4,940	594	5,909
M'Kean	9,217	21,167	276,820	17,852	299	24	844	892	1,197
...ber	171,792	162,399	4,798,787	247,390	8,026	4	12,525	8,122	16,304
Mifflin	79,109	47,725	4,149,675	150,424	3,858	4	8,495	40	4,006
Moe	60,855	75,897	2,000,748	80,182	2,188	10	8,075	860	8,242
Montgomery	289,231	42,815	20,290,748	763,509	11,481	48	27,767	198	8,169
Montour	67,182	38,002	2,614,949	122,208	2,361	......	8,014	111	2,148
Northampton	80,059	7,128	2,585,675	82,267	1,639	4	2,021	......	1,879
Northumberland	185,086	62,682	5,766,803	242,407	5,025	1	5,794	14	4,779
Perry	111,292	104,969	8,817,790	130,178	4,125	8	5,001	89	6,084
Philadelphia	60,706	4,970	18,659,960	277,969	4,451	87	9,169	49	1,288
Pike	19,079	47,503	959,200	81,536	564	......	1,289	427	1,428
Potter	28,732	56,281	730,986	46,809	671	59	1,976	1,144	2,197
Schuylkill	81,599	82,909	8,097,598	169,674	8,180	2	4,400	99	4,231
Somerset	165,824	210,442	8,874,520	181,688	6,852	4	11,651	66	15,265
Sullivan	17,044	47,465	814,155	22,445	507	24	1,488	724	1,943
Susquehanna	195,798	183,287	5,882,470	231,075	5,288	5	13,886	5,406	17,164
Tioga	106,799	147,939	8,404,497	170,532	8,245	......	7,469	3,461	9,892
Union	182,049	74,881	5,800,718	184,087	5,295	10	6,288	44	5,562
...ngo	98,862	187,191	2,149,697	181,222	3,841	......	6,340	2,251	8,166
...m	49,258	92,780	1,593,186	90,893	1,788	22	4,208	1,669	5,863
Washington	844,046	170,165	14,943,098	341,856	12,055	2	12,284	465	13,418
Wayne	59,569	90,869	2,188,166	103,046	1,603	11	4,963	2,276	5,839
W...land	864,208	145,524	12,576,848	552,353	14,288	......	16,650	67	23,281
Wyoming	46,709	54,386	1,628,580	66,090	1,894	......	3,451	956	8,847
York	806,812	110,940	18,695,948	546,848	10,845	206	15,479	277	18,563
Total	8,628,619	6,294,728	407,876,099	14,742,541	860,398	2,259	580,224	61,527	562,195

23

AGRICULTURE—FARMS AND IMPLEMENTS, STOCK, PRODUCTS, &c.—*Continued.*

COUNTIES.	LIVE STOCK.				PRODUCE DURING THE YEAR ENDING JUNE 1, 1860.			
	Sheep.	Swine.	Value of Live Stock.	Value of Animals slaughtered.	Wheat, bushels of.	Rye, bushels of.	Indian Corn, bushels of	Oats, bushels of.
Adams	7,728	20,571	$559,996	$118,487	818,842	51,197	298,979	261,779
Allegheny	82,138	85,175	1,016,518	165,941	526,836	47,416	438,966	916,103
Armstrong	41,231	19,361	610,949	79,485	197,647	86,434	195,501	470,742
Beaver	81,911	18,560	510,145	90,560	244,112	86,839	226,258	829,481
Bedford	19,027	16,153	515,537	76,976	218,302	88,282	206,344	210,808
Berks	9,524	43,311	1,611,327	427,676	577,608	469,540	811,947	880,769
Blair	10,227	9,712	848,614	73,615	267,349	60,825	145,851	173,017
Bradford	60,403	17,729	1,359,459	230,794	304,675	54,849	371,143	510,176
Bucks	14,579	29,104	1,644,793	394,126	403,909	229,649	1,157,781	1,168,710
Butler	82,696	25,465	804,392	113,822	231,595	121,781	237,339	585,684
Cambria	18,267	5,946	270,653	43,918	42,898	18,947	58,947	193,082
Carbon	841	2,041	63,717	18,767	7,825	28,568	21,852	20,952
Centre	16,763	20,174	548,955	166,288	433,612	109,051	310,112	186,204
Chester	18,364	86,591	2,543,654	495,190	547,498	52,417	1,339,466	1,145,712
Clarion	26,860	18,150	402,946	99,741	165,460	112,010	111,534	279,287
Clearfield	12,232	7,265	277,637	60,054	80,588	81,040	55,948	168,870
Clinton	6,116	5,877	201,530	44,417	191,065	36,798	115,760	65,946
Columbia	8,392	12,783	864,982	97,620	153,700	102,193	149,530	160,364
Crawford	86,705	18,199	1,167,418	128,187	142,414	42,795	387,556	418,751
Cumberland	10,238	27,165	721,813	165,414	187,182	89,988	861,166	422,100
Dauphin	5,682	21,602	557,140	157,888	308,879	117,606	840,755	870,027
Delaware	7,424	11,267	763,480	280,755	121,096	1,909	214,209	169,754
Elk	1,586	676	60,086	7,749	4,749	6,265	10,076	24,040
Erie	66,705	15,417	1,070,519	157,571	147,825	10,203	48,692	433,765
Fayette	88,278	22,912	782,299	150,807	801,102	20,007	696,092	506,385
Franklin	18,375	84,532	888,580	196,765	887,062	77,102	539,976	803,447
Fulton	4,896	5,613	147,570	80,285	88,758	27,780	60,885	49,075
Greene	54,978	21,876	599,546	74,807	189,149	86,016	556,634	270,270
Huntingdon	19,686	15,262	581,228	129,568	865,278	79,406	221,392	280,186
Indiana	46,346	19,815	704,212	163,812	209,768	98,765	218,636	94,182

Jefferson	18,999	7,208	251,881	45,008	76,999	40,743	58,877	145,828
Juniata	6,809	10,152	284,806	78,250	187,187	32,438	138,688	102,493
Lancaster	19,876	57,535	2,340,587	517,879	1,365,111	151,067	1,803,312	1,578,321
Lawrence	76,654	15,504	508,040	61,871	168,246	32,820	205,620	292,218
Leon	2,974	14,875	490,452	135,887	274,095	75,122	241,939	872,542
High	5,297	18,818	725,382	162,999	261,301	827,505	897,048	289,669
Luzerne	18,496	16,864	654,805	139,236	165,828	125,604	290,122	287,797
Lycoming	14,230	14,197	429,382	97,581	285,925	95,274	262,466	106,308
M'Kean	8,726	890	65,647	11,469	1,962	585	10,172	29,974
Deer	80,652	28,680	846,511	118,164	206,729	50,895	268,710	385,976
Mifflin	7,471	11,382	855,556	78,328	305,994	26,640	218,896	191,018
Monroe	5,995	7,913	286,115	54,380	14,620	118,158	101,829	52,676
Montgomery	10,982	24,678	1,568,646	472,836	809,255	263,292	878,244	699,824
Montour	6,288	9,289	227,951	63,334	126,217	56,130	188,279	98,056
Northampton	1,501	5,483	200,462	42,180	165,147	70,596	136,668	46,980
Northumberland	9,986	17,748	548,073	107,602	289,522	120,354	282,087	194,676
Perry	10,154	13,516	844,973	79,870	190,697	91,098	155,271	144,142
Philadelphia	989	9,278	579,780	201,858	121,204	18,968	294,891	117,024
Pike	1,560	2,261	114,781	23,786	3,546	40,365	88,608	16,874
Potter	8,849	1,512	168,778	27,181	13,359	884	18,562	80,814
Schuylkill	5,872	10,877	881,210	96,459	64,928	122,052	165,556	121,505
Somerset	28,306	11,365	627,263	72,531	92,186	93,928	81,166	471,812
Sullivan	4,718	2,968	94,971	16,392	11,959	8,380	21,437	29,775
Susquehanna	42,971	11,345	978,359	116,360	83,788	83,942	237,343	865,649
Tioga	82,750	7,757	634,624	108,535	141,896	6,612	147,140	800,017
Union	9,981	15,911	471,890	94,198	353,015	78,804	180,563	282,332
Venango	41,689	18,616	416,289	79,193	98,189	49,185	109,042	255,146
Warren	22,026	8,189	301,628	45,826	83,756	5,614	83,898	156,480
Washington	870,944	44,470	1,636,439	169,812	563,182	26,874	804,540	855,943
Wayne	10,963	3,635	381,536	72,872	6,177	27,285	50,577	96,094
Westmoreland	61,344	42,238	1,696,849	250,896	668,476	82,355	889,711	1,161,656
Wyoming	8,809	5,104	260,337	54,005	62,734	40,239	116,849	88,682
York	18,681	34,603	1,186,715	289,816	578,828	191,686	707,161	582,817
Total	1,822,867	1,040,866	41,500,058	8,219,848	16,867,691	4,805,160	19,885,214	21,638,166

AGRICULTURE—FARMS AND IMPLEMENTS, STOCK, PRODUCTS, &c.—Continued.

PRODUCE DURING THE YEAR ENDING JUNE 1, 1850.

COUNTIES.	Tobacco, pounds of.	Wool, pounds of.	Peas and Beans, bushels of.	Irish Potatoes, bushels of.	Sweet Potatoes, bushels of.	Barley, bushels of.	Buckwheat, bushels of.	Value of Orchard products in dollars.
Adams........	....	28,697	5	87,689	1,461	80	2,412	$5,847
Allegheny....	72	215,802	1,460	257,408	6,092	10,525	22,802	38,180
Armstrong....	....	90,973	451	55,446	74	8,044	56,189	8,829
Beaver.......	....	211,878	876	76,597	481	5,082	85,231	18,952
Bedford......	1,680	87,791	....	84,695	....	1,204	18,400	1,086
Berks........	....	19,576	1,118	246,358	119	944	82,872	71,452
Blair........	200	26,278	....	25,192	4	8,686	5,226	1,276
Bradford.....	....	164,924	4,476	322,816	25	8,975	128,081	5,779
Bucks........	....	33,280	2,850	246,536	245	440	55,429	69,809
Butler.......	....	187,280	489	124,257	80	6,034	188,806	7,848
Cambria......	....	29,609	280	20,784	....	8,622	21,658	92
Carbon.......	....	1,761	29	20,768	40	....	10,511	4,990
Centre.......	....	86,628	84	55,568	....	11,263	6,919	....
Chester......	....	22,788	872	170,620	5,290	1,918	12,558	89,689
Clarion......	....	67,780	106	42,936	....	1,017	56,675	259
Clearfield...	....	81,498	490	24,862	1,068	180	85,159	4
Clinton......	....	15,659	20	85,690	17	814	10,960	4,688
Columbia.....	....	23,394	88	86,524	56	....	38,956	7,817
Crawford.....	....	208,068	781	165,662	....	1,175	92,389	28,675
Cumberland...	200	26,368	45	48,546	275	7,620	2,129	18,569
Dauphin......	50,200	14,982	1,801	115,827	2,816	889	9,216	17,467
Delaware.....	....	3,406	188	108,508	81	170	698	18,717
Elk..........	....	4,514	199	16,708	....	117	5,658	288
Erie.........	8,000	179,108	8,141	171,855	170	42,852	27,272	17,827
Fayette......	....	102,604	52	47,677	1,622	142	21,668	8,927
Franklin.....	....	44,192	1,687	51,898	196	2,568	3,800	84,819
Fulton.......	....	18,094	....	8,876	....	....	6,416	515
Greene.......	2,250	185,665	10	17,760	590	18	19,450	2,602
Huntingdon...	7,000	51,884	170	41,296	285	2,088	21,015	9,159
Indiana......	....	105,486	591	49,804	....	816	67,288	1,187

County								
Jefferson	......	3,827	374	28,746	......	808	80,897	1,047
Juniata	......	14,686	40	23,728	......	1,395	8,167	6,401
Lancaster	878,060	29,043	459	215,277	6,840	7,877	6,684	80,151
Lawrence	......	196,145	556	61,148	29	7,589	64,171	7,185
...en	......	6,713	......	46,718	00	360	871	2,477
Lebigh	1,?40	21,8?0	60	181,811	171	1,516	28,265	9,155
...ne	......	49,872	88?	188,047	......	291	116,178	8,335
Lycoming	......	85,220	5	86,278	40	1,809	52,609	5,586
M'Kean	......	9,657	676	17,604	......	92	8,689	1,059
Mercer	......	218,359	865	101,860	66	1,885	114,426	6,787
M...	......	21,068	11	34,821	0	2,057	4,406	1,907
Monroe	20	1,616	190	67,435	36	20	77,866	1,186
Montgomery	100	14,?07	604	238,824	49	1,785	15,641	19,100
...on	......	2,7?.	107	47,176	48	42	16,879	6,700
Northumberland	65,?50	96,670	......	47,330	......	660	1,194	3,582
Perry	......	24,469	8	121,496	210	82	84,427	7,829
Philadelphia	8,500	1,679	201	48,772	850	51	19,872	12,227
Pike	......	8,519	90?	385,849	53	848	7,205	18,432
Potter	......	22,048	2,8..	52,059	......	......	29,615	......
Schuylkill	......	15,255	70	43,780	......	848	15,997	1,467
Somerset	......	66,503	28	138,380	......	......	42,884	20,084
Sullivan	......	12,066	850	34,3?7	......	98	88,618	109
Susquehanna	......	91,450	1,977	27,349	......	......	17,802	832
Tioga	......	86,212	16,140	1??,086	5,12.	447	80,377	6,029
Union	......	25,149	2	158,4?9	18	6,888	60,954	8,645
Venango	800	80,114	81	78,6?6	......	260	12,782	8,046
Warren	2	54,498	2,080	97,287	......	70	100,878	629
Washington	......	983,167	262	48,603	1,579	14,868	28,868	5,926
Wayne	......	28,928	8,446	49,646	5,884	140	12,682	59,877
...land	......	161,351	1,246	180,388	1,248	2,824	60,786	8,059
Wyoming	17,970	19,339	78	108,299	......	150	62,0..	15,706
York	418,555	88,193	124	65,821	9,048	1,868	60,982	29,833
Total	912,651	4,481,570	56,281	5,980,782	52,172	165,684	2,198,692	725,0..

AGRICULTURE—FARMS AND IMPLEMENTS, STOCK, PRODUCTS, &c.—Continued.

PRODUCE DURING THE YEAR ENDING JUNE 1, 1850.

COUNTIES.	Wine, gallons of.	Value of produce of market gardens.	Butter, pounds of.	Cheese, pounds of.	Hay, tons of.	Cloverseed, bushels of.	Other Grass seeds, bushels of.	Hops, pounds of.	Hemp, dew rotted, tons of.
Adams	....	$4	624,424	1,180	36,639	8,600	1,655	88	....
Allegheny	480	48,807	971,484	8,644	35,836	459	834	403	....
Armstrong	....	5,279	489,103	1,339	16,847	527	472	76	....
Beaver	2,571	1,695	498,772	2,760	17,915	1,057	1,111	2,636	....
Bedford	55	55	846,587	1,010	18,094	....	89	6	....
Berks	16,825	17,116	1,873,294	8,927	83,257	406	1,924	1,153	2
Blair	2	....	203,088	1,758	18,637	1,887	50	80	....
Bradford	70	815	1,590,248	108,413	73,700	1,110	869	22	....
Bucks	875	2,464	2,336,182	6,838	62,842	14,864	5,017	2,587	4
Butler	6	5,902	699,764	2,208	31,195	1,062	998	1,157	....
Cambria	....	....	290,780	....	10,326	141	149	....	....
Carbon	4	40	31,890	850	3,041	79	50	63	....
Centre	....	75	414,715	....	18,530	6,119	....	....	8
Chester	889	8,457	2,092,981	88,012	96,316	9,775	8,122	2,364	8
Clarion	....	....	....	228	17,086	1,857	249	703	....
Clearfield	....	60	42,846	870	10,556	443	8	18	....
Clinton	8	....	140,456	125	6,696	1,800	11	232	....
Columbia	6	1,686	368,055	....	12,884	1,958	187	79	....
Crawford	51	71	1,267,486	810,584	70,784	277	267	54	10
Cumberland	5	4,326	782,587	2,517	81,788	2,077	977	833	....
Dauphin	28	9,356	575,668	114	27,814	1,566	1,733	91	....
Delaware	....	4,350	1,842,248	7,210	27,932	446	1,154	161	....
Elk	....	40	31,755	810	26,661	86	77	....	....
Erie	129	8,833	252,848	754,452	69,422	1,720	1,258	1,260	....
Fayette	....	4,692	553,565	19,650	22,096	1,822	986	108	....
Franklin	2	2,616	670,466	4,571	88,591	8,744	1,218	247	7
Fulton	....	....	100,260	100	4,752	88	86	....	....
Greene	....	4,804	459,180	20,775	15,086	108	948	4	....
Huntingdon	....	7,886	331,268	8,461	17,842	259	198	524	....
Indiana	....	164	470,251	4,284	18,189	888	748	27	....

County									
Jefferson		80	147,816	2,850	9,116	280	216	40	
Juniata	1,047	40	262,085		12,288	2,304	16		
Lancaster	90	14,035	1,907,848	18,848	96,184	10,829	8,187	470	
Lawrence	520	273	420,650	12,825	22,025	830	892	403	
Lebanon	995		417,074	100	25,602	1,115	1,075	8	
Lehigh		1,456	838,816		80,832	8,068	505	91	2
Luzerne	25	8,192	558,168	91,618	81,601	997	237	114	
Lycoming		5,481	800,401	120	15,035	1,302	5	27	
M'Kean	20		66,186	7,920	5,856		44		
Mercer	11	461	625,572	214,931	41,579	898	865	860	2
Mifflin		20	264,850	2,380	13,196	8,741	91	5	
Monroe	1,088	11	174,204		10,258	600	27	293	5
Montgomery	20	18,162	8,048,089	10,662	98,701	4,834	4,526	481	
Montour		4,879	276,941	90	10,429	2,888	101	222	
Northampton	27	1,200	205,100	789	7,126	853	22	279	2
Northumberland	5	1,472	501,619	7	20,310	2,448	1,727	470	
Perry	292	1,608	80,289	487	16,690	2,142	481	78	
Philadelphia		486,818	671,061	88	28,282	701	854		
Pike			99,517	870	4,479				
Potter	40		165,677	13,254	5,717	89	852	160	
Schuylkill	69	14,817	824,143	80	16,644	779	355	88	
Somerset		89	777,204	241	29,620	254	483	21	
Sullivan	5		90,250	455	4,719	89	129		
Susquehanna		170	1,020,578	121,019	50,105	274	608	90	
Tioga		16	724,281	57,890	37,614	58	1,268	58	2
Union		28	877,190		20,811	2,274	192	28	
Venango	58	400	819,870	4,008	15,663	618	166	10	
Warren		50	835,725	29,550	20,990	70	245	974	
Washington			860,568	20,805	41,269	457	8,109	66	
Wayne	68	17,818	891,814	22,906	25,880	9	95	1,585	2
Westmoreland	129	8,519	1,711,854	82,215	48,024	4,980	1,225	46	
Wyoming		29,460	211,215	21,140	9,788	198	4		
York	180	1,085	1,082,579	4,082	50,760	5,661	1,455	804	
Total	25,590	688,714	89,878,418	2,505,034	1,842,970	125,030	53,918	22,088	44

AGRICULTURE—FARMS AND IMPLEMENTS, STOCK, PRODUCTS, &c.—*Continued.*

PRODUCE DURING THE YEAR ENDING JUNE 1, 1850.

COUNTIES.	Wine, gallons of.	Value of produce of market gardens.	Butter, pounds of.	Cheese, pounds of.	Hay, tons of.	Cloverseed, bushels of.	Other Grass seeds, bushels of.	Hops, pounds of.	Hemp, tons of.
Adams	......	$4	624,424	1,180	86,639	8,600	1,655	88	......
Allegheny	480	48,807	971,434	8,644	35,836	459	8?4	403	......
Armstrong	......	5,279	489,108	1,339	16,647	527	472	76	......
Beaver	2,571	1,695	498,772	2,760	1?,915	1,057	1,111	2,636	......
Bedford	......	55	846,587	1,010	18,094	......	89	6	......
Berks	16,325	17,116	1,873,294	8,927	83,257	1,?06	1,924	1,158	2
Blair	2	......	203,088	1,758	13,627	1,887	60	80	......
Bradford	70	815	1,590,218	108,4?	74,0??	1,110	869	22	......
Bucks	875	2,464	2,836,182	6,4?3	?0,842	14,804	5,017	2,587	......
Butler	6	5,902	699,764	2,298	31,195	1,662	998	1,157	4
Cambria	......	......	290,780	......	10,326	141	149	......	......
Carbon	4	40	81,390	350	3,041	79	59	63	......
Centre	......	75	414,71?	88,012	18,530	6,119	......	......	......
Chester	889	8,457	2,092,?81	228	96,315	9,775	8,122	2,364	8
Clarion	......	66	42,845	870	17,086	1,357	249	703	8
Clearfield	8	......	140,456	125	10,556	483	8	18	......
Clinton	6	1,688	368,055	......	6,696	1,800	11	232	......
Crawford	......	71	1,267,486	810,584	12,884	1,968	187	79	10
Cumberland	51	4,3?6	782,587	2,617	70,784	277	267	54	......
Dauphin	5	9,850	575,668	114	81,785	2,077	977	833	......
Delaware	28	40	1,342,243	7,210	27,814	1,566	1,733	91	......
Elk	......	8,883	81,755	810	27,932	446	1,154	31	......
Erie	129	4,692	252,848	764,452	26,661	86	77	......	......
Fayette	5	2,616	553,565	19,550	69,422	1,720	1,253	1,260	......
Franklin	28	......	670,466	4,571	22,096	1,822	986	108	7
Fulton	2	......	100,260	160	88,591	8,744	1,218	247	......
Greene	......	4,804	459,180	20,776	4,752	688	86	......	......
Huntingdon	......	7,380	311,263	8,461	15,080	108	948	4	......
Indiana	......	154	470,251	4,2?4	17,842	2,769	19?	524	......

Jefferson		80	147,816	2,850	9,116	280	216	40	
...ita	1,047	40	262,035		12,233	2,364	16		
...ncer	90	14,035	1,907,848	13,848	96,184	10,829	8,187	470	
Lawrence	520	273	420,660	12,825	22,025	880	892	403	
Lebanon	995		417,074	100	25,602	1,115	1,075	8	2
Lehigh		1,456	888,816		80,382	8,068	505	91	
Luzerne		8,192	558,168	91,618	81,601	497	287	114	
Lycoming	25	5,481	800,401	120	15,035	1,802	5	27	
M'Kean			66,186	7,920	5,856		44		2
Mercer	20	461	625,572	214,931	41,579	893	865	860	
...in	11		264,859	2,330	18,196	8,741	91	5	5
Monroe			174,204		10,253	600	27	298	
Montgomery	1,088	18,162	8,048,049	10,662	98,017	4,334	4,526	481	
Montour	20	4,879	276,941	90	10,429	2,888	101	222	2
Northampton		1,200	205,110	789	7,126	858	22		
Northumberland	27	1,472	501,619	7	20,310	2,443	1,727	279	
Perry	6	1,608	802,189	487	16,690	2,142	481	470	
Philadelphia	292	486,818	671,661	88	28,282	701	854	78	2
Pike			99,617	870	4,479				
Potter			168,677		2,717	89	852	160	
Schuylkill	40	14,817	324,143	13,254	16,644	779	855	88	2
Somerset	69	89	777,204	241	29,620	254	483	21	
Sullivan			90,250	485	4,719	89	129		
Susquehanna	5	170	1,020,578	121,019	50,105	274	603	90	
Tioga		16	724,281	57,890	87,614	58	1,258	53	
Union		28	877,190		20,811	2,274	192	28	
Venango		400	819,870	4,008	15,663	618	166	10	
Warren		50	835,725	29,550	20,990	70	245	974	2
Washington		17,318	860,563	20,805	41,269	467	8,109	66	
Wayne	58	8,519	891,814	22,906	25,380	9	95		
Westmoreland	129	29,460	1,711,854	82,215	48,024	4,980	1,225	1,585	
Wyoming			211,215	21,140	9,788	198	46	4	
York	180	1,085	1,082,579	4,082	50,760	5,661	1,455	804	
Total	25,590	688,714	89,878,418	2,505,084	1,842,970	126,080	58,918	22,088	44

AGRICULTURE—FARMS AND IMPLEMENTS, STOCK, PRODUCTS, &c.—Continued.

PRODUCE DURING THE YEAR ENDING JUNE 1, 1850.

COUNTIES.	Flax, pounds of	Flaxseed, bushels of	Silk Cocoons, pounds of	Maple Sugar, pounds of	Molasses, gallons of	Beeswax and Honey, pounds of.	Value of Home-made manufactures.
Adams	7,550	690			511	2,708	$3,068
Allegheny	1,305	65		1,687		12,589	11,614
Armstrong	11,446	1,436		8,103	208	12,514	15,520
Beaver	9,917	499	10	8,890	429	19,102	14,517
Bedford		2		12,959	221		5,621
Berks	15,873	2,192	1		100	6,462	21,175
Blair	895	71		2,550	40	289	1,686
Bradford	10,100	463		198,891		62,924	89,858
Bucks	104,285	6,290		78	271	15,944	14,862
Butler	29,723	1,950	82	7,314	560	49,295	81,166
Cambria	2,517	225		39,655		4,189	9,970
Carbon	534	54			4,508	1,865	137
Centre				100		10	5,472
Chester	2,974	131		1,524	230	10,815	4,018
Clarion	2,719	167		5,577	527	77,981	16,678
Clearfield	100	7		1,030	134	6,201	7,701
Clinton	2,635	54				4,404	633
Columbia	15,127	905		14,310	517	20,428	14,202
Crawford	9,210	810	80	219,912	2,016	48,547	32,802
Cumberland	8,046	288	5			1,205	5,416
Dauphin	4,461	311	1			1,158	8,798
Delaware	228	5				1,621	2,226
Elk	50	1				561	10,621
Erie	18,729	860		9,394	446	28,239	28,681
Fayette	7,651	863		833,748	1,875	18,952	24,374
Franklin	1,224	221		86,630	8,967	1,810	4,246
Fulton	1,078	70		799	17	1,560	8,558
Greene	18,400	704		67,481	2,888	15,827	27,840
Huntingdon	2,841	448		6,356	788	12,684	10,582
Indiana	86,805	2,928		10,298	1,180	25,878	81,182

County							
Jefferson	8,189	181			2,295	2,886	5,126
Juniata	60	14	6			70	
Lancaster	7,818	564	2	20,781	1,564	7,468	14,058
Lawrence	16,546	1,644	22			23,120	2,602
Lebanon	2,281	169				294	8,287
Lehigh	18,812	2,840	10	19,768	148	8,926	9,816
Luzerne	4,748	292		1,480		26,521	17,888
Lycoming	2,858	196		45,674		7,808	2,260
M'Kean	850	7	1	64,242	8,856	8,094	1,769
Mercer	41,561	2,310		80	15	24,125	19,712
Mifflin	177	8		879	150	2,890	742
Monroe	4,548	251	40			8,274	6,057
Montgomery	29,164	8,014				7,175	8,360
Montour	5,867	447		26		5,678	8,107
Northampton	8,468	256			62		252
Northumberland	8,708	757	7	280	6	14,287	8,280
Perry	8,181	898	2	1,518		2,896	11,618
Philadelphia						1,229	156
Pike	460	22				1,167	175
Potter	1,818	42		184,887	2,106	18,066	9,529
Schuylkill	8,188	842	21	878,798	7,667	9,984	2,976
Somerset	18,580	1,456		65,000	1,669	4,778	26,887
Sullivan	225	12		167,181	472	10,869	5,764
Susquehanna	2,648	48	9	202,851	299	22,998	89,034
Tioga	2,656	198		2,065	528	83,468	18,462
Union	8,188	440		14,678	486	8,440	4,862
Venango	1,144	183		88,705	466	27,449	14,046
Warren	1,008	85	2	25,963		12,917	10,768
Washington	5,680	828		27,398	8,540	88,679	24,724
Wayne	4		5	81,242	819	12,272	10,051
Westmoreland	23,420	2,892		2,990	8,261	22,967	51,616
Wyoming	2,092	82				7,855	6,025
York	8,272	1,159	29			24,894	7,468
Total	580,807	41,728	285	2,826,625	50,652	839,509	749,183

24

MERCER COUNTY.

ADDRESS DELIVERED BEFORE THE MERCER COUNTY AGRICULTURAL SOCIETY, AT ITS ANNUAL MEETING, ON THE TWENTIETH OF SEPTEMBER, 1853, BY JAMES GOWEN, ESQ., OF MOUNT AIRY.

[It has been thought proper, in the preparation of this year's Transactions of the Pennsylvania State Agricultural Society, to re-republish this very practical address on account of the numerous errors occurring in it, through the great haste with which the last volume was hurried through the office of the State Printer, to meet the demand for the work by the members of the Legislature.—B. C. W.]

At a meeting of the Mercer County Agricultural Society, held on their exhibition ground, the 20th instant, the following resolution was offered and unanimously adopted, to wit:

Resolved, That the thanks of this society be tendered to James Gowen, Esq., for the able address which he has this day delivered to us, and that he be requested to furnish the society with a copy of the same for publication.

———

MERCER, SEPTEMBER 21, 1853.

JAMES GOWEN, ESQ.—*Dear Sir:* In pursuance of the above resolution, permit me, on behalf of the Mercer County Agricultural Society, to request that, at your earliest convenience, you will furnish the society with a copy, for publication, of the excellent address you delivered at their late annual-exhibition.

Yours, very respectfully,

W. MAXWELL.

SEPTEMBER 22, 1853.

DEAR SIR: In complying with the request of the Mercer County Agricultural Society, as I cheerfully do, permit me to hope that the address, when published, will serve as a memento of the kind feelings reciprocated by the members of your respectable society and myself, during my visit to your beautiful region, as well as, in some degree, to promote the interests of Agriculture in Western Pennsylvania.

Very respectfully,

Your obedient servant,

JAMES GOWEN.

W. MAXWELL, ESQ.

ADDRESS.

Mr. President, and Gentlemen of the Mercer County Agricultural Society:

When you did me the honor to invite me to address you, on the occasion of this your annual agricultural exhibition, my engagements at home were so numerous and pressing, that it seemed almost impossible that I should be able to comply with your invitation. The little time, too, that was to intervene, until I should have to appear before you, affording but so brief a space for preparation, with the distance I should have to travel before I reached you, all tended to increase the difficulties of the case. These difficulties could only have been overcome by the devotion that has almost, I might say, become a passion in me, for the promotion of Agriculture—a devotion that neither years of labor in the cause, nor the disappointments that sometimes. attended my best efforts, could either abate or measurably subdue; and there-. fore it is that I am here—here, for the first time, in Western Pennsylvania.

Another reason why I could not refuse your request was, that I was, as many of you know, among the foremost, if not the first, in calling the atten-. tion of the farmers of Pennsylvania to the necessity of organizing a State Agricultural Society, as a means of awakening every part of the State to a sense of the expediency of forming county associations, for. the purpose of eliciting and diffusing, mutually, the benefits to be derived from a combined effort in promoting the prosperity, intelligence and dignity of the landed interest—the much neglected, though most important interest of the country. Prominent then as I was, as a promoter of those organizations, it could not be that when one of those societies, which had sprung into existence through my efforts, and in accordance with the hopes and anticipations I had cherished, called upon me to address them on the occasion of their annual exhibi- tion, it could not be, I repeat, that either the fatigues of the journey, or home cares and engagements, could afford, to my apprehension, a satisfactory ex- cuse for declining a task which a sense of duty so sternly enjoined I should undertake. How well or ill I might perform that task, as affecting your ex- pectations, was not so much a consideration with me, as that I should prove myself willing to do the best I could for the cause I felt myself bound to serve and promote.

Agricultural exhibitions have ever been with me a favorite expedient,. whereby a laudable emulation and rivalry might be promoted among the tillers of the soil, and to serve as a rallying point, where, in the presence of each other, they might learn to have more confidence in themselves, and. by emulating the progress of others, snatch a spark of that spirit and enterprise, : so luminous now-a-days, in the track of the busy throng, that are pushing along and going ahead with railroad speed. It grieved me to perceive that the farmers, as a class, seemed regardless of the position, however low or ob- scure, assigned to them; appearing ever content to labor unrequited and un- honored; complaining not, nor attempting to reverse the decree that fashion, folly and pretension had recorded to their prejudice. Such should not, I thought, be the condition of the farmer. His calling or profession is in itself so intrinsically independent, that it seems strange (unless there is something in the soil with which he deals that deadens, or in the air he breathes that bewilders his faculties,) that he should not have the sense and spirit to stand more erect, and battle manfully for that lofty position, which is his rightful heritage!

To the husbandman, under Providence, is committed the bounties of the field and seasons, and upon his management depend, not only the wealth of the nation, but the daily sustenance of every man, whether rich or poor, high or low. Plenty and scarcity, fulness and famine, in a great measure depend upon the foresight, skill and energy of the farmer; he holds the veritable cornucopia, and so long as it is found in condition of teeming fulness, pouring out the invigorating comforts of sustenance, so long does the human family wax strong, rejoicing in the enjoyment of health and vigor! Let it give but a partial supply, or none, feebleness and languor, famine and pestilence, brood over all and enshroud every living creature! Is there a man so obtuse or insensible, whether mechanic or manufacturer, merchant or professional man, as not to perceive how indespensable are the functions of the farmer? Why should he not be held as ordinarily intelligent, with perceptions capable of penetrating the hidden operations of nature, so far as they lie within his sphere of action; profiting by all that is deducible from, or observable in her teachings? And is it not a reproach to us farmers, if we do not establish our claim to this high consideration, and prove that we are not the dull unenlightened drudges we are supposed to be—good but so far as material strength may serve, to toil with other working animals of the field!

Agricultural exhibitions are the precursors of improvement—they are eminently calculated to arrest the attention of the apathetic—to break in upon the dull monotony that prevades the locality where the fair is held. They are as interesting as they are instructive, and never fail, if properly conducted, of impressing a salutary and abiding influence upon the minds of all who have participated in their interesting display and innocent recreation. Within their enclosures are to be found the best specimens of farm stock, the choicest varieties of seeds, samples of the best crops, improved implements of husbandry, specimens of household manufacture, butter, cheese and poultry; all arranged for the inspection of the curious, and challenging competition. Who can look upon such a scene and not be struck with a deep sense of its utility, and what farmer, however enlightened, but may add something to his stock of knowledge, or have his doubts removed as to the excellence of some breed of farm stock, or the capability of some implement, which he had never used, for the work it was designed to execute? And who can be insensible to the advantages of such an opportunity for an interchange of opinion upon the theory and practice of culture and husbandry, upon soils, and the adaptation of crops and manures to each variety respectively? These, with the friendly greetings, the revival of old acquaintanceships, and the formation of new friendships, give to the scene a holiday freshness—a dash of rural felicity, that compensates for many a long and solitary day of toil upon the farm.

But exhibitions should be kept within their primitive and legitimate bounds. If they should be permitted to run into ridiculous frolic, fun and folly, then good-bye to all the hopes of improvement, cherished through their means, by those who labored sedulously to promote them. If mountebanks, venders of nostrums, cute sharpers and monstrosities, with all their base and degrading concomitants, be tolerated, and their iniquitous jugglery be played off before the eyes of unsophisticated farmers and their families, it were better that Agricultural Fairs and cattle shows were abolished; for who can answer for the consequences of such demoralizing scenes? Visitors are liable to be drawn off from the real objects of the exhibition by the lures of those impostors, and made the victims of their heartless impositions. Some youth, perchance, may be taken with the spirit of their adroitness and manner, and become affected with a moral leprosy that may cleave to him for the remainder of his days—a relish for their trickery will beget a distate for honest industry, and lead him into the ways of the idle and profligate, the humbug or mountebank, the gambler or pickpocket.

The State Societies are obnoxious to those objections; their exhibitions seem to be held more with a view of drawing together a monstrous crowd or multitude, to put money in the purse and to gain popular eclat, than to promote, earnestly and appropriately, the cause of Agriculture. Farm stock, implements, &c., are, it is true, in abundance; but then, where is the chance of fixing the attention of visitors upon these, or of holding discussions on their qualities, when along their borders and within their very grounds are to be seen the flaunting signs of mountebanks, offering to show wonders and sights unparalleled, and tricks incomprehensible, for a " 'levenpenny-bit!"— While a dozen of throats at a time, rise above the ordinary noise, vociferating at the highest pitch, recommendations of the infalliable nostrums they are vending, to credulous crowds gathered around their stands; and ever and anon, thimble-riggers and pickpockets are plying their nefarious trades, undetected amid the general confusion of this disgusting Babel! Another great source of evil springs of necessity from, or is incidental to, the inordinate desire for monster exhibitions, and that is, they must be held at or near to cities, in order that lodging may be had for the multitude, and in order to obtain the largest sum possible from the inhabitants, by way of bonus, for the favor of the exhibition, to aid in defraying the expenses of the show. Such places seldom fail of having their due share of rowdies and ruffians, and these are sure to precipitate themselves upon the exhibition grounds, and if not restrained by an overpowering police, will perpetrate various outrages, still further disgracing, and deepening the disgust which such a spectacle, take it all in all, cannot fail to produce.

These scenes are not imaginary—they are founded in fact, and are pointed at through a sense of duty, and under deep concern for the influence they may exert upon the public mind, especially upon the rising generation. If instead of presenting, as naturally they should, so interesting and respectable an assemblage as this now before me, with nothing to offend against propriety or good taste, but all in harmony with the peaceable and honorable pursuits of Agriculture, they exhibit scenes of depravity, wild and vicious incongruity, they must be regarded as dangerous nuisances, that should be abated for the same reasons that have placed horse-racing under the ban of public opinion. In this connection I observed recently that among the premiums offered at a forth-coming exhibition, east of us, were several to young females, under a certain age, for the best performance on horseback, or the best *female* horsemanship. Now, in the name of sense and propriety, what have such feats to do with Agriculture? If it were to train up candidates for the circus or hippodrome, the race-ground would be a more fitting arena for the purpose than the enclo-sure of an Agricultural Fair and Cattle Show. And how must the modesty of a young girl be outraged, if she be subjected to the vulgar gaze and com-ments of the crowd, and her sense of delicacy blunted, if she receive a pecuniary reward for the exhibition of her person and prowess? What should fathers, mothers and brothers think of the consequences likely to ensue to a daughter or sister thus tempted to forego the native delicacy and bashfulness inherent in the gentler sex?

Of the popular improvements agitated of late, Agricultural education has claimed, as its importance deserved, a due share of consideration; its benefits have been freely discussed and enlarged upon by the Agricultural press. In-ferences have been drawn and illustrations given, of the utility of the system of training practised in the Agricultural seminaries of Great Britain and Ireland, and other parts of Europe. Enlightened and patriotic travelers from this side the Atlantic, while sojourning abroad, have visited those schools, and have borne unqualified testimony in their favor; among these, I may mention Professor Bache, now the head of the coast survey, who, when appointed president of the Girard College, visited Europe for the purpose of looking into educational systems and training, bearing semblance to the insti-tution over which he was to preside; and here I may say, that it was a mis-fortune greatly to be deplored by the orphans of Pennsylvania, that the pecu-niary embarrassments of the city of Philadelphia, involving the college fund, suspended the opening of the college, and lost to it a president, whose profound scholarship and enlightened philanthropy so pre-eminently fitted him for the station, that never perhaps again will it be the good fortune of the college to pos-sess his equal. This feeble tribute to a good and gifted man cannot be consider-ed out of place here, when it is understood that he was not unmindful of the in-terests of Agriculture, but labored in its behalf. He visited Agricultural schools abroad, took notes of their workings, and brought home special reports of many of them. He did more; he collected, in farming districts abroad, a large collection of seeds, which must have required much time and pains; among them, the greatest and best varieties of wheat, put up in phials, sealed and labelled, that were ever seen before or since in this country; they would have proved of incalculable value, and through recurring harvests have made the name of Professor A. D. Bache as familiar among husbandmen as it is among men of science and learning of the present day ; but unfortunately the city councils, to whose custody the seeds were committed, neglected to distribute them until the wevil had entirely destroyed them.

The late Mr. Coleman, an intelligent and devoted agriculturist, during his agricultural tour, paid particular attention to these schools, and speaks of them in terms of commendation; but there the schools are in charge of well-bred men, men of education, trained and educated for the proper discharge of duties so important to the community. Normal schools are founded for the express purpose of training teachers and assistants for the agricultural schools. Indeed, no one would pretend to offer himself as a teacher, unless he could produce a diploma or certificate from some accredited institution. Such qualifications as these we do not possess here, nor can we have them, unless suitable persons are sent abroad to study a course of scientific agriculture at schools such as Temple Moyle, near Londonderry, or Glasnevin, near Dublin, in Ireland—either this, or procuring the services of some experienced professors from abroad to take charge, for a time, of a college, will be necessary, should we be able to found such an institution. "Begin right," is a good maxim, and I am sure there is nothing that demands the exercise of more caution, more discretion, than the choice of a principal of an agricultural college or school, upon the good or bad management of which such vast interests depend. We have, it is true, many able chemists, botanists, geologists, &c., but these, however clever in the abstract, would make but indifferent teachers of systematic, practical agriculture.

If your society should deem it expedient to establish an agricultural school, I would advise, as the best that could be done under the circumstances, that you devote a farm and suitable buildings to the purpose, and engage the best practical farmer available, to instruct your youths in the most improved methods, known to him and you, in the practice of culture and husbandry—and that you provide also a good schoolmaster, capable of instructing to the extent that is embraced in our grammar schools; the whole to be under the supervision of a committee, who should visit weekly, at least, to witness the operations, suggest improvements, correct abuses, and encourage merit. On this farm, experiments could be made in tillage, manures, seeds and crops, that would, if properly conducted, be of lasting benefit to the county, to an extent that could not possibly ensue from the efforts of any one individual on an isolated farm. The different breeds of cattle could likewise be experimented upon, and the best established. Simple nurseries of fruit and ornamental trees might be profitably propagated, while the students, by alternately working on the farm, garden and nursery grounds, and studying in school, would be confirmed in proper habits of industry and economy, and become respectable husbandmen and intelligent citizens—gratefully retrospecting with the poet —

"Thanks to their friends for their care in their breeding,
Who taught them betimes to love working and reading."

The products of the farm, the trees and cattle raised, with the income for tuition, to say nothing of the improved condition of the land, would, in a few years leave a balance in favor of this experimental farm and farm-school. But should you entrust its management to some cute, unscrupulous, self-styled Professor of Scientific Agriculture, who will presumptuously overwhelm you with strange terms of agricultural chemistry, taken from Liebig and Johnson, of which he knows not the import himself, and astonish you with strange implements, in no wise useful but in the line of humbug, then will you have to deplore the credulity that led you to trust to the prospectus of a quack, with its array of ill-gotten and ill-used names, endorsing his pretentions. Better than thus experiment, you had never heard of Scientific Agriculture.—The science that is substituted for honesty, whether in agriculture or any other culture, is a villanous science.

The little knowledge I have of the soil of your county, being a perfect stranger to it, or the practice that obtains with you, the crops usually cultivated, their culture or rotation, or the character of your husbandry, will not enable me to address myself so especially to your condition as otherwise I certainly would, in all frankness be inclined to do, even to the rebuking of your practice, did I know aught in it that was prejudical to your own interests or the cause of agriculture in general. I can but remark on things deemed applicable as I imagine them to be, in a county rather remote from a market, and where, owing to a sparse population, land is cheap, and farm hands proportionately scarce and dear, leading to a not very close or careful practice in culture, lest the time and labor bestowed in cultivating would be disproportioned to the value of the crop raised.

Assuming, then, that this is *prima facia* the case, as the lawyers would say, yet perhaps a closer investigation might reveal, or lead to a different conclusion, as to practice. I shall, however, attempt to enforce the rule that "whatever is worth doing at all, is worth doing well." First, then, is not the land your own, and must it not be conceded, that whatever tends to enrich or promote its fertility, enhances its value, and makes you the richer? It might happen, that though a good crop produced by thorough culture would not in itself compensate for the expense incurred in producing it, yet the farmer, in the long run, might be largely the gainer from the improved condition in which the land was left, by reason of the pains and labor bestowed upon it while cultivating the crop. It is not altogether to the market value of the one, or first crop, that the farmer is to look for remuneration, but to regard also, as an item of profit, the facility in producing, and the abundance of the succeeding crops, through having well and wisely broken up or prepared his land for the first or former crop. I need scarcely illustrate this farther, for every farmer, of ordinary experience, may calculate the profits and advantages, that follow in the train of one well done job in this connection on the farm. One good deep ploughing, removing stones and other obstructions, though consuming a little more time at first, will render that operation ever after of easy execution, so that in the end, much time shall have been saved, to say nothing of the fine crops that shoot up luxuriantly ever after, from the well prepared mold, in which their roots repose and feed, by reason of the comfortable provision the thrifty and skilful husbandman provided before committing the seed to the ground.

Now, let any one compare this course with the wasteful, careless and un-profitable practice of skinning, not ploughing, the land, leaving stones and impediments to be met with in cross-ploughings and after-ploughings, to jolt and throw out the plough. Manuring and seeding after such a preparation, is but a mockery, a thriftless labor, that dooms the land to barrenness and its owner to poverty! Crops, thus produced, can never remunerate—land, so treated, must ever deteriorate.

Take, for instance, a piece of meadow land, surcharged with moisture, sending up nothing but sour grass, unwholesome herbage, and weeds; is it wise or economical to be mowing year after year, the heterogeneous and noxious growth of such an acid, damp and ill-conditioned piece of ground—wasting time and labor in curing such a product? And then the folly of calling it hay, and cheating the poor dumb animals, who know it is not hay, but will reject it, except compelled through sheer starvation to eat it; and if they should eat it, in the shape of hay or pasture, they are sure to slink their calves, or take disease in different forms from such unwholesome, poisonous provender. Would it not be better economy, cheaper and more profitable, to ditch and drain such land, even at the expense of weeks' or months' time and labor—correct its acidity by a good dressing of lime or ashes, after it has been drained, and realize the profits and advantages of wholesome, sweet hay, and of rich and nutritious pasture of white clover, blue or green grass, that will tell profitably in the fine condition of the cattle, their beef, milk and butter? Will not every good farmer—and I doubt not but there are many such present—agree with me, that the greatest waste of time and labor is that bestowed hastily and sparingly upon farm land. Want of time, want of means, are the ever ready excuses of the negligent, the slovenly and unthrifty. They have not time to clean the cattle or stables—they have not time to secure the manure, or keep the manure heap in order—they have not time to put the implements in their proper places out of the weather, nor to mend the gearings, the wagons, &c., until, by neglect and exposure, rust and decay, they are beyond repairing—in short, they never have time to do anything well—are always doing too much, and never doing anything as it should be done!

24*

Another prevailing error is, the proneness to till or cultivate too much land, where the article is plenty and cheap. To cut out too much work at seeding is a dangerous practice, and is sure to end in waste and disappointment in harvesting. Better, by far, to measure the breadth of land to be seeded by the means certain, the number of hands available, with proper allowance for contingencies of bad weather, so that all that is seeded has a fair chance of being gathered and securely harvested. Would it not be well to reflect how disproportioned is the scanty crop, taken from a large breadth of ill-prepared land, to the labor of ploughing, harrowing, hauling and spreading, with the quantity of seed wasted on such a space? And would it not be better to break up less land, and thus afford it a chance of being well manured—abridge the labor, and reap an abundant crop—leaving so much of the land, at least, in such order that one need not be ashamed afterwards to meets its reproachful looks, in the beggarly uniform dress of briars, thistles, dock and mullein, that cover it, as rags patched together may serve to cover the nakedness of the sluggard, but unerringly reveal his unhealthy, poverty-stricken condition!

To exemplify the mistake of running over too much land, a little farther, let us suppose ninety acres devoted to the barbarous inflictions of skinning and starvation, compared to thirty acres, treated with civilized skill and christian generosity, and see how these two pieces of ground, individualizing them, will work for their owners. Or, suppose we say nine acres and three acres—nine acres say in wheat, with only about as much manure as would be sufficient for three acres. Ploughing, hauling on manure and spreading it, over so large a space, seeding and harvesting, would cost eighty dollars. Then suppose twelve bushels to the acre—more than an average of half the grain growers in this, or I might say any other State in the Union—equal to one hundred and eight bushels, at one dollar per bushel, is one hundred and eight dollars; from which deduct cost of labor, &c., eighty dollars, leaving twenty-eight dollars to be passed to the credit of the nine acre patch—a fraction over three dollars per acre for the use of the land and manure. Is not this a poor rent or interest Mr. Nine Acres has made for his owner? But little as it is, I could easily show it to be "beautifully less," as wags sometimes say; nay, instead of the paltry balance shown by the figures, *prove* that he has made a loss, if you will excuse the bull, by the condition in which he left the land after growing this wretched crop. Now let us see what Mr. Three Acres has done? Why he has made forty bushels to the acre, equal to one hundred and twenty bushels, which at one dollar per bushel as above, is one hundred and twenty dollars; from which deduct proportionate expenses, say twenty-seven dollars, and we have a balance of ninety-three dollars to place to the credit of the three acres—equal to thirty-one dollars per acre; but this is not all, the fine heart the land is left in, with the heavy crops of grass which may be expected to follow, maintaining its rateable superiority for a series of years ever after, over the nine acres, must be taken into account also. In making this comparison, much detail has been omitted that may be supplied by any one conversant with the capacity of the soil, when properly tested, my object being to shadow forth the advantages of the close, earnest and common-sense practice, in reference to producing, and keeping land in proper condition, and the disadvantages of the loose, thriftless, unmeaning plan of working and seeding, to reap nothing but disappointment and poverty.

Though raising of grain may not be considered a profitable business, at present prices and a distant market, yet, even under these circumstances, if forty bushels of wheat, and eighty of corn, can be raised to the acre, with oats and roots in proportion, there can be little doubt but such crops would be highly remunerative. The farmer who has the intelligence, spirit and perseverance to pursue a rational course of cropping and culture, can, on ordinary good land, realize these yields, while he will find the value of his land increasing and increased. It is pleasant to contemplete the position of such an one, with well filled barns, fertile fields, and fine flocks and herds, constituting a capital that places him in the enviable rank of a wealthy, independent Pennsylvania farmer!

Now it requires no witchcraft, or science, so called, to produce such results; all that is required is the intelligence to judge between a good and a bad practice, and the resolution to adopt the one and avoid the other—to discriminate between a ridiculous theory, and a rational system founded on facts and observation; between old prejudices and new notions; adopting those that bear the genuine impress of utility, and rejecting those that are mere counterfeits, of which there are so many put into circulation of late, that it might be supposed some new Pandora's box had been opened, specially to torment, fleece and plague poor farmers! We of the old school—the old guard—are generally found well fortified against the attacks of the Magicians and Don Quixottes of improvement run mad; though some of us, to my certain knowledge, have been badly taken in. But there is as much danger in resisting innovation too obstinately, as there is in yielding too easily. Much improvement has been made of late years in farm implements, and many excellent theories advanced by men of undoubted skill and science, and much valuable information diffused by the Agricultural press; whilst the dignity of farming as a profession is of more general acceptance with the community than it formerly was. In fact, it is somewhat fashionable now-a-days to be considered an agriculturist, theoretical or practical—a patron or a promoter of the science of rural economy; and I am right glad of it; but then this popular excitement has its drawbacks, in the swarms of Professors and Patentees who are loud in their professions and desires to serve the cause, in selling you an implement or machine that will work of itself, or a fertilizer that will save you the trouble of cleaning the stables, or keeping a nasty dung-heap, or a pamphlet that will instruct you to select a good milch cow by the cut of her hair—in lecturers that will unfold all the mysteries of vegetable physiology in a single lecture, provided you give them a dollar *and promise to keep their*

secret—in rural architects who will construct you a "Cataract Barn," as superb
as a Crystal Palace, that with steam will do the threshing, grinding, milling,
creaming, pressing, washing and cooking—turn the mangers and troughs into
crystal rivulets, whereat the horses, cattle, sheep and swine may drink while
reposing in their pens and stables—provided the mischievous "Jack Frost,"
on some winter night, don't turn the "cataract" into huge icicles, and the
milk into ice-cream *without* the application of potato starch—in professors
who will teach you scientific agriculture, including chemistry, botany, geology,
zoology, and all the ologies, with some of the *isms*, who, while teaching,
will be hard put to it to "learn themselves to spell" in the common primer
or rudiments of Clodhopperism! Such are a few of the novelties of fashionable agriculture, or rural economy—the excrescences rather, or fungi developments that at this time characterize the march of agricultural improvement.
But the experience that teaches burnt children to dread the fire, will lead to
more caution and prudence for the future, and place Quackery and Humbuggery at a discount, so far as agriculture is concerned.

It strikes me that grazing might be carried on to some advantage in your
county; indeed, there are few localities in Pennsylvania in which it might not
be profitably conducted to some extent, at least, if not as a leading business.
There is no department in our husbandry, to our shame may it be spoken,
more neglected than this; our culture and tillage will bear a comparison with
any other State in the Union, but in the quality of our cattle we fall short of
several of our sister States. This should not be; it is incumbent upon us—
nay, a duty we owe to ourselves and the commmunity at large, that we should
remedy this glaring defect. It is, indeed, a reproach that our fine farms should
exhibit such meagre, paltry herds as so generally disgrace them; not one in
fifty of these cattle, if stalled to feed, would repay the cost of forcing it into
condition fit to slaughter. By dint of long and high feeding, some tallow
might be produced, but it would be in vain to expect a good rib or loin of beef
from such an animal, no matter how long it might be fed. The offal will be
in undue proportion to the meat, and the feeder will be made to feel, as he
computes the diminution of his corn-crib with the increase to his purse, how
unprofitable an operation he had on hand. Suppose we look a little closer
into the folly of losing time and money in this way. Land, time and labor
constitute the capital of the farmer, and should he not, like the merchant, turn
his capital to the best account? The grass, corn and oats are the products of
the land, time and labor; and if these "don't pay," as the phrase is, when sold
at market, should he not think of some other mode of turning them into cash
that will make them pay better? He concludes then to feed these products
to cattle on the farm, to be driven to market; if so, should he be content to
feed the ill-shaped, bony, ravenous tribe that are never satisfied, and never
show any proof of having denuded the fields and emptied the cribs? If he
do, he will find out to his cost, that he will have gone to the worst market he
could possibly have resorted to, and be made to realize the bitter fruits of

having begun wrong. Every grazier, especially in such a region as this, should raise the cattle that he intends to feed, because he cannot feel the same confidence, in having through purchase secured the properties suited to his purpose, as he could have, if he had bred them from reliable sires and dams upon his own farm. As well might the vegetable gardener rely upon seeds raised at a distance, by others, as the grazier can depend upon the young cattle picked up indiscriminately by the drovers for sale. If, then, the grazier resort to breeding, the question naturally presents itself, which is the most profitable breed? This question I shall attempt to answer.

The cattle most relied upon by breeders, in Great Britain and Ireland, for feeding, are the Short-Horns or improved Durhams, and the Herefords. The North Devons claim some consideration in this respect. The milking properties of these, and some other breeds, will be considered presently.

The stately Durhams, the familiar name of the Short-Horns, owe much of their perfect forms to the great care bestowed upon them by the perseverance, skill and judgment of English breeders, who spared neither time nor money in refining upon them, so as to mould them in size and form to suit their ideas of perfection—imbueing them at the same time with the ease, gentleness, and sluggishness I might say, so necessary to early maturing, easy feeding and good handling; these properties, however necessarily followed, as the result of the form, symetry and constitution they were made, as it were, to take, by the artists who fashioned them; hence they were held as the paragons of the cattle tribe; and, it may be said, that in all the disputations touching their superiority, and there were many, prompted too often either by jealousy or prejudice, the palm of rivalry in size and early maturing of the Short-Horns was never seriously contested. The judgment of the present day is decidedly in favor of the Durhams.

The Herefords, as grazing cattle, take the next rank, in my opinion, to the Short-Horns. Though but little known in this country, they are of high repute with English graziers, and have more frequently, I believe, come in close competition, at Smithfield and the cattle-shows, with the Durhams, than any other breed. Why they are not more frequently to be met with here is matter of surprise, except it be that the few imported at first were held at prices as high as the Durhams, whose celebrity was previously established, and engrossed the attention of those who had the spirit and patriotism to pay a generous price for a good animal; the Herefords, therefore, were neglected.— From what I have seen of them—and when I had the opportunity of seeing them, I examined them with more than ordinary attention—I consider them good feeders, more capable of enduring the rough and tumble system that prevails here than the aristocratic Short-Horns.

The North Devons are also a favorite breed in England, and of late years, have attracted considerable attention in this country; they are a beautiful race, and exhibit a neatness and compactness that cannot fail to please a practised eye. In size and early maturing they fall short of either the Herefords or Durhams. I have seen, however, many large fat bullocks claimed to be Devons, or essentially so, but they were generally some eight or more years old, and must have consumed more feed than was compatible with profitable feeding. In New England, the Common or South Devons are numerous, and to my apprehension, a more profitable cattle than the North Devons. The distinction between these varieties is, that the North Devon is neater and of a deeper red than the South or Common Devon; but where the object is to have the largest and easiest fed cattle, a shade of difference in color can be of no importance. The animal that will fatten soonest, and make the most beef at the least expense, should fix the grazier's choice. These Devons are the most appropriate for crossing with the Durhams of any breed I am acquainted with; indeed I have never seen the result otherwise than advantageous in lifting the Devon to a higher standard. The Durham should never, if possible, be made to stoop lower than this, in view of producing a proper effect. A memorable instance of the judiciousness of such a cross was exemplified in the ox "Pennsylvania," an eight year old, slaughtered at Philadelphia, in 1841, whose live weight was three thousand three hundred and fifty pounds—dead weight of the four quarters, two thousand three hundred and eighty-eight pounds. The whole animal, when alive, showed unmistakeably the characteristics of the two breeds from which he was derived, and when dead, evinced no less the advantages of the cross in the quality of the beef, it being so finely marbled with fat and lean—a characteristic essentially Durham; this breed being more prone to distribute the fat thus, than stow it away in a corner as suet, or lay it on the outside, to be melted down for the tallow chandler's use.

Having slightly glanced at the breeds best adapted to the stall, I shall say a word now on their milking qualities; and in doing this shall introduce two other breeds, namely, the Ayrshires and Alderneys. These two breeds are well known, and are of much repute for the dairy. If the milking property alone was of such value as to compensate for the want of the feeding property we have been considering, it might be a primary object with the farmer to secure it at the sacrifice of the feeding property; but then this is not, nor ever can be the case with farmers in general. Especially in rural districts, far from market, the milk property, as compared with the beef, is of secondary importance. In and near cities, where the milk-men stimulate the cows, with still slops and other unwholesome food, and milk the poor animals to death, the quantity of fluid—it can hardly be called milk—that can be extracted from them, is the only thing worth looking at according to the sage opinion of these worthies. But farmers, even in dairy districts, should know that the cow that will give the most milk, and, when dry, can most easily be fed off, is, by all odds, the most profitable animal for their use. This being admitted, the question is in which of the breeds are best blended the two properties of milk and beef? I answer, unhesitatingly, the Improved Short-Horns and Ayrshires—while it must be admitted that this combination may be found in animals of other breeds, or of no distinct breed, but this depends upon individual constitutional qualities not common to the whole family. The Short-Horns and Ayrshires assimilate more in disposition and properties than any other two breeds; they exhibit in common the composure, love of ease and rest, so well calculated, in ruminants, to insure the most profitable results in milking and feeding.

That the large and seemingly over-grown Short-Horn or Durham should be a great milker, may seem paradoxical to some persons, but ask them why, and they never can give a rational answer. Their great length, breadth and depth can surely not deny to them the lactescent property of the cow; and if this bulk be composed of the material proper to make milk and butter, does it not follow that the more there is of the material, the more can be extracted from it? And, is it not likely, that in proportion to the great amount of the material, nature has, in like proportion, endowed the animal with the organs necessary to provide for the suckling of its young, or artificially to dispense to the human family its wholesome and nutritious milk? Who will be so bold as to deny that the structure or organs of the Improved Durham are not only excellent, but unsurpassed? Can their great health and fine constitution militate against their milking? Surely not. Let one of them have twins, or two calves put to her, and then mark how her great strength and constitution will stand their attacks and supply their cravings! Prejudice has been maintained and urged against the Durhams in Pennsylvania, through the envy and jealousy of some, who, not having the spirit to aid in supplying the country with fine cattle, at high prices, were wanting in generosity to those who from time to time attempted it, and who failed only long since to have accomplished it through a worse than "dog and manger policy," waged against them. Their motives were impugned, their cattle stigmatised and depreciated, their losses and disappointments were made subjects of ribald jest and provoking ridicule. False standards were set up by these selfish, prejudiced men; improvement halted, if it did not retrograde, and the Commonwealth was cheated out of the patriotic offerings of her devoted citizens. To the malign influence referred to, may be ascribed the wretched character of the cattle that disgrace Pennsylvania at the present day. Travel where you may, the eye in vain seeks for a creditable specimen. It is my belief, take them in the aggregate, throwing out the few Durhams, there is not one in ten of them that would make six hundred weight of beef, and which it would not be hazardous to eat, from constitutional defects, or from ill-treatment it had been subjected to from its unfeeling owner. Contrast this with Kentucky and Ohio, even Virginia and New York, and may we not blush, as an Agricultural State at our destitution? How many thousands of dollars, perhaps millions, have we not paid to Kentucky and Ohio for the splendid droves of cattle which they have supplied us with—and of what breed are they? Why, anything of a judge could tell at a long-shot distance they were essentially Durham. Let a Philadelphian, or any one from the eastern counties of Pennsylvania, go to Ohio and Kentucky, and inquire of the Rennicks, the Clays, &c., why they import so many young Short-Horn bulls and heifers, at such high prices, and they will be provoked to laugh at him for coming so far to put the question, when he could have had it answered at or nearer home by looking in at the Philadelphia drove-yard, or inquiring of one of the Philadelphia butchers. But I find I am at the shambles when I should be at the dairy.

What helped to give weight to the opinion, if not its origin, that the Short-Horns were bad for milk, was, that those who mainly bred and prized them in England, set but little value upon their milking, compared to their feeding properties. The heifer with her first calf was neglected, she had no milker but the calf, and when it was removed she went dry, for want of the necessary attention to milking, and keeping her milk veins in proper use. How then could a heifer thus treated, whether Durham or any other breed, prove a good milker? Then if any cow, while being at the pail, was shipped to this country, the irregularity of milking on shipboard was sufficient to break in upon her habit of milking ever after. Does not every dairy-man know this? And because these did not exhibit on their arrival, or even after, large and distended udders, and prove deep and enduring milkers, was it just to stigmatize the whole breed as worthless for the dairy? Besides, the importations for Ohio and Kentucky were made with no view of obtaining milk, yet these were disingenuously referred to, to swell and confirm the senseless charge that was sweepingly made against the Durhams.

Col. John Hare Powell, to his credit may it be spoken, made every effort to counteract these prejudices. For a series of years he imported Improved Short-Horns from the stock of Mr. Whitaker, who had taken great pains to develope and establish their milking properties, and was eminently successful. Mr. Prentice, Mr. Sheaffe and Mr. Lenox, of New York, had their cattle from Mr. Whitaker, and these were good milkers and fine handlers. Mr. Lenox's cow, "Red Lady," was the most beautiful animal I ever saw, except my celebrated "Dairy Maid," which was also bred by Mr. Whitaker. Colonel Wolbert, of Philadelphia, owned a beautiful Durham, called "Isabella," she was second to none for deep milking, but "Dairy Maid." Mr. Dennis Kelly's imported bull, "Prince of Wales," was of Col. Powell's importation, and ten years experience has proved him to have been unrivalled in getting superior milk stock; while in size, symmetry and fine handling, he seldom found a competitor. In the herds of Lewis F. Allen, of Black Rock, Col. Sherwood, of Auburn, Mr. Vail, of Troy, Mr. Morris, of Morrisania, and in the herds of several others of New York, great milkers were ever found; Mr. Canby, of Delaware, had also fine Durhams; among them, his cow "Blossom"—a great milker. Mr. Calvert, of Maryland, has had much experience in Durham stock and appreciates them highly; it was mainly owing to his enterprise and liberality, I think, that the Short-Horns were introduced to such an extent into Maryland. Mr. Evans, of York, Pennsylvania, owns a fine herd of Durhams, of good milking properties, the same that deservedly attracted so much attention at the State Agricultural Exhibition at Harrisburg. He now holds the rank as a breeder, which the Messrs. Smalls did some years since, and they in this respect were the successors of the late venerated Charles A. Barnitz, of same place. Joseph Cope, Paschal Morris, Mr. Bolmar, and some others of Chester county, did much towards the introduction of Durhams, and consequent improvement of the cattle in that quarter. George Cadwalader and Thomas P. Remmington, of Philadelphia, are now in the full tide of progress with valuable herds of Short-Horns, procured from every reliable source within their reach; may they be successful, and never be made to feel the vexations that beset the path of their predecessors.

The Ayrshires stand next to the Durhams in milking, and this I consider high praise. It has been remarked by some one—the author I do not recollect—that the Ayrshires could lay but little claim to a remote origin or distinctiveness of breed. Be this as it may, I cannot perceive the force of the objection; if, from careful breeding, even of late years, they have been made to exhibit peculiar or uniform points and properties by which they may now be designated. Can we suppose that any other of the crack breeds were, a century back, precisely the same, in form and quality as they are now? To think so, would be but paying a poor compliment to the generations that have passed away since then, if they had thus been unmindful of improving the breeds of cattle in their day; and it would be somewhat criminal in us if we do not attempt to improve them further still. I have also heard it said that the cross of a Durham and Devon would be equivalent to an Ayrshire—this I strongly doubt, unless a Devon dam could be found, having the same disposition and quality of milking that are usually found with the Ayrshire. As to the milking properties of the Herefords, I can say nothing from my own experience or observation, having had but few opportunities of even seeing them, and when I had, my attention was exclusively directed to their grazing qualities, of which, as I have already stated, I formed a very favorable opinion. The next breed in order are the Devons. In passing upon these as milkers, I feel a degree of hesitancy that even my frankness cannot wholly overcome, because time will not permit me to adduce the reasons and proofs I could bring forward in support of the opinion I have formed of them, and in the absence of these, the hasty glance I must needs take of them, and the conclusions I must arrive at, will, by many, be considered as partial and unwarranted.

Fair dairy cattle no doubt may be found among the common Devons of New England, where, and in Western New York, they form by far the greatest portion of the cattle used in the butter and cheese dairies. Now this, of itself, is no proof that they are better milkers than the common, native or mixed cattle, which, if found of same size and constitution, would equal, if not surpass, the New England Devons in giving milk and making butter; yet, although this may be the case, there may be peculiar qualities in the Devon's milk that may be more profitable or better adapted to cheese making, than the milk of some other cattle, and of this I have but little doubt—add to

25

this the hardihood and activity of the Devon, fitting it for the severe climate of New England, and you have the solution of the preference given to them by the dairymen of the Northern States. · But I do contend that, even among these Devons, but few if any can be found, that can lay claim to the deep milking so frequently found among our red and white, black and brindle-colored tribe of native cattle. If this be the case, as I firmly believe it to be, even with the common Devons as milkers, the pure North Devons fall still farther below a medium milking standard, for it is observable that the greatest promise of milk in the Devons, is to be found with those that are largest and lightest of color.

The North Devons are a beautiful, healthy, hardy breed of cattle, and must have formed a distinct breed or race at a much earlier period than any other of the favorite breeds of the present day. Nature has impressed them with characteristics more distinctly and deeply than other breeds. Their tenacity in retaining their color, temper and tractableness, is truly remarkable; you might as well think of rubbing out "Indian," in the Aborgines of our forests, as to think of wholly merging "Devon" in other races. It is owing to this, no doubt, more than to any special care by the New England farmers, that the red cattle of that region have, for so long a period, retained their charac-teristic distinctiveness. The North Devons make the best working cattle of any breed ; if this be so, and I believe it cannot be gainsaid, the activity, thews and sinews, and bone, that place them next to the horse for endurance and spirit, must deny to them, in a considerable degree, the disposition and quali-ties essential to constitute good milkers. Working and milking properties I hold to be incompatible in the same animal.

Of all the cattle under review, I consider the Alderneys to be the most unprofitable to the farmer; because they are undersized, ill-formed, and such hard feeders, that it is impossible to get beef on them ; and as to milk, it seems anomalous that they should hold the rank in this respect so generally conceded to them, except it can be traced to some freak of fashion that, as is too often the case, puts both judgment and propriety at defiance. The cry is they give rich milk and make yellow butter—so does almost every hide-bound, rickety cow, that may be picked up along the lanes or roadsides, give rich or thick milk, chiefly *because she gives so little,* and, by consequence, that little will make more cream than a similar quantity would of milk taken from a twenty to thirty quart a day cow; but in the twenty quarts would there not likely be as much, if not more, butter than could be produced from the eight to ten quarts a day animal ? If so, then we have the same quantity of butter, with the addition of double the quantity of milk, an item not to be overlooked, besides, we have that which is much better, a fine, healthy, large animal, that when it will be proper to feed off, will show some proof of the food she con-sumed in her beef and tallow. To compare this fine, healthy animal to the goat-a-kin thing called Alderney, would be ridiculous! ♦ The straw-color of the butter of the Alderneys, so much boasted, is no proof of its excellence,

The yellow, tinged with rose, is a more inviting and desirable color (evincing delicacy of flavor and richness, and giving assurance of the good health of the cow and suitableness of the food she had,) than the straw-color can convey to our apprehension. To test the richness of the milk of the cows referred to, let two calves of same age, size, &c., be provided, one to be put to suckle at the Alderney, the other at the large twenty quarts a day cow, and then see, in the course of five or six weeks, which calf will thrive more and make the better veal. This would be a fair common-sense test, for the result of which I should have no fears. Remember, I speak of Alderneys that are thorough Alderneys, not those that have had a chance game of admixture of blood for generations. Most of those to be met with have scarcely a vestage left of the Alderneys, except the high rump—muzzle, cheek and shanks hardly traceable —therefore, if a round-ribbed, plump animal, with something of a shoulder, a good fore-arm and straight limb, be presented to you, though she be of a dun or mouse color, class her as an "*Improved Alderney*"—improved, no matter of what other breed soever it has been derived. In habit, constitution, size, milking and feeding, the Alderneys, are all unfit for a farmer.

If in treating of cattle I have not already consumed too much time, I should like to say a word as to the bad treatment milch cows are but too frequently subjected to in almost every place; a treatment as unwise as it is cruel. If it were confined to cities, where the poor animals are drugged with still slops and other unnatural food, by milkmen, so called, to excite the cows to yield undue quantities of what they call milk, I would not think it necessary to refer to it here; but the cruel and improper treatment of cows is not confined to cities alone—go where you will you are sure to be shocked at the scenes of suffering and neglect these patient animals are made to endure, whether on commons, farms, stables or yards. If driven out after milking, or brought home to be milked, they never fail of being run, whiped or cudgelled by some unfeeling boy, who seems to think it part of his duty to deal them as many blows as he can while within his reach. Then but too often follow the blows of the milker, should the poor animals wince under the pressure on teats, lacerated perhaps by thorns, or made sore from other causes. No wonder that this treatment, with scantiness of food and sometimes of water, reduces the cows to the wretched condition in which they are but too often found in every quarter. Set a farm hand to clean the cow stable daily, to curry and brush the cows, and he will be apt to think you a fool, or that you mean to degrade him—if he comply, it will be with reluctance, and it is quite likely that he will take more out of their hides, or put more into them, than you bargained for. Ask the same worthy to groom your horse, and he will not fail to do it cheerfully. Why this prejudice, this folly? Does not the cow stand in a more interesting relation to us than the horse? He works for us and carries us, to be sure, but then do we partake of his flesh and blood while living, in the shape of milk, butter and cheese? and do we slaughter him for beef when we suppose him failing in strength? No. Well, then, why is not the same attention paid to the cleanliness and health of the cow as is bestowed upon the horse? The same care that produces so fine a condition in the one, could not fail of having the same effect upon the other—and I say that it is the height of folly, and positive injustice to ourselves, to withhold those attentions, from the cow. She is a second wet nurse to us and our children, and if this nurse be in ill health, will not her milk, cream and butter be imbued with her condition? Would we be willing to eat of the flesh of some of those wretchedly poor animals if they were slaughtered? And why should we not feel the same repugnance to use their milk? Let us be more careful in feeding these useful animals properly, keeping them comfortable and clean, and in good, healthy condition.

I have dwelt longer upon this matter, perhaps, than you may think its importance required, but regarding this as likely to become a dairy as well as a grazing district, I could not but deal with it fully, in a spirit of justice to you, and in humanity to the patient and much abused animal, upon whose condition so much of you and your children's health depends.

The cheapest and most economical way of producing a valuable stock, would be, to procure a thorough-bred young Short-Horn bull from some reliable breeder. Introduce him to none but the finest cows and heifers you have or can provide, of the common or mixed breed — indeed, all undersized, ill-conditioned animals on the farm should be removed at once. After having used this bull two years, or when his own produce shall have grown, let him be exchanged for another of equal purity of blood; and when he shall have served his two years, let him be likewise removed. At this juncture, say after six years, how much would a herd of some thirty head be worth under such management? Why, it would not be unreasonable to suppose them worth two thousand five hundred to three thousand dollars. How much would the herd have been worth supposing the thorough-bred Short-Horn bull had not been introduced? Perhaps not six hundred dollars.

From what has been said on breeds and qualities of cattle, you may determine by your own good sense assisting, what description of cattle is best adapted to your condition, but let me entreat you to select the best individuals to breed from, of whatever class, whether common, grade or distinct, and always aim at breeding up, but never down to a lower grade. Do not let your best calves go to the butcher, but the worst. If you thus begin and persevere, you will promote your own individual interests, confer credit upon your county, and at the same time add to the Agricultural wealth of Pennsylvania.

I can say but little from experience, even if time would allow, upon sheep husbandry. The annoyances from noise, bustle and dogs on the borders of a city, where my farm lies, rendered the keeping of sheep impracticable. This I regretted, for I should have been delighted with so interesting, and to my mind so profitable a branch of husbandry. Wool-growing is of vast importance to the country, and like every other branch of industry, he who studies it most, and practices it best, will reap the richest reward, and be entitled to the highest professional distinction.

Peter A. Browne, Esq., of Philadelphia, a gentleman of great research and untiring perseverance, has of late years devoted much of his time and talents to the subject of hair and wool; the breeds of sheep, the importance of breeding and crossing as affecting the quality of long or hair wool, and short or felt wool. It is, as illustrated by Mr. Browne, one of the most curious and interesting works that has been brought before the public of late, and which none but a mind such as his could have so minutely explored and elucidated The work should be in the hands of every wool grower. Much credit is due to its gifted author, for the able effort he has made to enlarge the boundaries of useful knowledge.

occasion to say, that it

pleasing task, to have spoken of agricul-ture and its attendants, in a different strain from that indicated by the undis-sembled remarks I have had the honor to make before you. There is no man, who appreciates more than I do, the beautiful in nature within the bounds of the husbandman's interesting vocation, or who can drink deeper of the inspiration that may be quaffed from the perennial fountain the seasons supply, to tempt or satisfy the eye and heart. There is not a fine tree, shrub or flower, hedge, field or lawn, but presents to my eye more than com-mon delight and attraction. 1 am no less a votary of Ceres, than I am a wor-shipper in the temple of Flora; and who that know me, and have witnessed my habits and pursuits for years, but must admit, that I have shown myself to be a faithful and zealous laborer within the domain—the charmed circle of these Divinities! Notwithstanding all these habitudes and predilections, I chose, while addressing you, the rugged, rather than the flowery path; to aim at the useful rather than the ornamental—to expose, rather than to gloss over defects—to risk censure for the sake of truth, rather than gain applause by pan-dering to a morbid taste, or bolstering a vicious system!

Too much of this plating and gilding is apparent of late. Men who never tilled a piece of land, planted a tree, raised or exhibited an animal in all their lives, are now, by false coloring and idle pretension, transformed into Tulls and Lowdons—leaders at Agricultural Clubs and Societies, where their twat-tle and professions pass frequently for sense and experience with those that know no better. Some of these are ever displaying their operations over a vast and boundless field; while others of them are busy at cutting out work in the moon or in the "Isle of Sky." To use an old "salt" or sailor's ex-pression descriptive of a fresh water sailor, "they are always found in every-body's 'mess' but in nobody's 'watch.'" The end of all this will be, if not timely checked, that the true disciples of improvement will become lukewarm when they see the position assumed by mere professors and pretenders. The masses, or rank and file, that have just been clearing their eyes for a reading spell, will pitch their books, like physic, to the dogs—the subscriptions to the

Agricultural journals will diminish till, ere long, there will not be patronage sufficient to maintain, as is the case in Pennsylvania, a respectable periodical. In other words, when Agriculture finds such *things* sitting on and under his skirts, he will, in his strength or madness, jump out of his coat entirely, choosing rather to be coatless than to furnish a garb or covering for moon-shine philosophers and Pangloss professors.

Do not, I pray you, think me a seeker of adventure or renown, in combating abuses ; but, on the contrary, let me assure you that there is nothing of the Knight-errant in my whole composition. To the many calls that have been made upon me to come forth from my pleasant retreat, to take the field in the way you have marshalled me, I have ever made refusal, except on one occasion, not very long since, at Lancaster ; and, if I shall be permitted to consult my own taste and inclination, henceforward, this will be the last time I shall serve the cause in the manner I consented to *serve* it, at your special instance and prompting—if, indeed, I *have served* the cause, and at the same time, gentlemen, obliged you, I shall feel amply recompensed for the effort now ended.

INDEX.

A.

B.

C.

S.

T.

U.

W.